BOTH SIDES NOW

THE GEORGE GUND FOUNDATION
IMPRINT IN AFRICAN AMERICAN STUDIES

The George Gund Foundation has endowed
this imprint to advance understanding of
the history, culture, and current issues
of African Americans.

Both Sides Now

The Story of School Desegregation's Graduates

AMY STUART WELLS

JENNIFER JELLISON HOLME

ANITA TIJERINA REVILLA

AWO KORANTEMAA ATANDA

UNIVERSITY OF CALIFORNIA PRESS
Berkeley Los Angeles London

University of California Press, one of the most
distinguished university presses in the United States,
enriches lives around the world by advancing scholarship
in the humanities, social sciences, and natural sciences. Its
activities are supported by the UC Press Foundation and
by philanthropic contributions from individuals and
institutions. For more information, visit www.ucpress.edu.

University of California Press
Berkeley and Los Angeles, California

University of California Press, Ltd.
London, England

Library of Congress Cataloging-in-Publication Data

Both sides now : the story of school desegregation's
graduates / Amy Stuart Wells . . . [et al.].
    p.   cm.
Includes bibliographical references and index.
ISBN 978-0-520-25677-4 (cloth : alk. paper)
ISBN 978-0-520-25678-1 (pbk. : alk. paper)
1. School integration—United States—Case studies.
2. Minority high school students—United States—Case
studies.   I. Wells, Amy Stuart, 1961–.

LC214.2.B68   2009
379.2'630973—dc22   2008026056

Manufactured in the United States of America

17   16   15   14   13   12   11   10   09   08
10   9   8   7   6   5   4   3   2   1

This book is printed on Natures Book, which contains 50%
post-consumer waste and meets the minimum
requirements of ANSI/NISO Z39.48–1992 (R 1997)
(*Permanence of Paper*).

The publisher gratefully acknowledges the generous support of the African American Studies Endowment Fund of the University of California Press Foundation, which was established by a major gift from the George Gund Foundation.

For Trevor, Katie, Anna, Anthony, Destiny, Rae Ana, Michael Anthony, Michael K., and Jacob—our next generation. May you all see from both sides and not become disillusioned.

For the community members, educators, and class of 1980 graduates from the places of both sides—we have tried to do justice to your story in the hope that others can understand the complexity of your experiences and resist the urge to simplify the lessons learned from school desegregation in the United States.

But now old friends are acting strange
They shake their heads, they say I've changed
Well something's lost, but something's gained
In living every day.

I've looked at life from both sides now
From win and lose and still somehow
It's life's illusions I recall
I really don't know life at all.

Joni Mitchell

Contents

Foreword by Vanessa Siddle Walker xi

Acknowledgments xix

1. The Class of 1980 1

2. Six Desegregated High Schools 39

3. Racially Mixed Schools in a Separate
   and Unequal Society 77

4. We're All the Same—Aren't We? 115

5. Close Together but Still Apart: Friendships
   across Race Only Went So Far 155

6. Why It Was Worth It 199

7. More Diverse Than My Current Life 236

8. But That Was a Different Time 264

9. The Souls of Desegregated Folk 292

Notes 321

Index 339

Foreword

Given the tenacity of his commentary on double consciousness, mixed schools, and the color line, the capacity of W. E. B. DuBois to introduce the significance of the present work should come as little surprise. Writing during a period when school boards across the South were implementing varied forms of massive desegregation and noting unequivocally that the "United States has a long history of ignoring and breaking the law," DuBois posed a central, albeit generally ignored, query: "During the 25 or 50 years while the southern South refuses to obey the law, what will happen to Negro children?" (Jones 1978: 7). His question was simple and forthright. Its answer, however, has not been so direct.

What happened to the children? DuBois's question haunts us into the present. To be sure, some previous scholarship provides discernible categorical responses to his query. For example, in the literature are first-hand accounts of the intimidation, isolation, and mistreatment black children experienced as they entered previously all-white settings (Beals 1994; Baker 1996; Morris & Morris 2002). Supplemented by television documentaries such as *Eyes on the Prize* that captured the countenance of angry mobs who would impinge upon the right of black children to attend previously all-white schools, this line of scholarship vividly answers DuBois's ponderings about the experiences of children by elevating the violence and mistreatment that occurred. When linked with historical scholarship revealing the extent to which the experiences of black children in southern desegregated schools mirror the experiences of other black children in desegregated schools in the North in the previous century (Jones 1978; Mohraz 1979), one answer to DuBois's question is that the short-term effect of school desegregation on black children has consistently been school-level mistreatment.

Other scholars have taken a more long-term view of the question and arrived at a different conclusion. This second line of scholarship counters stories of mistreatment with descriptions of outcome variables that describe the success of the children over time. In their answer to DuBois's question, rising test scores and graduation rates are examples of the effect of desegregation on the children. Moreover, this literature demonstrates the increased access to social and professional networks that occurred for black children after desegregation (Orfield 2005; Braddock & Eitle 2003; Poll: Integration Improved 2004). In contrast to the portraits of individual mistreatment, this second group of studies implicitly posits that in the fifty or more years while some school boards constrained full implementation of the law, the effect of desegregation on the children has been long-term success.

Both strands of scholarship are significant tributaries in explaining the effect of desegregation on children. Yet neither line of investigation fully delves into the nuances implicit in DuBois's question. If we are to address his ponderings comprehensively, the experiences of children must be explored in the context of teaching and learning at the school level and must include a reflection over time and a conceptual link with the social and cultural milieu of the era. Between the recountings of mistreatment and beyond the descriptions of improving test scores and job opportunities, what actually *happened* to black children in the day-to-day process of education and how did these experiences influence their behaviors over time? Although DuBois did not include other ethnic groups in his question, a reasoned extension would also ask how white children or Latino children fared. Moreover, what has been the effect of their experiences in the fifty years while courts have embraced and then retreated from the laws governing school desegregation (Orfield & Eaton 1996)? Research in school segregation, desegregation, and resegregation has generally left questions as delicate and pivotal as these underexplored.

Both Sides Now is groundbreaking in its intent to provide a broad, inclusive answer to DuBois's decades-old question. In the pages that follow, Amy Stuart Wells, Jennifer Jellison Holme, Anita Tijerina Revilla, and Awo Korantemaa Atanda reveal the results of 550 interviews from six cases of school desegregation across the country where graduates completed their high school education in 1980. They question specifically how the children interacted while attending desegregated schools and how they have lived since. Using the voices of informants and drawing upon history, political science, sociology, and legal studies, they lead us into desegregated school environments to provide an up-close perspective on the reported experiences of the children while they were still in school. With masterful portrait weaving, they also navigate the home and work settings of graduates to reveal an answer to the question of what happened to the students over time. More than can be captured in traditional quantitative descriptions of test scores and other measurable forms of success, Wells and associates unveil through first-person accounts a world of teaching and learning and school climate often masked in traditional desegregation studies.

The findings herein are compelling. The stories of their informants create a portrait of desegregation that simultaneously depicts racial progress and uneasy contradictions. In their descriptions of racial progress, the authors laud the ways in which graduates of desegregated schools embrace the importance of their experience. In particular are explanations of the extent to which all participants in the class of 1980 valued their cross-racial friendships. However, using DuBois's lens of double consciousness, the authors also dissect the difficulties within the desegregated schools they studied. In poignant language they describe the limitations of these cross-racial friendships, the blatant tracking practices, and the unequal dissemination of knowledge, especially information about college. They depict the ways students and teachers in the settings were forced into a color blindness where all parties celebrated seeing one another as raceless, a retreat that included omitting conversations on weighty issues such as race and inequality. Coupled with a curriculum that failed to address alternate views of the world, these graduates emerge as the products of a system that deemphasized race even as they daily experienced inequities that were part of its unspoken influence.

As compelling as the descriptions of the students' experiences during their high school years is the juxtaposition of their past experiences with their present realities. While students uniformly emphasize the value of having been part of desegregated school environments, their reports reveal troubling descriptions of adult lives more segregated than their prior schooling. The pages introduce us to white graduates such as Larry, who live comfortable lives in all-white worlds while wistfully acknowledging that they are not providing for their own children the desegregated opportunities they experienced. Larry's reality represents more than 50 percent of the white graduates. Sadly, many have not maintained for their children the very world they proclaim to value. Of course, one interpretation of the failure of these graduates is explained by Feldman (2004), who provides the historical context to demonstrate the ways students came of age during the rising tide of conservatism that dominated politics beginning in the 1980s and that made the public mind disdainful of "liberal" causes such as school desegregation. His narrative chronicles extensively the ways in which race linked with politics during this era, and his interpretations unveil political structures that dismantled many desegregated schools. As his interpretation suggests and the authors here affirm, these 1980 high school graduates may have been more influenced by the societal tide surging around them than the treasured memories of the schools they admired.

In sobering ways the explanations these graduates offer for their complicity in accepting the housing, legislation, and socioeconomic factors that limit school desegregation in the present era also unwittingly mirror the reported values of some white parents in a previous generation. In the 1960s white parents in selected settings adamantly postulated that their refusal to accept busing was not a rejection of integration in the abstract but a refusal to have their children suffer "for a social experiment" (Ramsey 2008: 109). Indeed, Douglas Davidson, recounting Charlotte's desegregation—which is one of the sites the authors use as a case study—recounts that the Concerned Parents Association argued that they were "not segregationists" (Douglas 1995: 144). In both these settings white parents excuse their actions that limit desegregation while elevating expressions of their intent. Like some in the generation of their elders, the white 1980 school graduates the authors study also believe in the value of diversity, but many choose lifestyles that negate their values. Rather than their desegregated school experiences forging avenues for continued desegregation, even integration, in their adult lives, both cases capture the real tension that desegregated schooling experiences did not repudiate: that the struggle for racial equality was intended to destroy the manifestations of overt racism but never designed to disrupt economic progress or overthrow deeply held cultural norms of white privilege.

The story of progress and contradictions in *Both Sides Now* is not limited to white graduates. Black graduates report adult experiences only slightly more hopeful. While they live in more desegregated housing than their white counterparts, report jobs in diverse settings, and are more adamant about finding diverse schooling settings for their children, they also confine their social and religious activities primarily to other African Americans. In other words, just as they were bused across town in some cities to desegregate schools, so they now artificially position themselves in jobs and neighborhoods that reflect the valued diversity of the previous era, while simultaneously retreating into the familiarity of a black neighborhood for their closest ties. Such behaviors reflect the significance of increased job opportunities and social networks that desegregation scholars have identified but add vexing dimensions that reveal the extent to which race remains a central variable in ethnic relationships.

For adding to the scholarship the first-person accounts of the complexity of the schools and the experiences of the students therein, these authors contribute significantly to the extant literature. With balanced hand they chronicle the vision of a desegregated world the schools represented and the ways in which graduates of the era embraced an America that would be just in its schooling practices. In some described cases, as that of Julia, a Jewish woman who is adamant that her remembered experiences be replicated in those of her children, the findings give reason to hope. However, the authors deserve commendation also because they refuse to retreat from the complexities in the schooling experiences, both in the described high school memories and the activities and beliefs over time. Indeed, their careful presentation of these complexities reveals the extent to which the practices of desegregation have failed to achieve the vision for which its proponents hoped. Their portrait does not diminish the importance of desegregation, but it strikingly uncovers some of the issues with which desegregated schools still need to contend to deliver educational experiences more equitably across a diverse student body and to ensure that the visionary goals of desegregation are not abandoned by adult practices.

I confess, however, that for me the book is more than the filling of a gap in the academic literature. Indeed, this narrative also compels me personally. In 1980 I was a first-year teacher of seniors in a newly built suburban desegregated school on the black side of an industrial town in North Carolina. As I read the vivid accounts of student struggles, both then and now, I have been intrigued to imagine that these participants are symbolically *my* students and that I was one of the teachers described in these pages. In entering this shared space of identity, I allow my mind to recall my students by name, and I remember black and white teenagers laughing as they interacted in class settings and extracurricular activities. I recall our collective joy when we successfully competed against the former all-white high school on the other side of town to see who would achieve the highest test scores. Although some of the concerns about teachers and structures in the schools the authors describe in this book also resonate with my experiences, especially tracking, ours was a school headed by one of the few black high school principals who survived school desegregation in North Carolina. In ways I did not recognize at the time, this principal extended his previous experiences with black children in a segregated school by insisting on a top faculty who would commit to practices that increased student achievement. Despite some failures, in many ways our world was the success story of desegregation for which many Americans hoped.

The findings in *Both Sides Now* are thus troubling. As I remember the excitement and easy familiarity of the era and contrast it with the experiences recounted of similar students in this book, I wonder if the students I remember with such fondness continue to value the school they left behind. Based on cursory conversations with a limited sample, I suspect many do. But do they value those memories enough to insist on similar experiences for their children? The answer to that question is unknown. As a first-year teacher, I engaged in a rare digression from a lesson plan on the day Ronald Reagan was elected to the presidency to offer my views on the policy changes his election signaled. My students listened politely, some skeptically. Yet, neither they nor I could have foreseen the world of yuppism, Republicanism, and conservatism that would unfold in the following years. In fact, the success of the desegregated school of my memory is reportedly undermined by changing demographics, school policies, and administrative and teaching staff. It has become a typical urban school with all of the challenges we now associate with schools whose students are predominately black and Latino at a low socio-economic level (Eaton & Orfield 2003; Singham 2003). I find it difficult to comprehend that some of my white students could have become complacent about its loss or so uncaring about their experiences there as to sacrifice the opportunity for their own children to attend the school. Yet, like many former students of similar age described in these pages, I have little reason to believe they have escaped unscathed from the changing world around them.

Both Sides Now is brilliant for inviting me and others, academically and personally, into the world of graduates of desegregated schools. For some readers the intersection will be scholarly as they struggle with the new research questions these findings will surely generate. For others the intersection will be personal, challenging individuals and institutions to recapture the promises by learning from some of the failures of school desegregation policy. This response will challenge our collective acquiescence to the housing and employment patterns and the income gap that limit equality in schooling opportunities in a new, more restrictive, and more segregated school climate. For all, the book will open a window on a period that is too often a recounting *about* children and policies rather than a focus on capturing the children's ethnographic rendering of their own lives.

And so DuBois manages to leave another salient quote for a new generation. What happened to the children? In this text the authors provide a robust, well-written, and well-documented answer to the question. What has happened appears to be that the children have become romantic about their experiences, often ignoring the inequality inherent therein, and simultaneously complacent about their present-day actions. It is not the answer we might have liked. But *Both Sides Now* provides the answer we need.

Vanessa Siddle Walker

REFERENCES

Baker, L. (1996). *The Second Battle of New Orleans: The Hundred-Year Struggle to Integrate the Schools.* New York: HarperCollins.

Beals, M. P. (1994). *Warriors Don't Cry: A Searing Memoir of the Battle to Integrate Little Rock's Central High.* New York: Pocket Books.

Braddock, J., and T. Eitle. (2003). "The Effects of School Desegregation." In J. A. Banks, ed., *Handbook of Multicultural Education,* pp. 323–46. Menlo Park, CA: Jossey-Bass.

Douglas, D. M. (1995). *Reading, Writing, and Race: Desegregation of the Charlotte Schools.* Chapel Hill: University of North Carolina Press.

Eaton, S. E., and G. Orfield. (2003). Rededication Not Celebration. *The College Board Review* 200: 29–33.

Feldman, G. (2004). "Prologue." In G. Feldman, ed., *Before Brown: Civil Rights and White Backlash in the Modern South,* pp. 1–20. Tuscaloosa, AL: University of Alabama Press.

Jones, F. C. (1978). "Desegregation in the 1970s: A Candid Discussion." *The Journal of Negro Education* 47 (1): 2–27.

Mohraz, J. J. (1979). *The Separate Problem: Case Studies of Black Education in the North, 1900–1930.* Westport, CT: Greenwood Press.

Morris, V. G., and C. L. Morris. (2002). *The Price They Paid: Desegregation in an African American Community.* New York: Teachers College Press.

Orfield, G. (2005). "The Southern Dilemma: Losing Brown." In J. C. Boger and G. Orfield, eds., *School Resegregation: Must the South Turn Back?* pp. 1–25. Chapel Hill: University of North Carolina Press.

Orfield, G., and S. E. Eaton. (1996). *Dismantling Desegregation: The Quiet Reversal of Brown v. Board of Education.* New York: New Press.

Poll: Integration Improved Education for Black Students. (2004). The Associated Press. http://www.ipsos-na.com/new/ap/.

Ramsey, S. (2008). *Reading, Writing, and Segregation: A Century of Black Women Teachers in Nashville.* Urbana, IL: University of Illinois Press.

Singham, M. (2003). "The Achievement Gap: Myths and Reality." *Phi Delta Kappan* 84: 586–91.

Acknowledgments

This study would not have been possible without the generous support of the Spencer Foundation, the Joyce Foundation, and the Ford Foundation. The first author also benefited greatly from two fellowships while working on this project. She launched the study when she was visiting scholar at the Russell Sage Foundation and completed the final editing of this book manuscript as a fellow at the Center for Advanced Study in the Behavioral Sciences. While we are greatly indebted to these foundations and institutions for their faith in us to carry out this timely and important research, the arguments stated here are entirely ours, based on our five years of interviews, document collection, and analysis, and do not necessarily reflect the views of the foundations.

Over the life of this study, our research team has expanded and shrunk as some researchers signed on and others moved on to new pursuits. The findings presented on the following pages would not have emerged without the dedication of several research associates who left before it was finished. Amina Humphrey, Alejandra Lopez, Janelle Scott, Jolena James, and Camille Wilson Cooper all influenced this study in significant ways. We are grateful for their contributions and know that our work would have been far less insightful had we not had the opportunity to work with each of them.

Any study of nearly 550 interviews with more than 500 people relies heavily on tape transcription. We have benefited greatly from the hard work of superb tape transcribers. Linda Roehmholdt, Annie Petrossian,

Julianne Phillips, Yuvetta Robinson, Johanne E. Zell, and Juan Menchaca worked wonders—sometimes listening to the same tape two or three times to do justice to the words of our interviewees. We are forever indebted to them for their persistence, accuracy, and understanding.

Many other part-time graduate and undergraduate students worked on this study, performing technical and administrative tasks that were critical to our day-to-day functioning as a multisite research project. These students include Angelica Marin at UCLA and Dave Yang, Amy Wooten, Lance Ozier, and Anna Tuite at Teachers College. Thank you also to Diane Katanick and Christy Bagwell at Teachers College for critical administrative support.

We were further supported by the guidance of an advisory board of distinguished scholars in the field of education. James Anderson, Patricia Gandara, Roslyn Mickelson, and Jeannie Oakes—experts in the study of school desegregation and equal educational opportunities—read many pages of our material, helped keep us focused and methodologically sound, and provided much-needed encouragement throughout the course of a study that was logistically and intellectually challenging.

Additional scholars and leaders in the field of education offered invaluable advice. Special recognition goes to Annette Lareau, Anna Neumann, and Vanessa Siddle Walker for listening the longest. Others who have been helpful in numerous ways include Marv Alkin, Jean Anyon, Michael Apple, Carol Ascher, Darlyne Bailey, Jomills Braddock, Charles Clotfelter, Kevin Dougherty, Michelle Fine, Megan Franke, Edward Gordon, LaRuth Gray, Jack Greenberg, Pamela Grundy, Ellen Condliffe Lagemann, David Lapin, Arthur Levine, Henry Levin, Pat McDonough, Gene Maeroff, Lamar Miller, Aaron Pallas, Ted Shaw, William Spriggs, Alan Sadovnik, and William Trent.

Heartfelt thanks go to the hundreds of people who let us interview them and who provided us with historical documents, guided tours, and access to their twenty-year high school reunions. Through your insights, laughter, and tears, we have learned more about the complexities of school desegregation in America than any other research team before us. This study is both about you and for you. We have worked hard to bring your understanding of race and education to a larger audience, which can benefit from your vision of what was, what is, and what could be.

Most importantly in terms of the final stage of this long process of researching and writing this book, we want to thank our editor at UC Press, Naomi Schneider, for believing in this book and its potential contribution to society. Your insights and understanding are greatly appreciated. We are also extremely thankful to Marilyn Schwartz, our managing editor, for keeping us on track, and to Elisabeth Magnus, our copyeditor, for shortening and tightening our sometimes rambling prose with grace while remaining true to our meaning.

Last, but not at all least, we thank our families and significant others for putting up with our travel, late-night analysis and writing, and hours of discussion about what we learned. We could not have done it without you, and this is your accomplishment too.

ONE The Class of 1980

On a hot July afternoon, Larry Rubin was sitting on the large wooden deck behind his spacious, newly built suburban home in northern New Jersey.[1] Drinking cool water and wearing a T-shirt from the prominent university he had attended two decades before, Larry watched three of his four sons playing on their backyard jungle gym—a well-equipped structure that rivaled those of many public playgrounds. Their squeals echoed off the tall trees that provided privacy from the nearest neighbors almost an acre away. His wife, Laura, carrying their infant son in a baby sling, pushed one of the older boys on a swing. The Rubins had just returned from a beach vacation, and Larry was enjoying an extra day off before returning to work in a family-owned business.

Life was good for Larry and his family. Like so many white, upper-middle-class families, they had benefited from the shifts in the American economy since the early 1980s—twenty-five years in which those in the highest income bracket, the "fortunate fifth," made more money and acquired wealth much faster than everyone else.[2] They had a home that would fit comfortably in the pages of *House Beautiful,* a well-equipped minivan, and the American Dream of a large plot of land in a safe and secure suburb, far removed from the most vexing social problems of large cities and poorer communities.

Yet something was nagging Larry, who remembered his own child-hood of the 1960s and 1970s as being both less and more than that of his sons. Larry grew up in Englewood, New Jersey—a racially and

socioeconomically diverse town not too far from his current home—
where he had far fewer amenities than his own children because his parents were not as well off financially as he is today. His mother was a
nurse and his father a professor at a small college. During high school,
Larry recalled working in restaurants over the summer while his more
affluent classmates went on teen tours or to sleep-away camp.

But in another way, Larry realized, he had opportunities that his sons
are missing out on—the public schools he attended in Englewood taught
him unique lessons about life that he greatly values to this day. From the
moment he entered kindergarten in 1967 to his high school graduation in
1980, Larry went to school with students from both sides of the railroad
tracks that literally divide Englewood by race and class. In ninth grade he
and his classmates were joined by more well-to-do white students who
came down the hill from a nearby K-8 school system in Englewood Cliffs
to attend Englewood's Dwight Morrow High School. By the late 1970s,
Dwight Morrow High was 57 percent black, 36 percent white, and 7 percent Hispanic. The white students ranged from very affluent to lower
middle class in terms of their family backgrounds, while the black and
Hispanic students ranged from middle class to poor. A large percentage—
some say more than half—of the white students were Jewish, creating a
dynamic mix of race, class, and religion in one school that Larry and his
former classmates all say they have not experienced since. Larry, a white
middle-class Jewish boy and a member of the mostly black football and
track teams, found himself at the center of this mix, and he loved it.

"I was proud of a place that was diverse in population," Larry said.
"For the most part, I felt like we all got along, it was definitely . . . there
was a mix socially. I think I had a lot to do with [that]—not that I caused
it, but I was in the middle of a lot of social mixing happening, and I think
helped make it safe for people to get together . . . and I loved being a
white guy who could walk in those worlds."

His sons, on the other hand, are growing up in a more "lily white"
environment and—while there are a handful of Asian and Indian families in the town—have hardly any exposure to African Americans or
Hispanics. In that way, he said, his sons lack the kind of daily experiences that gave him a deeper appreciation of people on the other side of

the color line. Through their synagogue he and his older children are involved in community service, helping in homeless shelters and Red Cross centers in Englewood. But Larry worries that these interactions teach very different lessons from the ones he learned. The mostly black clientele in those settings are extremely poor and down and out—people who need help for a whole host of reasons; they will not be his sons' interracial friends and teammates.

Indeed, the more affluent and racially homogeneous community in which Larry and his family now live is "very much in a different world" from Englewood and Dwight Morrow—even if it is only miles away. Larry rarely sees or talks to his black friends from high school; he said their paths rarely cross. Since he went to college three months after high school graduation, most of his friends and the people he interacts with regularly are white and upper middle class. While he has seen a handful of his former black friends from Dwight Morrow— at a high school reunion and occasionally on the streets of Englewood where his parents still live—he commented on the separate and unequal "paths" he and these friends took after high school. "I have such warm feelings and memories of being with all these people, and we didn't save any of it. . . . I'm not friends with them now. . . . I think I went off with my white world. . . . People live lives for the most part along color," he said.

As Larry's life—and many of his classmates' lives—became far more racially segregated after high school, so did Dwight Morrow High School. Fewer white students enrolled each year, until, by the 1990s, there were virtually none. The school's once prominent reputation and its track record for sending students on to Ivy League colleges had evaporated, along with its political support among the more privileged members of the town and the local community's commitment to keeping it one of the top-ranked public high schools in the state.

Thus, while Larry now resides near his old high school—he noted he could jog there and back for exercise—he never considered moving back into the town of Englewood and sending his children to school there. Speaking of his old high school, Larry said, "It is what it is. It's just the reality. I mean, it's sad to me [because Dwight Morrow] had a soul, it had a feeling; it wasn't just this building. And I think it was just as important, just as rich an experience for black students as it was for the white students, as it was for me."

The racial segregation that envelops his adult life and defines it in stark contrast to his life as a child and teenager bothers Larry because it symbolizes the limits of this country's so-called social experiment known as school desegregation. He argued that much more could have been done to make the society as a whole more racially integrated and equal at the time—in the 1970s—when the public schools were struggling with these issues pretty much on their own. He said that when he and his classmates were in high school they had created a foundation for integration that, while it was not perfect, was a beginning—a base that could have been built upon to push for integration in other realms of society. "There were things going on where we could have taken this . . . being in an integrated environment—and maybe done more."

Absent such social and political efforts to build on what the children of school desegregation began, Larry said, "We went to school with each other. . . . We got along nice, we all threw our hats up together, and then we don't talk [to] or see each other anymore. . . . We didn't make the world an integrated place. It's just not."

Like many in his forty-something generation, Larry vacillates between his guilt over the individual pathways he and many of his classmates took and his anger at the larger society and its political leaders who, especially in the past twenty-five years, have neither supported nor sustained racially mixed institutions. The relatively brief period of history—from the late 1960s to the early 1980s—when school desegregation was implemented in hundreds of school districts across the country was not enough. According to Larry:

> I find it's so complicated for me, because I lived this certain life, and I don't live that life now. But I feel that . . . anybody who is different than me is equal to me as a person, before whoever, before God or before—we're just equal. But I don't live an equal life. . . . I'm trying to live the good life, but I want other people to live a good life too. And I know . . . I feel those things because I went to Dwight Morrow, I have this background. And if someone didn't, you know,

they don't think about these things—I'm very mixed on what did this background do to me.

. . . . .

As this book illustrates, Larry is not alone in his confusion about what attending a racially mixed school did to him. We spent five years talking to people like Larry—Americans in six diverse towns who graduated from desegregated high schools more than twenty-five years ago. We emerged from our cross-country travels with a profound understanding of the untold story of school desegregation in the United States. We found that despite pundits' claims that school desegregation is a failed social experiment, the millions of people who lived through this anomalous chapter of American history in the 1970s have a far more complicated tale to tell. Yet when we began this research no one had asked them whether *they* thought school desegregation was a success, a failure, or a bit of both.

Through thousands of hours of interviews with the graduates of school desegregation—as well as the educators who taught them and the community leaders who fashioned the policies that brought them together—we learned that this grand American "experiment" of enrolling children of different racial backgrounds in the same schools was simultaneously hopeful and dispiriting. In other words, much like the contradictory meanings of race that most Americans carry around in their heads, the stories of these graduates are double-sided, reflecting both how far we have come as a nation since the days of Jim Crow and how little progress we have made in moving toward an equal and integrated society.

Their stories are *hopeful* because virtually all of the graduates we interviewed said that attending desegregated public schools dispelled their fears of people of other races, taught them to embrace racial and cultural differences, and showed them the humanness of individuals across racial lines. In comparing themselves to peers and spouses who did not have similar integrative experiences, they are quick to note how much more comfortable they feel in multiracial settings or in places where they are a minority. They told us that while their years attending racially and ethnically diverse public schools were not always easy or tension-free, they were highly valuable preparation for an increasingly complex and global society.

At the same time, many of the graduates, especially blacks and Latinos, found their desegregated schooling experience *dispiriting* because it too often underscored how separate and unequal their lives were outside school. For instance, the racially segregated neighborhoods they lived in created logistical barriers to desegregation, namely long distances to travel to racially mixed schools. Usually, but not always, this logistical burden was placed primarily on black students, who often traveled great distances to attend racially diverse schools in white communities.

Furthermore, the resegregation within desegregated schools—across classrooms and spaces where students congregated when not in class—was real, palpable, and strongly reinforced by the distance between the homes, families, and cultures of the different racial and ethnic student populations. It was further reinforced by unequal opportunities prior to and outside high school and by too many educators who were biased against students of color in assessing ability and intelligence and who, at the same time, thought it was better not to talk about race and thus to not deal with racial issues at all. Still, despite all this, some of these graduates recall meaningful attempts that they and their classmates made to reach across the wide racial divide and function as equals in a society that told them they were anything but.

In the end the larger societal message prevailed. Regardless of the cross-racial bonds formed within these schools, the adults who graduated from them went on to lead lives that were, for the most part, far more segregated than their high schools. The white graduates were more likely to have reaped the benefits of an economy that for the last twenty-five years has greatly increased income inequality, rewarding the rich and the upper middle class while leaving the lower middle class and the poor behind. It was not that these white graduates actively avoided more racially diverse adult experiences but that their economic success relative to that of their parents led them to live in communities and engage in social networks that were, by virtue of their privilege, likely to be predominantly white. Even when they did find themselves in more diverse settings, they were generally associating with Asians as opposed to African Americans or Latinos.

Meanwhile, the black and Latino graduates of these schools, with few exceptions, worked harder than their white counterparts to escape racially isolated adulthoods—in part because they knew from their high school experiences that they could compete in mostly white settings where they would have greater access to status and opportunity. Yet even these black and Latino graduates who pursued and gained entry to more integrated workplaces and neighborhoods maintained mostly same-race social networks and friends. Thus the vast majority of the graduates we interviewed felt that school desegregation had been valuable to them on many levels, but they had learned that the racial mix they had been exposed to on a daily basis at school was not sustainable as they moved on into adulthood in a still-segregated society.

We concluded, after analyzing all these stories, that school desegregation did fundamentally change the people who lived through it—making them more accepting of those who are different from them and more comfortable in racially diverse settings—but that it had a far more limited impact on the larger society, which has remained highly separate and unequal along racial lines.[3] In fact, when these students graduated from their racially diverse public schools, there were very few neighborhoods they could move to or institutions they could join that looked like their schools. As a result, middle-aged graduates of desegregated schools such as Larry are perplexed. They told us that they believed, back in the late 1970s, that they were being prepared for the "real world," which they envisioned as an ever-more-integrated society. They thought that as first-generation graduates of desegregated schools in many cases they were at the forefront of major social changes. Yet after graduation they arrived at this so-called real world only to find it far more racially segregated than their schools had been, with few signs of meaningful change.

Thus we learned that racially diverse public schools of the late 1970s were doing more than other major institutions in our society—except perhaps the military—to bring people of different racial and ethnic backgrounds together and foster equal opportunity. But they could not, on their own, fulfill the promise of the Supreme Court's 1954 landmark *Brown v. Board of Education* ruling, which declared that racially separate schools were inherently unequal and implied that our best hope for greater equality lay in integrated public education.[4] At the time of the *Brown* ruling, it may have seemed plausible to the Supreme Court justices that the schools could carry such a heavy burden,[5] but our interviews with 540 people suggest, in hindsight, that this was too much to ask of one institution.[6]

Still, we should not interpret the attempts of officials and educators across the country to racially desegregate their public schools between the late 1960s and mid-1980s as a collective failure. We know from prior research on the quantifiable effects of school desegregation on students that there are numerous short- and long-term benefits, and our study certainly confirms many of these findings.[7] And when we note that the graduates we studied tend to lead far more racially segregated lives today than they did in high school, we do not mean to imply that their school experiences led them to seek segregation as adults. Indeed, as we explain in later chapters of this book, many of these graduates, especially the black and Latino graduates, live in more integrated communities than the average American. Furthermore, our interview data suggest that white graduates of desegregated schools are more willing than most whites in the United States to live and work in racially diverse settings.

Still, absent a broader societal effort to break down what sociologists call structural inequality, or the rigid patterns of racial segregation that are embedded in the policies and practices of our society, graduates of these and other desegregated schools are likely to lead adult lives that are more separated by race than their public schools were. These patterns— in the housing market, the labor market, and places of worship and other voluntary organizations—tend to channel people of different races in this country in different directions, almost always resulting in more advantages for affluent whites. Individuals can and do try to counter these trends—most often in workplaces although occasionally in housing—but such options are limited, since pervasive racial segregation and inequality mean that racially integrated neighborhoods remain the exception and not the rule for most home buyers. Even work settings, which are increasingly diverse by necessity because of our country's changing demographics, tend to be highly stratified along racial lines, with darker-skinned workers doing more menial jobs, often in physical spaces and work schedules separate from those of their higher-paid colleagues. This form of "segmented diversity" means that much interracial contact at work reinforces racial inequality and contributes to the large gaps in income and wealth across racial and ethnic groups.[8]

What we learned, therefore, is that efforts to desegregate public schools for a short time in the mid-twentieth century were simply the beginning of what should have been a long and comprehensive journey toward a more integrated society—a journey that has been aborted instead of expanded since that time. We write this book wondering when and if our leaders will ever wake up to the rapidly increasing diversity of this country—now that only 66 percent of the general population and 58 percent of the school-age population are non-Hispanic whites[9]—and recognize that the ongoing racial segregation in housing and now increasingly in our public schools needs to be addressed.

As we were finishing this book, the U.S. Supreme Court, in June 2007, provided a disappointing answer to this question by ruling that school integration plans that take the racial identity of individual students into account when assigning them to schools are unconstitutional. This ruling addressed issues of race-conscious policies in two cases—one from Louisville, Kentucky, and one from Seattle, Washington—where district officials had provided families with multiple choices of schools and then attempted to assign students to their first-choice schools while also balancing each school according to race. This effort to balance the students by race, therefore, meant that in a small number of cases students were assigned to their second- or third-choice schools. Parents of a few white students who did not get their first choices sued each of these school districts, arguing that their children's rights had been violated because of their race.

The Court's ruling in these cases—*Parents Involved in Community Schools v. Seattle School District No. 1* and *Meredith v. Jefferson County Board of Education*—significantly narrowed local officials' options to racially balance school enrollments and stabilize their districts by making schools more equal. Furthermore, the ruling will most likely have widespread implications for the kind of race-conscious policies that are still permissible in public education or any other sector of society, according to the separate opinion of Justice Kennedy, who embraced the goal of racial desegregation in public schools but not the means by which most school districts achieve that goal, namely taking into account the race/ethnicity of each student.[10] Kennedy suggested that other means that take the race of a neighborhood into account when building new schools or drawing attendance boundaries are permissible, as is targeted recruitment of students according to race. But the mechanisms that have been most helpful in actually creating and maintaining racially diverse schools—paying attention to the race of each student and making a student's race/ethnicity one factor in deciding who goes where—are no longer allowed.

Thus, even if policy makers do turn their attention to these pressing issues of racial segregation, they will have far fewer mechanisms they can use to make a difference. At the same time, they should be encouraged by our findings, knowing that millions of graduates of desegregated schools would agree with them if they chose to support the value of integration in an increasingly diverse society.

Yet even absent a Supreme Court ruling curtailing school districts' racial integration efforts, talk of racial integration is one thing and actually making meaningful change is something else. After all, many of the white graduates of diverse high schools are themselves relatively privileged forty-somethings currently ensconced in the status quo. Thus we would expect that most of those who, like Larry, are better off today economically than they were in high school would resist radical change that could result in a redistribution of opportunities in this society. Yet we argue that even within these political confines there is room to do much more than has been done in the last two decades to create a more equal and integrated society.

The story of these graduates of desegregated schools—a cohort of Americans who, more than any others, have seen our racially divided society from "both sides"—helps us learn some important lessons from the past that reconcile the contradictory legacies of the civil rights movement. As we explain in the following section, while there are clear signs of progress over the last half-century since the *Brown* decision, there is far less progress than many had hoped to see. For instance, we have witnessed the expansion of the black middle class and thus a great deal of mobility for many African Americans, but at the same time we see entrenched racial divisions and long-lasting inequality continuing to confound a society that refuses to look too closely for explanations. This book helps us understand critical aspects of the last forty years of American history that explain some of these two-sided results. The life course of the high school class of 1980 is particularly illustrative. These graduates were born in the midst of the civil rights movement and came of age in the 1980s. Thus they have a unique perspective on the dramatic social and political changes that occurred during the late 1970s and early 1980s in particular—changes that continue to affect racial politics and domestic policy today. In this way, they help us understand how we got where we are today and what is needed to make meaningful change.

RACIAL INEQUALITY AND SEPARATENESS: THE CLOSING AND REOPENING GAPS

Since the high school class of 1980 was born in the early 1960s, there have been significant advances in racial equality in this country. From the mid-1950s to the early 1970s, different branches of the federal government supported meaningful civil rights policies such as the *Brown* decision, the Civil Rights Act of 1964, the Economic Opportunity Act of 1964, the Voting Rights Act of 1965, and two other critical school desegregation rulings: *Green* (1968) and *Swan* (1971), which finally forced school districts to dismantle state-imposed segregation.

The Progress of the Civil Rights Era

Overall, from the mid-1960s until the mid- to late 1990s, disparities between blacks and whites in terms of educational attainment and household income narrowed fairly dramatically, leading to a significant increase in the black middle class.[11] For instance, the black-white gap in high school completion rates for people ages twenty-five to twenty-nine declined from 20 percentage points in 1967 to about 7 points by 1997. During the same time period, the median household income for blacks increased by 24 percent.[12] As a result, the proportion of African Americans considered middle class rose from about 10 percent in 1960 to about 50 percent today.

The evidence suggests that the civil rights policies, along with a shift in what was socially acceptable in terms of racial hatred and discrimination, the hard work of many African Americans, and the growth in government jobs, which blacks are twice as likely to hold, led to meaningful progress.[13] Furthermore, there are signs that these gains are positively shaping the opportunities of the next generation of the black middle class. In 1999, for instance, 60 percent of all black freshmen entering selective colleges had a father who had graduated from college, and 25 percent came from families earning more than $100,000 per year.[14]

Another sign of mobility among African Americans is the departure of large numbers of middle-class blacks from central cities to suburban communities, following a trail blazed by middle-class whites decades ago. According to the 2000 Census, about 40 percent of all African Americans now live in suburban communities, where more and more "people of color are increasingly making the dream of suburban home ownership a reality."[15]

While these statistics depict noteworthy gains for African Americans in the last four decades, a closer look at the data reveals that the most significant improvements occurred—or had their foundations laid—in the first half of that forty-year period. From the early 1980s onward, the picture is far less rosy, even as our nation has become increasingly racially and ethnically diverse. Gaps in economic and educational outcomes for whites and African Americans remain wide and, in some cases, have increased since the class of 1980 left high school.

Remaining and Widening Gaps

Despite the growth of the black middle class in the last half-century, in the last thirty years the gap in median family income between blacks and whites has closed by only 4 percent, from 58 to 62 percent.[16] Even in the late 1990s, when the African American poverty rate hit a historic low of 23.6 percent, it remained nearly 2.5 times the poverty rate of whites.[17] The African American unemployment rate in 2005 of 10.8 percent was 2.3 times the white unemployment rate of 4.7 percent.[18] And blacks, even those who have held the same job for many years, are far more likely to be laid off during an economic downturn, making their income status far more precarious.[19]

Meanwhile, a statistic with longer-term implications for inequality along racial lines, the median net worth of black families, was still less than one-tenth that of whites ($6,100 versus $67,000) in 2005.[20] Richard Rothstein argues that there are several reasons for the ongoing racial gap in wealth, many of which speak to the rampant racial discrimination in the housing market after World War II, when both the federal government and private lenders discouraged or prohibited blacks from buying homes in the suburban communities where values have appreciated most.[21]

Indeed, recent research on housing segregation in the United States is not encouraging. One set of authors sum it up as follows: "Despite the decline in group inequality and rapid expansion of the black middle class, residential segregation remains a striking feature of the urban landscape in many large metropolitan areas with significant black populations."[22]

Racial housing segregation has varied across place and time to some extent but not across social classes or urban-suburban boundaries. For instance, as the authors above note, the larger the black population in a given metropolitan area, the more segregation there will be within that context. Thus major cities that attracted millions of African Americans during their migration from the rural South to the urban North in the first half of the twentieth century are extremely segregated. Meanwhile cities and towns with smaller black populations, particularly those in the West, show signs of greater integration. Related to this phenomenon is a geographic difference in segregation, with the cities in the Northeast and Midwest more segregated than those in the West and South.[23] According to a study on racial segregation in the twenty-first century: "Desegregation has been slowest precisely in the places African Americans are most likely to live. There, racial isolation can be extreme. For example in the Chicago, Detroit, and Cleveland metropolitan areas, most African Americans live in census tracts (roughly, neighborhoods) where more than 90 percent of the residents are black and fewer than 6 percent are white."[24]

Indeed, this high degree of housing segregation in the metropolitan areas where most blacks reside is pervasive across urban-suburban lines and social class boundaries. In other words, segregation is a defining feature of the suburbs as well as the cities and for the more middle class as well as the poor. Even as more working- and middle-class black and Latinos move out of poor neighborhoods into the suburbs, the color line moves with them. The literature on housing segregation suggests that levels of segregation experienced by black households in particular are "uniformly high across all income categories" and that "white and black households at all levels of income, education and occupational status are nearly as segregated as are whites and blacks overall."[25]

Thus in many metro areas today the inner-ring suburbs—especially those that are less affluent and have more moderately priced houses—have become all African American and/or Latino. Meanwhile, the affluent whites have either moved back into expensive enclaves in the cities or moved farther away to the outer suburbs or "exurbs." It is not uncommon to find these mostly white exurbs dotted with so-called McMansions, or huge newly built homes, often ensconced in gated communities. As one of the fastest-growing segments of the housing market, these gated communities further separate white and affluent Americans from darker-skinned people, who generally enter the gates only to clean houses, manicure lawns, and care for the white people who live inside.[26]

Looking historically at the ebb, flow, and persistence of racially segregated housing in this country, we should expect the data to look better by now. Historically, residential segregation worsened during the first two-thirds of the twentieth century as millions of blacks migrated from the southern fields to the northern cities. By 1970, housing segregation in the United States had reached staggering levels, the result of state-imposed and state-supported policies of discrimination as well as white resistance to integration. After this highpoint in 1970 some progress was made, particularly prior to 1990, as small numbers of blacks moved into predominantly white neighborhoods, but few if any whites moved into all-black neighborhoods.[27] In fact, today the average white person in the United States continues to live in a neighborhood that is 80 percent white and only 7 percent black. Meanwhile, a typical African American lives in a neighborhood that is only 33 percent white and more than half black.

Thus the post-1970s progress in terms of housing segregation has not been great enough to undo the extreme segregation that was systematically put in place over several decades. Furthermore, reports based on the 2000 Census data find that in the 1990s we made less progress toward integration than we did in the 1980s. In fact, according to one report on these data, we appear to be losing ground as our "growing ethnic diversity in the nation is accompanied by a high degree of residential separation."[28]

This ongoing segregation exacerbates a system of inequality, as whites and more affluent Asians are able to move into communities with fewer working-class or poor neighbors. Through this spatial separation of those with more resources from those with less, affluent communities can ensure that they have the best public services, including public schools. Removed from needy communities physically and politically, the well off are less likely to care about those who are poor.[29] Meanwhile, middle-class blacks are far more likely than middle-class whites to live in poor neighborhoods with all of the social problems associated with concentrated poverty. In this way "separate translates into unequal even for the most successful black and Hispanic minorities."[30]

While a host of present-day forces maintain this high-level of housing segregation, the literature suggests that white racial attitudes and unwillingness to live in neighborhoods that are more than 20 percent black are central factors. Indeed, one study noted that while blacks' preferences for neighborhoods that are at least 50 percent black as well as income differences between whites and blacks play a part, whites' attitudes play the most essential role in maintaining racial segregation.[31] Furthermore, the authors note that much of the research suggests that the best way to change whites' attitudes is to improve their knowledge of blacks through either interracial contact or education on racial issues. Still, their conclusion based on their findings is that interracial contact and *not* racially isolated education is the best and perhaps the only way to meaningfully change whites' attitudes: "Optimism lies in the finding that neighbourhood and workplace contact affect white preferences in favour of integrated neighbourhoods. Inter-racial contact has been on the increase, especially in the workplace and this augurs well for future integration. On the other hand, the results lend little support for the hypotheses that greater integration will result as the percentage of whites with college degrees [from racially isolated schools] expands."[32]

Interestingly enough, the high school graduates of 1980 that we studied carried their interracial contact experiences with them into adulthood, where they encountered a separate and unequal housing market. While our findings support the argument stated above that prior interracial contact in their schools did indeed make individuals more open to the idea of housing integration, their willingness on its own proved to be too small a factor in most cases when it was challenged by their choice of neighborhoods, most of which were far more segregated in terms of race and class than their high schools. Furthermore, like many Americans, these graduates state that they are most likely to have interracial contact in their workplaces, but those workplaces, as we noted above, are often highly stratified by class, status, and race in ways that make workplace interaction more hierarchical across racial lines. And unlike their high schools, which were also stratified because students were too often tracked into separate and unequal classrooms, the graduates' adult workplaces do not have the extracurricular programs, including athletics, student government, and drama, that often brought them together across racial lines when they were in school.

Layered Inequality

To fully appreciate the context of the class of 1980's adulthood and what has happened to these graduates since they left high school, we must examine some critical and defining economic changes over the last two and a half decades. If the entrenched racial segregation discussed above were not enough, we have seen, in the last twenty-five years, another, overlapping form of inequality develop along social class lines. Indeed, by the time the class of 1980 entered the workforce, the postindustrial global economy had begun to fuel greater economic inequality, with huge and growing gaps between the haves and have-nots.[33]

Since the late 1970s, we have seen the rich get richer while the poor and middle class have just tried to hang on to what they have, often while working more hours and sending more family members off to work. Unlike the prior era (1950s–70s), which saw a compression of incomes and the creation of a stronger and better-off middle class, the last quarter-century has led to deeper and wider divisions in terms of income and wealth.[34] According to one report, between 1950 and 1970, for every dollar earned by the bottom 90 percent of the population, those in the top 0.01 percent earned an additional $162. But from 1990 to 2002, for every dollar earned by the bottom 90 percent, those in the top 0.01 percent earned $18,000.[35]

By the time the high school graduates of 1980 were looking for adult jobs, serious social and economic changes were occurring that led to a legitimization of the "deserving rich." Between 1989 and 2000, when median hourly wages grew by just 5.9 percent, CEO compensation increased by 342 percent to an average of $1.7 million per year. "In 1978, the average CEO made 37 times what the average worker made; by 2000, the average CEO made 310 times what the average worker earned."[36] By 2004, the United States held the distinction of having the greatest income and wealth disparities of any advanced industrial society.[37]

Because this growing income inequality was laid down on top of several layers of racial segregation and inequality that so strongly defined our country by the mid-twentieth century, it should come as no surprise that the vast majority of the "fortunate fifth" who have most benefited from these economic shifts are whites. In other words, the new form of extreme income inequality did not replace the preexisting racial inequality; it just exacerbated it. Indeed, one analysis of 2000 Census data reveals that the decade (1990–2000) of widespread prosperity "did not yield greater income or neighborhood equality for blacks and Hispanics."[38]

To make matters worse, the growing gap in income and wealth between the rich and nonrich has coincided with a political backlash against public policies, including affirmative action and school desegre-gation, designed to correct or even out major inequality in American soci-ety along several dimensions, especially race.[39] Efforts to end such policies have been legitimized by a general acceptance of wide economic disparity as "natural" and thus not requiring intervention. Indeed, resis-tance to such policies has been most fervent among whites who are in the "unfortunate four-fifths" at the bottom of the social class hierarchy.[40] This translates into an ongoing racial divide among middle-class and poor Americans, ensuring that the interests of the very rich and powerful will not be challenged by a meaningful political coalition of have-nots.[41]

For better or worse, the adult lives of high school graduates of 1980 have been profoundly shaped by these trends toward more socioeco-nomic segregation and inequality and an ongoing racial divide. Many of the graduates we interviewed have benefited economically from these shifts, even as they have wondered how their priorities and those of the society could change so drastically in just half their lifetime. And, as we discuss in a later chapter, many of these graduates became even more aware of how dramatically different the current era is from their childhood years when they had children of their own and faced deci-sions about where to educate them and with whom. Similar to the way in which the broader society influenced their school experiences many years ago, the growing racial and ethnic diversity in the United States, coupled with the rise in inequality over the last twenty-five years and the backlash against policies that try to correct it, has led to more racial sep-arateness in our public schools and a growing gap in educational out-comes across racial lines—the very gap that their desegregated schooling experiences were designed to fix.

Public Education: Becoming More Separate and More Unequal

Intertwined with the growth of the black middle class over the last fifty years, significant gains have been made in equalizing educational oppor-tunities since the beginning of the civil rights movement. Yet, like the economic developments discussed above, these gains are less than many had hoped for, and while we witnessed a rapid narrowing of the gap between the educational outcomes of students of color and those of white students beginning in the 1970s, these gains have stagnated or reversed since the mid-1980s.

Table 1 shows the narrowing and widening black-white gaps on several educational indicators from the early 1970s until 2000. As the data clearly illustrate, many indicators of black and Latino students' achievement and attainment show impressive progress during the years when meaningful civil rights policies were being put in place in schools and communities around the country.

It seems more than coincidental that these years during which the black-white achievement gap was closing correspond with the years that students of different racial and socioeconomic backgrounds were more likely to be in the same schools and thus in closer proximity to the same curriculum, teachers, and school resources and status.[42] This was also the period of American history when African American students were least likely to be enrolled in high-poverty schools.[43]

Since the mid-1980s, shortly after the graduates we studied had moved on to college or work, public schools in the United States became more separate and unequal—more racially and socioeconomically segregated, with larger gaps in terms of resources, curriculum, and opportunities between the most affluent suburban and the poorest urban schools. According to reports issued by the Civil Rights Project, levels of segregation for black and Latino students have been steadily increasing since the mid-1980s. In fact, between 1991 and 2002 the percentage of African American students attending predominantly black schools grew as much as 10 percent in some areas of the country. Meanwhile, the percentage of Latino students attending predominantly Latino schools grew by as much as 18 percent in some states.[44]

In 2002–3, the average white student attended a school that was almost 80 percent white, while the average black and Latino students attended schools that were 30 and 28 percent white, respectively. Thus, while the U.S. student population in K–12 schools is still majority white, most students of color attend schools that are substantially segregated—70 percent or more black and/or Latino.[45]

Table 1 Indicators of educational achievement and attainment by racial/ethnic groups from the early 1970s to 2000

Educational Achievement or Attainment Measure by Years[a]	White	African American	African American–White Gap	Latino	Latino-White Gap
% Aged 16–24-Year-Olds Who Dropped out of High School[b]					
1972	12	21	9	34	22
1986	10	14	4	30	20
2000	7	13	6	28	21
% Aged 18–24 Who Completed High School[b]					
1972	88	72	−16	56	−32
1986	90	82	−8	64	−26
2000	92	84	−8	64	−28
Average NAEP Reading Scores for 13-Year-Olds[c]					
1971	261	222	−39	n/a	n/a
1984	263	236	−27	240	−23
1988	261	243	−18	240	−21
1999	267	238	−29	240	−27
Average NAEP Math Scores for 13-Year-Olds[c]					
1973	274	228	−46	239	−35
1982	274	240	−34	252	−22
1986	274	249	−25	254	−20
1999	283	251	−32	259	−24

SOURCE: Kathryn Hoffman, Charmaine Llagas, and Thomas D. Snyder, *Status and Trends in the Education of Blacks*, NCES 2003–034 (Washington, DC: U.S. Department of Education, National Center for Educational Statistics, September 2003), http://nces.ed.gov/pubs2003/2003034.pdf (accessed January 22, 2008).

a. Different measures are for different years because the National Center for Educational Statistics' reports on these measures come out in different years.

b. Data for these measures were derived from a graph, so the specific numbers for any one year or racial group may be off by 1 percent.

c. NAEP is the National Assessment of Educational Progress, a battery of tests given to a random sample of students across the country.

Hand in hand with this increasing racial and ethnic segregation is a more intense concentration of poverty in predominantly black and/or Latino schools, making the separate schools more unequal. As Gary Orfield and Chungmei Lee report, 88 percent of high-minority schools— those with enrollments that are more than 90 percent minority—are also high-poverty schools, meaning that more than 50 percent of the students receive free or reduced-price lunches. The corresponding share of so-called low-minority schools (those with less than 10 percent students of color) that are also high-poverty schools is 15 percent. The reality of segregation by race and poverty means that, while the majority of white students attend middle-class schools, minority students are more likely to attend racially segregated schools in which most of their classmates are poor.[46] This highly concentrated poverty in schools, Orfield and Lee note, is one of the single best predictors of student failure and dropout. "Segregated schools are unequal and there is very little evidence of any success in creating 'separate but equal' outcomes on a large scale."[47]

In the meantime, our society—especially our school-age population— has become much more racially and ethnically diverse. As we noted above, according to the National Center for Education Statistics (NCES), in 2003 the percentage of students in the public schools nationwide who were white had dropped to 58 percent—down from 78 percent in 1973. Meanwhile, Hispanics or Latinos now constitute 19 percent of the K–12 public school population—more than triple their 6 percent in 1973. Another 16 percent of these students are African Americans, and the "other" category, which includes a wide range of Asian students as well as Native Americans, is 7 percent.[48]

Thus we find ourselves with a far more diverse school-age population and more segregated and unequal schools than thirty years ago when the class of 1980 was in high school. And while some have argued that the increase in racial segregation has more to do with the shrinking white population,[49] others respond that multiple factors contribute to greater racial isolation in public schools and that demographic shifts in the overall population do not entirely explain it. Indeed, if that were the case, white students would be far less isolated and there would not be such profound proportional differences in segregation levels across regions and contexts that have made drastically different efforts to overcome school segregation via public policies in the past.[50] Arguably this very real impact of public policies on racial isolation within schools is even more ironic in the current era of educational reform, which, as we demonstrate below, appears to be guided by the "separate but equal" doctrine that the *Brown* decision denounced.

Current Educational Policy

Indeed, over the last twenty-five years in particular, the educational policy priorities in this country have shifted away from fostering integration and diversity in the K–12 system toward trying to educate all children to high standards within the context of increasingly racially and socioeconomically segregated schools. Paradoxically, this shift has coincided with widening gaps in achievement and attainment along racial and ethnic lines, after these gaps had begun closing during the peak years of school desegregation, from the mid-1970s to the mid-1980s. The response of the federal government to this trend was to take the concept of standards one step further. In his first year in office President George W. Bush sponsored federal legislation, the No Child Left Behind Act of 2001, which requires more testing for students and a strict accountability system of sanctions associated with schools' failure to make progress in meeting benchmarks for student outcomes. Furthermore, test score data are broken down by student "subgroups" defined according to race/ ethnicity, poverty, gender, disability, and limited English proficiency. This provision, in theory, will help schools and the government ensure that no children are being left behind.[51]

In the years since its passage, however, the rhetoric of No Child Left Behind has not matched its reality. Thus, in addition to a plethora of complaints from school officials about how onerous the policy is to implement, researchers and educators have argued that the sanctions and punishments associated with school failings under this act are laid down upon a highly unequal educational system in which some students— particularly those in high-poverty schools—have access to far fewer resources and opportunities.[52] Furthermore, the law has been underfunded since the year it was passed, meaning that the inequalities in the educational system are not being offset by federal funding targeted toward poor students.[53]

Yet despite the alarming levels of inequality beneath the surface of the standards movement, the majority of policy makers, journalists, and commentators seem convinced in recent years that the best way to achieve greater equity in the American educational system is not through policies that try to address the segregation and concentration of poverty or the inequality across school sites but rather through policies that hold separate and unequal schools equally accountable for student outcomes. Accordingly, President Bush claimed that his new policy would attack "the soft bigotry of low expectations" for low-income students and students of color,[54] thereby closing the educational gap by forcing teachers who work in poor schools to hold their students to higher standards; but at the same time the federal government has done little to overcome the inequality in the educational system and the larger society that so profoundly influences students' achievement and life chances.[55]

Some of the most prominent news coverage of the fiftieth anniversary of the *Brown* decision in spring 2004 focused on how school accountability systems or court cases providing poor schools with more "adequate" (but not equal) funding had replaced desegregation as the promise of greater educational equity.[56] While more funding for poor school districts serving poor students of color is worth fighting for, suburban-dominated state legislatures have been loath to allocate such funds even when state judges rule that they must. Also, there is little reason to believe that, if all else remains the same—especially the high concentrations of rich and poor students in different rich and poor communities and schools—adequate funding will create equal educational opportunities.[57]

In essence, it appeared as though the *Brown* anniversary commentators were settling for the promise of *Plessy v. Ferguson,* the 1896 Supreme Court ruling that argued for "separate but equal" accommodations for black and white train passengers, despite the lack of evidence that such a condition can or does exist in the field of education. In this way, the coverage of the *Brown* anniversary allowed white Americans to absolve themselves of any responsibility for the perpetual segregation and inequality in our society and to lay the blame and burden of the achievement gap back on educators and poor students and their families. The angle of much of the anniversary coverage was that all that was needed to close the gap was more standardized testing and punitive measures for educators and students who did not raise scores sufficiently or in a timely manner.[58] This is an example of both a misguided and an exaggerated understanding of the role of schools in society as the single institution that can equalize the many inequalities that most adults turn their backs on every day.[59]

Thus it appears that we have arrived at the beginning of the twenty-first century with racial inequality and severe segregation firmly in place and a political climate in which no one is willing to do anything about it. We have accomplished this at the same time that most whites in the United States argue that enough has been done to solve racial problems in this country—"been there, did that" with the civil rights movement. Any ongoing inequality, they are now thoroughly convinced, is simply the result of black (and Hispanic) people's laziness or lack of family values.[60]

Meanwhile, most people of color, especially blacks and Latinos, see our recent history quite differently. They have an insight into race in America that most whites do not because of what W. E. B. DuBois termed "double consciousness."[61] Yet as we discuss below, some scholars have argued that there is also a white version of double consciousness about race that is quite distinct in its meaning and implication.

AMERICA'S DOUBLE CONSCIOUSNESS

Throughout the history of the United States, different social observers have reminded Americans that a large gap exists between our rhetoric of equality and liberty for all and the reality of our situation. Gunnar Myrdal, a Swedish economist who traveled this country for many months in the early 1940s, argued that the gap between what he called the American Creed and the conditions of the American Negro presented an ever-raging conflict that had to be resolved if our democracy was to be maintained. The Negroes' lack of rights and freedoms, Myrdal stated, represented a glaring inconsistency with the tenets of our constitution and democratic society.[62]

Myrdal's well-publicized book, a growing impatience and effective protests on the part of African Americans, and cries of hypocrisy from our Cold War enemies were three of the main factors that led this country into the civil rights movement of the 1950s and 1960s, which in turn provided the impetus for many of the federal Great Society policies of the 1960s and 1970s.[63] And while not all white Americans were as convinced as Myrdal in the 1940s or 1950s that the government needed to address racial inequality with fairly bold public policies, as time went on and the Jim Crow era of state-mandated segregation and separate drinking fountains faded into the past, most whites came to accept some degree of change as necessary and good.

For instance, public opinion data show that attitudes changed rather dramatically in the years following the 1954 *Brown* decision. In fact, the proportion of Americans of all races who believed that the Supreme Court was right in its *Brown* decision increased from 63 percent in the early 1960s to 87 percent in the mid-1990s. And in the South, where only 19 percent of the people agreed with the landmark ruling in 1954, in the 1990s, only 15 percent said they did *not* agree with the ruling. This marks a dramatic shift in attitudes in the region of the country that had most strongly resisted change.[64]

Still, support for the *Brown* decision, which struck down the use of blatant, state-sanctioned racial segregation, and support for what some consider more aggressive or proactive public policies such as affirmative action and school desegregation plans that require busing students across towns are two different things.[65] But as the 1960s, with its economic expansion and sense of national prosperity and optimism, gave way to the 1970s, with its economic stagnation and sense of disillusionment following Watergate and an unsatisfactory ending to the war in Vietnam, whites' views toward the civil rights movement and the war on poverty, which had never been overwhelmingly positive on average, began to sour.[66]

A conservative political movement would soon change the policy agenda in education and other public policy arenas. By the time the class of

1980 graduated from high school, in the midst of the Iranian hostage crisis, an economic recession, and a severe oil shortage, Ronald Reagan's presidential campaign was already fueling a powerful backlash against the civil rights movement and the Great Society policies of the 1960s and 1970s.[67]

The result of this backlash of white voters against policies of redistribution and greater access and opportunity for poor people and people of color has been a political era in which ongoing racial inequality is defined in very personal and individualistic terms.[68] The new "common sense" is that racism no longer exists and that the civil rights movement removed the barriers to mobility for African Americans, so that the only logical conclusion to be drawn about poor people, especially black or Latino poor people, is that they have created many of their own problems.[69]

Meanwhile, most blacks and Latinos argue that many of their problems still stem from racial discrimination and institutions and policies that maintain advantages—or privileges—for whites. The housing market would be but one example of such a structure in which racial discrimination helps to maintain segregation, which in turn allows whites to earn more from their property investments than do blacks or Latinos. In 1992, for instance, 29 percent of poor blacks and 21 percent of middle-class blacks agreed that "whites want to keep blacks down."[70]

Clearly, the ongoing problems of racial inequality and segregation look different from different sides of the color line. But complex and conflicting attitudes about race and equality also exist within racial groups—and within the souls of individuals.

Black Double Consciousness

More than forty years before Myrdal published his well-known book on the American dilemma, W. E. B. DuBois, an African American sociologist with keen insight into social phenomena, published a collection of essays on race titled *The Souls of Black Folk*. In the first essay, DuBois states boldly that the so-called "Negro Problem" is a "concrete test of the underlying principles of the great republic" and that "blacks' souls bear this burden in the name of this land of their fathers' fathers, and in the name of human opportunity."[71]

Two of DuBois's critical points in this book have been embraced by many readers as its defining principles. First, DuBois wrote persuasively that the problem of the twentieth century would be the problem of the color line. Second, he wrote about a sort of "double consciousness," a second sight that blacks possessed because they lived on one side of that color line, behind a veil of racial inequality and segregation through which they could see much more than they themselves could be seen.

> The Negro is sort of a seventh son, born with a veil, and gifted with second-sight in this American world—a world which yields him no true self-consciousness, but only lets him see himself through the revelation of the other world. It is a peculiar sensation, this double-consciousness, this sense of always looking at one's self through the eyes of others, of measuring one's soul by the tape of a world that looks on in amused contempt and pity. One ever feels his twoness,—an American, a Negro; two souls, two thoughts, two unreconciled strivings; two warring ideals in one dark body, whose dogged strength alone keeps it from being torn asunder.[72]

It has been said by DuBois and the many scholars who draw on his work that this double consciousness is a gift of a deeper insight that allows African Americans to see and understand life on both sides of the veil of race—or the color line that divides blacks from whites. For instance, Charles Lemert argues that the double consciousness is a *"gift of second-sight*—that is, the gift of a power that comes to those who, while held in contempt, exploit the shadows to see the world more deeply."[73]

Meanwhile, others have described DuBois's notion of double consciousness as *both* a gift and a burden. Lawrie Balfour writes: "It is second-sight, a way of seeing that which escapes notice by the White majority" and allows blacks to observe the distance between the American ideals—or the Creed—and American practices of systematic racial degradation. This double consciousness then "provides insight into the content of American promises as they are not understood by those who have the luxury of taking those promises for granted."[74]

In other words, to those who possess the double consciousness, the American promises embodied in the Creed that Myrdal describes cannot be taken for granted and must be fought for continually. That is the gift and the burden—the insight into the injustice and the responsibility to try to make this society good on its promises.

DuBois argued that the history of American Negroes is the history of this very strife and the longing to merge their double selves into a better and truer self—one less conflicted but still ever watchful and insightful. Yet in this merging, DuBois wrote, the Negro wishes neither of the old selves—the African or the American—to be lost. What the Negro wants, DuBois writes, is to be both a Negro and an American, without "having the doors of Opportunity closed roughly in his face."[75]

Henry Louis Gates Jr., in a *New York Times* article with the same title as this book, notes that DuBois wanted to make the American Negro whole and believed that only desegregation and full equality could make this psychic integration possible.[76] Our study and interview data from African Americans and Latinos who attended racially mixed schools suggest that to some extent this psychic integration did occur for people of color who attended desegregated schools in the 1970s.[77]

As we show in subsequent chapters of this book, these graduates of color have come to understand many things about themselves vis-à-vis their white classmates and teachers. Thus many have learned that in a white-dominated society they are more likely to gain access to the resources and opportunities they need to compete and succeed when they are in close proximity to whites—no matter how much these whites resist their presence or try to make them feel inferior. The schools and the classrooms that were predominantly white carried the reputations and the connections to take these students on to the best colleges and universities or job opportunities. Once schools and classrooms become predominantly black and/or Hispanic, they have learned, they will be perceived as far less desirable no matter what is going on inside in terms of teaching and learning.

In addition, the black and Latino graduates from the schools we studied learned that although the racial inequality and segregation outside schools definitely dictate the formation of cliques and friendships along racial lines, these barriers can be bridged in subtle ways that promote greater understanding and trust across racial lines. As one African American graduate of Shaker Heights High School reported: "It worked for most . . . seeing that there was some natural divisions at lunch, but being able to bridge that in the classroom, being able to bridge that in intramural sports, being able to bridge that with friendships through those events . . . that was the best teacher that anybody could have ever provided. You couldn't have taught that in a debriefing session for adults, you know, trying to get into the mind of a sixteen-year-old."

For this generation of African Americans, born in the midst of the civil rights movement and participants in many of the policies and programs designed to confront racial inequality, the veil behind which they view the white society and its understanding of them has been partly lifted. It is still there, and they still sense their "twoness" of being black and being American, but they are one step closer to the kind of psychic integration DuBois saw as the answer. But being only one step closer to something that has been so long in the making—so much longer than any writer in 1903 could have imagined—and seeing that the next generation may be on the verge of taking a half-step backwards makes the goal less desirable today than it was at the beginning of the twentieth century.

While much has been written about black double consciousness, far less has been published (at least in English) about the double consciousness of Latinos or whites. Interestingly enough, the work of Theresa Martinez partly applies the DuBoisian ideas of "two warring ideals in one dark body" and the veil to the analysis of what Gloria Anzaldúa has called "mestiza consciousness," adding issues of gender and sexuality to the analysis of oppression of people of color.[78]

Another social theory that explores a form of "double consciousness" is "whiteness" theory, which examines the manifestation of white privilege. In fact, a growing number of social theorists are considering the two-sidedness of that privilege in a manner that relates to the yearnings and contradictions of the white graduates we interviewed.

The New Double Consciousness of Whites

One of the more interesting developments in the study of race in the last two decades is scholars' efforts to uncover and depict whites' understanding of race, their own racial identity, and the persistence of racial inequality in American society.[79] Theories about whites and their identities as raceless and as "the norm" against which all darker-skinned souls must be judged have helped to explain many white people's attitudes toward people of color and their frustration with public policies, such as affirmative action and school desegregation, that take race into account. These writings on whiteness help explain the general understanding on the white side of the color line that there is far more equality and integration than in fact exists and thus the firm belief among many whites that the government needs to do little or nothing else to help people of color. In fact, to do more is, according to many whites, a form of favoritism and reverse discrimination.[80] At the same time, in the post–civil rights era, these same whites claim to be strong supporters of equal opportunities for all and see slavery and Jim Crow as evils that we have now, thankfully, overcome. As Derald Sue notes, "Most Whites were socialized into oppressor roles yet taught concepts of social democracy, fairness, justice, and equality."[81]

Howard Winant's theories of white racial identity in particular help us make sense of the often conflicting ways in which the white graduates from our study talk about race and their own lives. Winant espouses a theory of "white racial dualism" that he calls a way of extending to whites the "Du Boisian idea that in a racist society the 'color line' fractures the self." Winant argues that this idea can be extrapolated to whites at the turn of the century as the very idea of whiteness has been "deeply fissured by the racial conflicts of the post–civil rights period." Since the 1960s and the civil rights movement's language and rhetoric of equality and diversity, Winant notes, racial discourse that openly espouses the racial superiority of whites and thus justifies the exclusion of blacks and other people of color has been less accepted and less able to function in the public sphere. Therefore, he writes, "white identities have been displaced and refigured: They are now contradictory, as well as confused and anxiety-ridden, to an unprecedented extent. It is this situation that I describe as white racial dualism."[82]

According to Winant, this crisis of "whiteness"—in which the very meaning of whiteness is cast into doubt—does in fact relate to the greater, although limited, degree of racial equality in the post–civil rights period. For example, the growth of the black middle class is one of the developments that challenges the historical meanings of whiteness, especially for whites who are struggling to maintain their own middle-class status in an increasingly unequal labor market. While these whites are far less likely to be wearing white hoods, burning down black houses and churches, or advocating for state-sanctioned segregation than their ancestors were, they may well feel that their very identity is threatened by social changes since the 1950s in particular and thus may consciously or subconsciously resist further change. According to Winant, therefore, the crisis of whiteness is simply the latest defense of white supremacy, which "now covers itself with the fig leaf of a formal egalitarianism."

In other words, whites now too must cope with a double consciousness, though from a different standpoint in relation to the veil of racial inequality. Winant states: "On the one hand, whites inherit the legacy of white supremacy, from which they continue to benefit. But on the other hand, they are subject to the moral and political challenges posed to that inheritance by the partial but real success of the black movement (and affiliated movements)."[83]

This form of white double consciousness leads to dualistic and often contradictory allegiances to both privilege *and* equality, both color consciousness *and* color blindness, both treating everyone "equally" regardless of skin color or histories of unequal treatment *and* supporting policies and programs that help remedy past injustices.[84] That whites can simultaneously hold all these views—with some remaining more fixed in one allegiance than the other—helps explain their often confusing and contradictory views on racial issues. We learned, for instance, that in the course of one hour-long interview it was not uncommon for a white graduate to speak fervently in support of each of these positions.

Of course this theory of white racial dualism also suggests that it may be easier now than in the past for whites to sway politically between supporting and strongly opposing certain race-specific policies. Politicians and journalists can convince whites to shift their allegiances in one direction or another on issues related to race and opportunities.[85] And several authors have argued that conservative political leaders, particularly during the 1980s and 1990s, did just that. Icons such as Ronald Reagan talked the American public into a strident repudiation of policies and programs that assisted blacks or Latinos in gaining access to education, housing, and employment by framing all of the above as "reverse discrimination" and calling for a completely "color-blind" society. According to Walter Allen and Angie Chung, under the Reagan and George Bush administrations these new "rearticulations of race" wrapped in the gospel of color-blindness as fairness resulted in dramatic cutbacks on welfare programs, affirmative action policies, social services, education, health care, and prominority business branches.[86] Such a political philosophy serves what James Baldwin explained as the "consciousnesses of white Americans who aim to achieve racial equality by putting the past behind them without examining its traces in the present."[87]

In fact, this is clearly the direction the U.S. Supreme Court is headed in, and the Court's 2007 ruling in the Louisville and Seattle school integration cases moves one giant step toward that goal. During the two hours of oral arguments in those cases in December 2006, both Chief Justice Roberts and the Bush administration's solicitor general implied that race-conscious policies—those that take the race of students into account to achieve the goal of racial integration—were by their nature unconstitutional except when used to dismantle state-sanctioned or de jure segregation erected in the era of Jim Crow. According to the solicitor general, "The Constitution puts a particular premium on avoiding express racial classifications."[88] Thus, despite years of implementing race-conscious policies as a way to overcome a legacy of racism, the federal government— at least the Supreme Court and the president—are turning their backs on such efforts, implying that any lingering racial inequality needs to be solved in other ways. As Justice Roberts wrote in the majority opinion in these cases, "Where resegregation is a product not of state action but of private choices, it does not have constitutional implications."[89] Further, Roberts went on, citing other federal court rulings, race is a "*group* classification long recognized as in most circumstances irrelevant."[90] Therefore, he concluded that government action based on race is generally prohibited. And in what is perhaps the most famous quote from the Supreme Court's ruling in these two cases from Louisville and Seattle,

Chief Justice Roberts wrote: "The way to stop discrimination on the basis of race is to stop discriminating on the basis of race.[91]

This strong embrace of a color-blind philosophy in a country still powerfully defined by race and a history of racial oppression—even as older, blatant forms of racism are eschewed—forces whites to look for new explanations for ongoing segregation. According to Eduardo Bonilla-Silva, contemporary racial inequality is reproduced through "new racism" practices that are subtle, institutional, and apparently nonracial.

> In contrast to the Jim Crow era, where racial inequality was enforced through overt means . . . today racial practices operate in "now you see it, now you don't" fashion. For example, residential segregation, which is almost as high today as it was in the past, is no longer accomplished through overtly discriminatory practices. Instead, covert behaviors such as not showing all the available units, steering minorities and whites into certain neighborhoods, quoting higher rents or prices to minority applicants, or not advertising units at all are the weapons of choice to maintain separate communities.[92]

This is the new common sense in a color-blind white America—where whites will talk at great length about how they do not judge people by the color of their skin but they will spend an extra $200,000 to purchase a home with no black neighbors and few if any black students in their children's schools. They will have very few black friends and will, in some instances, go to great lengths to disassociate themselves from blacks, especially in status-based institutions such as schools and private clubs. In this way, their white racial dualism—their DuBoisian double consciousness—tends to place them structurally in the safe spaces of white privilege. At the same time, being color-blind allows whites to ignore just how separate and unequal our society has become in the midst of rapidly changing demographics.[93]

According to Bonilla-Silva, who writes extensively about "color-blind racism" and its impact on politics and public policy:

> Taken together, whites' views represent nothing less than a new, formidable racial ideology: new because the topics of color blindness have replaced, for the most part, those associated with Jim Crow racism; formidable because these topics leave little intellectual, moral,

and practical room for whites to support the policies that are needed to accomplish significant racial change in this country. Furthermore, because color-blind racism seems reasonable and has frames that are so different from those typical of Jim Crow racism, and because its style is so slippery, this new ideology provides an almost impenetrable defense of postmodern white supremacy.[94]

More recently, as Bonilla-Silva points out, Larry Bobo and Philomena Essed have written about "laissez-faire racism" and "competitive racism" respectively. According to these theorists, racial ideology today is usually not portrayed in old-fashioned racist speech but rather is able to effectively safeguard racial privilege by applying the principles of liberalism to racial issues and problems in an abstract manner. It also protects the status quo by focusing on cultural differences between whites and minorities, particularly those with dark skin, as the reason for ongoing racial inequality in labor markets, income, and educational attainment. Although the ideas endorsed by most whites today may sound like "racism lite" or may seem devoid of racism altogether, they help to support the racial status quo. For instance, whites may say in opinion polls that they strongly support the idea of racial integration but at the same time strongly oppose any policies or programs that might bring such integration about. In this way, they will argue that policies such as affirmative action violate the American creed of freedom and liberty.[95]

Many of the white graduates of racially diverse schools whom we interviewed definitely dabble in laissez-faire racism—and some embrace it more wholeheartedly than others. But they are also, we believe, more perplexed about the separateness and inequality that surrounds them because it is a structural feature of our society that is in contrast with some, but not all, of the lessons they learned about race in their public schools. Though they frequently buy into the color-blind argument and insist that neighborhoods are racially segregated mostly because blacks and Latinos want to be with their "own kind," they are also more likely than whites with a racially segregated upbringing to at least explore complex questions and explanations of the current state of our racially divided society. School desegregation did fundamentally change them, they will tell you. Most say they are appreciative of the souls of black (and brown) folks, they are less quick to blame black poverty on blacks' laziness or lack of responsibility, and they are more likely to see many positive dimensions of black culture. These insights, we believe, on the basis of our research and several recent quantitative studies that support our conclusions, are partly the result of their having glimpsed, even briefly, behind the veil of racial inequality and segregation.[96] They still share a white racial dualism, shifting and swaying between contradictory positions, and they no doubt benefit heartily from their white privilege, but in the end they are, as a whole, less comfortable with the most simple color-blind explanation: that all is well with our society and that "if those black folks would just work harder and have fewer babies, they could be well off like us."

WHY THE CLASS OF 1980?

For Americans born in the early 1960s—the group at the tail end of the baby boom and pre–Generation X—the civil rights movement is but a fuzzy memory of their childhood. It was something that began before them and was happening all around them when they were young children. They may have known that something significant had happened when Martin Luther King Jr. was killed in 1968, but they were too young to understand the struggle that preceded this event and how significant the formal dismantling of Jim Crow was at the time. Their impressions of this period of American history were shaped, no doubt, by their own racial identity and their parents' views of its importance or foolishness. But they were also shaped by their school experiences. And it is the class of 1980, more than any other cohort of students before or after them, that has looked at racial equality from both sides now—from experiences in both desegregated and more segregated contexts, from the pre-Reagan and the post-Reagan political eras—and that consequently has a unique vantage point from which to view our country's ongoing struggle with race.

In the fall of 1967, when Lyndon B. Johnson occupied the White House and Martin Luther King Jr. still lived, a new crop of kindergartners entered public schools across the country. Full of the hope and promise that marked the era into which they were born, these children would travel through the educational system at a time of tremendous change. On their first day of school, the federal government was on the verge of finally forcing hundreds of school districts to implement the *Brown v. Board of Education* decision. Thirteen years later, they would graduate from public schools that were, on average, far more desegregated than those they had entered.

Thus we chose to study the history of six high schools and the members of the class of 1980 who attended them during the late 1970s because their era was the beginning of the peak years of school desegregation implementation in this country. By 1988, efforts by the Reagan administration to dismantle school desegregation policies had begun to pay off, and resegregation was on the rise.[97] National data show that members of the class of 1980, therefore, were on average more likely to have classmates of other races than were students in any class before them or in classes from the mid- to late 1980s onward.[98]

Our research suggests that the late 1970s was a particularly pivotal moment in the history of school desegregation policy across the country. By this time in many towns the initial protests and racial conflict that had occurred when students were first reassigned to desegregated schools had subsided to some degree. According to many people we interviewed, the late seventies were a relatively sedate time when strong and vocal opposition to desegregation had died down. The promise of a new more racially integrated society was still alive, at least in school districts that had not already lost most of their white students.[99]

Yet among people who, like the class of 1980 members we interviewed, had firsthand experience with desegregation, survey results show that this experience changed them. For instance, a 1978 survey of graduates of desegregated schools showed that 63 percent of blacks and 56 percent of whites said that their school desegregation experience had been "very satisfactory." Only 8 percent of blacks and 16 percent of whites said the experience was "unsatisfactory."[100]

At the same time, as we noted above, the late 1970s was a transitional period, following Watergate and the Vietnam War. A conservative political movement would soon change the policy agenda in education and other social welfare arenas. The class of 1980 graduated from high school in the middle of a crippling economic recession, an oil crisis that led to long lines at the gas pumps, and the humiliating and protracted Iranian hostage crisis. Ronald Reagan was about to be elected president and would launch a major assault on the public policies of the civil rights era, including school desegregation, that had helped blacks and Latinos gain access to education.[101]

Thus the class of 1980 came of age during the Reagan years. Over the twenty-five years following their high school graduation, many in this cohort sought jobs and a college education, married, bought homes, had children, met new friends, and joined new religious and social institutions. Meanwhile, the public schools gradually became more racially segregated, and little progress was made in reducing the level of segregation in housing and other realms of society.

Indeed, while many people in this society have been affected by the political shifts of the last three decades, the cohort that left high school in the spring of 1980 was especially vulnerable. These changes, coming at a very formative phase of their lives, caused them to later question many of the ideals they had come to believe in as they made their way through school. These shifting ideals are reflected in the annual survey of college freshmen conducted at UCLA, which found that the percentage of college freshmen who agreed that "developing a meaningful philosophy of life" was "essential or very important" declined from about 85 percent in 1967 to about 39 percent in 2003, with most of the decrease occurring after the 1970s and early 1980s. Indeed, in the fall of 1980, about 60 percent of freshmen agreed with this statement. Meanwhile, the percentage of freshmen who said that "being very well-off financially" was "essential or very important" increased from about 40 percent in 1967 to about 74 percent in 2003, with the major rise occurring from the mid-1970s to the mid-1980s.[102]

By the time they had become adults and were making difficult decisions about their own jobs, homes, and families, the political terrain had changed so dramatically that many were caught off guard. The year many in this cohort graduated from college, 1984, was declared by *Newsweek* magazine to be the "The Year of the Yuppie." According to the popular news magazine, the "young urban professionals have arrived" and are bent on making a lot of money, "spending it conspicuously, and switching political candidates like they test cuisines."[103]

Caught between their older siblings who had worn go-go boots or been flower children and the new era of materialism, consumerism, and individualism, members of the class of 1980 exhibit their own chronological double consciousness that transcends and intersects issues of race and equality. Thus many members of the class of 1980 carry with them the spirit of hope of the 1960s and 1970s—hope that inequality could be eliminated or greatly lessened in their lifetime. Many also carry with them valued experiences in racially desegregated schools. Yet they embarked on their adult lives in an era that rewarded those who focused more on themselves and their own accumulation of wealth than on the problems of others or the greater good.[104] This politically schizophrenic life span has contributed to the confusion and contradiction in the voices of the African American, Latino, and white graduates we have interviewed.

In this way, the double consciousness about race and politics expressed by class of 1980 graduates is symbolic of the political and social soul of this country and the many shifts and changes it has endured since the early sixties. Their collective sense of loss about the interracial experiences they had in high school and no longer have as adults mirrors a sense of longing that many Americans have for a time when there was less focus on individualism and material gain and more emphasis on people coming together across various boundaries and creating a more fair and just nation. At the same time, most of these graduates, like most Americans, find themselves embedded in a society that pushes them away from such values.

For all these reasons, we felt compelled to study racially mixed high schools in the late 1970s and the long-term effects of these school experiences on their graduates of the class of 1980. Those graduates recount powerful experiences of cross-racial friendships, racial inequality, and missed opportunities within their racially mixed schools and the larger society. It is time we hear their stories.

TWO Six Desegregated High Schools

Racial segregation in schools is an institutional complex.
The establishment and maintenance of a system of segregated
educational facilities depends upon segregation not only
of pupils, but of teachers, administrators, politicians,
worshipers, and the residential segregation of white parents
from Negro parents. Segregated education depends upon and
feeds upon segregated churches, segregated businesses,
segregated recreational facilities, and segregated
neighborhoods.

Raymond W. Mack

When this passage was written in the 1960s about the politics of nine American communities undergoing school desegregation, this country was just embarking on what many thought was an effort to dismantle the "institutional complex" of racial segregation.[1] Yet we learned, forty years after Mack's book *Our Children's Burden* was published, not only that segregated education *depends* upon segregated communities but also that desegregated schools and their efforts to bring students together are severely limited when the neighborhoods, churches, businesses, and recreational facilities are pulling them apart. These segregated components of the institutional complex that had sustained segregated schools for so long also worked against desegregated schools' success in fundamental ways. They made it logistically more difficult for students of different races to socialize and interact outside school and also perpetuated a set of beliefs about race and status that profoundly shaped students'

experiences within the schools. The inability of school desegregation policies to consistently accomplish their most ambitious goals is best
explained within this larger context by a full consideration of the influence of these other forces.

This chapter and the three that follow it describe the social forces that
limited the success of desegregation in the schools we studied. Chapters
6 through 9 focus on the graduates of racially mixed schools today and
how, despite their appreciation for having attended diverse high schools,
most of them remain segregated in much the same way that they did in
their lives outside school when they were teenagers. Along the way, from
adolescence to adulthood, these graduates developed their own understandings of race and segregation that are double-sided and contradictory. They went to school together in part so that they could learn to get
along as adults, but most of them remain far more racially segregated as
adults in a manner that speaks to the persistence of racial segregation in
every aspect of the institutional complex outside their schools.

To write a book that could illustrate this fluid relationship between
schools and the larger society, we had to conduct a study that enabled us
to see it more clearly. In designing our study we were struck by how little
prior research had examined the social context of school desegregation
or paid attention to the ways in which the racial inequality that surrounded schools so profoundly affected the daily experiences of their
students.[2] Thus we set out in 1999 to conduct in-depth case studies of six
high schools nestled in six school districts that had undergone some form
of desegregation by the late 1970s.[3] Our overarching research questions
were: How do graduates of racially mixed schools understand their
school experience and its effect on their lives—their racial attitudes, educational and professional opportunities, personal relationships, and
social networks? And how did the policy context of their experiences
shape these understandings? To answer these questions, we knew we
needed careful and thoughtful qualitative methods to gather rich and
historical data. Given the nature of these questions—to really understand how graduates of desegregated high schools *made sense* of their
experiences and what those meanings were—we knew we could not
simply mail out surveys. Thus we set out to examine these schools in

light of political and historical trends and to conduct lengthy interviews with policy makers and activists in those towns, educators who had worked at these schools during the late 1970s, and at least forty members of the class of 1980 from each site. Our hunch was that to truly understand the effects of school desegregation on a cohort of students who lived through it we had to know something about their local communities. In this chapter we describe our research methodology and each of the towns, school districts, and schools that we studied.

CHOOSING OUR DISTRICTS, SCHOOLS, AND GRADUATES

We started our study wanting to know more about how the people who had lived through school desegregation made sense of it—what they thought they had gained or lost from such an experience and why. Yet we knew, for all the reasons mentioned above, that to generalize to any meaningful themes about how people came to understand their experiences in racially mixed schools more than twenty years after the fact we needed to examine those experiences across very different local contexts and schools.[4] Thus we chose to sample these towns and districts to achieve the greatest diversity across them because common themes that emerge in diverse places are especially meaningful.

To do this, we sought school districts with significant desegregation plans that varied in terms of size, region, racial and ethnic makeup of the general population and the students, social class of residents, and the policies by which the districts were desegregated. From an initial list of about twenty potential school districts that we compiled by asking school desegregation experts from different regions of the country for suggestions, we chose six: Austin, Texas; Charlotte, North Carolina; Englewood, New Jersey; Pasadena, California; Shaker Heights, Ohio; and Topeka, Kansas. Two of these districts—Englewood, New Jersey, and Shaker Heights, Ohio—had only one high school. In the larger districts, however, we had to choose among many high schools; we did so by looking at the racial and social class composition of their enrollments and at the role they played in desegregation efforts throughout each district. The schools we chose had to be "racially mixed" in the mid- to late 1970s, in the sense that no one racial/ethnic group constituted more than 70 percent of the total student population and that these schools were no more than 25 percent off the racial balance of the school district for any one race/ethnicity. But within that window we wanted the schools to be as different from one another as possible so that we could look at similar issues across distinct contexts. We ended up choosing six schools:

- *Austin High School*, Austin, Texas (Austin Independent School District). Desegregated via majority-to-minority transfers from several attendance areas. Racial makeup during the mid-1970s: 15 percent African American, 19 percent Hispanic, 66 percent white.

- *Dwight Morrow High School*, Englewood, New Jersey (Englewood Public Schools). Desegregated by receiving white students from the neighboring town of Englewood Cliffs via a sending-receiving plan. In addition to the Englewood Cliffs students, Dwight Morrow enrolled all public school students from the racially diverse town of Englewood. Busing and student reassignment began at the elementary level in the Englewood Public Schools at that time. Racial makeup of Dwight Morrow during the mid-1970s: 57 percent African American, 7 percent Hispanic, 36 percent white.

- *John Muir High School*, Pasadena, California (Pasadena Unified School District). Desegregated originally by drawing from several diverse attendance areas and in the 1970s via mandatory busing. Racial makeup during the late 1970s: 50 percent African American, 12 percent Hispanic, 34 percent white, 4 percent Asian/Pacific Islander.

- *Shaker Heights High School*, Shaker Heights, Ohio (Shaker Heights City School District). Desegregated as the only high school in a district experiencing an influx of African American students from Cleveland. Efforts were made in Shaker Heights to integrate neighborhoods, and student reassignment began at the elementary level. Racial makeup during the 1970s: 39 percent "minority" (mostly African American) and 61 percent white.

- *Topeka High School*, Topeka, Kansas (501 School District). Desegregated via assigned attendance areas; student reassignment began at the elementary and junior high levels. Racial makeup during the

1970s: 20 percent African American, 8 percent Hispanic, 69 percent white, 1.4 percent American Indian, 1.4 percent Asian.

- *West Charlotte High School,* Charlotte, North Carolina (Charlotte-Mecklenburg School District). Desegregated via a court order that created a district-wide desegregation plan and reassigned students from white high schools to this historically black high school. Racial makeup during the 1970s: 48 percent African American and 52 percent white.

These six high schools and the districts in which they were nested varied along many regional, social, and political dimensions that profoundly affected the day-to-day experiences of students. The diversity across these six places is central to the main themes of this book because the graduates' stories were both significantly different and surprisingly similar. In other words, certain specific social dynamics related to race and class were quite distinct because of the differing mores and traditions of the Northeast versus the Midwest versus the South or Southwest of the United States. The particular racial and social class mix of each school also mattered a great deal. Thus the two schools we studied that were 50 percent or more black by the late 1970s—Dwight Morrow and John Muir—offered distinct social milieus in which many of the students of all races listened to black music and the schools had high-stepping and "unconventional" marching bands. This is a sharp contrast to Austin High, which was socially defined by its white and affluent students. Similarly, across the six schools there were striking differences in the degree of interracial dating. There was virtually none in the southern schools of Austin High or West Charlotte and very little in Topeka, but interracial dating was not unusual at Shaker Heights High and was most common at Dwight Morrow and John Muir.

To add another level of complexity to this project, in deciding which members of the class of 1980 to interview at each school, we sought a wide range of graduates that reflected the racial makeup of each school back in the mid-1970s. Furthermore, within each racial or ethnic group we tracked down, whenever possible, graduates who differed in academic success, socioeconomic status, the distance of their residence from school, and their involvement in high school activities. We also sought variation in terms of their postsecondary education and current residence, making a concerted effort to interview out-of-town graduates.

And we interviewed small numbers of nongraduates—those who either dropped out or transferred out of the schools before graduation. We attended the class of 1980's twenty-year reunion at five of the six schools to obtain contact information and permission to call many of those in attendance. But we also used the alumni lists compiled by the reunion organizers of the schools to seek out several graduates who had not attended the reunions.

DATA COLLECTION AND ANALYSIS

Our data collection occurred in three overlapping stages. In the first stage we studied the schools and their districts by collecting historical documents, such as yearbooks, school board minutes, newspaper articles, and legal documents and by interviewing policy makers, lawyers, educators, and community members who had been involved with the six districts and schools in the 1970s. In the second stage we conducted in-depth semistructured interviews with forty to fifty African American, Latino, white, and occasionally Asian and mixed-race graduates of the class of 1980 from each of the schools. The third stage of data collection entailed "portrait" interviews,[5] or detailed second interviews, with four to six of the graduates from each of the six schools, whom we selected because they embodied the major themes that were emerging from each site and reflected the racial diversity of the class of 1980 at their particular school.

At the end of the five years of data collection we had conducted 540 interviews, including 268 graduate interviews (242 initial interviews, 26 portrait interviews). These interviews focused on the graduates' experiences in their families, communities, and, most importantly, their schools during their high school years. Of the 242 graduates interviewed, 136 were white, 79 African American, 21 Latino, 2 Asian, and 4 mixed race. Our open-ended interviews with policy makers, activists, school officials, lawyers, educators, and graduates focused, for the most part, on the effect of school desegregation on their communities, schools, and lives.

After each taped interview had been transcribed verbatim, we read all of the transcripts and "coded" or merged and reorganized all the data according to the central themes and issues that were most important in each interview. These themes were then merged and integrated with the themes emerging from other interviews from the same site and ordered according to their salience across all the interviews for each site. Then we identified cross-case themes and differences. In this way, our findings emerged from the data after we had read through every transcript and document, coded all the material, and identified what was most salient to the people we interviewed. In this type of qualitative case study work, the findings are the most powerful themes that develop from the data. Yet these themes did not come forth from the interview transcripts and documents in a simple, coherent, and uncontested fashion. Rather, they appeared in a complicated, messy manner that reflects the complexities and often the contradictions of the human experience. Insights into these nuances in people's lives and understandings about complex issues such as race are the unique gifts of qualitative research—themes that cannot be uncovered via survey research.

Each theme or subtheme discussed in this book represents a large body of data—primarily concurring or dissenting quotes from hundreds of interviews. The quotes cited in this book, therefore, represent sentiments or understandings that are far more broadly held among the members of our sample. Time and space required us to pick only a handful of quotes to illustrate each theme.

Below are brief descriptions of the six schools and their local contexts to provide the background information needed to make the following chapters more meaningful. In chapters 3 through 8 we present the central themes or findings that were prevalent in one way or another across all six sites. The often subtle differences that made these same general themes look different across places and races are the contributions of this kind of research to our often overly simplistic understanding of social issues.

DESEGREGATION HISTORY IN THE SIX SCHOOLS

Austin High School, Austin, Texas

In many ways, Stephen F. Austin High School symbolizes the complexities of the city of Austin itself. As the capital of Texas, Austin has seemingly resisted becoming too Texan and has stood out as more politically liberal and more artsy than the rest of the state. At the same time, there is a somewhat elitist air about a place that is self-defined as a bit more hip and intellectual than other nearby cities. But like the so-called "limousine liberals" of the East and West Coasts—the rich people who vote for left-leaning candidates—Austin residents can take the "progressive" label only so far when their city is as divided by race and class as most other cities in the United States.

Historically, Austin has been composed of three ethnic groups: white, Hispanic, and black. Each of these populations is a mixture of both new and long-standing residents who come or stay for a variety of reasons. Because Austin is the capital, state legislators and politicians live and educate their children there. The University of Texas at Austin is an internationally renowned research university that draws scholars from all over the country and the world. During the 1990s, the booming technology industry in Austin brought professionals and businesspeople to the area. Because of Austin's proximity to Central America, large numbers of Mexican and Latin American workers have immigrated there in recent years. But other members of Austin's Hispanic community have resided there for many generations, some dating back to the years when Texas was part of Mexico. Likewise, Austin has been home to African Americans for many generations, beginning with slavery. By 2000, the city of Austin was about 11 percent African American, 28 percent Hispanic, 55 percent white, and nearly 6 percent Asian.

Over the years, Austin became divided into fairly distinct and separate areas where different racial and ethnic communities live. There is the affluent and most white West Austin, centrally located just west of the downtown and north of Town Lake, which is where the Colorado River divides the northern and southern parts of the city. North of West Austin is the northwestern quadrant of the city, which is also predominantly white and upper middle class, although not as affluent, for the most part, as West Austin. The east side of town, divided from the west side by a highway, is where most of the people of color live—African Americans farther north and Hispanics more to the south. Farther south, across Town Lake, is a mixture of middle- and working-class whites to the west and Hispanics to the east.

Close to the center of these racial and ethnic dividing lines, Austin High School was founded in 1881 as the "high school department" of the Austin Public Schools. The second public high school to open in Austin was Anderson High School, a historically black school on the east side of town. Because Latinos were not racially classified as black, they were allowed to go to Austin High from the beginning, but they were never fully integrated into the school in terms of social space, curriculum, and ownership of the school. Echoes of this separation and second-class status were still alive and well in the 1970s. Nevertheless, the fact that Latinos attended Austin High before official desegregation is viewed by some as proof that Austin High was more progressive since it was "naturally integrated." In a sense, Latinos may be perceived to be lucky not to have been segregated out of Austin High, which has been and still is to some extent the high-status high school in the district where the children of many state leaders, including former governor George W. Bush, were educated. However, we know that Latinos did not always have access to equal educational opportunities within this "integrated" school. Then, when Anderson High School was closed in 1972 (see discussion of this in chapter 3) and the black students were dispersed across the city, a portion of them ended up at Austin High School because of its proximity to the black community, making it a more triethnic school in a triethnic city.

In fact, even though Austin High has moved many times—it has been housed in seven different buildings over the years—it has always been located near the city's center. This centrality has enabled Austin High to maintain its racial and ethnic diversity in a segregated city simply by being the designated school for students from several different surrounding communities. Furthermore, during the late 1970s and 1980s, black and Hispanic students were able to transfer to Austin High School via an early voluntary school desegregation plan called the majority-to-minority transfer program. This "M-to-M" program allowed students to transfer from schools where they were in the racial majority to schools where they were in the racial minority. For all these reasons, by the late 1970s Austin High's student population was 15 percent African American, 19 percent Hispanic, and 66 percent white at the same time that Austin Independent School District as a whole was 15 percent African American, 26 percent Hispanic, and 57 percent white. Thus, although Hispanics were underrepresented and whites were overrepresented, Austin High School was almost a decade ahead of the rest of the Austin Independent School District (AISD) in achieving a more reasonable racial and ethnic balance. Not until 1980, when the adults we interviewed were preparing to graduate, did a federal court consent decree require AISD to racially balance all of its schools via busing, altering attendance zones, or other integrative actions. In fact, it was not until 1978 that AISD was forced to integrate Hispanics with Anglos as opposed to considering Hispanics to be white for the purpose of balancing the schools—a strategy this and other districts had used to "desegregate" black students by placing them in predominantly Hispanic schools.

THE CLASS OF 1980 AT AUSTIN HIGH

In 1975, Austin High School's new lakeside campus was completed on the city's affluent west side. It is a large grayish concrete structure sitting on a narrow parcel of land between Town Lake, known as "the lake," on one side and a major highway on the other. Thus this urban high school has a somewhat suburban feel to it, in part because it is a relatively new structure and in part because it is cut off from the rest of the city on its little island of grassy land between the water and the road. The class of 1980 was one of the first to matriculate all the way through the new school.

The late 1970s are described by most of the people we interviewed as a high point in the history of Austin High School. The school was considered the best high school in the area, and its students excelled in academics and athletics. The top students were going on to the most prestigious colleges and universities, and the all-important athletic program yielded competitive teams in several sports. Although there was virtually no discussion of race or desegregation in the school or classrooms, strong cross-racial bonds were forged on the playing fields of Austin High, especially among the male students.

Inside, Austin High School was well equipped, with a large athletic/ physical education wing on the first floor, several floors of classrooms, long hallways with functioning lockers, freshly painted walls and stairwells, large trophy and display cases, and an administrative wing on the second floor. This was not a poor dilapidated urban school by any stretch of the imagination. Thus, while only the West Austin contingent of students were highly affluent and other students ranged from solid middle class to poor, Austin High School had, at the time the class of 1980 was there, many of the institutional advantages that "good" suburban high schools have, including a strong college prep curriculum, highly sought-after teachers, and a new facility. But that does not mean that all students across the many lines of race and class received equal access to all these opportunities.

Indeed, the racial and social class divides and the ways in which race, ethnicity, and social class were tightly intertwined within Austin High School strongly influenced the experiences of its 1980 graduates. The majority of the white students in that class came from the affluent central West Austin area. In fact, many of these students came from particular sections of West Austin, especially Terrytown, that were known for their extreme wealth. According to one of the white Austin High graduates who had been born and raised in West Austin, "Pemberton Heights is without doubt the fanciest neighborhood in Austin, and Terrytown is right next to it."

Because of its association with these most affluent sections of the city, Austin High School has historically held the reputation as an elite school. As Harriet ("Hattie") Allen, an African American 1980 graduate, explained, West Austin is the "old money" neighborhood, so Austin High "was considered the elite school, the school to go to. Like I said, all the school board members' kids went to school there. Every doctor, lawyer in the city, their kids went there. The mayor's kids went there!"

Within West Austin, the one area lacking glamour and prestige was a small section called Clarksville, where the black servants of rich whites had settled during the antebellum era so that they would be close to work. Of course, back then there were few public schools, and by the time these were well established they were divided by race in Texas, so having black servants live in close proximity to rich whites did not have any implications for who would go to school with whom. But by the 1960s, when the federal government began paying more attention to what school districts were doing vis-à-vis racial segregation, the children of Clarksville were integrated into the mostly white neighborhood West Austin schools, including Austin High School.

At the same time, in the late 1970s, Austin High was also enrolling—through both its attendance zones and the majority-to-minority transfer program—students from the east side of town—the barrio to the south and the African American community in the northeastern quadrant of the city. Also, according to the woman who was the principal of Austin High when the class of 1980 was there, by the late 1970s or early 1980s the school began to enroll some white working-class or middle-class students from the south side of town for the first time. These less affluent white students were—and still are—referred to as the "river rats" because they come from the other side of the Town Lake. This term, no doubt, also accentuated the social class distinctions among the white students—between the "rats" and the more affluent west side students.

Thus student identity in terms of race, ethnicity, *and* social class was very important at Austin High School and made school desegregation all the more challenging. The graduates talk a great deal about cliques that were divided not only by race and ethnicity but also by class, creating a complex hierarchy in which the mostly white and affluent West Austin students tended to dominate socially. Still, the boundaries that were crossed in this school—on the athletic teams and in other less formal settings—were often not only racial and ethnic but class boundaries as well.

A white woman who came from a working-class family and had lived in several different areas of Austin as she grew up explained in great detail how she had been intimidated by the rich white students from West Austin when she was a student at Austin High. In a voice that still echoed the emotional pain she had experienced more than twenty years earlier, she recalled that on a few occasions she had felt intimidated by Hispanic or black students in junior high school but said she had been "more intimidated by the whites because of money when I got to high school."

Thus the social class dynamics within racial groups, particularly among white students of different backgrounds and neighborhoods, were profound and often more problematic to the less affluent white students than any negative encounters they had with students of color. And in many ways this is the most important lesson of Austin High School: power and privilege are multidimensional and layered within the experiences of each student, and social class complicates the lessons of school desegregation in many unexplored ways.

Since the 1970s, a growing number of white families with children have moved out of Austin to more homogeneous suburbs, particularly Westlake, and the Austin Independent School District has lost about half of its white population in those decades. The district was 65 percent white in 1970 and only 37 percent white in 2000. Still, the board of education, in an effort to maintain the status and prestige of Austin High School, the district's flagship high school, has managed to shape attendance patterns in a way to maintain its diversity while keeping it predominantly white. By 2000, the school was 8 percent black, 37 percent Hispanic, 54 percent white, and 2 percent Asian. Interestingly enough, the school's most recent demographics somewhat mirror that of the entire city population, which is now about 11 percent black, almost 30 percent Latino, 55 percent white, and the rest Asian or "other." In many ways, then, Austin High School was and still is a microcosm of a complex and changing southern city.

Dwight Morrow High School, Englewood, New Jersey

Englewood is a community of about twenty-five thousand people located conveniently and strategically less than a ten-minute drive from the George Washington Bridge, which spans the Hudson River and connects suburban New Jersey to New York City. The folklore of Englewood—shared with us by many people we interviewed—is that the town was founded more than one hundred years ago by affluent New Yorkers who built large estates high in the hills that line the eastern edge of town. Once the George Washington Bridge was built in the early 1930s, Englewood became a bedroom community for wealthy Wall Street bankers and lawyers.

The wealth, power, and influence of these early white and mostly Protestant Englewood families was central to the town's growth and development because almost everyone else who moved there after them did so to work for rich people. Italians came to Englewood to build their large houses on the hill; the first African Americans migrated there from the South and from New York City in the 1930s to clean their houses and care for their children; and the Jews came to sell them merchandise. This, according to the legend, is how the town was settled and how it grew into four separate and unequal "wards."

By the early 1960s, all the pieces of a diverse but divided town were in place and have, for the most part, remained fairly fixed to this day, with the exception of the growing Latino population. In the First Ward, which encompasses the northeastern quadrant of Englewood, the mansions of the wealthiest residents are perched in the hills, set back from the road on expansive plots. Near the southern border of the First Ward is an elite and expensive private high school called the Dwight Englewood School.

Down the hill to the south and closer to the highway that leads to the bridge, Englewood's upper middle class have lived for years in the Second Ward. The houses in this ward are not nearly as grand as those in the hills, but they are, for the most part, large comfortable suburban homes on generous wooded lots and in close proximity to the bridge for those who commute into New York City. While Jews are not new to Englewood or this ward, in more recent years—since the 1980s, most residents believe—large numbers of Orthodox Jews have moved into this ward to be closer to the private religious schools where they send their children.

The west side of Englewood—literally on the other side of the railroad tracks from the First and Second Wards—is where the poor and middle class have lived for decades. Historically, poor and middle-class blacks lived in the southwestern quadrant of town, known as the Fourth Ward, along with some working-class whites. The houses in the Fourth Ward range in size and quality from very modest brick homes to larger wooden New England–style structures, many of which house more than one family. By the middle of the twentieth century the Fourth Ward had become predominantly black, and several housing projects were built there, which attracted more low-income residents from New York City and elsewhere. The poverty down in the valley, in Englewood's Fourth

Ward, still stands in sharp contrast to the wealth in the hills. Several people mentioned that when it rains for many days, the water and mud from "the hills" flood the Fourth Ward.

The northwestern quadrant of Englewood, the Third Ward, has been, and still is, mostly middle class and more racially diverse than any other part of the city. The Third Ward has been where black middle-class families have lived alongside Jewish families in comfortable single-family homes. Yet the Third Ward has experienced white flight over the last twenty years, and this trend shows no sign of reversing, according to census data and the perceptions of several people we interviewed. For instance, a former Englewood mayor who lives in the southern end of the Third Ward said people are shocked to hear that she, as a single white woman, still lives there. One of the white graduates of the class of 1980 who grew up in the Third Ward near the former mayor's house said that although his parents still live there the neighborhood has become increasingly black and the property values are declining. Dwight Morrow High School, Englewood's only public high school, is also in the Third Ward.

Overall, Englewood is clearly a racially and socioeconomically diverse town. Yet it is also a highly segregated and unequal town with a public education system that white and nonpoor families have abandoned. In fact, by 2005 the Englewood public schools were 94 percent African American and Latino. Furthermore, as we discuss in more detail below, the vast majority of white students who were enrolled in the district by 2005 were students who had transferred in from other districts to attend a separate and unequal magnet program housed in the high school but segregated from the black and Latino students enrolled in Dwight Morrow's nonmagnet section. Meanwhile, the city of Englewood is still almost 50 percent white, about 39 percent African American, and 11 percent Latino, according to the census data, and the residential population under the age of eighteen in Englewood is 36 percent white. This racial balance in terms of who lives in Englewood has remained relatively stable since the class of 1980 graduated, while the school district population has shifted from more than a third white to virtually all black and Latino. The story of how these shifts in school enrollments occurred over time in a northeastern city with no recent history of Jim Crow or explicit, state-sanctioned discrimination illustrates the power of racial ideology and how it shapes people's—even politically "liberal" people's—opinions of good and bad schools.

SCHOOL DESEGREGATION IN ENGLEWOOD

Indeed, Englewood's struggle to desegregate its public schools weaves together many common themes about race and education in the United States. First there was the African American community's powerful political resistance to separate and unequal public schools in the 1960s, when the Englewood public schools were still predominantly white. This black activism was supported by national organizations such as the Congress of Racial Equality (CORE) and the National Association for the Advancement of Colored People (NAACP), as well as some middle-class whites in Englewood's Third Ward, who backed the call for desegregation in part because they were liberals and in part because their local elementary school was becoming predominantly black while other schools in the district remained almost entirely white.

In the early 1960s, when the local elementary schools in Englewood reflected the racially segregated neighborhoods and the schools in the Fourth Ward and southern section of the Third Ward were seen as inferior, the black activists of Englewood, their children, and their supporters staged sit-ins at City Hall and in predominantly white elementary schools. They also led a boycott of the all-black elementary school in the district and sent their children to "underground" schools in people's basements. Meanwhile, a group of about a thousand white people called the Committee to Save our Neighborhood Schools organized to protest against desegregation programs.

The Englewood Board of Education gingerly tried to balance the demands of desegregationists with those of its economically powerful constituents in the more affluent areas of the district and to address (or not) the self-fulfilling prophecy of white and middle-class flight from the "declining" public schools. The board did close the historically all-black school in the Fourth Ward and tried to racially balance the other elementary schools by reassigning students. In fact, by the time the class of 1980 began kindergarten in the fall of 1967, their schools and classes were far more desegregated than those of students ten years older.

In this way, the story of Englewood shows that African Americans can succeed in gaining access to better educational opportunities, especially when such gains coincide with the self-interest of a segment of the white middle-class population who want to ward off white flight and declining property values in their neighborhoods. The legal challenges, protests, boycotts, and sit-ins did indeed lead to changes in the student assignment plans for the elementary and middle schools, despite opposition from some of the wealthier white families. Furthermore, this activism inspired many people—both black and white—by allowing them to believe that change could occur through organizing and protest. As the daughter of a now-deceased African American activist and politician in Englewood explained to us: "I guess I wish people knew more about the Englewood school fight, because it really talks about the possibility and the strength and power of the grassroots organizations. These were people who just got together and said, 'Okay, how can we do this thing?' And they did it."

Thus the history of Englewood teaches us about promise and possibility. In later years—the mid-1960s through the 1980s—the protests and outrage were directed against the resegregation of students by tracks within Englewood's Dwight Morrow High School and the lack of black history and literature in the curriculum, but these efforts were ultimately less successful. Indeed, like the other sites in this study, Englewood also teaches us that the struggle for greater access can go only so far—that separateness and inequality along race and class lines will reemerge *within* schools almost immediately.

DWIGHT MORROW HIGH SCHOOL AND THE CLASS OF 1980

A first-time visitor to Englewood who happens upon Dwight Morrow High School could easily mistake it for a private prep school or a small college. Set off from the road by a plush and rolling lawn, Dwight Morrow's main building is English Tudor style with dark red brick and a stately Gothic bell tower. Inside, classrooms have wood floors and leaded windows, and one even has a fireplace.

Across the driveway is the far less impressive "South" building. This boxy brick building was built in the 1960s when Dwight Morrow's enrollments were high and when a neighboring school district without its own high school, Englewood Cliffs, entered into a sender-receiver relationship with the Englewood Public Schools and designated Dwight Morrow as its high school. Soon afterward, school buses carrying mostly white and upper-middle-class high school students from Englewood Cliffs began winding their way down the large hill in Englewood, past mansions and grand estates, to the valley where the high school stood in all its architectural glory.

Back in those days, Dwight Morrow enrolled 1,600 students; half of them were African Americans who lived in the diverse but segregated town of Englewood. The other half consisted of white students drawn from both racially diverse Englewood and the virtually all-white Englewood Cliffs. At the time, Dwight Morrow was recognized as a high school that sent a cadre of students on to Ivy League colleges each year; had many talented teachers; and hosted renowned performing arts, visual arts, and photography programs. In fact, Dwight Morrow's "artsy" reputation was buttressed by its many famous alums, including John Travolta, Sister Souljah, and Sarah Jessica Parker, to name a few.

Furthermore, in the sixties and seventies, the school was known for its racial diversity—one of only three high schools in Bergen County that was not predominantly white at the time—and in some ways, given the political activists of Englewood's black community, it symbolized the civil rights movement's hope for racial integration and equality. Many of the students, like Larry Rubin in chapter 1, who attended Dwight Morrow back then, knew they were a part of something that was special and unique in affluent northern New Jersey. Students recall being taunted and subject to racial slurs by students at white and afflu-ent suburban schools when they would show up for a sporting event. Sydney Morgan, a black woman from a middle-class and politically active family in Englewood who graduated from Dwight Morrow in 1980, recalled being threatened by racists in other nearby New Jersey towns: "We would have problems, for example, like sporting events, when we went to certain towns, we actually sometimes had to have police escorts in the towns because, you know, they'd throw rocks and bottles at the buses."

At the same time, while the students at Dwight Morrow for the most part got along across racial lines, there was within-school segregation, in that the top-level classes and the more aesthetically pleasing cafeteria in the "old" building were both predominantly white. Most, but not all, black students were in lower-level classes and ate lunch in the cafeteria in the South building. In fact, in 1974 the federal government temporarily withheld a grant from Englewood because of significant overrepresentation of black students in special education classes in the district as well as allegedly unfair disciplinary action taken against black students. With this legal action, the Englewood School Board began trying to address the issue of separate and unequal educational opportunities within their schools, a move that may well have spurred faster white flight from the district.

By the time the class of 1980 entered Dwight Morrow High School in the fall of 1976, blacks made up about 57 percent of the students, the white population was less than 40 percent, and there was a small but growing Latino population. Each year that the class of 1980 attended Dwight Morrow, fewer white students showed up in ninth grade from Englewood or Englewood Cliffs. Shortly after this class graduated, between 1982 and 1987, the white population in the school dropped from 32 to 12 percent of the total. By 2000, the school was less than 5 percent white and the total enrollment was less than six hundred, which meant that the second building—the one built to accommodate the influx of Englewood Cliffs students—was no longer needed.

In the mid-1980s, Englewood and Englewood Cliffs ended up in state court fighting over whether Englewood Cliffs could end the more than twenty-year-old sender-receiver relationship that, on paper, assigned their middle school students to Dwight Morrow High School. At the point the lawsuit was filed, the number of Englewood Cliffs students enrolled in Dwight Morrow had dropped from nearly 120 in 1982 to about 60. In that same time period, the number of Englewood Cliffs students enrolling in nearby Tenafly High School—a public high school in the mostly white and affluent town just to the north of Englewood—had increased from

11 to 48. While Englewood Cliffs students could not simply transfer into Tenafly High School for free because of the sender-receiver relationship with Englewood, they could pay a nonresident tuition fee to attend. By the early 1980s, the Englewood Cliffs School District had begun providing their middle school parents, upon request, written instructions on how to apply to Tenafly High School for admission on a tuition basis.

In 1987, during the trial in which the Englewood Cliffs School Board was trying to end the sending-receiving relationship with Dwight Morrow, the school board's attorneys argued that the quality of education at Dwight Morrow had declined and thus that Cliffs students should have other public school options. The Englewood lawyers argued that when Cliffs families began pulling out of Dwight Morrow the quality of the academic program was as strong as it had been in prior years and that these families were leaving for racial reasons. Englewood won the legal battle when the state judge ruled that the Englewood Cliffs families' motivation for not attending Dwight Morrow High School was race and not school quality, but it is clear from the picture today that the district and the high school lost the war for more equal educational opportunities for black students.

Although the court ruling was symbolically important because it defended Dwight Morrow's reputation, it was a pyrrhic victory. By the time the trial was over, the school was less than 15 percent white, and only twenty-one Englewood Cliffs students were enrolled. This might not have been problematic if the white flight that occurred had not resulted in a chipping away of Dwight Morrow's programs and reputation. But we have learned from teachers that many of the resources and course offerings that were available at Dwight Morrow in the 1960s and 1970s when more white and affluent students attended are now gone. Thus, in some ways, the false accusations made by Englewood Cliffs parents and board members in the early 1980s came to pass in the 1990s as the political clout and status of the school declined in the community and the support for public education in Englewood waned.

In 2002, in an effort to end what the New Jersey Commissioner of Education called the "thirty-year-old desegregation problem" of Englewood, the New Jersey State Department of Education and the Bergen

County Vocational School District partnered with the Englewood Public Schools to launch a new academically challenging and career-focused magnet program—the Academies @ Englewood—as a school within a school at Dwight Morrow High.[6] This magnet program within the larger, otherwise racially isolated high school was designed to draw students from all over Bergen County while attracting more high-achieving students from Englewood and Englewood Cliffs back to the public schools. Students who are admitted to the competitive program, with its merit-based admissions process, receive an extra dose of science and technology curriculum and, through the additional state and county funding that they receive, have access to more and better resources than Dwight Morrow High School.

The Academies @ Englewood—AE for short—is housed in the newer, less aesthetically pleasing South building on the Dwight Morrow campus and attracted an initial freshman class of 114 that was about a third white, a third black, and a third Latino. Four years later, when this class graduated from high school in 2006, the AE program was composed of 469 students—about 22 percent white, 25 percent black, 22 percent Latino, and 28 percent Asian.[7] While the Academies @ Englewood has been widely touted as the answer to the harms of racial segregation that have been so clearly inflicted on Dwight Morrow and Englewood as a whole, the question remains whether having a separate and unequal program housed within a racially isolated district and school exacerbates the problem. After receiving some initial complaints to that effect, Englewood officials have taken a few baby steps to better merge Dwight Morrow and AE—what the principal now refers to as DMHS/AE—by allowing Dwight Morrow freshmen "an opportunity to share classroom time with Academies students."[8] How far the merger of the all–black and Latino Dwight Morrow students with the more diverse group of high-achieving AE students from all over Bergen County can go, given the history of white flight, has yet to be determined.

Today there is little to celebrate in Englewood for those who embrace the goal of school desegregation, especially in a small town that is so diverse in terms of race, ethnicity, religion, and social class. Public schools in such a suburban town could be, if all the children attended, models of integrated education. The sit-ins, boycotts, and protests of Englewood, the battles for racial justice that were fought there, are reminiscent of a time when such political action appeared most effective and there was hope for meaningful change. At the same time, the history of Englewood shows just how hard it is to overcome white privilege in the end.

John Muir High School, Pasadena, California

John Muir High School was once the crown jewel of one of California's most esteemed school districts, Pasadena Unified. Traditionally, Muir High School enrolled the children of Pasadena's wealthy elite and the intellectuals who worked at nearby Cal Tech and the Jet Propulsion Laboratory, as well as students from the affluent white community of La Canada to the northwest. It was a school with a reputation for academic excellence that was also renowned as a sports "powerhouse."

Muir High School is located on the west side of town, where African Americans, and later Hispanics, were forced to settle when they moved to Pasadena in the first half of the twentieth century. The city's early racially restrictive zoning laws, and later the racially restrictive covenants used by many homeowners in Pasadena, as well as distinctions in the size and price of houses, ensured that black and Latino families could not move into the increasingly affluent east side.

Thus, beginning in the 1930s, Muir was the district's only racially diverse high school for many years. Yet despite this diversity and relative racial harmony at Muir throughout the thirties, forties, and fifties, Pasadena itself was a city rife with racial tension and discrimination. A white former school board member who served in the late 1950s and early 1960s gave an example of the extent of discrimination against blacks in Pasadena. He recalled that the city had a municipal swimming pool that barred blacks from swimming except on "Cosmopolitan Day," which was the day before they cleaned the pool: "That's gone now, of course, but they were barred from a lot of things in Pasadena. Traditionally they could work as maids on Orange Grove Avenue for the people who came out for the winter . . . and as far as hiring them even as clerks, that was out. They could be garbage collectors, but that's about it."

Thus, despite the image of California as being more open and pro-gressive than the Jim Crow South in the 1950s and early 1960s, many restrictions were placed on blacks. As a white parent activist noted, the years before the sixties in Pasadena "were the days when a black person couldn't even go into . . . five and dime stores and order a glass of coke. Oh no, they couldn't be waited on. It was like the South."

Even in the late 1970s, black and Latino students said that they rarely if ever went to the east side of town. Quentin Dennis, a black graduate of Muir from the class of 1980 whom we introduce in more depth in chap-ter 6, said he knew very little about the east side of Pasadena, where the majority of white people lived by then and where Pasadena High School was located: "When I was a young person, we never went east of Lake [Street]. . . . I never knew that there was another part of Pasadena. We only went to our west . . . boundary. The only time I went east of Lake was when my mom took us to Sears, and that was a big deal. So PHS [Pasadena High School] to us was this new school where all the white kids went, it was nice, and Muir was west-west Pasadena."

The discriminatory practices that left Pasadena racially separate and unequal applied to the city's schools as well. While Muir had been racially diverse since the 1930s, the school district systematically enforced segre-gation in its elementary and junior high schools by busing black students past their local school to the "black" school and busing whites to all-white schools. As one of the white plaintiffs in the Pasadena school desegrega-tion case noted, in the 1960s she was bused from her predominantly white neighborhood past Washington Junior High, which enrolled large num-bers of black students, to Elliot Junior High, which was predominantly white. Similarly, a former administrator who was working at the Pasadena Unified School District office when a federal judge ordered the board of education to desegregate its schools stated: "We did a lot of busing in the sixties, of the worst possible kind. We bused white kids out of schools in their neighborhood to go to white schools, past schools that were close. When the federal judge accused the district of deliberately segregating itself in the sixties, he was flat-on right."

Meanwhile, by the early 1960s, the growth of the African American population on Pasadena's west side had led to a sharp increase in the percentage of African American students at Muir High School. At the same time, La Canada, a wealthy white community that was not part of the city of Pasadena but had been part of the Pasadena Unified School District and had sent its students to Muir for high school, seceded from Pasadena schools and built its own high school. While it is difficult to gauge all the factors that contributed to this secession, many people in Pasadena thought the main impetus was race. As one Pasadena administrator put it, in 1960, when La Canada voted to form its own school district, its population was more than 90 percent white. "There isn't much doubt that the major reason that they formed their own school district was that they were unhappy about their kids having to go to Muir High School."

The pullout of nearly 1,200 mostly white La Canada students from Muir shifted the demographics of the school, making it nearly majority black. The resulting racial imbalance was exacerbated by Pasadena's school board, which redrew attendance boundaries to reassign the children of white families from Muir to the newer, predominantly white Pasadena High School. Muir parents fought this reassignment in court, claiming that this was a pattern of growing discrimination against Muir and against black students in the district.

As Ray Cortinez, a former principal and superintendent in Pasadena, recalled, there were legitimate reasons for that court case, *Spangler v. Pasadena Unified,* filed by one black and one white family, both with children in Muir High School. He said that the district had a truly "two-tiered system," with west-side schools lacking certified teachers and decent, clean facilities: "Money was not spent on John Muir or the middle school. . . . So there was real reason for the lawsuit, and the people that brought it . . . were assigned to Muir and did not feel that their children were afforded the same opportunities in every way, whether it was teachers, facilities, money spent on education, as some of the other schools. And I have to say I agree with them."

In 1970, Pasadena became the first district outside the South to be ordered by a federal judge to desegregate its schools. The *Spangler* case and the ensuing court order to desegregate initiated years of political turmoil in the district, with the city divided between supporters of the court order and its opponents. But ironically enough, because Muir High School had been the more racially diverse high school in the district, it was the least affected by the court order. Thus, while some whites were reassigned to Muir via the court order, the predominantly white Pasadena High School was more directly affected, as hundreds of black students were quickly reassigned there. Indeed, many African American students felt connected to Muir, a school where interracial relationships among students had always been far more common than at Pasadena's other high schools.

THE CLASS OF 1980 AT MUIR HIGH

Still, during the 1970s, in part in response to the desegregation plan, white students continued to leave the district and Muir High School. By the time the class of 1980 attended Muir, white flight had caused the student population to shift from majority white to majority black. By the time the class of 1980 arrived, the school was very racially diverse, with a student body that was 34 percent white, 50 percent black, 12 percent Latino, and 4 percent Asian and Pacific Islander.

Most of Muir's educators responded to these demographic shifts by attempting to ignore race as much as possible, believing that the most progressive approach was to adopt the attitude that race did not matter. Thus Muir graduates, like those in most of our other sites, told us in interviews that race was rarely discussed in their classes and that the curriculum did not reflect different cultures or perspectives. But despite the lack of focus on race in the formal curriculum at Muir High during the late 1970s, the graduates remember being very aware of race. For instance, many remembered vividly that white students were more often assigned to upper-track classes while African American and Latino students were regularly assigned to lower-track classes. Furthermore, although graduates report having gotten along well across racial lines for the most part, they also recall incidents of intimidation—by black *and* white students—that were not addressed by administrators.

This avoidance strategy by the Muir staff had negative repercussions for a school that was on the brink of resegregation and had been increasingly fighting its growing reputation as the district's "ghetto school."

Today, Muir is the struggling, predominately low-income and minority institution that, in the late 1960s, many parents feared it would become. The goal of racial integration in Pasadena Unified is long gone, and many people are left with lasting scars.

Shaker Heights High School, Shaker Heights, Ohio

Shaker Heights is a suburban community bordering the city of Cleveland and one of a handful of communities in the United States that has become known for its progressive policies promoting both school and housing integration. As a result of these policies, both the city of Shaker Heights and the Shaker Heights Public Schools have remained racially diverse for over forty years. This is all the more remarkable given that Shaker is an inner-ring suburb, bordering the city of Cleveland, in one of the nation's most hypersegregated metropolitan areas, where it is not unusual for neighborhoods and public schools to transition from all-white to all-black in a few years. To successfully maintain integration, both the city of Shaker Heights and the Shaker Heights schools have, over the past forty years, been walking a fine line, trying to maintain diversity while at the same time making the city and the schools attractive to white families, who are often skeptical of the "quality" of diverse schools and neighborhoods.

HOUSING AND SCHOOL DESEGREGATION
IN SHAKER HEIGHTS

In the early twentieth century, Shaker Heights was founded as an elite, all-white suburb with housing stock that varied from more than ample to extravagant. When a handful of black families began to move into Shaker in the 1950s, residents began to mobilize to prevent the rapid white flight that had created havoc and massive racial turnover in the city of Cleveland and other inner-ring suburbs, such as nearby East Cleveland. They formed community associations and by the late 1960s convinced the town leaders to adopt prointegration measures. These policies were later codified and institutionalized in a housing office run by the town and funded by the public schools and other tax dollars.

The office, called the Shaker Heights Housing Office, provided loans to whites to make downpayments on homes in transitional or more racially mixed neighborhoods, as well as to African Americans (and other nonwhites) who wished to move into predominantly white neighborhoods. However, because many African American families could not afford the home prices in those more affluent neighborhoods, the end result was that most of the monies from the program went to white families. The housing office crafted very explicit race-based policies aimed at keeping whites in, or attracting white buyers to, transitional neighborhoods and encouraging nonwhites to move to white neighborhoods

At the same time that the housing integration efforts were occurring, the Shaker Public Schools also took steps to integrate. The resulting voluntary school desegregation program was similar to the housing policies in that it was designed to encourage whites to make prointegrative moves into the district's predominantly black schools, while encouraging blacks to transfer to predominantly white schools. More experienced teachers were transferred into the predominantly black schools to make them more attractive to the white families. Students graduating from the ten elementary and two junior high schools then matriculated into the district's only high school.

By the 1970s Shaker Heights High School prided itself on being one of the premier public high schools in the country, with large numbers of National Merit scholars and graduates going off to Ivy League universities. Shaker Heights High was also one of the few schools in the country to be integrated through proactive housing policies that provided incentives for residential integration and concerted efforts to prevent white flight. Thus many of the people we interviewed in Shaker spoke of the integration that had occurred here as both voluntary and "natural," as opposed to other places where *desegregation* connotes court orders and strife. Most of the graduates from the class of 1980 expressed enormous pride at graduating from such a renowned high school and being from a community known as much for the quality of its schools as for integration.

Throughout the 1970s, more African American families poured over the city-suburban line from the east side of Cleveland into the western areas of Shaker Heights, where the relatively less expensive housing was built. These parents, while middle class, were lower income and often less well educated than the upper-income white and black families who were already living in Shaker. According to longtime residents we interviewed, these newly arrived black parents in the 1970s often worked two jobs to be able to afford to live in Shaker Heights and give their kids better educational opportunities than they had had in the Cleveland public schools. Some divided the larger houses in Shaker into dual-family homes to make ends meet, creating more densely populated neighborhoods and schools.

This demographic shift seemed to shock the educators in the high school, especially the teachers. In the 1950s and 1960s, the few African American students in the high school fit in relatively well with the school structure: they did well in class and assimilated quietly into the school's traditions and reputation. Thus the influx of larger numbers of African American students from Cleveland in the 1970s created some upheaval in the Shaker school community, which had been nationally recognized for doing everything "right."

The high school, while still ranked among the top high schools in the country by various popular magazines during this era, faced a growing achievement gap between its African American and white student population. Indeed, the more recently arrived African American students posed a new challenge to the teachers, especially at the high school. The teachers argued that these students had been less well prepared for high school by the Cleveland school system and thus were not up to the challenge of the Shaker curriculum.

Because the African American students from Cleveland were perceived as being "behind" and "not up to the challenge," they were often assigned to the lower of the high school's four academic tracks or levels. Indeed, the ability grouping in Shaker Heights High became quite elaborate, at one point consisting of five separate tracks, although it was down to four by the time the class of 1980 arrived. These tracks were quite racially distinct, with the white students dominating the highest-track classes and the lowest-track classes being disproportionately African American. Furthermore, although Shaker Heights High was renowned for its racial diversity, race was rarely discussed inside the school walls. Indeed, there was an unspoken assumption that, despite the racial distinctions across classrooms and levels, race was not an issue and should not matter.

By the late 1970s, the school district began to pay more attention to the racial disparities in enrollment between the different tracks. Some parents—particularly African American parents in the community—called for an end to the tracking system. However, as a former white school board member noted, many believed that this would drive whites away from a school system that was already on the brink of resegregating:

> I think it was a fear that if done away with, it will be harder to keep good students coming to the school because people in Shaker Heights can afford to send their children to private schools, and one of the great attractions for them is the level [tracking] system because it provides an excellent education, and there's a great percentage of children that go on to college, and those do very well on tests, placement in national tests, SATs, and so forth. And if that happened [abolishing the tracking system], then we'd probably have more of an imbalance in the schools; it would become less balanced, let's put it that way. So there's always that tension, and so far those levels have been maintained.

Still, the graduates from Shaker's class of 1980 almost uniformly report fond memories of Shaker Heights High and think of their years there as a special time in their lives that was never again replicated in their more segregated adult lives. Indeed, most graduates report that their years in Shaker public schools were the one time in their lives when they felt they had true friends from other racial and ethnic backgrounds. Furthermore, most graduates said they were shocked when they went off to college and work and found the "real world" to be much more seg-regated and less tolerant than Shaker Heights High.

Today many Shaker graduates actively seek out diverse neighbor-hoods and schools for their children, and many—more than at any of the other schools we studied—have returned to Shaker Heights in an effort to re-create some of those experiences for their children. Yet these gradu-ates also feel pressured by the test scores published in local papers that make them doubt the "quality" of racially and socioeconomically diverse schools, which generally have lower average scores than more affluent and predominantly white schools. Thus, though little has changed at the school but the student population, which has become more nonwhite since 1980, Shaker Heights High has been profoundly affected by the more recent federal and state policies requiring ever more testing and a local press that is keen on publicizing scores and ranking public schools accordingly. As a result, more and more people in the metro area have begun to seriously question whether Shaker is the school it once was.

These scores have also been a source of controversy in the school itself, as the community has been embroiled in debates over the existence of a test score gap between its white and African American students. By the time we completed our data collection in 2005, Shaker Heights High School seemed poised at a critical moment—as a school that was fighting for its reputation, trying to counter the tide of public perception against racially diverse schools and to hold on to its white population, which hovered around 40 percent.

In fact, there was an overwhelming sense that Shaker Heights High, once a model integrated high school, might well be headed in the direction of its neighboring school districts by losing most or all of its white and more affluent students to private schools and/or outer-ring suburban school districts. As one Shaker Heights High School teacher explained, referring to school desegregation: "People say that if it doesn't work here, it's not gonna work."

Topeka High School, Topeka, Kansas

Topeka High School is one of the main architectural attractions in Topeka, Kansas, because of its elegant Gothic design and thus its stately presence in a town dominated by plain but functional state office buildings. The high school was built during the Depression as part of the Works Progress Administration (WPA) program, and it cost over $1 million, which was unheard of at that time. But growing enrollment in what was then the city's only high school required a new school building. Inspired by at least three British landmarks, Topeka High School looks more like a private liberal arts college than a public high school.

But perhaps as important as its impressive architecture is Topeka High's central location in a city that is divided racially and socioeconomically and now has two additional high schools, each located in more racially divided neighborhoods. Today most black and Hispanic families live on the east side of the city, where Highland Park High School is located, and the more affluent whites live on the west side of the city close to Topeka West High School. In the middle, literally butting up against the heart of downtown Topeka near the state capitol, stands Topeka High School, drawing, as it has done for decades, its diverse student population from the near-east and near-west city neighborhoods. Against the backdrop of the school district's decades-long struggle to racially balance the elementary and junior high schools in Topeka, the flagship high school has always pulled students from across color lines. Indeed, a little-known fact about Topeka, the site of the most famous school desegregation case in America, is that until the late 1950s it had only one high school—Topeka High—which enrolled both black and white students many years prior to the *Brown v. Board of Education* case. Before the famous 1954 ruling declaring de jure segregation unconstitutional, Kansas state law allowed, but did not require, districts to segregate schools by race.

But racial segregation was alive and well within and across many of Topeka's schools, and at Topeka High School there were separate black and white basketball teams, dances, and extracurricular activities. Black alums we interviewed who attended Topeka High School in the thirties, forties, and fifties described the internal segregation as a "school within a school" and complained that teachers and administrators treated the black students like second-class citizens. Blacks were not involved in theater or school plays. And according to several black interviewees, although Topeka High School had a swimming pool—quite a luxury for a high school in those days—the white administrators opted not to fill it with water because that would mean blacks and whites would be swimming together in the same pool, a racial taboo at that time.

By the time the class of 1980 arrived at Topeka High School, which was then a tenth- through twelfth-grade school, many things had changed since the 1940s and 1950s, yet some had remained the same. By the late 1970s there were three high schools in the district instead of just one because the city of Topeka had annexed the predominantly black and Latino area of Highland Park and its public schools too. Then, in 1961, Topeka West High School was built on the predominantly white and more affluent west side of town. This growth to the east and west left Topeka High School at the center of a racially divided city and school district and thus gave the school an identity as the diverse high school; hence it was derogatorily called "Congo High" by white students from Topeka West and was considered a very "white" school by students from Highland Park High. Because of that mixed identity, some students (mostly those from the east) tried to transfer in and others tried to transfer out (mostly to the west).

By the late 1970s, some but certainly not all of the within-school segregation that had so profoundly shaped students' experiences at Topeka High in the earlier era had disappeared. For instance, there were no longer separate black and white teams or squads or dances (at least officially). In fact, the school had quotas for certain extracurricular programs, such as cheerleading, to ensure that the squad reflected the diversity of the school. Still, the classrooms remained fairly segregated at the high end of the spectrum, with the top-level classes enrolling few black or Latino students. But given the demographics of the school at the time—69 percent white, 20 percent African American, 8 percent Hispanic, and 3 percent "other" (American Indian and Asian)—Topeka High, for the most part, did not have lower-level classes that were all black or all Latino. In fact, most graduates from the school who were not in the most advanced courses—more than in any other school we studied—remember their classes as being very racially diverse.

Furthermore, the mid-1970s had been an era of activism around equal educational opportunities in Topeka in general and at Topeka High School more specifically. Thus in 1969 the Black Student Union was formed, and its members demanded that the district hire more black teachers and counselors and add a black studies program. In the spring of 1970 black students staged walkouts and boycotts to draw attention to these issues, and some, but not all, of their demands were met.

Also in 1970, Topeka High's Mexican American students marched to City Hall to protest unfair treatment at Topeka High School and in the district in general. They demanded more Mexican American counselors, teachers, administrators, and coaches as well as courses in Mexican American history and Mexican American representation on the drill and cheerleading squads. By the late 1970s, as the political climate and activism of the late 1960s and early 1970s was fading, most of the Mexican students' demands remained unmet.

In fact, as the class of 1980 matriculated through the Topeka Public Schools, issues of race and ethnicity became less contested, even as deep-seated problems remained unresolved. The 1980 graduates we interviewed from Topeka High recalled that most of the racial unrest, tension, and, at times, fighting among the students had occurred in the early to mid-1970s, when they were in junior high school. They remembered stories of older siblings getting into racialized fights in the high school, and many of them had vivid memories of potentially explosive situations in their junior high schools. But by the time these students got to high school, the tension had died down. A white male graduate of Topeka High School's class of 1980 told us that he had not seen any racially motivated fights when he was in high school. The earlier incidents, he argued, could have just been a reflection of the time: "I know that kids are kids and—not justifying it—[but] kids get to scraps now and then. But I never saw a real divide based upon race. I didn't experience that. I know that when my oldest brother went to Topeka High in 1972, 1973, and 1974 there were some racial tensions, but I think that was systematic of what was going on in the country more than just the school because it was happening everywhere in towns."

Still, like graduates from the other schools in this study—and perhaps even more so—members of the class of 1980 from Topeka High School told us that the topic of race was a taboo in their school. They did not discuss it in class; nor do most of them recall their teachers talking about the 1954 Supreme Court decision in *Brown v. Board of Education,* the landmark case that was brought by an African American family living less than five miles from their high school.

In its stoic midwestern fashion, Topeka High School taught its students to move forward pragmatically without contemplating the larger meaning of the era of history they were creating. The graduates of this high school are, as a result, very matter-of-fact in their understanding of what they lived through but as confused as anyone about what it means today, as they find themselves in more segregated adult spaces. And their alma mater, the most racially stable of the six schools we studied, remains at the center of a city that is increasingly diverse but still divided.

West Charlotte High School, Charlotte, North Carolina

Charlotte, North Carolina's famous school desegregation case, *Swann v. Charlotte-Mecklenburg*, was decided by the U.S. Supreme Court in 1971 and became one of the most important school desegregation decisions because it sanctioned the use of transportation—or "busing"—of students to racially diverse schools. Over the next thirty years, thousands of students enrolled in the Charlotte-Mecklenburg Schools were bused to desegregated schools outside their neighborhoods.

In Charlotte and in most school districts undergoing desegregation, the burden of this busing was placed on the African American or Latino students, as many of the segregated schools that had served these students were shut down, and they were reassigned to predominantly white schools outside their neighborhoods. Meanwhile, white students were more often allowed to stay close to home for more years of their schooling.

DESEGREGATING DE JURE SEGREGATED SCHOOLS IN CHARLOTTE

The long story of school desegregation in Charlotte, North Carolina, begins in 1960, when the city's public school system merged with the surrounding and increasingly suburban Mecklenburg County School District. As a former administrator in the Charlotte-Mecklenburg Public Schools and a district historian explained: "The two districts—city and county districts—consolidated in 1960, and it's my opinion that consolidation made it possible for us to completely desegregate the school system ten years later in 1970. I know the judge's order was the thing that prompted that, but the fact is that we were a consolidated district, city and county, and because of that it was one unified school district. So you didn't have people who would flee to the suburbs, for whatever purpose, whatever reason. And that's what basically happened in some districts."

Thus this distinctly southern feature of a countywide school district, which was still segregated according to state law at the time of the merger, would prove to be the most important factor in undoing the de jure system. The process of desegregating the new city-and-county system began in the 1960s and early 1970s, when several black schools— three of them high schools and one of them the oldest black high school in the city—were shut down. The last remaining black high school, West Charlotte High School, was housed in a fairly new facility in a middle-class black community of fiercely loyal graduates and activists. West Charlotte was the pride and joy of the black community in Charlotte at that time. To shut it down would have been the ultimate slap in the face to the black children and families. Politically, it simply could not be done after the district had closed so many other black schools. But politically, the school board knew, it would be very difficult to desegregate a historically black high school in a black neighborhood by bringing in white students. In fact, the most interesting aspect of the role that West Charlotte High School played in the local school desegregation case is that it went from being the sticking point in the negotiation process over desegregated student assignments to being the symbol of the success of school desegregation in Charlotte—all in a matter of a few years.

Under the first student assignment plan ordered by Judge McMillan in 1969 and implemented in 1970, black students from West Charlotte, many of whom were middle class, were bused out to nine predominantly white high schools, and white, mostly working-class students were bused to West Charlotte. But this first assignment plan did not desegregate West Charlotte because many of the white students did not show up. Thus "what to do with West Charlotte" remained a central tension throughout the period of 1969–74 as various parties proposed solutions and the district tried implementing several different desegregation plans.

Finally, an agreement that some of Charlotte's most affluent and politically powerful leaders signed on to reassigned white students from the affluent Southeast area of the city—along with middle-class blacks and other white students of varied socioeconomic status from all over the city—to West Charlotte High School. One of the architects of that plan, a white woman who was a public school parent, teacher, and community activist, recalled that the assignment of affluent students from Southeast Charlotte to West Charlotte High School was the hardest piece of the puzzle because busing those particular students out of their neighborhood had been avoided up until this final phase of negotiations in 1974. Yet as this activist noted, it made sense given the proximity of those two communities—Southeast Charlotte and West Charlotte—to each other. Furthermore, not busing the most affluent white students—a political strategy that had been used in many other cities, including Boston[9]—sent the wrong signal to the rest of the community: "[It] made sense geographically. And because they [the affluent white students] had been sheltered from busing through the whole beginning years, and it was symbolic in a way of fairness—sort of became a symbol—that everybody was going to be involved, [we were] not just shipping black children to white neighborhoods, but the other way was going to happen too, and you couldn't avoid it by being rich and living on the right side of town."

Meanwhile, plenty of incentives—some might say "bribes"—were put into place at West Charlotte High School as soon as it was decided that the children of some of the wealthiest and most influential white residents of the city were to be "bused" there. For instance, the first white principal of West Charlotte High School was assigned there the same year the affluent white students arrived and was seen as one of the incentives to help ease the transition for the white families. This former principal recalled in an interview that several aspects of West Charlotte changed when the wealthy white students were sent there. For example, the school simultaneously began enrolling more affluent black students and developed a special magnet school within a school—an alternative education program called the Open Program—which was designed to attract more middle-class families. As this principal recalled, the school's test scores went up shortly after the affluent white students arrived and these changes took place: "The SAT scores just went way up, and I got all of these inquiries from around the United States, asking how in the world did we do it. My [answer] to them was very simple, we've changed populations. That's the kind of thing that happened. A lot of the more affluent black and white kids came there to the Open Program."

Thus, between 1969 and the mid-1970s, the racial makeup of West Charlotte shifted from about 100 percent black to about half black and half white. What's more, West Charlotte High School in many ways came to symbolize the success of school desegregation in Charlotte, since many of its students excelled academically and athletically. When the class of 1980 matriculated through this school, it was on the ascent, becoming one of the premier high schools in the district.

Since the early 1990s, when the Charlotte-Mecklenburg School District administration began slowly dismantling its school desegregation programs in favor of color-blind school choice programs, West Charlotte has lost virtually all of its white student population. In 2002 the district was declared "unitary," meaning that its federal court order to desegregate students was lifted. Since that time Charlotte's public schools have become increasingly racially segregated, with some schools 90 percent African American and others more than 80 percent white. Nearly half of the African American students in the district now attend racially segregated, predominantly black schools, including West Charlotte High School.[10]

By 2006 West Charlotte was nearly 90 percent African American, almost 6 percent Latino, and about 3 percent Asian. Only twenty-eight white students, or 1.7 percent of the student body, were enrolled. Like the school desegregation plan that it came to represent, the glory of West Charlotte High School is now seen as a thing of the past. It is a "has-been" school, currently defined by low test scores and middle-class flight. As one former West Charlotte math teacher who had been there throughout the desegregation years noted: "West Charlotte was always an extremely delicate thing. It had to be nurtured; it could not be left alone if it was . . . to succeed. . . . The school board stopped nurturing it. They stopped doing that, so the percentage of blacks increased. . . . So the percentage of whites was really going down."

. . . . .

These brief historical sketches of the six high schools we studied and their surrounding communities provide a backdrop for the cross-case themes that unfold in the following chapters. The unique contexts of these schools lend themselves to variations on the themes presented in chapters 3 through 5 in particular. Yet at the same time these divergent milieus make the similarities in the stories of school desegregation all the more powerful. Indeed, some of these themes are so compelling across the divergent sites that we can venture to generalize from the specifics of these six places to social theories of racial contact, experience, and understanding. When we do this, school desegregation policy—as the sole force against racial segregation—does seem, in hindsight, fairly short-sighted and overly optimistic. To imagine that one institution, the public schools, could overcome such deep racial divisions was as much a leap of faith in the 1970s as it would be today. But it was a leap that these and hundreds of other communities took, and their stories can help us imagine a new future.

THREE Racially Mixed Schools in a Separate and Unequal Society

Sitting in her office at a city-run agency in Austin, Texas, Christine Almonte speculated about what she had gained and what she had lost by attending the predominantly white Austin High School instead of the mostly Hispanic Johnston High School more than twenty years ago.[1] Like Larry Rubin in suburban New Jersey, Christine does not have a simple answer about what school desegregation meant to her. But Christine's assessment of her schooling, unlike Larry's, embodies the trade-off—and the resulting double consciousness—that many students of color express when talking about their desegregated lives as teenagers. As a Mexican American who was born in the United States but still identifies strongly with her cultural roots south of the border, this tall, thin woman with shoulder-length brown hair said that she had both "loved" her high school years and, at the same time, felt alienated from the popular white students and underappreciated by the educators there.

In the course of several hours of talking about her schooling experiences, Christine wavered more than once. She suggested, on the one hand, that she would have been much better off attending Johnston High School, her neighborhood school, where she could have been one of the top students in her graduating class and possibly won a college scholarship. On the other hand, she acknowledged that she had benefited from attending Austin High, the most prestigious high school in the city, because it was more challenging academically and she did not end up hanging out with the "wrong crowd" and dropping out of school, as some of her peers who attended Johnston High did.

Christine's story begins with her mother, who graduated from Austin High School in the 1950s, when blacks were still segregated into separate schools. Hispanic students, meanwhile, as we noted in chapter 2, were counted as "white" by the Austin school district and allowed to attend some of the predominantly white schools, depending on where they lived. Christine's mother grew up in a highly educated family; both of her parents had gone to college, and one of her brothers became a doctor, another a pharmacist, and another a CPA. While Christine's mother did not finish college herself, she read a lot and was, according to Christine, very knowledgeable about education; she assumed that her seven daughters would all go to college after high school.

By the time Christine was ready for high school in the mid-1970s, Austin High had, as we noted, maintained its reputation as the most academically and socially elite school. But in the mostly Hispanic East Austin neighborhood where Christine and her family lived, students were assigned to nearby Johnston High School. At that time, Johnston's student body was completely Hispanic and black and had a poor academic reputation and little status or prestige in the town of Austin. This reputation and lack of status was related to the racial and socioeconomic makeup of Johnston's students and the self-fulfilling prophecy of schools that are not affiliated with families of privilege. According to the research, segregated black and Latino schools like Johnston are far more likely to have fewer resources, less qualified teachers, less challenging curricula, and lower expectations than schools serving mostly white and affluent students.[2]

While attending her local junior high school, a mostly Hispanic and black school in East Austin—"You could probably count the Anglos on your hand in that school"—Christine was singled out by her teachers as one of the highest-scoring students in her grade. They told her parents that she should not go to Johnston because it was a bad school and that she should go instead to Austin High School via the majority-to-minority transfer program. Christine's mother was also worried that if her daughters went to Johnston High School they might get involved in a "bad crowd." So she sent her three youngest daughters—Christine and her two older sisters—to Austin High.

Christine and her sisters transferred to Austin High School together in 1976 as Christine was entering ninth grade. One of her sisters was beginning her senior year of high school, and the other was a sophomore. Two of these three daughters—Christine and the sister who was a senior— went to Austin High against their will. The third, who is only a year older than Christine, did not object. In hindsight, Christine explains, this is the sister who most rejects her Hispanic heritage and who is married to an Anglo man. The story was more complicated for Christine and her other siblings, who wanted both to be successful academically and professionally and to hold on to more of their Mexican heritage.

Christine's four oldest sisters had already graduated from Johnston High School by the time she began at Austin High School. Thus the experiences of Christine and her six siblings who collectively graduated from two separate and unequal high schools are quite telling; they reflect the range of possibilities and disappointments related to school desegregation in this country.

When recalling the different outcomes of the two sets of sisters, Christine noted that those who went to Johnston High School all did reasonably well—not really any better or worse than she and her sisters who went to Austin High School. She noted: "I don't think there's any difference, certainly not in our education level, 'cause they are all very bright people, you know, too. And I don't think they're any less . . . or more Hispanic or, you know, than I was 'cause I went to a white school."

In fact, Christine said that her sisters who went to Johnston High "turned out pretty darn well." Two of these sisters got four-year college scholarships out of Johnston, which was the lowest-performing high school in the district at that time. But she also said that one of the main reasons these sisters did so well in school was that they had parents who kept them in line and did not allow them to hang out with the wrong people. She is not sure that the same family context would have saved her and her two other sisters had they gone to Johnston.

This is the sort of double-guessing that Christine engaged in many times in our interviews with her. At one point she said she thought that if she had stayed at Johnston, "I could have gotten a scholarship without trying . . . I probably could have been a top graduating, 2 percent or, you know, 1 percent of my class had I gone to that school." Yet at other times, or even at the same time, she considered whether her life as a student at Johnston High School could have gone in the totally opposite direction: "I could have totally gone . . . with a bad crowd and not ended up being worth anything, you know. So . . . there's no way of knowing."

She wonders whether at Johnston the teachers would have overlooked her because she would not have been any different from other Hispanic or black kids. "Or maybe I would have been recognized as, she's really smart—let's work with her, you know, to get a scholarship, or you know, get her grades going. You know, I don't know. I'm just guessing."

What Christine does know is that while she benefited in many meaningful ways from her time at Austin High School, she also had to endure subtle forms of discrimination against Mexicans and being a member of a lower-status ethnic group within the social and academic hierarchy of a highly stratified school. Thus Christine's discussion of her years at Austin High School is also riddled with contradictions and double consciousness. When asked what attending Austin High did for her, she said: "Academic-wise . . . it's always been a good school; it still is a good, high-achieving school. . . . It helped me to do well in my academics. . . . In that sense I think I did well, the school did well for me . . . it kept me academically high, I would say."

In the same breath, she described the sense of inferiority she had experienced in a high school that enrolled so many white students from affluent and privileged backgrounds and how they often made her feel self-conscious and insecure: "But I think at the same time . . . I would think that it's also made me be the kind that . . . I have to prove, I'm still out to prove . . . to everybody, even from that experience that . . . you're not better than me . . . and I'll probably carry that forever."

These scars, etched into the souls of some, but not all, graduates of color and, in some instances, the less affluent whites across our sites, reappear in descriptions of the social hierarchies and cliques, especially at Austin High, where the hierarchy was that much more pronounced. As Christine recalls, "I was real active. I joined a lot of organizations and

I had a lot of friends. I was, you know . . . I would say popular *for being, you know, a Hispanic.* I was smart. I, you know, made good grades and never got in trouble. I was a good student."

Thus the upside of attending Austin High School from Christine's perspective was that she went to an academically rigorous school and graduated in the top 10 percent of her class. At the same time, she was involved in a wide range of activities, from the drill team to the Spanish Club and volleyball team to the student council and the Vocational Office Education Club. She said she had a lot of fun and made a lot of friends— mostly Hispanic but some white and black as well.

Still, her regrets include not studying hard enough so that she could make a 4.0 average. She said that while she did graduate in the top of her class at Austin High, she thinks she would have had more scholarship opportunities with a higher grade-point average and a ranking as one of the very best students at Johnston. When asked why she did not try that hard, she said: "Nobody pushed us. My parents didn't push me. The school didn't push me. My friends weren't into it, you know, just all those reasons. . . . I never did anything extra, I never did any extra work, any extra homework, any studying for tests . . . nothing that probably really could've put me way above if I really would have put an effort to it."

Partly as a result of not being pushed and partly as a result of not having enough information about the different levels of classes offered at Austin High at the time, Christine ended up taking "whatever was required to graduate" and nothing extra—none of the highest-level courses that were filled with white students at the time. "I don't remember that [high-level courses] being offered. . . . I was always a good student. I mean, I made good grades. . . . So I guess if it was never brought to my attention then I just left it alone and did the minimal of what I needed to do to get out."

The other difficult aspect of being a Hispanic student from the "other side of the tracks" attending a predominantly white high school on the affluent west side of town was the invisible social boundaries over which no one dared step. For instance, Christine talked about becoming friends with white students on the volleyball and drill teams in particular. She noted that working with other students on these racially and ethnically diverse teams practically "forces" you to integrate while practicing, fundraising, or traveling together.

Yet the boundaries of the outside world dictated just how far these friendships could go. As Christine recalled, these boundaries were such that Hispanic or black students could be accepted to the extent that they were teammates—"We practice together, we do fun things together." But, she noted, if white teammates had some girls over to their homes for a sleepover or parties, she and her Hispanic friends never got invited. "We knew there were parties, or things, events, going on. We weren't invited to 'em."

Christine recognized that these "boundaries" divided students by race, ethnicity, and social class in Austin High. She recalled that while most of the Hispanic students at Austin High were not affluent, they were also not poor. "And I would say the majority of the Hispanic kids that went to Austin High were your middle class. You know, they had stuff. They weren't really 'poor' poor, but they were, of course, nowhere near to, you know, the Anglo people with their status and their income level and stuff like that."

One of the things that struck Christine about these race and social class distinctions from more than two decades ago is that in many ways they are still prevalent in her adult life. She lives on the east side of Austin, in an older neighborhood that is still predominantly Anglo, but most of the whites are elderly people who have lived there for a long time. Christine moved back to the less affluent east side after she divorced her first husband, who still lives in West Austin. She said she had moved back east because she wanted to stay close to where she grew up. "I'm very close to my Hispanic culture. . . . You know, I'm not ever gonna move out of that area. . . . I could care if I have degrees or whatever, but that's still my home base."

Since high school, Christine has worked in various office support positions in the public sector, where she said she works with people of all different backgrounds and has been treated unfairly on more than one occasion—denied opportunities for advancement that she felt she had earned. She attended college on and off and even earned her paralegal certificate but was still working on her bachelor's degree when we interviewed her more than twenty years after her graduation from high school.

Christine's son from her first marriage was in middle school at the time we met her, and he lived mostly with her ex-husband and his wife in their expensive home in West Austin. Her son was attending a virtually all-Anglo private school that her ex-husband wanted him to attend. Christine was not happy about having her son in that school because of how it had affected his attitude toward people who were not affluent. She explained: "You know, my ex-husband makes a heck of a lot more money than I do. His wife is an electrical engineer. She makes [a six] digit figure. You know, they live in a very nice part of West Austin, you know, with the pool, the maid, the whole bit, you know, kind of stuff. . . . There's just . . . there's a difference. And he's [her son] learning to grow up in that environment."

Christine and her second husband, on the other hand, live a much more modest lifestyle and, she said, stay closer to their cultural roots as Mexican Americans. She worries that her son is missing out on that and on the kind of racial, ethnic, and socioeconomic diversity she experienced herself at Austin High. Thus, despite the many issues and problems she faced during her high school experience, she explained that she thinks attending a racially diverse school is important for children of all walks of life: "I think it's real important. . . . People need to realize what a real world is. . . . You know what a diverse world is, and a diverse world isn't all white. But I think they need to prepare students more . . . for that. And to offer the opportunity to all the students."

. . . . .

As Christine so vividly explained, there were many advantages to going to the prestigious high school on the "other side of the tracks." There were also a fair number of disadvantages, but most of these were the direct or indirect result of the larger context of racial and ethnic inequality in the city of Austin and our society as a whole. In other words, the aspects of Austin High School that Christine and other students of color found to be most problematic were reflections of the contradictions of the American Dream as it is juxtaposed with ongoing segregation and inequality across race and class lines. Thus Christine's story introduces the main themes of this chapter, which push us to consider, not simply whether school desegregation "worked," but the much more complex question of what it could possibly accomplish when schools were, for the most part, the only institutions trying to bring people together across racial lines in these local communities. Thus the ambivalence in Christine's voice echoes the many trade-offs—the "twoness"—of students of color whom an equity-minded educational reform such as school desegregation can only take so far before they (and it) hit the roadblocks put in place by the larger, mostly segregated and unequal society.

This chapter, therefore, explores the relationship between the larger context of these students and their schools and what "school desegregation" looked like in different places at that time. Looking more closely at the details of the court orders (or whatever desegregation policy existed) and then the experiences of students and educators within these six schools, we found that the schools and communities we studied often reproduced racial inequality by maintaining the privilege and advantages that whites—particularly affluent whites—have in the larger society within the context of desegregated schools. Yet at the same time these schools provided spaces where students and educators crossed the color line in ways they had never done before and have not done since. As we discuss below, these schools were, indeed *desegregated*. But they were not *integrated*.

Thus we argue that the school desegregation policies that were in place in these six school districts were better than nothing but simply not enough to change the larger society single-handedly. We illustrate how difficult it was for the people in these schools to live up to the goals of school desegregation given the larger societal forces, including racial attitudes, housing segregation, economic inequality, and racial politics, working against them. We also document how deeply committed some of these actors—both educators and students—were to bringing about change.[3] In this way, we explore the double consciousness of the desegregation policies themselves and the people called on to participate in them.

The people we studied speak to larger lessons about the role of schools in society and the futile but worthwhile efforts of lawyers and judges to use schools as one of the very few tools for social change. As we argued in chapter 1, desegregated schools of the 1970s embodied both the hope and the disappointment of *Brown's* promise to lessen racial inequality in the United States. We should not view the disappointments as simply an indictment of the idea of school desegregation or the legal levers that allowed it to happen in hundreds of school districts across the country.[4]

But we should use the findings from this in-depth historical study of six unique communities to help us better understand the burden we placed on the public schools to solve a systemic, societal problem that affects every dimension of our lives, from where we live and how much money we make to whom we pray with and who our close friends are. Racial inequality and segregation did not begin in the public schools; thus we should not expect remedies in the public schools to solve the problem by themselves. But we can rely on racially diverse public schools—to the extent that current and future policies allow them to exist—to be critical sites in the struggle for a more just society.[5]

In this chapter we explain the many ways in which the goals of school desegregation were undermined by larger societal forces. Lawyers and legal scholars who helped make desegregation a reality and who continue to fight for racial diversity in educational settings need more detailed information on this complex view of the history of school desegregation in the United States to move forward with new legal strategies.

THE POWER OF WHITE PRIVILEGE IN RACIALLY MIXED SCHOOLS AND DISTRICTS

Some of the most prevalent themes to emerge from our study illustrate the distance between the *intent* of school desegregation policy—to fulfill the Fourteenth Amendment rights of African Americans and Latinos— and the actual results these policies achieved. In the communities we studied, powerful whites were able to maintain their privileged status even in the context of an equity-minded reform movement such as school desegregation.[6]

In each of the six districts and schools in our study, policy makers and educators tried to make desegregation as palatable as possible to affluent and middle-class white students. On a political level, this made perfect sense. The idea was to stave off white and middle-class flight, which would leave the public schools politically and economically vulnerable. However, in concentrating on appeasing white parents, school districts often reinforced a sense of white entitlement while disregarding the needs of students of color and poor students. This happened in both blatant and more subtle ways and shifted the focus of these policies from remedying past discrimination on the part of whites to providing a form of educational welfare—a gift from whites to blacks and Latinos.[7]

Across the school districts, therefore, we saw the disillusionment of African American and Latino advocates, educators, and students as they watched a "remedy" they had once thought would solve the educational problems of students of color compromised to the point of being less effective. While they acknowledged many gains that resulted from efforts to desegregate public schools and create more diversity within these educational institutions, they voiced clear disappointment about how little progress had been made overall and the price that communities of color had to pay to accommodate the demands and threats of whites.[8] These African Americans and Latinos expressed their realization, currently known as "desegregation fatigue," that, given the relative economic, political, and social clout of whites in each of these communities, policies such as school desegregation could go only so far.[9]

Hattie Allen, an African American graduate of Austin High School who got along with most white students but never felt accepted by them, had this to say about whether the government should mandate more school desegregation: "I had strong feelings about government and how important it is to things like desegregation. But you know, laws don't change what's in people's heart. So the law, yeah, in theory opens up opportunities where you need to be able to go to school with these kids who are getting a better education . . . but the flip side is that . . . pain and suffering you have to endure as a result of the resentment and the anger [of knowing] that these people don't want you there."

Some of our findings related to these issues are not new to the literature on school desegregation. For instance, other authors have highlighted many of the shortcomings of desegregation policy, including the closing of black schools, the loss of black educators' jobs, and the dispro-portionate burden of busing that black students bore.[10] We, however, add a sense of double consciousness to the discussion. In other words, we think it is important to celebrate the accomplishments of *Brown* and the role that public schools and the courts have played in trying to right the wrongs of racial inequality in our society. But at the same time we want to explain from the context of these six communities how inadequate school desegregation—as a single policy affecting but one of many racially unequal institutions in our society—was in overcoming the legacy of white and wealthy privilege.[11] Our goal in moving this discussion to a more double-sided take on these issues is not to absolve the schools and educators of all wrongdoing but to examine them within the broader social context in which they were enmeshed and try to consider future policy proposals in light of what has happened in the past. As one Latino former school board member in Austin explained to us, desegregation amounted to "societal problems . . . being dumped on the children."[12]

In the sections below, we discuss the many ways in which the privi-lege of whites in an unequal society overrode the interests of people of color. What this history illustrates so clearly is the multiple problems associated with policies that end up being implemented by the same people who often created and maintained the segregated system that these policies are supposed to dismantle.[13]

Placing the Burden of Busing on Blacks and Latinos

As other school desegregation scholars and observers have noted, it was common practice across the country, and particularly in the South, for the historically black or Latino public schools to be the first to close once districts were forced—whether by judges, the federal government, or their own defensiveness—to desegregate their schools.[14] This meant that black and brown students were more likely to be riding buses longer distances at younger ages than most white students in desegre-gating school districts.[15]

In five of the six school districts that we studied, at least one histori-cally black school was eventually closed. Furthermore, in five of the six districts, black students, parents, and activists felt that their communities bore the burden of achieving racial balance in the schools. We learned from our data that this burden did not merely relate to the issue of inconvenience—black students having to get up early and get home late. Rather, the consistent closing of black schools, often without question or public debate, was often a harsh blow to the pride and dignity of the black communities. It sent a strong message that there was nothing of value in the black community or the Latino community, nothing that whites wanted or needed.

A particularly egregious example of this occurred in Austin, Texas, shortly after Christine Almonte and her classmates entered kindergarten, as the first phase of school desegregation in the Austin Independent School District began. This first phase entailed closing black schools on the east side of town and transferring students out of those neighborhoods to other schools, many with large Latino populations. One of the black schools that was closed early on was Anderson High School, which, as we noted in chapter 2, was the city's second oldest high school, with a long tradition and strong ties to the African American community. Prior to closing this historically black high school, the federal judge overseeing the desegregation case in Austin made one attempt to reassign nearby white students to Anderson. A longtime district administrator recalled what happened next: "You know, people [at Anderson] got revved up for that. . . . The black kids did a lot of work on trying to get ready for these [white] kids. And, of course, the [white] kids didn't come. So there was like total flight, you know. Well, that was a downer as well. That was another unfortunate situation that helped solidify an adversarial deal because feelings were hurt."

Thus, despite the huge amount of pride that members of the black community had in Anderson High School and their efforts to "fix it up" when they thought white students were going to enroll there, the white students never showed up. In hindsight, given the history of racial discrimination and segregation in cities such as Austin, it is not surprising that white families did not want to send their children to historically black or Hispanic schools. Most of these schools were inferior to the white schools in terms of resources and facilities, a fact that only underscored the harms created by years of racial and ethnic segregation. Furthermore, the communities in which these schools existed were more likely to be poor and unfamiliar to whites, particularly affluent whites.

Still, we know from school desegregation history that such schools, with a great deal of extra support and funding, can be made more appealing to white families. For instance, in Austin, several years after the effort to enroll white students in the old Anderson High School failed, another, newer high school on the east side of the city (in a mostly Hispanic area) was temporarily desegregated after district officials put additional resources and facilities into that school to attract and retain white students. Similarly, as noted in chapter 2 and later in this chapter, in Charlotte, North Carolina, the school we studied—West Charlotte High School—was historically black. In that city as well, district officials provided the extra resources needed to ensure that white students would show up to their newly assigned high school in the black community.

But from the perspective of the African American leaders we interviewed in Austin, the white officials and parents clearly gave little thought to the symbolic meaning of the failed effort to desegregate Anderson High School, which was the black community's pride and joy. After this act of white resistance and defiance, the judge rescinded the plan that reassigned white students and ordered a new plan that resulted in the closing of all the black schools, including Anderson High School, in 1972 and the one-way busing of black students out of their community. The longtime Austin administrator we cited above noted that this alteration of the desegregation plan was both a good and a bad step. It was good in that it was more effective in creating racially balanced schools, but it was bad in that it reinforced the idea that what the black community had to offer was not worthwhile and that black schools were inherently inferior. He said, "When you tell people that their schools are inferior to some degree, you're telling them they're inferior."

To make matters worse, the manner in which Anderson High School was shut down was particularly insulting. At the time of Anderson's closing, the Austin School Board committed to building a new "Anderson" high school in the northwestern, mostly white section of the city, in part to appease blacks who were angry and frustrated about the demise of their school. Members of the black community thought that the new Anderson would carry on the history and rich tradition of the original Anderson High School and thus should house some of the memorabilia, such as trophies and plaques, from the now-defunct black school. Yet they soon learned that such memories of the old, all-black Anderson High School were not welcome in the new, predominantly white school. As one African American community leader explained, the people leading the new Anderson High School said that they did not want the trophies or anything else from the black Anderson High School. He said the "new" Anderson was related to the "old" Anderson in name only, a statement that "insulted and infuriated the Afro-American community, justifiably so."

An African American graduate of Austin High School whom we interviewed recalled that she would have gone to the old, historically black Anderson High School had it not been torn down before she entered ninth grade: "They closed that school back in the seventies and kept the name but moved it to the west side of town so the white kids could go to it. I felt bad about that and I felt robbed . . . because all those old black schools were torn down. They won all the state championships and all that stuff, and I wanted to go and be a part of that. My mother went to Anderson High School. I wanted to go to Anderson High, but they moved that school out of the east side of Austin."

Ironically, more than twenty years after attending Austin High, this African American graduate explained that she had benefited from the academic program there and thus had wanted her two sons to go there. But she told us that her sons had opted to not go to Austin High "because they didn't want to be in a 'white school.'" She said they had told her, "Oh mama, that's a white school."

As we noted in chapter 2, in the 1970s Austin implemented a majority-to-minority transfer plan, a voluntary desegregation plan through which students of any race could transfer from a school in which they were in the racial majority to a school in which they would be a racial minority. This program did not succeed in fully desegregating the district, however, because no white students opted to transfer to the predominantly black or Hispanic schools on the east side of town. As one local Hispanic politician noted, "The majority-to-minority transfer rule did not meet the test of integration because all the burden for moving was on the minorities. No white guy would say, 'I want to go into a minority school.'"

Other sites in our study were similar to Austin in placing the burden of busing on African American and Latino children as schools in their neighborhoods were closed or unable to enroll many white students and they were put on buses in larger numbers and at younger ages than white students. For instance, in Pasadena the school desegregation plan paired black, Latino, and white elementary schools so that all the students—black, white, and Latino—from the two schools went to one building for kindergarten through third grade and then to the other school for grades four through six. But all of the K–3 schools were in the previously predominantly white schools in the white neighborhoods, which meant the youngest students of color were always sent the farthest. By fourth grade, many white parents had enrolled their children in private schools to avoid sending them to schools in black or Latino communities. As several people we interviewed noted, private schools flourished in Pasadena at that time.

In Charlotte, North Carolina, one of the most comprehensive school desegregation plans in the country was implemented three years after the 1971 U.S. Supreme Court ruling in *Swann v. Charlotte-Mecklenburg Board of Education*.[16] In this case the Court held that, if it was necessary to achieve racial balance, school districts should reassign students to schools outside their neighborhoods and use transportation such as busing to get the students to these schools.[17] Thousands of Charlotte students were bused every day to schools across town, but the African American students from the west side of town were bused in greater percentages, at younger ages, and for many more years on average than most of the white students. This was partly because of the demographics of the district and the high concentration of black students in certain neighborhoods, but it was also the result of deliberate choices made by the judge, lawyers, and district officials to appease white parents and stave off white flight.

According to one of the lawyers who represented the black plaintiffs in *Swann*, the biggest problem with the plan was that those in charge placed a far greater burden on black families than on white families. He said the Court purposely decided to close the K–3 schools in the black neighborhoods and put all such grade schools in the suburban and predominantly white areas of the county. This plan was implemented, the lawyer argued, "so that white kids wouldn't have to go to school in the inner city, and that supposedly made it easier for white parents to send their kids to school."

Meanwhile, all the black high schools in the city of Charlotte and Mecklenburg County, except West Charlotte High School, were closed, and their students dispersed to predominantly white high schools. One of these historically black high schools, Second Ward, was shut down quickly over the summer of 1969 with no prior warning given to the students or their families. Although the Charlotte-Mecklenburg School Board had been telling the Second Ward students, most of whom lived in a very poor community on the edge of downtown near the school, that they would be getting a new high school to replace their dilapidated facility, the board decided instead to abruptly close and demolish the school, scattering the students, some of whom were just starting their junior and senior years of high school, across several other schools.

It appears that the school board's decision on the fate of Second Ward High School occurred in a mere two-week time frame as Charlotte's school desegregation case was wending its way through the federal courts. A white teacher we interviewed who was returning from his Peace Corps assignment in the Philippines in the summer of 1969 said he was hired by the Charlotte-Mecklenburg Public Schools to teach high school math. Shortly thereafter, he remembered learning that he was to be assigned for that fall to Second Ward High School. Then, he said, about a week later, he learned that Second Ward's name had been changed to Metropolitan High School. A week or so later, he received a letter from the district informing him that Second Ward/Metropolitan High School had been closed and that he had been assigned to West Charlotte High School. He noted, "So I went from Second Ward to Metropolitan to West Charlotte, all in about two weeks!"

While an official reason was never provided for the decision to abruptly tear down the school, several people we interviewed noted that the mounting pressure of the court case most likely forced the school board to contemplate the idea of desegregating white students into the oldest and poorest black high school in the city. In fact, Second Ward was geographically much closer to the affluent white neighborhoods from which students were eventually reassigned to the more middle-class black community of West Charlotte.

District officials defended the decision to close Second Ward, citing the extremely poor condition of the school's buildings and the fact that the neighborhood around the school was undergoing urban renewal. Of course, that does not explain why they could not build a new Second Ward High School on that site in 1969 instead of closing the school. African Americans in Charlotte seem fairly convinced that Second Ward had to close so that the board would not be forced at some point to assign white students there. They also suggest that urban renewal and the subsequent removal of blacks and their beloved old high school from the nearby community were part of a larger plan to move blacks out of the predominantly white eastern part of the city to make room for more office buildings, hotels, and highways for sub-urban commuters.[18]

According to one African American community activist in Charlotte who attended Second Ward High School and went on to become a school board member in the 1990s, a bond referendum was passed in the 1960s that was supposed to pay for the new Second Ward High School:

> Like in '63 the bond referendum passed, '63, '64, '65, '66, '67, they were telling the public they were going to rebuild the school [Second Ward]. In less than a year's time something happened politically, and they said, "No, we're going to close it." People were shocked, people were crying, because they'd never heard that before, all of a sudden, "You're going to be the last class, we're closing Second Ward." And the community was shocked, but because urban renewal was moving a lot of people out of [the neighborhood by the school], the political struc-ture wasn't in place to fight it. You had blacks who worried about where they were going to live because the bulldozer was coming. So it just went off the face of the map like that.

The students from Second Ward were rapidly reassigned, and many of them—some say more than half—either were sent to or chose to attend the nearest black high school, West Charlotte, which had traditionally enrolled the more middle-class black students. The irony was that not only were these Second Ward students being reassigned to a similarly segregated school, but West Charlotte and Second Ward had been long-time rivals, with heated debates in the black community about which school had a stronger football team. In fact, one of the most highly anticipated events of the year in Charlotte's black community had been the Second Ward–West Charlotte football game. The winner of that game took home a huge trophy for the year.

The teachers who were at West Charlotte High School at the time recall the tension between the Second Ward and West Charlotte students when they were thrown together in the same school in the fall of 1969. These teachers said that students from the two schools would sit on opposite sides of the classrooms from each other, segregating themselves according to their schools of origin. The math teacher who had just returned from the Philippines described this tension as it affected his first semester of teaching at West Charlotte, right after the Second Ward students enrolled there: "You talk about a segregated school. . . . Those West Charlotte and Second Ward blacks were as segregated as you could possibly get. They were amazing. . . . I had an Algebra III class, and it had five rows of desks. I had two rows of Second Ward people, and two rows of West Charlotte people, and I had an empty middle row. [laughs]"

Still, the civil rights attorney who helped bring the *Swann* case, when asked if he would proceed differently if he had a chance to negotiate the plan again, said he was not sure. He noted that the plan, which allowed far more white students, especially in elementary school, to stay in their own neighborhoods and placed much more of the burden of busing on the black students, forcing them to leave their local communities, often at a very young age, garnered more acceptance of the court order from the white community.

Thus in Charlotte, as well as in Pasadena, Austin, Englewood, and eventually Shaker Heights and Topeka, African American and Latino children were more likely to bear the logistical burdens of integration.

Meanwhile, black communities lost many of their neighborhood schools—some because they were decrepit and others simply because no whites would ever go to them. Often these white parents pulled their children out of the public schools anyway, leaving African American parents, educators, and activists angry, hurt, and frustrated.

Ironically, the high school in Charlotte that we chose to study, West Charlotte High School, is one of the few historically black schools that survived the implementation of school desegregation by enrolling large numbers of white students in the 1970s and 1980s. Nevertheless, the story of West Charlotte—the extra resources it received and the recruitment of some of the top teachers across the district to attract the white students as well as changes the school went through once the white teachers and student arrived—provides some of the most solid evidence of the ways white privilege can assert itself even within the context of a historically black school.

According to the white former principal of West Charlotte who was assigned to the school by the board of education once the affluent white students were bused there, his goal at that time was to help make the white students feel comfortable at the historically black school. Looking back on that era more than twenty years later, he said he now thinks he went too far. "I made lots of mistakes, and one of the mistakes I made was that I think that I tried to make it too white too quick."

When asked what he meant by "too white," he said that, for instance, he took down pictures of former West Charlotte educators—some of the most esteemed members of the city's black community. He also moved some of the coveted West Charlotte trophies from where they had been prominently displayed when it was an all-black school and put them in a place where they were less visible. Other traditions and customs of the formerly all-black high school were discontinued. He noted that "that was the wrong thing to do. . . . I wouldn't do it now."

This perception of what happened to West Charlotte when the affluent white students showed up is corroborated by many other interviewees. While the marching band, with its rhythmic performance style more in keeping with those of historically black high schools and colleges, including several dance moves that many white band members found challenging,[19] and a few other activities maintained their black high school identity, much of what West Charlotte High School had been before school desegregation was homogenized or conformed toward "white norms" of the culture of schooling. In some ways this was a positive change, especially to the extent that the affluent white families that came to West Charlotte brought resources and political power to the school. But in other ways this homogenization of West Charlotte's tradition and history was a missed opportunity to move toward more meaningful integration—as opposed to merely desegregation—of black and white students and their communities.

In other words, one of the most salient findings from our study is that when members of two or more different racial/ethnic groups that have been historically segregated are merely *desegregated*, or brought together with little conscious effort to consider the terms upon which they will coexist within the same space, the group with the most power and status in the larger context—whites—will, unless they are in the minority, dominate academically, socially, and culturally within the desegregated school or organization. In the context of these six schools and communities, this meant that whiteness became the norm, and the racially diverse schools, for the most part, operated on white people's terms of whose knowledge and experiences were valued and who had greater status and prestige socially. Had the goal for these schools been to create greater *integration*, the educators would have made more of an effort to value and embrace the traditions and experiences that black and Latino students brought with them from their schools. The difficulty of doing this, particularly in the politically charged context of implementing a massive school desegregation plan, was perhaps most pronounced at West Charlotte High School, given its history as a black school. As the former principal and other staff members from the school admitted, far more could have been done to celebrate what had been good about West Charlotte before the white educators and students arrived in 1969. While many of the white students did try to embrace some of this historical culture of the school, especially with regard to their pride in the band, most of these efforts were symbolic and too superficial to fundamentally challenge the dynamics of race and power that permeate this society.

Of course, as the central themes of this book illustrate, the educators at West Charlotte and the other schools were not operating in a cultural or political vacuum. They made the choices they did when they did because that is how they made sense of race and what was "normal" and "good" at the time and because the white families in these communities had more clout and voice than the families of color. Thus there was a great deal of focus on making the white students feel at home in desegregated schools, particularly in a historically black school in a black neighborhood.

A white graduate of West Charlotte, Betsy Hagart, who grew up in a lower-middle-class white neighborhood and whose parents strongly opposed their daughter's attending a high school on the black side of town, noted that the school had been fairly "homogenized" (meaning that it had become more like a white school) by the time she got there in 1977: "As far as the traditions, I didn't really know that West Charlotte had [any]. . . . It was like our school at that time, and there weren't any old, like, you know Yale and Harvard and all those have . . . you know, steeped in tradition and it's passed down from class to class. I didn't feel that at West Charlotte. There was no definition of the school, so we just kind of made it our school while we were there."

The school that the students and their educators made "while they were there" lacked the soul of the school that had preceded the arrival of white students. As we discuss in chapter 5, there was some social integration of the students in terms of friendships and teen culture—for example, music and clothing. But the formal structures and the official cultures of these schools, including what was taught and the public symbols of the schools, were normalized in a way that was more in line with the histories and experiences of white students, particularly those who were not low income. French sociologist Pierre Bourdieu explains this advantage that wealthy students have over others as their "cultural capital," their understanding of the world that is legitimized and rewarded in the educational system as the "proper" norm.[20] When we add the racial inequalities that remain so tightly woven into the fabric of this country, the concept of cultural capital becomes even more complex, with hierarchies of race and class intertwined in favor of those who have the lightest complexions and the most money.[21] Furthermore, as Bourdieu so eloquently argued, the cultural differences in terms of what children pick up formally and informally through their out-of-school experiences become intertwined with structural inequalities, such as laws, regulations, unequal income and wealth, and spatial separation. In other words, instead of creating the "equal status" that sociologist Gordon Allport claimed was necessary for meaningful "intergroup contact" when bringing members of different racial or ethnic groups together within institutions such as schools, the educators and leaders of desegregated schools often inadvertently perpetuated the unequal status of white, black, and Latino students by trying to keep the norms the same while the student bodies were changing dramatically.[22]

In a study of how white teachers perceive racism within racially diverse schools, Julie Kailin found that most of the teachers she surveyed operated from an "impaired consciousness" of racism and were more likely to blame the victims of racism or remain silent when they witnessed their colleagues committing racist acts. Kailin recognized that these teachers lived and worked within a larger social context that condoned their consciousness, but she added that it was important to realize that within the schools the educators were members of a group that did have some power and ability. "In a society in which we have racial domination, racial assumptions and categories left unchallenged and unlearned will be reproduced in institutional practices."[23]

Thus at West Charlotte, within a few years of school desegregation, white teachers were found teaching most of the advanced classes, which had always been taught by black teachers before. And, as we discuss below, the vast majority of the students in these upper-tier classes were white as well. White students and their parents also took on many of the leadership roles in various student organizations and the PTA.[24]

Yet even with the extra resources that were placed in West Charlotte and the ascent of white students and adults into positions of power and prestige within the school, we learned through our interviews that it was not unusual for white students assigned to West Charlotte (nicknamed "West Chocolate" by many whites in the community) to have their doctors write letters to the board of education saying that for either physical or mental reasons they could not endure the bus ride to the black neighborhood where the school was located and should be exempt from the busing plan. Another white West Charlotte graduate who grew up near Betsy and whose parents were also angry about her going to the black high school said she personally knew several people who had tried to use a doctor's note to get out of going: "Some doctors did lie. I had friends who got to go to [East Mecklenburg High School] because they had 'scoliosis,' you know? And now, when I look at that, I'm going, you know? How unethical! But . . . you know, it happened."

Unequal Knowledge of and Access to High-Track Classes

The relative privilege and power of white parents and students influenced not only the way in which students were assigned to desegregated schools but also who had knowledge of and access to certain classes within racially diverse schools. We recognize that many factors affected the resegregation of students across classrooms within desegregated schools, including the often unequal schooling that blacks and Latino students had been receiving prior to desegregation, the higher poverty rates and lower education levels of their families, and these students' hesitancy to demand access to predominantly white classes where they often felt marginalized.[25] But we also have a great deal of data to suggest that, even when prior achievement levels of white and black students were similar, white students were given more information about and easier access to the higher-level classes, whether honors, accelerated, or Advanced Placement (AP) classes.

From blatant tracking practices that labeled students as "gifted" or "nongifted" in elementary school and then channeled them through the grade levels in the "appropriate" classes to more subtle forms of sorting students that entailed requirements such as teacher recommendations to get into the best classes, the schools and districts we studied managed to create consistent levels of within-school racial segregation. Like the more frequent busing of black students out of their neighborhoods, the preferred access to high-level classes given to whites was in part a strategy to appease white parents. The time frame we studied is important in this regard because it was the late 1970s, when tracking and grouping practices were becoming more sophisticated and hierarchical as the AP program was rapidly becoming more prominent, especially in high schools serving students from upper-middle-class backgrounds.[26] Scholars of tracking as well as many of the people we interviewed in the six sites question whether the rise of more complex within-school tracking structures was not directly related to the concurrent rise in the number of schools across the country that were racially desegregated.[27] According to the black community leader who was on the school board in Charlotte for many years: "See, what you do is you desegregate schools but you resegregate the classrooms. That's the pattern across the country. . . . They'll say, 'All right, you got to come to this school, but we're going to put you in this class now.' So you actually have school desegregation but classroom segregation."

At all six of the high schools we studied, high-achieving white students talked about seeing many of the same students in all the upper-level classes. "Schools within schools" was a phrase that was used regularly to describe the special, predominantly white configuration of advanced classes and students within desegregated schools. A white 1980 graduate of Shaker Heights High School who was in most of these advanced classes noted that while not always the exact same twenty students were in every upper-level class, "it would be very unusual to see somebody, like a new face in one class that you didn't see in any other class."

At Dwight Morrow High School in Englewood, New Jersey, which was only about 36 percent white when the class of 1980 was there, a white student who enrolled in mostly high-level classes commented that the more "academically stringent" the class, the fewer black students were in it. He noted that his AP biology class had enrolled only one or two black students and his calculus class only one, even though the school was almost 60 percent black. When asked if the racial makeup of the high-level classes was something that students at Dwight Morrow talked about, this white graduate stated that while there was not much open discussion, students were aware that "there was, like, two societies going on at the academic level."

This white student, who benefited from all the cultural and economic privileges of white families in the school system at that time, was aware that many of the African American students in the lower-level classes lacked the information they needed to go on to college, including which classes would look best on their transcripts and when or why they should take the SATs. On the other hand, white students tended to be very well informed regarding what it took to get into college. He commented: "There were people that knew that you're gonna do this stuff [college prep], and they just kind of marched along and did it, and there were other people who were totally out of it. Most people were just not included in it."

Other white graduates who were in upper-tier classes across the six schools recognized the same unequal knowledge bases across racial and social class lines. Even when they were more likely to chalk this up to "family values," as many did, implying that what really mattered was whether a student's family valued education as much as theirs did, they would still admit some degree of an unequal playing field when it came to the hidden curriculum of how to win the college admissions game. Meanwhile, it was also clear from our interviews that the vast majority of African American and Latino students in these schools had, at the time, a much hazier understanding of this hidden curriculum and a vaguer sense of the tracking system and why it mattered in terms of college admissions. Furthermore, we learned across the six sites that for the most part the high school guidance counselors were more helpful to those who already had help in terms of college applications from their families.

Thus one of the most powerful themes to emerge from Dwight Morrow interviews was that the African American graduates seemed to have much less understanding of the tracking system overall. The white students, on the other hand, whether they were in the most advanced classes or not, tended to be more aware of where they and their classes fit into the hierarchy. The situation was similar at other schools in our study. For instance, Christine, the Latina graduate of Austin High School profiled at the beginning of this chapter, noted that, looking back at her high school years, "I was never aware that there was maybe like an advanced, upper-level class for those that made As, and they were all predominantly white. I think they kind of put those students all together; they were making all As and they were going to go with a certain instructor and all be in the same room together." Meanwhile, one of Christine's Latino classmates who also lived on the east side of Austin and attended Austin High School via the majority-to-minority transfer plan remembered being placed in a "fundamentals of math" class his sophomore year. He referred to the class as "loser math," in which they did very basic addition and subtraction: "It was an insult to me. I don't know how I ended up in that class. . . . But I ended up passing it. I tolerated it, . . . but when you look back I shouldn't have been in that class. I was way smarter than that. My grades were nowhere near [that bad]."

This lack of information among students of color about the tracking hierarchy and the lack of discussion regarding the resegregation by classroom of desegregated schools were powerful themes across the sites we studied, but there were exceptions. For instance, a white graduate of Shaker Heights who took the most advanced classes in English, social studies, and science and more "regular" classes in math recalled that her advanced classes were about 95 percent white. This student remembered talking with one of the few African American students in her AP government class during her senior year; she said the two of them would walk home together every day and occasionally would talk about how there "were too many white males" in the AP classes: "I recall that there was a lot of discussion . . . about too many white males in government, and we've got to change that, and whether it's females or other races, we've got to change that. It was almost like we felt . . . we knew we were on the cusp of being the next generation of lawmakers or whatever we wanted to be, and we felt a great strength and anticipation at the ability to really be different and do something. . . . I just really remember that, we were all just so excited."

Despite such optimism, a classmate of these two students noted that it was standard practice at Shaker High at the time to refer to the lowest tier of classes as "ghetto classes" because they were predominantly black. But it was very rare for students to have spaces where they could discuss this rather blatant resegregation by race within their desegregated schools. As a result, they made sense of it in a de facto manner that usually lacked any critique of the broader inequalities that perpetuated it. Yet there was plenty of evidence that the roots of the resegregation problem were far deeper than most students surmised, and some discussion about the deep-seated nature of these problems would have been helpful in terms of the lessons the students learned. For instance, it was clear from our data that often students had been "tracked" into their gifted slots well before they got to high school. Quotes similar to the following one from a white West Charlotte graduate were common in our data from white student interviews: "I was tested at the end of second grade and stayed in the same [high] track through high school."

In many instances students from different racial backgrounds had different access to these early opportunities to join the high track. As an English teacher at Muir High School in Pasadena noted, the honors-level classes were composed of mostly white students primarily because such within-school segregation had existed in the elementary and middle school. Prior to the 1970s and court-ordered desegregation, the students of color had limited opportunities to participate in the gifted program instituted in the elementary and middle schools, known as the "Mentally Gifted Minor" program, because many of the schools they had attended did not offer this program. Thus, the teacher at Muir noted, "it followed that they would not be in the high school program for five years because you have to bring them up, you know, through the rest of the levels . . . so they're prepared to do honors."

But the teacher stated that after five or six years, while she did begin to see more African Americans in the honors-level classes, not many Latino students enrolled in them. She added that today students are still "grouped and tracked" in the third grade into honors classes, a practice she referred to as "criminal" because by high school good students are hesitant to take the honors classes if they have not previously been labeled as "honors" material.

Meanwhile, a retired English teacher from West Charlotte High School told us perhaps the most revealing story about tracking and race. When this white teacher was in her first year at West Charlotte, the students were still all black because the teachers had been desegregated a year before the students. This teacher and a small cohort of colleagues were among the first white teachers to be assigned to the historically black school. She talked about her students in the all-black honors classes her first year at West Charlotte as being very "bright"—some of the best students and the best classes she had ever taught. But she noted that the following year, when the white students arrived, even though she thought the honors-level black students were as good as the honors-level white students who came into the school, the honors classes became predominantly white in a school that was only 50 percent white. She said that in those first years of integration she used to look out at all the white faces in her honors classes and wonder where all those high-achieving black students had gone: "What did happen to them [the high-achieving black students] when the school became integrated and the high-level classes became predominantly white?"

Across the racially diverse high schools in our study, at least two separate and unequal academic spheres existed. While many students of color felt that they did not have enough information or access to the different academic options, many of the white students who had been identified as gifted since they were in elementary school saw the upper-level classes as their manifest destiny. They did not ask where the high-achieving black students had gone; too rarely did they even know that such students existed within desegregated schools.

The Effects of Segregation Outside the Schools

In spite of the obstacles to meaningful integration in racially mixed schools and the profound influence of white privilege on the design and scope of desegregation policies, the majority of the class of 1980 interviewees recalled becoming friends or at least acquaintances with one or more people of another racial group while in high school. As we discuss more fully in chapter 5, these relationships developed primarily through extracurricular activities—athletics in particular, especially among the boys. But student government, drama, band, and chorus, for example, brought boys *and* girls together across racial lines. Furthermore, in a few of the schools, as the class of 1980 neared graduation, racial barriers seemed to diminish (see chapter 5).

Still, social cliques at these schools were mostly segregated along racial lines. According to the graduates, their very best friends—those they did things with outside school—were almost always the same race. Of course, many important social psychological theories regarding racial identity formation in students help to explain this phenomenon in diverse schools across the country.[28] Our findings offer yet another related but distinct explanation: that racial segregation, discrimination, and inequality in the local communities surrounding these schools perpetuated racial isolation in terms of friendships and social networks within the schools. In other words, students who had grown up in racially segregated neighborhoods that were sometimes clear across town from each other, attending segregated churches and temples, having parents and relatives with very few friends or co-workers of other races, and in many cases attending less diverse elementary and middle schools, arrived on their high school campuses with far less familiarity with students of other races and a much higher comfort level with their same-race friends. For instance, a white Topeka High graduate, when asked about cross-racial friendships in high school, sounded conflicted when she contrasted her in-school and out-of-school experiences: "I can't say that I ran around with a lot of black kids, but I did have [black] friends at school, and they were in different classes. I don't remember outside of school doing a lot of running around with kids from other races. . . . It kind of went back to being with who you knew and stuff like that and where you grew up."

Layered on top of this were students' fears of the separate neighborhoods where some of their classmates lived. This fear was especially powerful among the white students and even more so among their parents, who were reluctant to allow their children to attend parties or social events in the black or Latino neighborhoods. For instance, the white West Charlotte graduate who grew up near Betsy recalled that her parents would not have allowed her to go to a party in a black neighborhood: "You know, they just would have said, 'No, you can't come.'"

White parents could also be reluctant to allow black or Latino friends to come to white students' houses. One white Austin High graduate who grew up in a less affluent area of West Austin had a very good friend named Rita who was a Latina. She explained that while her mother would rarely allow her to bring Latinos into the house, she made an exception for Rita: "I can remember bringing her [Rita] to my house and asking her to stand outside for just a few minutes, and I went in and called my mother and asked if I could have a friend come in. . . . She said yes, and I said, 'Well, she's Mexican. Would that still be okay?' My mother said, 'Rita only.' I mean . . . it wasn't an open-door policy."

This kind of fear and distrust was certainly not unidirectional; many graduates of color talked about not feeling welcome in white neighborhoods and homes. According to an African American graduate of Topeka High School who was popular and a star athlete at the school, outside school the white and black students kept to themselves because it was unusual for students—or anyone else—to cross the color lines. He said, "You didn't really go over to the white kids' house."

In addition, we learned that in several of the communities we studied, the spatial separation accompanied by a lack of mass transportation so typical across the United States added to the sense of distance and separation across racial lines.[29] A white West Charlotte graduate, in talking about how the students would "split up" racially outside school, noted, "You had a big . . . geographic, mileage, radius of travel to get around because [the affluent white neighborhood] was pretty much located in the center, the center of the city, West Charlotte's on the west side of town, and then the other group that was bused in, they were from the northeast side of town. So we were quite a distance away from one another."

Thus we have learned that for the most part students in these desegregated schools stepped over color lines only when they were in school—if they did it there—and that outside school the racial apartheid of their communities continued to divide them. This iterative relationship between the schools and their local context is critical to understanding what school desegregation accomplished as a policy that dramatically changed only one social institution in the society while others remained segregated. It also raises the question of what could have been accomplished if school desegregation had been implemented simultaneously with more forceful social policies designed to tackle housing segregation, income inequality, and the need for more public transportation.

The Self-Fulfilling Prophecy of Becoming a "Bad" School

A final finding related to the way in which the promise of *Brown* has remained unfulfilled in the context of an ongoing unequal and stratified society is that the reputations of the six high schools we studied have tended to rise and fall with the demographic changes of their student bodies. We found that as the racial makeup of racially mixed schools became predominantly nonwhite and the enrollment of upper-middle-class students declined, the public's perception of the quality of those schools tended to decline, echoing the rationales for closing black schools in the 1960s and early 1970s. This phenomenon was particularly marked for the two schools in our study that had shifted from majority white to majority nonwhite in the late 1970s: Muir High School and Dwight Morrow High School. Two additional schools from our study, West Charlotte High School and Shaker Heights High School, have faced the same issues more recently as they have become majority-nonwhite schools in the last decade. Austin High School, meanwhile, has managed to maintain its majority-white student population, though barely. Topeka High School has been the most racially stable.

In this section we will highlight the experiences of Muir and Dwight Morrow because the white flight from these schools peaked during the era we studied. We think the lessons learned from the experiences of these two schools have a general relevance because, according to our interviews, the experiences of students and educators at West Charlotte in more recent years are similar and both Shaker Heights and Austin High School appear to be facing some of these issues today.

INCREASING RACIAL DIVERSITY, DECLINING REPUTATIONS

Both Muir and Dwight Morrow had maintained reputations as good and even elite schools as recently as the early 1960s for Muir and early 1970s for Dwight Morrow, before they had begun to lose their wealthiest white students. But both of these schools experienced a large degree of white flight, leaving them with predominantly students of color by the late 1970s. As the African American and Latino populations began to increase in these two schools, people in the local communities began to question their quality. Former educators and graduates of these schools talked about the changing public perceptions and explained how their schools had been unfairly maligned by both the public and the media. Both educators and graduates firmly believed that during the early phase of these changes the declining reputation of their schools had had little to do with the quality of programs offered, since these had not changed, especially for students in the high-level classes.

For instance, Dwight Morrow High School shifted from a predominantly white student population in the late 1960s to a predominantly African American student population by the late 1970s. As we noted in chapter 2, when wealthy white parents from both the city of Englewood and Englewood Cliffs began to enroll their high school students elsewhere there was a lot of discussion about the decline in the quality of the education program at the school, even before the teaching staff, course offerings, or Ivy League acceptances had changed much from the school's "glory days." A former Dwight Morrow teacher observed, "As the population in the school changed, that's when the reputation began to change. As there was a change in the population then they said, 'Oh the quality of education is not as good.'" A Dwight Morrow guidance counselor, when asked why this change in perception had occurred, noted: "I think a lot of it is just racism, I really do, because even—I mean, I was in Teaneck High School in 1959, and Teaneck and Englewood and Hackensack had the only black kids in the whole area, and you'd always hear something about Teaneck, Hackensack, or Englewood. Now, this is at a time when the schools were academically superior schools, so it wasn't like you could point [to] . . . the academic part. And I just think it snowballed until you had the white flight and there was always this perception."

As we noted in chapter 2, John Muir High School in Pasadena suffered similar public perception problems as its African American and Latino student populations increased. Muir had once been the jewel in the high school crown of the Pasadena School District, serving the children of wealthy white West Pasadena and La Canada families. After predominantly white La Canada seceded from the district in the early 1960s and built its own high school, pulling about a third of Muir's white students out, Muir's reputation began to decline. Many educators believed that this reputation was further damaged by the school's geographic location in the heart of what was becoming a heavily black area of Pasadena. As one former teacher explained: "Muir was known in the community as *that* school on *that* side of town. Strictly racial. . . . At one point if you drew a line down the middle of this town . . . it was pretty much black and white on either side. And in those days there weren't a lot of Latinos. . . . So [Muir] was pretty much, you know, a ghetto school, if you will—this was the mind-set. There are people in this community that still think that way." According to another teacher who taught at Muir in the late 1970s, many rumors were going around Pasadena about safety issues at Muir. He recalled that people were saying, "'This is a very dangerous place and people get knifed there all the time, they have shootings, they have this'—that wasn't true. If that was true I would have transferred to another school. I mean, I'm not suicidal. . . . And these stories just passed through the community."

THE MEDIA AND PUBLIC PERCEPTIONS
OF RACIALLY DIVERSE SCHOOLS

The rumors and perceptions of these schools were often far removed from the educators' and students' daily experiences. While many teachers and students blame racism for the misperception, our respondents were also quick to point out that the local media fed these misperceptions by consistently covering minor racial incidents at these schools while ignoring the good things that were happening there as well as the problems in more predominantly white schools.

In Englewood, for instance, virtually all of the Dwight Morrow educators and the majority of the class of 1980 graduates whom we interviewed spoke of the negative reporting by the local news outlets, particularly the local newspapers. As one frustrated white graduate of Dwight Morrow noted:

> I think it was more this notion that the media was making DM out to be a bad school, that it was a problem school, that it was a dangerous school, and I just felt that it was being portrayed inaccurately. While I didn't deny that there were problems and there were squabbles here and there, I think they were minor, and I think if it happened between

two white people in an all-white school no one would have made a big deal about it. But because it happened between a black and a white person . . . people read a lot more into it.

A longtime African American teacher at Dwight Morrow also found the news coverage inaccurate, with reports that girls were getting raped and guys were carrying knives at the school: "In the thirty years that I've been here, I've never seen a guy carrying a knife or a gun. I mean, there have been idle threats, people have gotten beat up—that happens in any school—but to say that it was a place that was violent, it's not true at all."

As a white teacher in the Englewood Public Schools for many years noted, the local newspapers not only highlighted negative incidents in the community's schools but downplayed anything positive that went on there: "I remember one year our math club won the state championship, and it was a paragraph on like page 28 of the [the local paper]. But on the front page . . . was 'Student at Dwight Morrow Brings Knife to School.' And no one ever even acknowledged that this math club had won the state championship."

The educators and graduates of John Muir High School expressed similar frustration with the media. They complained particularly about coverage from the local newspaper, which they believed favored Pasadena High School (PHS), in the white area of town, over Muir. A black 1980 graduate of Muir, like many of his classmates, observed that Muir always got a "really bad rap" in the local paper. Meanwhile, he argued that the media never reported on anything bad that happened at Pasadena High, even if Muir students knew of incidents there. A white graduate echoed these sentiments, noting that "any—any—any negative publicity that they could scrape up from Muir, they would! And did!" Meanwhile, this graduate's wife, also a Muir graduate, said, "If there was a fight at PHS, it was a small mention, . . . you know, in the back of the paper. If it was a fight at Muir, it was front-page." And an African American former teacher said she thought Muir had "always gotten a bad rap" because of where it was located or because it was more black and Hispanic than other schools. She told us that the reports of violence and other disturbances were wrong: "I was never afraid to work here. . . . There were some experiences that maybe weren't so hot, like breaking up fights and making sure things did not happen, but those are normal things connected with education. But as far as it being the roughest and toughest, I don't think we had any more incidents than the other high school. It was just that Muir was always highlighted." This teacher told us about a group of Muir teachers who went so far as to have meetings with the local newspaper staff to try to convince them to stop their negative reporting. The teachers were not successful.

SELF-FULFILLING PROPHECIES IN THE ABSENCE OF WHITE PRIVILEGE

More than twenty-five years after the class of 1980 graduated from these schools, data suggest that both Dwight Morrow and John Muir have become more like the schools that newspapers were reporting them to be in the 1970s: troubled by the multiple harms of racial segregation and concentrated poverty.[30] Total enrollment in both schools is down, and there are virtually no white students left, except for those in a separate and unequal magnet school program started by the state of New Jersey on the Dwight Morrow campus in 2002. The range of course offerings has dwindled, leading to a more watered-down curriculum. Average test scores are also down, leaving these high schools ranked very low on their state assessments.[31]

These two high schools, along with the now predominantly black West Charlotte High School, stand as a testament to the old adage that "green follows white." In other words, one of the primary motivations behind pushing for desegregation was that schools with large percentages of white and wealthy students enrolled are more likely to have resources, the best teachers, higher expectations, and a challenging curriculum.[32] Either through parental donations or political clout, such schools usually get what they need to make their schools the very best. In turn, these schools tend to embody the status of their highest-status students—if there is a critical mass of such students—since their prestige as educational institutions is intricately tied to the prestige of the students they enroll. This status is then bestowed upon the students who graduate from these schools, a badge of honor they wear on T-shirts and sweatshirts that allows them far easier access to high-status colleges and universities and jobs.[33] Once these higher-status white and affluent families leave, over time, predominantly black and Latino schools too often come to resemble the poor reputations that often precede their actual decline. In other words, racially diverse public schools that maintain high status and a "good" reputation are incredibly fragile institutions. Once public perceptions of them change, they tip out of balance, are suddenly labeled as "bad," and quickly lose most of their white students, particularly those from more affluent families. Their declining reputation has long- and short-term negative implications for the students who remain after the whites have left.

The greatest irony that emerges from studies such as ours is that from the perspective of African American and Latino parents, students, and educators it is hard to live with white privilege and hard to live without it. In other words, because white privilege pervades so many aspects of our society, schools with large numbers of white and affluent students are likely to be the most prestigious. When these schools also have significant numbers of black and Latino students in them, they are likely to be fairly segregated by classrooms, with white students constituting the majority of the students in the highest-level classes. At the same time, once the white students leave and upper-level classes become more predominantly black, Latino, or both, the reputations and eventually the quality of the schools decline because the resources and status decrease.

Interestingly, the three schools from our study that lost the majority of their white populations were the three schools most likely to challenge, albeit rather meekly, the automatic privilege of whites and the status quo within their schools. For instance, of the six schools that we studied, Muir and Dwight Morrow had moved further along the path toward instituting a multicultural curriculum than the other four schools (see chapter 4), and it was in Englewood and Charlotte that African American parents and activists challenged the tracking system in Dwight Morrow and West Charlotte High Schools. But in the end such challenges appear to have been pyrrhic victories, as these three schools lost not only their white students but also the prestige and status in their communities that they had once enjoyed and benefited from in numerous ways.

RACIAL POLITICS MAKES FRAGILE SCHOOLS

Placing these six racially mixed high schools from the late 1970s in their broader social, political, and historical contexts helps us rethink the current, overly simplistic debate about the "success" or "failure" of school desegregation policy in this country. Indeed, rather than portray the struggles of these schools as evidence that we have fallen short of the ideal of a racially more equal and just society, we want to point to these stories as evidence of how far we have come and how much further we need to go.

Much of the burden of righting the historical racial wrongs was placed on the public schools, while the rest of the society, except for the military, continued along its separate and unequal path. Since white privilege was not strongly challenged in other realms of our society, we should not be at all surprised that it was barely challenged at all in racially mixed schools. What we learned from our six schools and their graduates is that, despite what many adults thought back in the 1970s, their journey toward equal educational opportunities was not complete once white, black, and Latino students walked through the same school doors; it had only just begun.

A white school district administrator in Charlotte who was one of the many principals of West Charlotte High School in the 1970s reflected on how different people's understandings of the goals of school desegregation had been back then. He said that at the time liberal white educators often experienced a tension in that they supported desegregation and racial equality in theory but also wanted to teach the predominantly white high-track classes and did not want to delve into the issues of resegregation. Many of these educators were not ready to close the black-white achievement gap at that time. The administrator noted: "Our moral issue [in the 1970s] was to get two groups of people together who had never been together before and let them succeed—or let the institution succeed—as a result of creating that kind of grouping. I think the moral dilemma today is, you got to go deeper than that. It's not enough just to put two groups of people together. Those two groups of people had to be put together and come out on equal terms. I don't think that was in our thought process at the time."

Another central paradox of this study is that by the time a critical mass of educators began to critique how and what they could and should try to accomplish in racially mixed schools, the number of such schools was declining. For instance, while we were completing our interviews in Charlotte, the Charlotte-Mecklenburg schools ended their court-ordered school desegregation plan. West Charlotte High School, as we noted, is predominantly black once more.

FOUR We're All the Same—Aren't We?

Betsy Hagart grew up in the 1960s and 1970s in a middle-class, all-white neighborhood on the east side of Charlotte, North Carolina. As a middle-class white girl, she blended into her community and her nearby elementary and junior high schools, where there were very few black students and no students from backgrounds of real poverty or affluence. Her parents had moved to this part of town so that she and her younger brother could attend East Mecklenburg High School, like her mother, aunts, and uncles before her.

It came as a surprise to the whole family, therefore, when they learned that Betsy had been assigned to West Charlotte High School, a historically black school on the other side of town. Unable to afford private school, Betsy's parents had few options. In the fall of 1977, as she was entering the tenth grade, Betsy boarded a school bus with other students from her neighborhood and headed for the other side of the tracks—literally and figuratively.

More than two decades years later, Betsy remembered her parents being "furious" because they wanted her to go to East Mecklenburg and had no choice in the matter. She noted that while her father, who was retired from the military, was probably the "least prejudiced person" she knew and was "color-blind" and very open-minded, he was not comfortable with the busing, in part because he looked at it from an economic standpoint. "Dad said, 'My taxes are going to go up to pay for all this gas.'" Betsy's mother, meanwhile, had spent her early childhood in

South Carolina, where her family had had black servants and where she had first learned to see blacks as inferior. Betsy said that her mother was very upset to have her children bused to the black side of town.

This strong opposition was not unusual for white parents in Charlotte at the time; in fact, there was no shortage of unhappy parents in their community. Betsy's junior high school class was split in two, with half going to East Mecklenburg and half going to West Charlotte, depending on which side of the street the students lived on. Whether these white parents were "color-blind" like Betsy's father or more traditional in their racial views like her mother, it was challenging for them to come to terms with what a federal judge and their school officials were telling them they had to do, namely send their children to a high school in the middle of the black community. The fact that this reassignment of their children was a court-ordered remedy for years of systematic segregation of blacks into one part of the city and into separate and unequal schools did not make it easier for most of these parents to swallow. It is difficult, for white Americans in particular, so steeped in a tradition of individualism, to accept courts' or school officials' infringing on their liberty in the name of correcting prior infringements on other people's liberties. This is particularly true when the "other people" are African Americans, whom many whites have considered (and still do consider) to be inferior and less capable.

Yet over the years that followed Betsy's initial transfer to West Charlotte, the city of Charlotte became known for its citizens' relatively peaceful acceptance of school desegregation once the courts had ordered it. This was the city, after all, where in the 1980s Ronald Reagan tried to rouse a crowd to cheer in opposition to school desegregation policies and received a deafening silence. But in the mid-1970s, the mandatory reassignment of white students to a black high school in a black neighborhood was considered fairly radical.

To make matters worse, Betsy and her friends had heard "horrible things" from the older boys who lived across the street and were graduating from West Charlotte as she was getting ready to go there. She said they "scared us to death" telling stories about knifings, shootings, and students getting beat up and locked in lockers and screaming for help.

"And the media didn't help because they were full of the same, you know, horror stories."

It is no wonder that this tall, thin teenage girl was petrified when she first set foot on the West Charlotte campus. "I was sick to my stomach, you know, I was just terrified. . . . I kept to myself at first, which is very unusual for me." But Betsy quickly realized that all the hype did not match the reality of West Charlotte. She said that as soon as she got to know some of her classmates and got a chance to look around and see that the acts of violence were very rare and that fighting was as likely to occur between students of the same race as it was between students of different races, she began to better understand how white people's perceptions can be distorted by race. What's more, Betsy's own personal experiences began to directly contradict the myths of this historically black high school.

Betsy still gets excited when she tells what she calls her "favorite West Charlotte story," which she describes as being "on the flip side of the racial issue." Within the first few weeks of being bused to West Charlotte along with other students drawn from thirteen different junior high schools across the school district, Betsy was singled out by a large white girl. She noted, "I didn't even know her. She wasn't in any of my classes. She just decided she hated my guts. And she was about six and a half feet tall, and I only weighed like a hundred and ten pounds. I was a stick."

Scared that this white girl would beat her up, Betsy didn't want to go to school, and she tried to avoid the girl by going different ways to class. This went on for about two weeks, while other students would come up to Betsy and tell her things like "This girl is after you. She's going to kill you. She just hates your guts."

Finally, Betsy said, she could not take it any more, and she decided to confront the girl—in the middle of the large quadrangle in the center of West Charlotte's campus where students gathered for lunch and breaks. "I met this girl face to face in the quadrangle. I was scared to death. I was shaking. My legs were trembling. And I said, . . . 'I don't know why you hate me. I don't even know you.' She goes, 'Well, I'm just going to kick your butt.' And so I said, 'Fine.' And I guess just the fear—she gave me a rage, and I threw my books down. All of a sudden I heard a male voice behind me, 'Don't worry about it, Slim. We've got your slack.'"

"Slim" was Betsy's nickname because she was so skinny. And when she turned about to see who had said that, she saw six black students from her gym class lined up like a wall behind her. "I could not believe it. . . . But the girl, she just turned around and walked away."

Betsy, the forty-year-old adult, more than two decades removed from the skinny adolescent version of herself, still laughed when she told this story. She said that what she found to be most ironic was that she, as a white girl who had been scared to go to the "black" school, ended up being rescued from another white girl by a group of black students, who took it upon themselves to intervene on her behalf:

> I mean, I just thought that was such a funny incident to happen when white people are so worried about the black people. . . . But after that it just . . . changed something for me. It just changed that fear, and it changed a lot of the prejudice that I had carried because of stories told to me by my neighbors. So at that point I just . . . I really lost a lot of my prejudice. And that's why I'm so grateful, to this day, that I did go to a desegregated school because I feel that just with family values, with my friends' ideas, I think I would have been extremely narrow-minded, extremely prejudiced growing up.

In fact, shortly after she began attending West Charlotte High School—then a tenth- through twelfth-grade high school—Betsy began to understand racial issues in a deeper and more insightful way. For instance, she recalled the daily bus rides from east to west, from her white neighborhood to the black neighborhood, and the black man who drove the bus. His name was Calvin Jacobs, and over the course of the year Betsy grew to love him dearly. In more than one way, Calvin and the bus he drove helped Betsy and at least some of her white classmates transition to a new place and a new perspective.

In the morning, the bus route's last stop between the mostly white east side of town and West Charlotte High School was at the Piedmont Courts, a housing project on the near west side that had a reputation as a very dangerous place. By the time the bus arrived at Piedmont, it was already fairly full of white students. Unfortunately, the bus did not have enough seats for everyone once the Piedmont students got on, and some students were forced to stand during the last stretch of the route. Usually, according to Betsy, it was white students who stood because they were intimidated by the black students from Piedmont and gave up their seats.

Betsy recalled being scared of the Piedmont Courts kids and said she and her friends would leave seats for them on the bus because they would enter the bus with a tough attitude. She said that, looking back on that experience, she understands why those students displayed such an attitude and got on the bus acting so tough and intimidating. She said, "Just think how they would feel getting on a bus, you know, with these little white students who are, well, . . . you know, fairly well dressed and they are not because they came from a project. They didn't have the money. That's all they had was the attitude." She said that she thinks these students were really afraid and intimidated themselves, so they put on this big front: "We're big and tough and scary, you know, to cover that up. . . . Looking back, that's what I really think it was." Betsy added that she feels bad about it now because she wishes she had tried to reach out to those black students and offer them a seat next to her instead of only sticking with her "buds."

While the white students did not reach out to the black students on the bus (or vice versa), other important transitions did occur. According to Betsy, the best aspect of the bus ride was Calvin himself. Betsy talked about how all the students loved him and how good-natured and nice he was. "Just getting to know Calvin helped us too, not to be, you know, so fearful."

It was in her effort to defend Calvin that the self-proclaimed "timid" and "scrawny" teenage Betsy got herself into her only fight—and in fact the only fight that occurred on Calvin's bus that year. It all started when a white girl with whom Betsy had gone to elementary school was talking on the bus and started using the word *nigger*. Betsy said she was not sure exactly what happened; all she knew was that she kept hearing "nigger this, nigger that" from this girl. "And it, for some reason, just hit me wrong, and I jumped out of my seat, and I jumped on top of her and I was shaking her, and I said, 'Don't you ever say that,' 'cause Calvin, our bus driver, was like sitting driving the bus right in front of her. And . . . all I could think about was how awful that's probably making him feel." Betsy recalled telling this girl, as she was shaking her, to never say that word again while other students on the bus were trying to pull the two screaming girls apart. Looking back on that moment on the bus, Betsy admits that it was a weird thing for her to do "to actually attack someone I'd known almost all my life because of racial slurs. And then afterwards I was like, I cannot believe I did that."

She said that Calvin thanked her afterwards. And what's more, though the girl she had started shaking was mad at her for a while, even she got over it; she said she was sorry to Calvin, and she and Betsy became friends again. In fact, at the end of that first long year of busing, all the white students who rode Calvin's bus pitched in and bought him a plaque that read: "Through rain, snow, sleet, and a flat tire . . . Calvin Jacobs never failed to get us home safely."

Interestingly enough, the plaque emphasized the bus ride *home*. This is, most likely, because life at West Charlotte High School was complex and filled with potential minefields as the first generation of desegregated students made their way through. Betsy and her classmates who graduated in 1980 entered tenth grade at West Charlotte only three years after the final desegregation plan for the district had been put in place. Their cohort, like those at the other five schools we studied, bore the responsibility of healing the wounds of the past and building new bridges across racial lines. Several of Betsy's experiences in her first year at West Charlotte brought her and many of her classmates closer to some shared understanding of people on the other side of the color line. But these personal experiences could take the students only so far when the perceived goal of desegregation, according to the adults involved in the process at the time, was for everyone to become truly "color-blind."

At West Charlotte High School, like the other schools in our study, the educators tried their hardest to ignore race—to make it a nonissue when, of course, it was *the* central issue that made their time at West Charlotte so distinct from the time they spent in their neighborhoods, churches, and so on. At that time, it made sense to these adults to ignore the very factor that had caused so much controversy and upheaval in their communities as the details of desegregation were ironed out. Betsy reported that the educators at West Charlotte did not discuss racial issues at all during the entire three years she was there. She said the main focus was on discipline and what would happen to students who violated the rules. "It was pretty much 'You're all students here. You follow the student rules.' That's how they dealt with it. So that's kind of hard because when you're young and you're thrown into a different, new situation you really need that guidance."

The curriculum at West Charlotte and the other schools did not challenge this color-blind perspective; in fact, it often perpetuated it. When asked what she would have done differently had she been a West Charlotte educator at the time, Betsy said she would have gone from class to class, maybe with a school psychologist, and "talked straight to the students." She said she would not have been afraid to directly address the racial issues and would have allowed students to share their experiences and learn that they were not the only ones who thought a certain way. For instance, she remembered that it was not unusual for white students at West Charlotte to believe that black students were not as smart as whites. "We just thought it was a fact."

Betsy said that in retrospect she is bothered that she and her white classmates would think that about the black students and that there was never any discussion about these beliefs or any effort among the educators to address any these views. But in many ways it is not surprising that Betsy and her white classmates believed that blacks were less intelligent, given that these white students were products of a southern society predicated on white supremacy. Meanwhile, their school was also highly segregated across classrooms by race, with the remedial classes almost completely filled with black students. But this backdrop was all the more reason to allow students the space to debate issues of racial inequality and ideology and their historical antecedents.

Lacking such educational experiences, Betsy has struggled to come up with her own way of understanding race. She is torn between her desire to be "color-blind"—thinking that everyone is the same no matter what their skin color—and her underlying belief that people do differ culturally along racial lines: "But you know, even in spite of all that, I don't think we're the same, not to this day. And I don't mean it as a prejudice, but I, in my heart, believe that white people, black people, Asian people, Hispanic people, we're not all the same. . . . I don't have to treat anybody better or less than the other person, but we are different."

Betsy said that she has to be aware of these differences so that when she is interacting with people she can remember that they may have a very different culture, a different background and upbringing, and that she may be offensive without being aware of it. But Betsy, like virtually all the white graduates we interviewed, has a far more difficult time relating racial distinctions and backgrounds to the structural inequality— for example, housing segregation and unequal access to jobs and income across color lines—that has so profoundly shaped her city and her world. Because discussions of these larger frames that constrain human agency were not part of her high school curriculum, or any of her still-unfinished college coursework, it is hard for Betsy and most whites in the United States to see past the differences in the ways people may act across racial groups and acknowledge the differences in the ways people have been treated on the basis of race in this and other countries.

Ironically, today Betsy works in the one industry in which systematic racism has had the most profound structural effects—the housing industry. When we interviewed her she was working for a mortgage company and was aware of all the regulations regarding what appraisers could and could not do in terms of indicating the racial makeup of the neighborhoods or the buyers or sellers of the homes. She also noted that she could not accept any pictures of a house that included people because that could lead to discrimination based on the race of the people in the picture.

Betsy was also aware that very few blacks worked in the mortgage industry, yet at the same time she noted that the two black women who did work in her office were often excluded socially. She said, for instance, that it was not unusual for her to go to lunch with three other white women from her office and not think to ask the two black women if they would want come along. "It's kind of like I assume they'd wouldn't want to go or something. So I still have, you know, little quirky things still that have carried over."

As an adult, whether at work or with friends, Betsy said she hangs out with mostly white people. Yet she struggles with her own sense of not belonging in certain settings because of social class differences. She noted that she and her husband, who is a blue-collar worker, are behind many of their peers in moving up the economic ladder. Thus she said she does not really have much in common with the crowd her former college roommate hangs out with, which includes a lot of professionals—dentists, doctors, and pilots: "I don't do the same things they do 'cause I don't have the money. . . . I can't talk about skiing in Vale or Aspen or whatever, you know. 'Well, I went to Wal-Mart last week and they had a special.' [laugh]. . . . I tend to hang with my buds, who are all pretty much about the same economic level."

Thus while Betsy says that she learned important lessons at West Charlotte High School—lessons that to this day make her much more comfortable in racially diverse or even predominantly black settings—she remains most at home with people more "like her" in terms of race and class. That is reflected in her neighborhood and church—but not in the school that her daughter attends.

Since the 1990s, the Charlotte-Mecklenburg School Board has been slowly adding more school choice options for parents and dismantling its student assignment patterns that sustained the desegregation plan that Betsy participated in back in the 1970s. In the fall of 2002, the school desegregation plan in Charlotte was completely dismantled. Thus, when Betsy's daughter started school in the 1990s, there were many choices of racially diverse schools. Betsy said she appreciated these choices and was glad that her daughter was not forced to go to a particular school without any say, the way she had been: "If you take away people's feeling that they have some say-so in their own family, you're going to get anger regardless of what the issue is. So I think that the way they did it was a mistake, but the idea behind it was a good idea, and I still believe in . . . desegregation. I believe that we should be mixed. It helps all of us learn more about each other."

We interviewed Betsy shortly after her daughter had started middle school. The family had chosen a school that was on Betsy's way to work so that Betsy could drop her daughter off and then pick her up after her after-school program. Betsy said that because it was a school of choice that drew students from all over the district it was racially diverse. What's more, Betsy noted that her daughter is "totally color-blind, which is amazing and I love it." As a result, Betsy said she makes a point not to ask her daughter what race her friends are. "I've got to stop myself from saying that, 'cause like, what does it matter, you know? If she wants to go spend the night at someone's house, I need to stop that thinking, that habit, 'Well, is she black or white?' What does it matter?"

But clearly race does matter in Betsy's life today, as it did when she was a child growing up in the midst of the turmoil related to school desegregation. She is insistent that she would not be who she is today if she had not attended West Charlotte High School, an experience that shaped her taste in music and her understanding of how to treat other people. She illustrates this with a story about the night of her twenty-year high school reunion, when she went out for a postreunion drink with some of her old "buds" at a bar. She recalled that the husband of one of her high school friends—not a West Charlotte grad—began telling racial jokes. She said he was drunk and loud. Much as she had gotten frustrated with the white girl on her school bus who used the "n-word" in front of Calvin, Betsy recalled getting really uncomfortable with this man's jokes. But she hadn't wanted to ruin the evening, so she said to him: "'Maybe you should know, maybe [your wife] didn't mention this,' I said, 'but my father is black.' And I said it dead serious. People fell silent. Everybody's looking at me. [The husband] goes, 'I am so sorry. I did not mean to offend anybody. I was just telling jokes.' The table cracked up."

She said that while her friends at the table knew she was lying, the drunken spouse did not, and he stopped telling the jokes, even as everyone else got a huge laugh over his having been duped about her racial identity. That more recent experience, Betsy noted, helped her remember a lesson she had learned riding Calvin's school bus in the late 1970s: no matter how hard whites try to deny it, they are not color-blind at all. The distinction, then, is not between the enlightened color-blind whites and those backward folks who still see race and therefore must be racist. Rather, the central dividing line between whites on the issue of race lies between those who place most of the blame for ongoing racial inequality on blacks or Latinos themselves and those who are uncomfortable with such an explanation, even if they are not sure exactly why. Whites who fit in the first category scapegoat blacks and Latinos—their culture, their work ethic, their attitudes—as a way to explain differences across racial lines in poverty, unemployment, lack of health care, and so on. Whether or not they tell racial jokes matters less than if they overtly or secretly agree with the derogatory sentiments conveyed in those jokes. Whites who fit into the second category know that this scapegoating is unjust. They may not always be able to articulate the complex and multiple ways in which racial inequality is reproduced and reinforced within the educational system, labor market, and housing market, but they know that it is not easily explained away by blaming the victims.

These different ways that whites tend to make sense of race in the U.S. context are not set in stone but are fluid and evolving as individuals have experiences that change their perspectives. This is what happened to Betsy and many of the white graduates we interviewed in high school. Even the whites who share this racial sensitivity do not necessarily live in racially integrated neighborhoods or work in racially diverse settings or even go to lunch with black colleagues. But they tend to see and feel racial inequality in a way that many white people do not, even if they lapse in and out of that understanding from time to time. According to Betsy, "Yes, even to this day. I still hear some of the racial slurs, and it just hurts something inside of me . . . even like when I jumped [the white girl] on the bus; it hurt something inside of me. I don't know why. I still don't understand that. It's weird."

· · · · ·

The goal of color-blindness in the six high schools we studied was paradoxical, given how central race was to Betsy and the other students' lives in desegregated schools in the 1970s. Clearly, race mattered to the students; it defined their preconceived notions, their attitudes, and their fears. Thus to try to become color-blind was, for these educators and students, an attempt to deny the reality of race in their daily existence. It was also a convenient, if unintended, way for adults and teenagers to ignore the historical and present-day structural—meaning economic, political, and social—forces both surrounding and within their schools that reproduced segregation and inequality along racial lines. In other words, a color-blind perspective allowed all the privileges that whites enjoyed (and still enjoy) simply by not being black or Latino—such as access to certain neighborhoods, wealth, educational opportunities, and jobs—to go unexamined. It is far easier, after all, to proclaim that race does not matter when you are standing on the top of a racial hierarchy than when you are being crushed at the bottom of it.

Yet for all the problems that a color-blind agenda presents and reproduces, it also had a temporary positive aspect in a time of racial turmoil and change, particularly in places such as Charlotte, where years of racial tradition were being challenged. For instance, in the students' and educators' efforts to overcome fears and negative stereotypes of the racialized "other," a color-blind approach was helpful in allowing them to see "people as people." In this complicated double consciousness of race, white students such as Betsy who have moved beyond racial scapegoating want to see past the bigotry of their parents' generation to view people of color as people with needs and desires similar to whites'. But being "color-blind" is, as we noted above, a double-edged sword in that it simultaneously helps whites to move through life without seeing their own privilege or its impact on the welfare of whites versus blacks or Latinos in this society and thus the deeper distinctions between opportunities on one side of the color line versus the other. Color-blindness is one of the few perspectives that can accommodate both of these conflicting but simultaneous yearnings. Yet it is also a view that leaves too many white people in this society caught in a perpetual double consciousness of white guilt about a horrific racial history in this country and an uneasy and unfocused understanding of the relationship between the past and the present.

It is important to remember that these former students' experiences were historically located in the 1970s, just as the more recent political backlash against race-based policies such as school desegregation was developing and as cruder forms of resistance to such policies—such as throwing rocks at buses of black students and blocking their entrance to predominantly white schools—were becoming less acceptable. Thus their time in high school marked a turning point in racial politics in the United States when opposition shifted from racial slurs, picket signs, and flying objects to seemingly more reasoned arguments in favor of "race-blind" policies in the Ronald Reagan tradition.[1] Therefore, what being color-blind meant back then, in a politically different age, is somewhat distinct from what it means today, as several of our interviewees noted. This was certainly the view of a white graduate of Shaker Heights High School named Maya Deller, who said that as a Jewish girl growing up in the 1970s she had a strong sense of justice and fairness: "We were supposed to be color-blind because that was the pendulum then. . . . In the fifties race means everything. In the seventies, race means nothing, you know? But that's not reality and that's not—it's like a very juvenile and immature way of perceiving the world because the world is never one way or the other."

But since this cohort graduated from high school, many more powerful conservatives have made political arguments to do away with policies of racial preferences or set-asides that were established during the civil rights era. The U.S. Supreme Court ruling in the Louisville and Seattle cases takes us one step closer to that goal. Thus, as we noted in chapter 1, the call for a color-blind society has, in the last twenty-five years, become a political rallying cry in the United States, particularly for whites who argue that we have done whatever needed to be done to correct our history of racial discrimination. Now, the color-blind argument goes, it is time to dismantle affirmative action, school desegregation, and other race-based programs and move forward without focusing on race, treating everyone exactly the same.[2] According to a Louisville, Kentucky, lawyer who was an advocate for ending school desegregation in that town: "We're a diverse society, a multiethnic society, a colorblind society. . . . Race is history."[3]

Color-blindness, therefore, or the importance of *not* seeing color, as it has played out in recent decades, is a seemingly benign and even deferential outlook toward race that often allows whites to blame blacks or Hispanics themselves, rather than discrimination against them, for any ongoing inequality. There are interesting and important connections, however, between what color-blindness became in the national racial politics of the 1980s and beyond and what it was back in the 1970s as adults and children struggled to make sense of school desegregation at the more local level of schools, communities, and classrooms.[4] In both the more recent politicized version of color-blindness and the ways it manifested in the 1970s, there was (and is) a profound lack of awareness on the part of whites that they benefit from their racialized privilege. To the extent that white privilege is not recognized, then, the assumption is that once interpersonal discrimination is corrected—once people are treated as people—little else can be done to address inequalities. Even assuming that more blatant forms of racial discrimination are a thing of the past is problematic on several levels, but beyond that, assuming that such public displays of hatred are the only racial problems in this society is quite naive. And, as we noted, while some whites, particularly those who attended desegregated schools, are more frustrated with this view and ongoing racial inequality than others, they have little understanding of exactly how it is perpetuated or how to interrupt it. That history and its legacies were not taught in their color-blind schools.

In the 1970s, when the public schools were left to deal with the day-to-day struggles of implementing civil rights policies such as school deseg-regation, educators, administrators, and students often found it easier—or at least less painful—to adopt a superficial motto, an argument that "we are all the same" and that "race does not matter."[5] Thus there was also something more naive or "juvenile," as Maya would say, about the color-blind ideology that pervaded these six schools at the time: it was about bridging large racial divides as opposed to dismantling public policies. Still, the advantages that whites have in this society simply by being white went unexamined, which meant these schools were organized around norms about education, knowledge, and ability that often put students of color at a disadvantage. Our data and other writings related to race and white privilege in the U.S. context demonstrate that when race goes unex-amined in this way whiteness becomes the de facto norm and those who are not white or do not "act white" are seen as not normal—substandard on several levels.[6] In such a situation, the goal of racial equality and the dream of a truly color-blind society are elusive.

Still, we must, on some level, distinguish between the color-blind stance adopted by people who were brought together on a daily basis in public schools with colleagues and classmates of other races—often for the first time in their lives—and the widespread color-blind stance adopted by many whites today in their more abstract opposition to race-specific policies. These two views are somewhat distinct at least in their origin if not their effect. The former seemingly grows at least partially out of a sense of being uncomfortable, awkward, and even naive at the level of day-to-day interactions. The second grows out of an undeserved feeling of injustice on the part of whites—the sense that hardworking and upstanding whites are being discriminated against in favor of lazy and unethical blacks and Hispanics.[7] But both attitudes evade more meaningful racial change.

This chapter presents the findings that emerged from our data related to the theme of color-blindness. These findings explain not only what color-blindness looked like in the six schools but also how it shaped and was shaped by the experiences of the educators and students. Finally, we argue, on the basis of additional findings from our study, that the color-blind ideology perpetuated in these schools contributed largely to the uncertainty and contradictions—the double consciousness—about race that many of these graduates, especially the white graduates, express today. In other words, for many whites the efforts to become and then to be color-blind in school may have helped ensure their attraction to a present-day political color-blind ideology, even if they struggle with such a view more than whites who did not experience school desegregation.

This partially explains how many of the whites we interviewed could argue, in the course of one hour, that "people are people" and thus that "everyone is the same" while at the same time trying to explain that a larger percentage of African Americans and Latinos/Latinas in our society are poor because of their problematic culture or their failure to place enough emphasis on education and getting ahead. A few moments later they might comment on the injustice of racial profiling and note how few opportunities young black men have to get a good education, access to college, and a decent job.

In this way, these graduates provide a clear view of the ongoing American dilemma of race. White Americans want to think about race only on the individual level—how individuals treat each other—but many, especially those who have had cross-racial friendships and experiences, sense that there are broader, society-level explanations for the ongoing racial inequality. Thus they might try to explain away this inequality by blaming the victims of it, decrying the injustice of it, and simultaneously avowing that we are all the same in this color-blind society. This double, almost triple consciousness of white people striving to be color-blind even as so much of the society they live in is defined by race is difficult to capture in large-scale surveys or quantitative analyses. Only by interviewing a wide range of people who lived through profoundly racialized programs such as school desegregation can we begin to capture it.

SIX COLOR-BLIND SCHOOLS

Particularly in Topeka, Charlotte, and Austin, but to a lesser extent in the other three sites as well, the vast majority of educators and graduates we interviewed cited color-blindness as *the* central goal for their desegregated schools in the late 1970s. While this goal of color-blindness seemed to be more imperative for the white graduates and educators than for those of color, what was so striking about this finding was that it was not simply a "white thing"; rather, it reflected a powerful ideology that permeated these schools and silenced discussions of race.

As a result, we saw many ways in which the color-blind attitude left important issues about race unexamined. In fact, many of the adult graduates we interviewed noted that there were times during their high school years when they would have appreciated educators' greater openness to talking about race and helping students deal with underlying racial tensions and misunderstandings. Furthermore, these schools, as discussed in prior chapters, were divided internally by race, with the highest-level classes consistently enrolling a disproportionate number of white students. Thus race clearly did matter in terms of who took which classes and who had the best opportunities, making the myth of color-blindness even more specious.

Janet Schofield writes that the color-blind perspective, which she also found to be common in a desegregated school she studied, does have a number of negative effects. Most important, "the decision to try to ignore racial considerations—to act as if no one notices, or should notice, race—means that policies that are disadvantageous to African Americans and other nonwhites are often accepted without much examination or thought."[8] For instance, a color-blind perspective can easily lead to ready adoption or tolerance of policies that resegregate students across classrooms.

Thus, Schofield argues, a color-blind view may reduce initial discomfort and tension in daily interactions between students and teachers, but it has detrimental consequences in the long run, especially as it affects school policies and curriculum.[9] Such detrimental consequences can include disproportionate suspension rates for African Americans and other nonwhite students—practices that are perpetuated if "school faculty and staff think of students only as individuals rather than facing the difficult issue of whether the school may be treating certain categories of students differently than others."[10]

Yet on the surface color-blindness was often seen as the "fair" and "right" thing to do in the context of these six high schools, especially in the southern schools, where a system of legal, race-based segregation had only recently been dismantled. In these contexts, it seemed wrong—almost impolite—to talk about the very thing that had divided the members of different racial groups for so long. Furthermore, the vast majority of the graduates and educators we interviewed at all six sites said that most of the students in their high schools "got along" across color lines, partly because they did not see race. They also told us that it was easier for the graduates and educators to be color-blind than it was to learn how to talk about race and to deal with the discomfort of discussing such sensitive issues.

Thus the vast majority of the people we interviewed were convinced that their success in eliminating racism was based on their ability to transcend or even deny race and be color-blind. As a white graduate of Austin High School noted when we asked her if her teachers talked about race in class, "[Race] wasn't a big deal. I mean, it really wasn't something we talked about, it wasn't a big deal."

Despite such quotes—and there are many just like this one in our data—it is clear from our interviews that the goal of color-blindness took these students and educators only so far. Below we illustrate how the educators, in particular, made sense of their goal of color-blindness and their degree of investment in it. This is followed by a section on the students' (now adult graduates') memories of how color-blindness promoted peace and "getting along" but at the same time left them feeling that important issues or tensions were not being discussed.

Color-Blindness as a Central Goal

The ideal of color-blindness clearly originated with the teachers and administrators in all six high schools that we studied and was then handed down to the students. In fact, it was a rare exception to find an educator who had taught in one of these schools in the late 1970s and did not espouse this color-blind ideology.

Two central themes emerged from the educators' explanations of *why* being color-blind was so important. The first had to do with their prior experiences, particularly in the early 1970s, when in several of the districts and schools we were studying there had been a great deal of racial tension and even "rioting" and fighting. In these settings, particularly Topeka, Austin, Pasadena, and Charlotte, color-blindness was seen as the best way to "keep the peace" and to "keep a lid on things" that might otherwise erupt. By not talking about race and being color-blind, the rationale went, educators could prevent such incidents from happening.

The educators' second major rationale for the color-blind perspective was the simple and generally well-meaning argument that "people are people" no matter what color they are and that we need to treat people as individuals and not as members of a particular racial or ethnic group. This view was then seen as the most helpful way to get people to look beyond race and to emphasize personal connections across racial and ethnic groups.

BEEN THERE, DONE THAT: KEEPING A LID ON RACIAL TENSION BY NOT TALKING ABOUT IT

According to the educators and students we interviewed, by the late 1970s the peak years of racial tension and fighting in most of these schools and communities had already passed. For instance, a former math teacher from West Charlotte High School recalled that during the early seventies, in the first years of school desegregation, when she was teaching at a high school on the east side of town, they had to close the school down occasionally because of racial violence. She remembered that on the days following such outbursts the students would come to school and they would have a sort of "rap session" in classroom "to talk things out and stuff." But by the time she was transferred to West Charlotte in the mid-1970s, things had quieted down quite a bit, and there were no school closings or rap sessions.

Similarly, as discussed in chapter 2, virtually every graduate we interviewed from Topeka High School had heard from older siblings or friends about the race "riots" that had taken place at that school in the early 1970s. One such graduate said that his older brother, who had attended Topeka High from 1972 to 1974, had told him about at least two occasions when the police had to be brought in to keep order. As a result Topeka High developed a reputation as a "tough school," but according to this graduate such views were greatly exaggerated because what was going on there "was symptomatic of what was going on in the country more than just the school, because it was happening everywhere."

This graduate was accurate in his assessment of what was happening in other parts of the country; at least, in all six of the school sites we studied, the late 1970s was a relatively tranquil period compared to prior years. And in the towns that had seen a great deal of racial unrest related to school desegregation or other race-based policies—most notably Topeka, Austin, Pasadena, and Charlotte—the years of the greatest turmoil had occurred before the class of 1980 entered high school.

Furthermore, because all six of these high schools had already been racially mixed at least a few years prior to the arrival of the class of 1980, most of the teachers remembered that the bulk of the staff development on race and how to deal with racial diversity had occurred in the early seventies when there was more racial unrest. In these early days of desegregation, some district and school leaders were trying to ease the transition into desegregation through teacher workshops, small student group activities, added course electives, or onetime events. The teachers who

were at these schools at that time recalled (sometimes vaguely) participating in such workshops and also seemed to remember some student
assemblies, new courses, and special student or faculty committees that
dealt with race. As one white teacher who taught English at Austin High
School explained, "I think in 1980 everything was all over, anything con-
troversial or any unhappiness, you know, that was all settled, and we
were settled in as a school."

Perhaps the most conscious efforts on the part of school administrators to address issues of race were mandates, usually coming from the
school district offices, for high schools to have racial quotas for high-profile
extracurricular activities such as cheerleading or student government.
Such quotas, which were in place in varying degrees in Topeka, Austin,
Pasadena, and Charlotte (see chapter 5), were as much about the external
image of a school—for example, an all-black or all-white cheerleading
squad was not the right "image" for a racially mixed school—as they
were about equal access. But they were clearly race-conscious and not
color-blind policies, although they were rarely discussed in that way. By
the time the class of 1980 matriculated to these high schools, such policies were well established, well accepted, and rarely challenged.

Thus, even when educators were making a conscious attempt to balance popular activities, there was no place for students to dialogue
about race or the racial balancing policies. There was an awareness of
such quotas, which in some instances benefited white students more
than black or Latino students, and an acknowledgment of their impact
on students' experiences in high school. Thus students would talk at
Austin High, for example, about the slot for "one black cheerleader,"
but they had different reactions as to whether such policies were a good
or bad thing, and no place to discuss their thoughts except among their
friends.

As one white West Charlotte graduate noted, although there were no
explicit discussions of race in her high school in the late 1970s, issues of
race were everywhere:

> No, there were no discussions of that. But, but was it a known fact that
> we had three white candidates, three black candidates, and three at-
> large [for student government elections]? Yeah! And—I don't even

remember the ballot, but the ballot probably said it! I mean, you know, I—I don't know. But did we sit around and have round tables about . . . how to be better people and like each other and live together in harmony and all that stuff? No! No. But were there white kids in the Gospel Choir? Yes! . . . And we'd have, you know, the black guys come to the choir with cornrows, and [the African American choir teacher] would tell them, . . . "Get rid of those cornrows, you know? Just because you're a black boy—don't be wearing those cornrows." So . . . was there a discussion? No. But was race everywhere? Yeah!

Thus, while race was not regularly discussed in these schools, it was *lived* in a very real and intuitive sort of way. With no forum or dialogue in which to make better sense of the racial differences they experienced every day, many of these graduates walked away from high school with fairly superficial understandings of race and its role in American society, understandings that would not lead to challenging the racial status quo.

Indeed, by the late 1970s, except for these racial quotas on a handful of extracurricular activities in four of the six high schools, programs or forums for students or faculty to deal with racial diversity and tensions had declined drastically since the early days of school desegregation. The assumption was that the difficult task of making school desegregation work was behind them. The relative calmness of the late 1970s reinforced the general belief among the educators that there was no need to talk about race because everyone "got along" across racial and ethnic lines. As long as there were no racial riots or physical conflict, teachers were under the impression that the social environments of their schools were positive.

In Pasadena, Shaker Heights, and Austin, we heard educators and community members compare their relatively calm school desegregation process to what was happening in Boston and places in "the South" (meaning the Southeast), indicating that in comparison their schools were much more progressive in terms of people getting along across racial lines. According to a white social studies teacher at Muir High School in Pasadena whose son attended Muir and now lives in Florida, his adult son told him, "Dad, you would not believe race relations in Florida. You would not believe how horrid they are. Black people don't like white people. White people don't like black people. . . . It's not at all what life was like when I was growing up . . . at Muir."

Consequently, in these desegregated high schools, a lack of fighting or any form of violence came to be a sign that everything was okay. And many educators told us that they believed that this peace—as superficial as it may have been in some instances—was a direct result of their concerted efforts to *not* see race, to be color-blind.

SEEING PEOPLE AS PEOPLE

In the absence of any perceived need to be otherwise, educators were, for the most part, very proud of their goal of color-blindness, especially as they reflected on the historical presence of racism in their schools, communities, and homes. In fact, they recalled being very vested in seeing "people as people." For instance, a white teacher who had worked at West Charlotte High School when the class of 1980 attended said she believed that being color-blind meant that people—not just students but also faculty—were capable of loving and caring for one another. She explained that this was the spirit of that school in the seventies and eighties, and in fact she became teary when recalling what a special place West Charlotte High School had been back then: "We just saw each other as people. . . . I guess, to be corny about it, we were color-blind. We saw people as people . . . and the potential they could offer, and loved and cared for each other. Again, it just seemed like color didn't seem to make a difference to anyone. . . .We just, again, viewed people as people. Not emphasizing . . . I mean, we emphasized the fact that we were *not* emphasizing color of skin."

The majority of the educators insisted that race was not an issue and that it did not matter to teachers what color their students were. For instance, a white teacher from Shaker Heights High School told us, "I never had a problem with color. I was raised to see people as who and what they are." An art teacher from Topeka High said that desegregation had resulted in their school becoming a much better place after people learned to trust and stop fearing one another. He noted that many people worked hard to make these changes so that race would not be an issue: "I think there [were] some real efforts by people to try to make it so that it is more equal. [Silence] I think for a lot of people there, race [didn't] matter. It's more of 'How is this individual doing? How can we help them with what's going on?'"

Interestingly enough, many black as well as white teachers spoke of their desire to see their students as people rather than to see their color. We discovered, for instance, that one of the few African American teachers at Austin High School at that time had a strong color-blind stance. When asked to summarize the highlights of desegregation in Austin, Texas, she answered, "I was not over there [at Austin High] for social priorities, social promotion, or advancement of the races. I was there to teach, and I taught them all the same way. . . . I would prefer to see no white, no black, no blue, no purple. I just wanted to be the best human being that I could be."

This teacher, like all but a handful of the more than 150 teachers we interviewed, made a concerted effort to *not* consider or be considered by race. Clearly, she wanted to extend her desire for color-blindness to her students. Yet ironically, within this ostensibly "color-blind" context, at least some of this teacher's white colleagues at Austin High School said they were so fearful of offending her that they went out of their way to avoid bringing up the issue of race at faculty meetings, even when racial incidents occurred. According to one of these white teachers in charge of the faculty meetings, "I remember at those meetings I would try so hard, it was just silly, but I tried so hard not to say anything that might offend her [the African American teacher] at faculty meetings." It was in part this fear of offending that prevented her and many others from engaging in meaningful dialogue about race—as it shaped the experiences not only of the faculty but also of the students. In part because of this de facto color-blind stance of many teachers in these six schools, black and Latino students' relationships with educators varied greatly across the schools and within them, and also across the race/ethnicity of the teachers. This was often related to the curriculum and the ways in which teachers did or did not carry over the color-blind theme into their approach to teaching social studies or English in particular.

Color-Blind Curricula and Classrooms

The curricula at the six high schools rarely reflected a color-conscious way of understanding the world. In other words, it was unusual for the class readings and assignments to present history or experiences from an

African American, Latino, Asian, or Native American perspective. This is partly because the call for a more multicultural curriculum had not become as widespread as it would in later years, when researchers and educators began realizing how important this was, particularly in racially diverse settings. But it was also partly attributable to the color-blind mode that most of these educators were in at the time.

Indeed, one of the more surprising findings from this study was just how little the curriculum in the racially mixed schools we studied changed during the 1970s, considering that the racial makeup of the students in most of them had changed a great deal. For the most part, the schools offered a white, Eurocentric perspective on the world. When changes were made to the curriculum, they were usually marginal changes, such as the addition of elective courses that only a few students took or a special assembly in reaction to specific demands by students of color. Even in Topeka, Kansas, the city at the heart of the *Brown v. Board of Education* case, 1980 graduates do not recall learning much about race or racial inequality in school. One Topeka High graduate who is now a lawyer noted that she had no idea how important the Topeka-based school desegregation case and the resulting *Brown* decision were until she went to law school many years later. While other Topeka High graduates do remember the *Brown* decision being mentioned, if not in high school, then in junior high, they do not remember teachers explaining the significance of the case in terms of racial integration and the civil rights movement. One of these students told us: "Watching the History Channel, and now as I've become more worldly and been out in the world, I . . . it's [the *Brown* decision] just something that I'm much more aware of, and I had no idea when I was at Topeka [High School] how big a deal it really was."

At Muir High School in Pasadena, the graduates and educators reported that for the most part the curriculum did not reflect different perspectives. The lack of diversity was the result of several factors, including the fact that Muir teachers had a great deal of autonomy in their classrooms and there was no systematic effort to expand the core curriculum in the 1970s to include nonwhite authors. Students' exposure to a more multicultural curriculum depended entirely on the individual teachers, and thus student experiences were not consistent. While a few teachers made a concerted effort to include nonwhite authors and perspectives, the vast majority of teachers were far more traditional. As one former counselor at Muir said, "As far as the teaching goes, [desegregation] didn't really start to affect the canon until about the mid-1980s, so we were still teaching the Dead White Man for a long, long time."

In an even more pronounced manner, the graduates of West Charlotte High School stated that race and the history of racial conflicts and segregation in the United States were taboo subjects in southern schools at the time. According to one white West Charlotte graduate who came from a very affluent family in the southeastern part of the city, there was much more discussion of race in the northeastern liberal arts college she attended than there had been at West Charlotte. And when asked about discussions of the Civil War in high school, she laughed, noting: "We didn't talk a whole lot about the Civil War growing up in school. The South lost, and it wasn't a big topic of conversation, so I laughed that you would say that. No, I don't remember black/white analysis, you're going a lot deeper than we were. I was sixteen years old—we were trying to survive, and we were trying to past our tests."

Meanwhile, in the Northeast, Dwight Morrow High School offered elective courses that focused on black history and culture, and reportedly black and liberal white teachers made a greater effort to weave African American studies into the required classes. Several of the white graduates, including Larry Rubin from chapter 1, felt that they had almost learned too much about black history and not enough about the traditional Eurocentric canon, which was more highly valued in their college contexts. Yet the black graduates of Dwight Morrow felt that the opposite was true, that not enough of the African American experience had been reflected in their classes. In trying to explain these differing perspectives, Sydney Morgan, an African American graduate of Dwight Morrow, who was in many of the upper-level classes that were predominantly white, thought for a few moments and then said that if the white students had gone to school elsewhere they probably wouldn't have gotten any black history or literature, so even the little bit they received at Dwight Morrow seemed like a lot to them.

And for black students, you know, I myself know that when I went to college, I took Afro-Am history classes and there was a lot that I learned that I didn't learn in high school, so that's probably what caused the discrepancy. . . . For example, I think it was sophomore English [at Dwight Morrow], one of the books that we read was the *Autobiography of Malcolm X*. And I can remember some of the white students feeling that it was stupid and a waste of time to read that. . . . Whereas I remember being forced to read *Winesburg, Ohio*, which to this day—I remember the name, [but] couldn't tell you anything about the book. So it wasn't very relevant to my life. So I think it was a difference in perception.

As would fit with Sydney's theory, the absence of race in the curriculum was more often noticed and critiqued by the graduates of color we interviewed, particularly those who had been taught different lessons in their homes, communities, or college African American history classes. For instance, one African American 1980 graduate of Austin High School talked about the difficulties he had accepting and relating to his high school history teacher: "He was a good teacher, it's just that I didn't believe in what he was teaching. 'Cause everything was white . . . and I used to get so tired and frustrated . . . sitting and listening to what all these great white people [had done]." The lack of diversity in the curriculum contributed to the distrust that many students of color felt toward their white teachers.

Obviously, this lack of attention to race in the curriculum was echoed in the omission of discourse about race in the classroom. In fact, the way students remember it, any efforts to bring up more complicated ways of making sense of history or literature that would relate to racial oppression or inequality were sometimes squelched by teachers who were either too nervous or too unfamiliar with differing perspectives to allow such discussions to occur. It seemed to the students of color we interviewed that when white teachers in particular strayed from their Eurocentric base to add something more multicultural, they were often in uncharted territory and thus less certain about how to present and teach the material.

A good example of the difficulties teachers faced when presenting more multicultural materials was conveyed to us by Sydney, the African

American graduate of Dwight Morrow High School in Englewood who compared blacks' and whites' reactions to racial content in the curriculum. Sydney recalled the time her white English teacher required the class to read *The Bluest Eye*, by Toni Morrison, a novel about a black girl who wants blue eyes. In the story, someone tells the girl that if she kills a dog she'll be given blue eyes, so the girl kills the dog: "And so, you know, I raised my hand and I said, 'Well, you know, when she killed the dog she kind of killed her own beliefs in everything that was ugly about herself,' and dah, dah, dah. [The teacher said,] 'No, I think you're reading it too deeply.' . . . You know, I mean, and that was the type of reactions that I would get out of this woman."

Sydney's mother had demanded that the school place her daughter in the advanced classes after she had been placed in regular classes despite her high grades. Thus Sydney was often one of a very few African American students in advanced classes. Through her experience in these classes she quickly learned that race was a taboo subject, even though much of her daily experience was grounded in race within the predominantly white classrooms.

The lack of a dialogue about race combined with the maintenance of a traditional Eurocentric curriculum became a de facto assimilationist project in these schools. In other words, students of color were required to fit into the norms of the schools, including rules and understandings about what was right, smart, and appropriate.[11] Many African American and Latino students were left to feel that the teachers did not value their input or perspective. When values, racial norms, knowledge, and history go unchallenged, so does the privilege of one racial or ethnic group over another.[12]

As a black West Charlotte graduate noted, he did not receive any black history until he graduated from high school. He said that later, when he looked back, he realized that a lot had been left out of the curriculum: "I was somewhat . . . in an environment where someone was telling me their own vision . . . or interpretation about the world and how society was, as opposed to telling it the way it really is. That was very disappointing, and I felt like I had been shafted or misled."

Occasionally, across these six schools, isolated elective courses were developed on such topics as black history, African American literature, or—at Dwight Morrow—Swahili or Hebrew. But such additions had usually been made in reaction to the racial unrest of the early and mid-1970s and were more likely to be found in the predominantly black high schools of Dwight Morrow and Muir than in the other four schools. For the most part, these classes remained on the margin, and the "color-blind" schools taught the curriculum of only one color—white—not to mention one gender and one area of the world. This was the norm.

Furthermore, graduates from both Dwight Morrow and Muir recall that classes such as black history or Swahili tended to enroll far more black students than white students. Thus, rather than leading to greater cross-racial understanding, these courses may have led to greater divides between the races with regard to understanding the role of African Americans in U.S. history. In fact, by marginalizing black history into its own separate class that mainly enrolled black students, these high schools were ensuring that black students would have a far deeper understanding of the role of white privilege in the development of the American society. One white graduate of Muir noted, as he looked back on his years in high school and the lack of any cross-racial dialogue: "Some of the things that they [Muir educators] did, like having a black history class that only black kids took, was stupid because one, it pitted an us-against-them situation, and two, while they were in there learning about black history and we were in our classes learning about, for lack of a better term, white history, when did we ever cross over? When did we get to better understand them, and when did they get to better understand us?"

Perhaps to partly compensate for the lack of multicultural curriculum or dialogue about race within the classrooms, three of these schools—Austin High, Dwight Morrow, and Muir—did acknowledge Black History Month or Cinco de Mayo or both. But for the most part these celebrations were about pageantry and performance and not about deeper discussions of racial inequality. As a black graduate of Muir recalled, the Hispanic students would perform dances and play music for Cinco de Mayo, and the black students would usually put on a choral performance for Black History Month. In fact, according to this student, it was the only time of the year that she saw the blacks really have the spotlight, because the rest of the year, when it came to "the stage and things like that, the Caucasians always participated in plays and the drama clubs, things like that. I don't think that was by design, I just think they had an interest in that and we didn't."

Thus, if nothing else, these holiday celebrations gave the black and Latino students the opportunity to gain the spotlight that was, for much of the rest of the year, shining most brightly on white students. But they did not translate into deeper discussions in the classrooms about the history of race and racial inequality in the United States. As a white Austin High graduate noted, these cultural celebrations generally took place in large, whole-school assemblies where the emphasis was on entertainment and not on the meaning or history of the cultural differences: "We had, as a whole school . . . assemblies. And we dealt with most of our cultural education that way. We all celebrated Cinco de Mayo, you know, all the different ethnic group holidays or important days, we celebrated as a school, more so than we did as a class, I think." Except for these performances, she said, race itself was not an issue that was discussed at school. She said, "Because it wasn't a big deal—I mean, it really wasn't something we talked about. It wasn't a big deal. It was all we knew."

The color-blind ideology, then, may have helped in some ways to bridge the racial divide in terms of individual relationships and to keep a lid on potential racial fights or conflicts, but it left many issues unexamined, many misunderstandings unresolved, and many feelings deeply hurt. Furthermore, as we demonstrate below, it did nothing to promote greater insight into the role that race was playing in these students' local communities and the society at large. Thus, as many theorists have noted, color-blindness as a goal can often be used to maintain white privilege by allowing educators and students to avoid addressing the many ways in which whiteness becomes the norm and thus goes unchallenged. Meanwhile, that which is not white is seen as not only different but also deficient.[13]

What we see when we look at more of the data from the interviews with these former students who are now adults is that in many ways they did adopt color-blind perspectives similar to those of their teachers and administrators. Still, they were more likely to question the value of color-blindness in light of what they were living through on a daily basis in their schools.

QUESTIONING COLOR-BLINDNESS

Given the attitudes of the educators in these six high schools, it should come as no surprise that these adults played virtually no role in helping students deal with or better understand the racial issues they faced in their racially mixed schools. Furthermore, we found that this was not just a high school phenomenon. The class of 1980 graduates, many of whom had been in desegregated schools since elementary school or junior high, said that except for a few occasions racial issues or desegregation were never talked about in any of their schools. They said they went to their racially mixed schools without ever really understanding the goals of desegregation.

Overwhelmingly, the graduates said they did not attempt to talk with their teachers about racial issues in their schools. As a white graduate of West Charlotte High School explained when asked if he remembered ever talking about desegregation in school, "No, I don't remember [laughs]. I don't remember anybody ever mentioning anything, really. We just all knew that we were being bused to try to balance out . . . the racial lines or whatever." Thus, while apparently race was salient on a daily basis and students knew that for many of them it determined where they went to school, it was not discussed in school.

On one level, most of the graduates seemed fine with this color-blind orientation. They reported that generally students "got along" with one another in these high schools even though some students, parents, and community members opposed the racial integration of the schools. As students, they seemed to understand, almost intuitively, why so many of the educators wanted to avoid talking about race. And looking back on the experience more than twenty years later, they saw some value in teachers' efforts to "keep a lid on" racial tension and to see people as people. In fact, the "people as people" theme comes through loud and clear in their discussions of race today and how they get along with people of different racial and ethnic backgrounds (see chapter 6).

Furthermore, it was clear from our interviews that the graduates—like many of the educators—saw race as a delicate issue that was to be avoided in part because students and adults of all racial backgrounds felt vulnerable talking about something that had divided society for so long. For instance, a white graduate of the predominantly black Dwight Morrow High School in Englewood indicated that race was a "terrible topic" that he could not discuss in school. When asked why, he said, "'Cause you didn't want to offend people. You didn't want to say something stupid. You didn't want to get into fights. You know, I think it was a culmination—that's kind of, that's a U.S. thing. In the U.S., it's kind of like a topic you don't talk about very much."

Students, therefore, did not expect race to be discussed by their teachers. Instead they assumed that color-blindness was a much more "natural" approach to dealing with race. Another white graduate of Dwight Morrow High School said, "It is a very touchy, a delicate issue. How could a public school, an integrated public school that is predominantly black, go try to tell or try to encourage something that might not be natural? I don't know if that is possible. And how much more natural can you be by just letting it happen?"

Thus more than half of the graduates we interviewed, and an even larger percentage of white versus black or Latino graduates, said they believed that the educators' effort to ignore race and not engage in formal discussions about it was the "right" or at least the "easiest" thing to do at the time. As a white male graduate of West Charlotte High School noted, there was no racial tension at the school when he was there. "I think one reason it was so successful at the time, and it clearly was, was because we didn't sit there and focus on it, we didn't try to figure it out, and we didn't say, this is so different."

Thus, as adolescents are wont to do, the 1980 graduates came up with their own ways of dealing with race absent any adult-led or classroom-based discussion. For instance, in Austin, an African American graduate who has fond memories of his experience at Austin High School recalled that to the extent that the students came together across racial lines they did it on their own with no support or encouragement from the educators. He recalled, for instance, the changes that occurred over the time while he was a student. He said that initially, in the lower grades, students were very separated by race, but eventually they learned to get along with one another. However, he claimed that the administrators had done nothing to assist the students in this process of making connections across race. He described the social environment of his high school:

> At the beginning there . . . it was separated basically. . . . At the end, I think it was . . . more of a togetherness, . . . and I can't give the administrators credit on any of it, 'cause I can't think of anything that they did. . . . I think the students just took it amongst themselves . . . to make it happen, . . . break down some stereotypes about the school and stuff. That wasn't created by the administration at all. . . . That was definitely the students just . . . being real, you know, and hey, you're friends, we're friends, . . . we're not looking at color and stuff, and that's the way it went down.

Graduates on all sides of the color line evoke a sense of accomplishment in their cross-racial friendships that suggests that while they wanted to see people as people, they were also keenly aware of race and aware of when and how someone crossed racial lines.

In the northeastern and Californian schools of Dwight Morrow, Shaker Heights, and Muir, graduates talked about the kind of racial joking and jiving that would occur on both sides of the color line. For instance, an outspoken and rather bold white Shaker Heights graduate named Dale Kane recalled another white student who was good at drawing and who drew cartoons that would be photocopied and passed around the school each day. One of his central characters in these cartoon strips was the father of a black student in the school who worked as a janitor and had a reputation as a drunk. According to Dale, this white student who was a cartoonist

> had a really mean cartoon he'd draw every day called *Old Man Jones*, and he'd put him into compromising situations and, you know, stupid behavior, ghetto behavior, and make fun of it, and even allude to the fact that [the janitor's son], you know, our classmate, was gonna follow in his father's footsteps, and stuff like that. So yeah, I mean, race was out there, it was not a, it was not a taboo subject by any means, and both directions, I mean people would speak about it. . . . A lot of times

it was explaining what was different or what, you know, we weren't aware of.

This story from Shaker High speaks both to the salience of race in the students' lives and to one of the consequences that occurs when students who have no place to discuss the larger framework of inequality or white privilege in our society take matters into their own hands. A similar de facto racialized culture of "joking" seemed to occur to some extent at Muir as well. As a white Muir graduate explained to us when asked if race was discussed much at this high school, "I don't recall specific, you know, scheduled . . . you know, discussions or assemblies or anything like that that focused on that." But he did recall talking about race a great deal with his friends more informally: "Oh, sure. We, actually, sort of had fun with it sometimes." He went on to explain that part of the way he and his friends made fun of each other was racially: "I mean, you just, I mean, it wasn't . . . it was not unheard of to say, 'Nigger, please!' you know, to one of your, one of your black friends, or to tell them the latest black joke that you just heard, and vice versa. Him telling me the latest white joke that he just heard. It wasn't, you know, it wasn't a thing where it was really thought about. . . . [pause] I mean, it didn't matter what color your mother was, she was still fair game for bagging on."

Yet on another level, underlying their insight into why color-blindness was necessary and, at the same time, why their racial "joking" was just a joke, lay the graduates' uncertainty about whether maybe talking more about race beyond the informal adolescent pranks would have been helpful. Those few graduates who remembered their schooling experiences as racially tense or chaotic, for instance, often said they would have liked for the educators at these schools to have played a larger role in helping students work through such issues. A white 1980 graduate of Muir High School in Pasadena said race was a "nonissue" for her, but she admitted that although she had never been harmed in any way she had been very fearful of being bullied by students of color in school. She told us,

> I guess it—for me, [school desegregation] was a nonissue, too, 'cause I didn't know any different. And I assumed people across the nation

went to schools with people of . . . all different colors. I did kind of wish that . . . I didn't have so much fear in school. And there didn't seem to be much . . . support, like I said, from the administration or from teachers. You know, if you were, if you were bullied by someone, . . . you were basically afraid to tell anybody for fear of getting even more bullied. . . . So what did that experience do for me? I don't really know! Except maybe, I mean, the experience of going to school where I felt kind of threatened I don't think served me much. Going to a school where there was, you know, diversity, I think, helped me a lot.

Clearly this graduate, even as she proclaims that race is a nonissue, would have benefited from discussions about race and racial tensions in her racially desegregated school. Twenty-plus years later, she and many of her classmates are still trying to make sense of their past experiences. But even those graduates who did not experience such racial tensions say that more constructive dialogue about race would have been helpful to them.

Other graduates spoke more directly about the foolishness of color-blindness at that time, but such interviewees were in the minority in thinking that much more should have been done. As Maya Deller, the Shaker Heights High School graduate we quoted above, told us, race does matter because of the different ways in which people make sense of race when they can draw on no larger framework or debate about the relationship between past discrimination and current conditions: "To pretend it doesn't matter is a lot of energy being spent on the wrong thing, 'cause it's denial. But if we could all . . . just say, 'You know what? It matters. It's an issue. People have different perceptions. Perceptions can be important, sometimes even as important as reality . . . and you got to deal with the perceptions.'"

Maya, who is a divorced single mother and a lawyer in a Cleveland law firm (see vignette at the beginning of chapter 6), likens the color-blind argument to the gender-blind argument that so many of her male colleagues subscribed to: "It's like when men say to me, 'I don't see you being a woman as an issue in your career development.' It's like, 'You know what? That's great that you don't see that, but you know what? It happened and it's true.' So that's nice that you can live in Lalaland, but that's not a reality." Here Maya gets closer than most of the white graduates we interviewed to relating the absence of a discussion of race to a denial of the larger, societal forces that create the broader inequality in which color-blind people must function. In retrospect, having a place in the high school curriculum to explore these broader, structural issues would have been helpful to her and other students in making sense of where they are today and how they got there.

Other graduates, even those who subscribed to the "color-blind" view, did note in retrospect that at times adults could have been more helpful in terms of the many changes they were experiencing within their schools, including influxes of new students of different racial backgrounds and white flight. In Austin, the African American student mentioned above felt that he could talk about race with his classmates but noted that the teachers would not condone such discussions, either because of their racial beliefs or because they were too scared, "Because, like [I] say, it was back in the seventies, so everyone was still touchy-feely. . . . They didn't wanna stir up anything . . . so I can't remember any of the teachers offering us an opportunity to share . . . 'What is [this student] about? What is her culture about?' . . . They said, 'Let's just get along.' . . . And that's why I say the administration gets no credit for that school becoming . . . so diverse and the cultures being able to get along with each other. It was strictly on the students."

Again, this student reminds us that the administrators and educators of his school were, in his opinion, not helping students interact with one another or understand themselves, their own culture or history. Students had to take responsibility for considering issues of diversity and difference and working through the difficulty of talking about race. As this student argues, teachers were "scared" to let students talk about race in the classroom.

The African American Austin High School teacher mentioned above who made an extra effort to *not* consider race was remembered by many teachers and students as the black teacher who had problems with the black students. When students went to her asking that she sponsor a black student organization, she refused, not wanting to be accused of favoring the black students. She recalled, "And although they wanted me to sponsor a black club, I wouldn't. I wouldn't, because I told them,

'You are here because you want to integrate. And I don't want to have something black sitting out. We want to try and integrate.'"

African American students told us that they resented what they perceived to be neglect from this teacher. Nevertheless, she was well accepted by her colleagues—even if they tiptoed around racial issues in her presence—and often, when they noted that race did not matter at Austin High, they cited this particular teacher as one who set the example of color-blindness.

The story of this one teacher at Austin High illustrates a larger theme in the data regarding the sense of community in all-black schools. We argue, on the basis of our many interviews, that losing contact with teachers of color who were more aware of black or Latino students' needs and cultural backgrounds was clearly one of the negative consequences of school desegregation for students of color. Yet it is also true that, like the teacher quoted above, not all teachers of color brought such a focus or desire to their teaching. Furthermore, graduates of color sometimes noted that it was white teachers who showed the much-needed empathy when they were struggling to fit in or feel accepted.

Thus, while the goal of color-blindness transcended racial boundaries and was embraced by educators and students alike, it was the educators who adopted it more fervently and uncritically, while the former students (now adult graduates) of these schools were more likely to see that being color-blind only took them so far. Yet although the students who were sometimes frustrated with the colorblind perspective were racially diverse, the color-blind view ended up serving the white students far better than the students of color.

IGNORING RACE DOES NOT MAKE IT GO AWAY

The "color-blind" theme that emerged so clearly from our data relates closely to many other emerging themes from our study, especially themes about how white privilege is reasserted in desegregated spaces. For instance, as noted above, the curriculum at these schools for the most part remained highly focused on "dead white men," as if nothing had happened to the racial makeup of the students, and adolescents, left to their own devices, tried to make sense of race in their own ways, which could include racially insensitive jokes perpetuating the unexamined perceptions that both Betsy and Maya discussed.

In addition, as discussed in chapter 2, we learned that the burden of desegregating schools in these six cities, as in so many other cities across the nation, was placed primarily on the African American and Latino communities. Once students arrived at these high schools that were desegregated in terms of having racially diverse student bodies, they were often racially resegregated inside the schools by a tracking system that ensured that very few students of color would be in the high-track classes. And of course, in contexts in which race was not discussed or debated, such resegregation was rarely if ever talked about; it was seen as the norm to have the white students in the top classes.

Yet despite this resegregation and reassertion of white privilege in these schools and communities the students made important cross-race connections and friendships, even if these friendships did not always carry over into their social lives outside the schools (see chapter 5). Thus it is not totally surprising that more than two decades later most members of the class of 1980—including Latinos, African American, whites, and the few Asian Americans we interviewed—saw their experiences in racially diverse schools as mostly positive, offering wonderful opportunities for learning how to participate in a racially diverse society.

These graduates reported that in high school "we all got along" and expressed a belief that attending a desegregated school, while sometimes challenging, was nonetheless "worth it" (chapter 6). Again, it seems more than a little paradoxical that these graduates were attending "color-blind" schools while they noted how much they valued their cross-racial friendships, even if these friendships went only "so far" and virtually all their "outside school" friends were of the same race. Furthermore, as we discuss in chapters 7 and 8, the vast majority of these graduates have found that in adulthood they are living in fairly racially segregated neighborhoods and, in most cases, sending their own children to far more segregated schools than the ones they attended. Yet when asked about how they came to lead more segregated adult lives, these graduates, for the most part, lacked a broader understanding of racial inequality and segregation in the U.S. society that would have helped them make sense of how things had come to be that way. This was especially true for the white graduates, who were quick to slip into double-consciousness explanations that simultaneously argue that people are people and then blame the victims of racial inequality or see racial segregation as unfortunate and unfair but also inevitable given people's choices and preferences.

As time went on, therefore, many of the white graduates, lacking a formal education in the racial structure of inequality in the United States, became more and more willing to fall back on explanations that blacks were "lazy and immoral," despite their personal experiences to the contrary and their underlying sense that this was too simplistic. In other words, a constant focus on "people as people" in high school, despite several indicators that their schools and lives were ensconced in a larger structure of racial inequality with a long history and far-reaching effects, did not prepare these graduates for adulthoods in which it would be extremely difficult for them to maintain meaningful cross-racial friendships while following the larger patterns of racial separateness that divide most adults in the United States. Hence, they currently believe in equality while living a life that contradicts it.

Thus it is clear why color-blindness is one of the most salient themes in the recollections and opinions of educators and students in the six high schools. Not only did the desire and goal to become color-blind pervade their experiences in the late 1970s, but according to our interviews many continue to struggle toward a goal of color-blindness as the answer to an unequal society. In fact, many of them thought that school desegregation was the first step toward creating a color-blind society. They credit the experience of attending or teaching in a racially mixed school with their current views of racial equality, or more specifically their view of race as a nonissue. At the same time, many of them feel that this view does not adequately address what they have been through.

We wonder whether their present-day struggles to make sense of race spring more from a high school experience in which race was positively framed as a nonissue and everyone strove to be more color-blind or from the current political context in which a race-blind policy agenda is seen by many people in power to be the solution to ongoing racial inequality. Eduardo Bonilla-Silva has found that such a color-blind view is embraced by many white graduates of segregated schools as well.[14] So we are not arguing that our informants' experiences in racially mixed schools had a negative impact on them; indeed, the data on the extent to which the graduates valued their cross-racial friendships and exposure in racially mixed schools strongly suggest the opposite.

Rather, we are saying that for the generation of students who lived through school desegregation the color-blind ideology of their high schools represents a missed opportunity to reconcile the contradictory lessons they learned (or failed to learn) about race in school—namely that in school they got to know individuals of other races whom they admired and were friends with while they groped for explanations for the broader and systemic racial inequality and segregation in the United States. Perhaps the greatest irony is that now, as schools in this country are becoming more open to multicultural curricula and are celebrating issues of diversity, they are at the same time becoming more racially segregated.[15]

A few of the graduates we interviewed are trying, twenty-plus years later, to figure out some of this racial confusion on their own. Amid their busy adult lives, they wonder whether the color-blind perspective has served them well, especially in light of the increasingly diverse national population and one of the more prevalent movements to have sprung up in reaction to color-blind politics: racial identity politics. According to one white graduate of West Charlotte, who wondered, like Maya from Shaker High, whether a color-blind ideology had prepared him for life in the twenty-first century: "[We] knew our mission was to make us all color-blind. That was the objective in that day, time. . . . In the late seventies, early eighties, the objective was to be color-blind and everyone be the same. That has since changed to embracing the differences through diversity, and it was [a] very different time and different objective." Yet this graduate, like many we interviewed, felt unprepared for this paradigm shift because the color-blind view had served so many of the graduates (especially the white graduates) so well for so long.

Little of this story of school desegregation in the United States is known because, as we noted above, most school desegregation research has ignored what happened inside schools. A lack of information and understanding about students' experiences of race and color-blindness in schools left school desegregation policy open to a strong critique by African Americans as ignoring sociocultural experiences or views of students of color.[16]

Yet we have learned in our research on these six high schools that what was happening in racially mixed schools during the late 1970s was much more than a de facto process of ignoring the sociocultural experiences and needs of students of color. It was also, to some extent, a proactive effort on the part of many educators to "move beyond racial differences" and foster a sense of "common ground" of human connections across race. As compelling as calls for such connections might be, especially after years of racial tension and fighting, these proactive efforts to be color-blind did not actually create a situation in which race did not matter in diverse public schools of that era. It is clear, in fact, that it mattered then and, in many ways, continues to matter a great deal.

FIVE Close Together but Still Apart

Fourth grade at the Robert E. Lee Elementary School in Austin, Texas, was a difficult year for Harriet "Hattie" Allen. It was 1971, and Hattie, an African American child from East Austin, on the "other side of the highway," had just transferred into the predominantly white and affluent Lee Elementary School in West Austin. Her teacher, a white woman, tried to label Hattie mentally retarded and have her sent to another school. She was one of only three black students in her class: one of the others was a boy who was academically advanced; the other was a lighter-skinned girl with long hair. According to Hattie: "I was an average kid, I didn't have long hair, and I have dark skin, so I kind of bore the brunt of my fourth-grade teacher, who was in fact an elderly woman who was not happy with black children coming into white schools, she had a fundamental problem. So I had a very difficult time adjusting in fourth grade ... [coming] from an all-black school where I felt comfortable."

But Hattie never went back to an all-black school; she spent the rest of her school days surrounded by mostly white classmates, and she graduated from Stephen F. Austin High School in 1980. Hattie will tell you that her mother, a nurse who worked at a hospital near Lee Elementary, was "ahead of the curve" when it came to school desegregation. She had enrolled Hattie and her brother in West Austin schools before the court ordered the school district to move students from one school to the next on the basis of color. Her mother had asked people at her work about the different schools and their reputations, and when she became concerned about the quality of education her children were receiving in their historically black elementary school, she knew how to work the system and gain access for her kids to schools that, at the time, most other black students could only dream of attending.

The distance between her mother's dream of finding better schools for her children and Hattie's personal trials and tribulations at these "better" schools mirrors the double consciousness many African Americans have concerning school desegregation. The trade-offs between what they must give up in terms of comfort, familiarity, and acceptance in a mostly black school and what they gain in often more prestigious, more academically competitive, and better-resourced white schools are enormous and hard to fathom in the abstract. Personal journeys such as Hattie's help us understand.

When we interviewed Hattie—once in 2000 and again in 2002—she was in some ways the same thin, energetic (self-proclaimed "hyper"), and enthusiastic person she said she had been in high school. She was employed as a social worker and was unmarried and had no children. She said she had few friends as an adult, especially few who were black. She told us that since her days at Lee Elementary she had constantly straddled white and black social spheres, never feeling completely comfortable in either one.

Hattie recalled, for instance, the popular white girls in her fourth-grade class, the cute outfits they would wear and the gymnastics classes they took. But Hattie's father worked as a janitor at that time, and her mother was a nurse with an associate's degree, so fancy clothes and gymnastics classes were not an option. "I wanted to go so bad, and my mother would say, like, 'We can't afford that,' you know . . . but she would feel bad. She would want me to be able to go."

Similarly, Hattie can remember how much her mother wanted her to be socially accepted by the white students. But Hattie knew there were boundaries: friendships with white students could go only so far, especially when it came to out-of-school activities. She noted that one of her white friends in sixth grade invited her to her house for a party, even though her other friends never invited Hattie to their houses. She said, "I came home, and I was excited, 'Oh, a friend invited me over to her house.'"

She recalled that her mother had been "so appreciative and grateful" that a white family had invited Hattie to their house. She said that going to a predominantly white school meant and that she and her parents were "stuck between a rock and a hard place because . . . you know, I'm very proud of my heritage and my culture and who I am and being African American, so it's painful for my mother to watch these kids being nasty to me."

Thus the thin, dark-skinned black girl from East Austin soon learned that she could "only befriend white kids so much. . . . For the most part I wasn't invited to the parties." Hattie said she was sure it was the parents of these white students who were drawing this line. "They were getting subtle messages—or not-so-subtle messages—about who was acceptable and who was not acceptable, and how close you could be."

Race and class, then, were the dividing lines between Hattie and her white peers. But the fact that she had any connection to these white students at all—even a connection that occurred only in school—created another division between Hattie and her black classmates. She said she was ostracized by most of her black classmates, especially when she got to Austin High School, which enrolled many more black students than there had been in her elementary or junior high schools.

She remembers feeling like an outcast in both the white and African American social circles at Austin High School and even in her East Austin neighborhood, where black kids would taunt her and be mean to her. She said that most students in "the black community" called her an Uncle Tom. "So really, I hate to say it, but the people who were nicest to me when I was in school were the white people. But they had their limits too, you know. . . . It was just very difficult, painful."

What made Hattie's years in desegregated schools so difficult was the fact that the social cliques within these schools were often sharply divided by race and class. Being a black girl who had white friends meant she could not hang out with black students in the same way that most blacks did. Thus starting off in a predominantly white elementary school "ahead of the game" of school desegregation and then learning to fit in within that setting as best she could meant that she moved forward through the grades with a better sense of how to be friends with white kids than did most of her black peers who came from segregated junior high schools to Austin High. And when they entered Austin High, they saw a predominantly white high school (66 percent white, 19 percent Latino, and 15 percent black) deeply divided by race, class, and space in terms of who was friends with whom and where they congregated when they were not in classes, which, as we noted, were also partly segregated by race. She recalled that even some of the teachers treated her poorly because she was friends with white students and thus "did not know her place."

While Hattie claimed that there was no racial fighting at Austin High, she said that the relative calm and "people getting along was superficial." And like her peers at the other schools, she noted that the adults in these schools did nothing to bridge the racial divides. "There was always this underlying tension that never was addressed. And it wasn't addressed because the adults didn't know how to address it. You know, there was no leadership in that regard."

Despite feeling that she was not completely a part of any of the separate and unequal social cliques and that the educators at the school were doing little to deal with racial issues, Hattie did "succeed" in high school according to many measures of adolescent social success. She was elected by the student body to be the one black cheerleader on the coveted cheerleading squad. She also played on the Austin High girls' basketball team and on the junior varsity tennis team and was involved in student council. Clearly, these various activities helped Hattie to cope; they helped her feel that she belonged.

Yet most of these extracurricular activities, especially cheerleading, tennis, and student council, were high status in the school, in part because many of the high-status (read white and affluent) students were involved in them. Thus Hattie's involvement in these particular activities projected her further into the popular white clique of students who were mostly from West Austin and created more distance between her and her black peers. But the girls' basketball team, which was racially diverse, was where she made her closest and dearest friend, who was also black. She said, "The only person I was really friends with was Lena, and that was because we were on the basketball team together, we both played point guard. . . . We had played basketball together since junior high."

Still, the process of becoming a part of these activities was not always what Hattie had hoped it would be. She recalled what happened after she was elected by popular vote to be a cheerleader. At the time, Austin High had strict, if rarely mentioned, racial quotas on highly visible activities such as cheerleading.

In essence, noted Hattie, it was a popularity contest. And whichever black girls got the most votes would become what were often only one or two African American representatives on the cheerleading squad. "But you know," she said, "the black people, when I got to be cheerleader, . . . they made it very clear that the reason that I was elected cheerleader was because the white people had voted for me."

While enough white students had supported Hattie's bid to be a cheerleader, there was less support among whites at Austin High School for her to play on the tennis team, which had no quotas and a long history of white privilege. Hattie explained that she had been playing tennis since she was ten years old, which was unusual for a black girl growing up in her neighborhood during that era. She said that her mother had signed her and her brother up for children's tennis clinics through an Austin recreation program. She said that they had played tennis often and had played with people who were very skilled at the game. So Hattie recalled that when she had showed up for the tryouts for the Austin High tennis team she beat a white student in the tryouts but the coach would not put her on the team. "I mean, it was okay for me to play basketball because that was an African American designated sport. But tennis . . . I wasn't supposed to be there, this was an exclusive, elite, white sport, and I didn't have any business there."

Hattie's sense of it was that the white parents more than the students themselves were strongly opposed to having a black student playing tennis for Austin High. She said, "You know, tradition dies hard. . . . The parents of the children who were on the tennis team—who were very elite children, I might add—their parents were probably, who knows, telling the coach, 'No black kid can be better than my kid at Austin High.'"

Still, to this day, Hattie said that she did not think the coach was a fair person. Instead of letting Hattie on the varsity team, the coach formed a junior varsity team with three or four students. According to Hattie, there had never been a junior varsity girls tennis team before, and "it was very painful." Hattie, by the way, went on to play tennis in college.

Whether it is actually true that Austin High had never had a junior varsity girls' tennis team before Hattie arrived and tried out for the varsity team is not really the point here. What is clear from Hattie's interviews is what she learned about the power of white privilege at Austin High and her other West Austin schools. Yet for the most part, she remembers the adults, particularly the white parents, as the biggest perpetrators. In fact, Hattie has many memories of the white students from affluent families being more generous, more open, and less prejudiced than their parents.

She explained that even when we change the laws so that black and Latino students can go to school with white students, that does not change what is in people's hearts.

> So the law, yeah, in theory opens up opportunities where you need to be able to go to school with these kids who are getting a better education, . . . but the flip side is that it's also . . . pain and suffering you have to endure as a result of the resentment and the anger that these people don't want you there. It wasn't so much the kids, the kids were just reflecting the attitudes of their parents. I mean, yeah, it's nice that desegregation happened, but then you just have a bunch of kids who are thrown together who don't like each other, don't know each other, and are espousing the values of their parents. The black kids included, you know.

She wouldn't or couldn't believe that her friends felt the same way their parents did, at least not back then, though now that these same white students are grown up with homes and children of their own they may well be ensconced in the same power structures their parents were—and even more so, given the growing gap between the rich and the poor since the 1970s and the growing pressure on parents to get their children into the "right" schools and colleges (see chapter 8). According to Hattie, "The people who had power and control want to keep power and control, you know, 'cause they have money and they're comfortable. That's what they want, is to be in control, and so what you have is people not wanting to share and people being uncomfortable on being confronted about that. Equality can never happen until people are willing to give up things like power and control and share that."

Another sign that race and class clearly mattered a great deal in Austin High School and that people with power were not keen to have their children associate too closely with those without such power was the community's complete rejection of interracial dating. In fact, only in Austin and West Charlotte high schools—the two "southern" schools in former Jim Crow states—was interracial dating such a taboo. Even though Hattie was not very popular among black boys, and her parents strongly discouraged her from dating when she was in high school, she did attend the senior prom with an African American student she had known since she was a child. They went as friends because, according to Hattie, her date was surreptitiously dating a white girl but could not take her to the prom.

In the end, Hattie admitted that in spite of the pain of not fitting in on either side of the color line, school desegregation was better than nothing and was an important learning experience for her because it clearly reflected how people function in the regular society.

> On the one hand I got what I feel like was a very good education, I had been exposed to and was familiar with white students, and had kind of learned how to fit in, and made some friends. But you know, the reality of it is, I didn't have any strong friendships, I was pretty much a loner in high school because the white kids would accept you to a point. . . . I never quite fit anywhere. The black kids didn't accept me because they were always taunting me and harassing me and saying very mean, hurtful, nasty things, you know, "You think you're white."

This memory of the double consciousness of school desegregation makes Hattie reflective. She frequently mentioned what an elite school Austin High was and how every doctor, lawyer, and politician in the city sent his or her children there. "The wealthiest of the wealthy were going to school there."

The perception Hattie and her mother held was that wherever such influential people were, the system would ensure that they had access to the best education. If she could be a part of their school, she too would gain from their political clout in the system. This was definitely true, and

Hattie said she had never regretted opting out of her poor neighborhood high school on the east side. But such choices, she is quick to point out, came at a price mostly because of the school's racially divided social milieu and partly because white privilege, which was part and parcel of the prestige of the school, strongly overshadowed the students' social interactions.

She thinks about the parallels between her life in high school and her life as an adult. She is a social worker in a racially diverse agency where she works side by side for eight hours a day with whites, blacks, and Latinos. Once again, however, as she experienced twenty-plus years ago, her friendships across racial lines go only so far—and often not even *as* far: "You know, it's more than working together in an employment environment. I think it's having people in your personal life that are different from you, and risking and growing and learning. You know, learning that, yeah, this person has some things that are very different about them, their culture is different from ours, their belief, their religion, whatever, but they also have some things in common with you, some very basic things that you have in common. I mean, I guess I feel kind of conflicted about school desegregation. I mean, my own experience makes me feel conflicted."

· · · · ·

Geri Delgato, a Mexican American graduate of Muir High School, was raised in the predominantly African American section of Altadena, which is part of the Pasadena school system. His extended family had lived in that area for many years and had sent many children to Muir. His father was a self-employed gardener, and his mother never worked outside their home. Geri had three siblings, and they were a very tight-knit family.

Recalling the Muir basketball team his senior year, Geri noted that it was a twelve-person varsity team, with ten African Americans, one white guy, and Geri, the only Mexican (he does not like the terms *Hispanic* or *Latino*). Unlike most of the Mexican students at Muir—the school was 11 percent Latino (mostly Mexican) at the time—Geri was known as a very good athlete. He also played tennis his first two years of high school and was a member of the marching band. In part because of his involvement in these extracurricular activities, he says he had little in common with most other Latino students. He sometimes felt that they did not accept him because he was different; other times he felt they respected him because he was one of the few Mexicans who was a star athlete.

As a result of his distance from what was a very tight "Hispanic clique" at Muir, most of Geri's friends were African American. Like so many other class of 1980 graduates we interviewed, he found that through his involvement in athletics and the marching band he got to know students of different racial backgrounds and was able to transcend racial barriers. He said his three best friends were African American basketball players. He also hung out with some white athletes, although other, economic barriers often separated him from white students. He noted, for instance, that some of the popular white students lived in large homes, drove expensive cars to school, and took expensive vacations that his family could never afford. He said, "From a socioeconomic standpoint, we were just worlds apart."

Furthermore, Geri did not take the most challenging classes at Muir, which he noted were generally filled with white students, and he referred to himself as a high school "underachiever." Still, he became the first in his family to graduate from college. He attended one of the California state universities and earned a bachelor's degree in business management.

After college, Geri married a fellow Muir graduate who is Southeast Asian, and he worked in various jobs in Southern California. He and his wife then moved to Memphis, and several years later to a Chicago suburb. Today they live in an upper-middle-class suburb south of Phoenix, Arizona. In fact, their community is so far away from the city it borders a rural area. On the way to their house from the city is a cattle yard with hundreds of cows and some wide-open fields with grazing horses.

As you approach Geri's house, the area becomes more residential, in the planned community genre. Geri lives with his wife and their daughter in a gated subdivision that looks very similar to the surrounding subdivisions. There is only one entrance and exit, and the residents are mostly white and upper middle class. All the homes are made of a brownish stucco. Geri's wife explained that with this latest move to Arizona they had not sought out a more racially diverse community as they had in suburban Chicago. She said that as they have gotten older they have been more concerned about their investment in a home and the quality of the public schools for their twelve-year-old daughter. Geri's wife explained, "So this neighborhood is not as diverse, . . . but the home is nicer and the area is nicer and the school is better."

When last we saw him, Geri was working for a large corporation as a customer development manager. He commented on how white and male dominated his industry is. He said, "You almost feel, you know, in some sense like a token."

Geri still values the racial and ethnic diversity he was exposed to at Muir. He is proud of what he learned there about getting along with people of all different backgrounds. He noted that too many people in this country lack that exposure and thus make assumptions about people who are different from them. He said he hoped to give his daughter that exposure through various activities outside her highly ranked public school in the suburbs.

· · · · ·

The stories of Hattie and Geri speak to several themes in the book and in this chapter on the social milieu of desegregated schools. As we know from the previous chapters, students in desegregated school were quite often resegregated across classes and had no forum for discussing race. We also know that the racial inequality in the local communities and the larger society profoundly shaped the design and details of their school desegregation plans, as the power and privilege of white people challenged and reconstructed policies designed to equalize educational opportunities.

All of these factors combined do not bode well for the formation of meaningful friendships across racial lines within these schools. And in fact, the social groups that tended to form in these schools did mirror the racial and social class (and occasionally religious) divides in the larger society. The most visible such divide was usually racial, although there were also profound divisions sometimes both within and across racial groups by social class or athletic ability. Still, the most popular students, at least in the predominantly white schools, were white students who were affluent and athletic or otherwise involved in high-status activities. As one wealthy white student from Austin High School noted: "We ruled the school."

Still, the majority of class of 1980 graduates we interviewed recalled becoming friends or at least acquaintances with one or more people of another racial group while in high school. These interactions and cross-racial friendships were most likely formed through extracurricular activities, which often, but not always, drew students from across racial lines. Athletics, in particular, tended to facilitate cross-racial friendships, particularly among boys who regularly bonded with other teammates—of all colors—as they were playing competitive sports, particularly football. At the same time, some sports, including water polo, tennis, hockey, or even basketball, were more racially segregated. But other activities, including student government, drama, band, and chorus, also brought students together across racial lines, even as traditionally elite or ethnic clubs, such as the Key Club or the Black History Club, generally pulled them further apart.

The six high schools varied to some extent in the racial and social class makeup of the students and the politics of the local communities. Yet in all of the sites, the graduates remember that while they learned a great deal from their interactions with students of other racial and ethnic groups, their closest friends tended to be of the same race, and the major social cliques remained racially identifiable. Even though graduates of these six schools informed us that "everyone got along" fairly well across racial lines, for the most part students hung out with their same-race friends outside school.

This ongoing segregation across racial and ethnic lines was partly the result of logistical and historical facts, such as who grew up with whom, who had attended elementary school and junior high with whom, who lived near whom, and who was "comfortable" with whom. But there is no denying that it was also the result of a powerful social hierarchy that

divided students not only by race but also by social class and other factors, including physical attractiveness and athletic ability. Most often the
more affluent or athletically talented subset of students who were in the
racial majority at a particular school constituted the most popular crowd.

This also meant that in the two predominantly African American
schools we studied, even white and wealthy students could be socially
marginalized to some degree. Although these students generally fared
better socially than most black students in predominantly white schools,
their social domination was not a given.

In the four predominantly white schools, even when an athletically
talented, middle-class African American student became "popular," his
or her connection to the most popular white students generally went
only "so far." For instance, he or she was rarely invited to many of the
important social events that occurred outside school—whether cotillions
or private parties at white students' houses.

Thus the stories of a few graduates point to important exceptions to
the rule of racially isolated cliques. Most notably, the star athletes or
cheerleaders of the minority racial background in any given school—
usually African American or Latino students but sometimes white
students—were more likely to be accepted into the "popular crowd,"
often making these popular cliques the most integrated in these schools.
Still, even popular "minority" students did not always feel fully accepted
within these groups.

Additionally, to the extent that there was any interracial dating in
these schools, it tended to be between the athletically gifted African
American and Latino boys and white girls. It was very rare to find
instances of white boys dating African American or Latina girls.

All of these findings related to the social realm of these schools suggest the many ways in which broader societal inequalities demarcated
by race, class, and gender were reproduced and occasionally challenged
in these schools, depending on which racial or ethnic group was in the
majority in each context. Despite such social hierarchies, which were
entrenched in the local community and easily permeated the school
walls, students reported that they had important cross-racial interactions
and friendships that they could not have had in a one-race school.

Furthermore, we found that in a few of these schools, as the class of 1980 matriculated through the high school and neared graduation, the racial barriers seemed to diminish and social cliques, once extremely segregated by race, became less so. As we will see in chapter 6, these interactions changed them in some fundamental ways that remain with them as adults.

The remainder of this chapter discusses first social cliques, then extracurricular activities as a setting for cross-racial friendships, and finally the limits of cross-racial friendships and interracial dating.

HIGH SCHOOL CLIQUES

As we have noted in prior chapters, most of the racial tension and fighting that did occur in these six communities was already pretty much a thing of the past by the time the class of 1980 got to high school. As a result, a common refrain among the educators and graduates from these schools who were there in the late 1970s was that "we all just got along." For instance, an African American graduate of West Charlotte recalled that students at her school blended and got along "across the board," regardless of race or class. "I mean, we were friends. We all—we all got along. . . . It was great."

Graduates of Shaker Heights High School were even more emphatic about the degree of racial integration in their school, with many black and white students coming together and forming friendships. As one Shaker High graduate, a white man, remembered it: "We were, in the late 1970s, highly successfully integrated. . . . There was no tension or conflict that . . . you were led to believe would exist, so everybody could get along together. There was a lot of togetherness."

Thus it appears that the lack of racial fighting or tension and the general interpersonal politeness across racial groups in most of these schools led the graduates to conclude that they did indeed all get along. Paradoxically, however, when we asked the graduates about who was friends with whom and who was popular, a far more elaborate picture emerged—one that was delineated not only by race but also by class and status. In this context, status included athletic ability, high academic achievement, or "good looks" as defined in very racialized ways—such as blond hair and blue eyes—at least for the girls.

In a book titled *Freaks, Geeks, and Cool Kids*, sociologist Murray Milner writes that many students in the racially mixed school he studied had known each other for most of their lives. Thus, he writes, their "micro" or individual history of interpersonal interactions with each other did not, for the most part, involve racist attitudes or behavior. "Nevertheless, the macro history—the collective memory and societal politics—of each group has not escaped the past."[1]

In other words, just as the broader context of white privilege profoundly shaped the organization of desegregated schools, so it helped to define the social hierarchies that students created within these schools. These hierarchies, which were flatter in some of the schools we studied than in others, and were particularly pronounced at Austin High School, were maintained through intimidation and acts of exclusion. Indeed, students sometimes used their status and power in a given context to exclude other students or make them feel inferior. According to literature in sociology and social psychology, such adolescent behavior is quite common in racially homogeneous schools.[2]

Yet in the context of racially diverse schools, such cliques and their hierarchies often appeared to be defined—or were most easily defined visually—by race,[3] although there was a great deal of evidence of the other divisions mentioned above. Racial "turf" seemed to matter as well. Thus, in the schools that had been historically white and still were by the late 1970s, including Austin High, Shaker High, and Topeka High, the popular white students (often but not always the most affluent white students) "ruled," although the degree to which they "ruled" and the segregation that accompanied such social hierarchies were much more pronounced at Austin High than at Shaker or Topeka. West Charlotte High School, with its history as a black school, its location in a black neighborhood, and the fact that it drew students from thirteen different junior high schools in the mid- to late 1970s, had a more complicated, and as a result more egalitarian, sense of "turf." Dwight Morrow and Muir high schools were both predominantly black at the time, so in these schools a delicate balance of popular black and white students dominated the social context in different but often complementary ways. Across these diverse contexts, then, students clearly saw race as a defining feature of their social lives in ways that reflected both the local societal contexts of these schools and the spatial arrangement of students in the buildings.

Racially Distinct Spaces

Graduates of each of the six schools we studied could tell you of particular places in those schools where particular groups of students used to hang out. These groups of students were not always racially distinct, but often they were. For instance, at Dwight Morrow High School in New Jersey, every graduate and many of the educators we interviewed described the racially distinguishable cafeterias—the one that virtually all the white students used in the older, North building, and the one that the majority of black students used in the newer, more industrial-looking South building.

In the same breath that he used to explain that there weren't many "huge racial issues" at Dwight Morrow, a white graduate of that school explained the "white cafeteria, black cafeteria thing." He said it was "kind of a joke" and that it "just happened" that way and he does not know why: "It may have been the cafeteria that you were closest to when you . . . got out of your class. I don't know. But that wasn't a big issue. It wasn't a problem, and if you were white you wouldn't, like, 'Oh, I can't go in the black cafeteria.'"

Despite this graduate's reassurance that the issue of separate cafeterias was not a big deal at Dwight Morrow, it was striking that all the white and black graduates we interviewed mentioned it. Many of the white graduates suggested that the separation resulted from the fact that more white students drove cars to school than black students and that the place where they could park their cars was much closer to the old, North building cafeteria, whereas the place where black students usually got off the school buses was closer to the newer, South building cafeteria. This may help explain cafeteria segregation in the morning but not at lunchtime.

Similarly, students at Topeka High School congregated around different entrances to the school in the morning on the basis of race and, to a lesser extent, where some of these students parked their cars. As more than one white Topeka High graduate and educator told us, the white students congregated at the west entrance to the school, the Hispanic students on the east side, and many of the African American students in the main hallway or outside the central, Tenth Street entrance to the school. The white students, according to one former Topeka High administrator, "would be to the west end as I recall, of the first floor, and then some upstairs too, either the second or third floor."

More than one white graduate argued that at Topeka High, as at Dwight Morrow, this racial separation in the morning was simply a reflection of how students got to school and where the white students in particular parked their cars. They said that with very little parking for students on campus they had to park in the streets of the surrounding neighborhoods. And groups (or cliques) of students would park together in the same neighborhoods—often on the same streets where their older brothers or sisters had before them. These different parking spaces often meant that most of the students with cars to drive to school—mostly white students—were walking to campus together, approaching the western side of the building where many of the popular white students congregated in the morning.

Meanwhile, Topeka High had an infamous back hallway on the first floor behind the cafeteria, where, it was rumored, white students should not go because it was the black students' turf. According to several white graduates of Topeka High, this back hallway was an area they tried to stay away from. As one of these former students explained: "That was an area where you could pretty [much] count on something happening to you if you got caught there between classes or after hours."

Yet no one we interviewed had ever had anything happen to them in that hallway, nor did they know firsthand anyone who had had a negative experience there. And the former administrator quoted above, who was an assistant principal at Topeka High at that time, said: "There used to be stories that Topeka High's halls were not safe, the back hall especially. But nothing ever happened in the back hall of Topeka High School. That was quiet, peaceful."

Still, the legend of the black hallway was already larger than life by the time these graduates arrived. The same could be said of a dark hallway behind the main office at Dwight Morrow, which the black and white students had nicknamed "Niggers' Alley," where, both black and white students report, a lot of "weed" was smoked and drug trading would occur. When asked who hung out in this infamous hallway, a black graduate of Dwight Morrow said, "All black. . . . It was blacks there and mostly your poor blacks, even some middle-class blacks that were off the beaten track that their parents had laid for them."

Interestingly enough, at Shaker Heights High School there was a well-known hallway called "Hippie Hallway," where students could smoke inside the school during breaks between classes; after all, this was the 1970s, when many high schools had smoking lounges. But the difference between the infamous back hallways at Topeka High and Dwight Morrow High and Hippie Hallway at Shaker High was that the latter was reported to be racially diverse in terms of who hung out there in the smelly, smoke-filled space. According to several Shaker graduates, including this white one, who was a frequent visitor to Hippie Hallway in his years at the school, "It was everybody. It was really everybody—anybody who smoked and, you know, there were black, white, Chinese, whatever smokers, and it was just . . . (a) it smelled awful, and (b) it was—like I said, it was a lot of the people who smoked." While one other white Shaker graduate said she sometimes saw little "pockets" of students congregating by race in Hippie Hallway, most recall it as a very racially diverse space in the school.

Meanwhile, during lunchtime at Muir High School, when most of the students went outside to enjoy the Southern California weather, they congregated in separate spaces according to race. As one former Muir administrator recalled, "It used to be that all of the white kids hung out over in a certain area, in what we called Salad Bowl . . . and all the blacks hung out over on this side under the pergola." A former Muir math teacher also remembered the racial divisions at lunchtime. "White kids would eat together. Hispanics would eat together. Blacks would eat together, and Asians [were] nowhere to be seen. . . . I don't know where they ate. Each one . . . each of the other groups had their little pockets."

As for lockers at Muir High, several graduates said that most of the white students had theirs on the first floor and most of the blacks had theirs on the second floor. In fact, according to some of the graduates we interviewed, black and white students would trade lockers with each other so that they could have lockers next to students of the same racial group. Another option was for students to double up with a friend so that everyone would be on the "right" floor according to race. As one white Muir graduate explained it to us, "I remember there was always a problem with the lockers. So, you know, you were, like, assigned a locker at that time. And everybody had a locker. And what happened is, you'd like, share with a friend or trade with your friend or never use yours or whatever."

West Charlotte, like Shaker High, was less segregated physically than the other schools, although the Open Program—a school within a school that was designed to help attract white students to the historically black high school—was disproportionately white. Early on, in the first years of the class of 1980's time at West Charlotte, the Open School Program students, including many from Southeast Charlotte, kept more to themselves throughout the school day. This led to a less dramatic version of spatial segregation within the school because the majority of white students enrolled in West Charlotte were not in the Open Program.

In 1997, psychologist Beverly Daniel Tatum published a now widely read book entitled *Why Are All the Black Kids Sitting Together in the Cafeteria?*[4] Her central message to her readers is that when people enter racially diverse schools and see all the black students sitting together, mostly away from white students, in one area of the cafeteria, they should not throw their hands up and claim that the effort to desegregate schools was a complete failure because the students "self-segregate." Tatum explains that such self-segregation, particularly within predominantly white schools, is important and necessary for the identity development of black children because it allows them to create spaces free of negative stereotypes where they can be themselves.

While such spatial separation may well be very helpful to black, Latino, or Asian students who attend predominantly white schools, we must question what such spatial separation does for whites. For instance, at Austin High School, like Topeka High and Dwight Morrow, students "hung out" in different parts of the school in the morning. Christine Almonte, the Austin High graduate profiled in chapter 3, explained the spatial divisions to us in this way: "Austin High had three floors, and . . . there was an area that all Hispanics gathered on the bottom floor. All the whites that were all the [West Austin students] were on the second floor, in the open common area. . . . And on the third floor was a mixture of blacks, whites, and leftover . . . you know, and the weirdos and people like that were always outside smoking, you know, they always had their little area where they were together that they kinda gathered."

As many white Austin High graduates explained, the most affluent West Austin clique dominated that second-floor area, and the white students who were on the third floor tended to be those from the other side of the river—from South Austin. In fact, the less affluent students of all races tended to find the second-floor social scene quite intimidating. As one Latina graduate explained it more than twenty years after her daily experiences in the school, "You know, you just didn't walk up on the second floor and try to hang out because the second floor belonged to the Anglos."

White Privilege Prevails

In the predominantly white schools, especially at Austin High, where black and Latino students were being bused in from elsewhere, the most affluent and privileged white students did in fact "rule" the school's social realm. The affluent white Austin High graduate quoted above as saying that she and her friends "ruled the school" explained the role of her clique of students from wealthy West Austin neighborhoods in the school: "We were *the* group. We were it. We just were all very involved in school. We all loved going to school, it was a great place to be, that's why." In further describing her clique of girlfriends from the affluent west side of town, which she noted was about 85 percent white and less than 1 percent black, this same graduate noted: "What did we call ourselves? I know some schools, they call them the 'socios,' but we weren't 'socios.' I don't remember what we called ourselves—'West Austin rich bitches,' that's what some people called us." When asked why this clique of rich white girls from the west side of town were the most popular, this same graduate speculated: "Probably we were the prettiest girls, the best parties, sought after for dates."

Some of the other white students at Austin High, especially those who were less affluent and lived on the south side of the river, aspired to be part of the popular West Austin crowd. As we noted, these more middle-class white students, derogatorily nicknamed "river rats" by their West Austin peers, were well aware of the social stratification and how their residence south of the river affected the way they were perceived. In fact, one white male graduate we interviewed from South Austin informed us that while he was not in the "A Group," which he defined as those who were "very wealthy from West Austin, and they were the popular ones," he was a member of the "B Group," which included students in the band or choir. The B Group was still a notch above the other predominantly white cliques from South Austin, which included the druggies and the "kickers," or "country" people.

This particular graduate noted that while he was not a full-fledged member of the A Group—and that river rats rarely were—he socialized with them and was invited to their cotillion dances, "and I mean, definitely if you were a minority you probably weren't invited." He said the West Austin parents hosted the cotillion dances each year, and "it was very elitist. . . . Looking back, I can't even believe I participated in that. But I was so honored to be asked at the time."

The "honor" that this white student felt as a result of being invited to these dances speaks to the clout the West Austin students held in the social realm of that school. Meanwhile, even as a handful of South Austin whites were drawn into the social circle of the rich West Austin students, the students of color from the east side of town felt more ostracized socially, as we have seen in the vignettes of both Christine Almonte and Hattie Allen. Similarly, a Hispanic male graduate of Austin High explained to us why he did not want to participate in his twenty-year high school reunion, which was being organized by graduates from West Austin: "I think I kind of felt, you know, like, well, why do I need to be a part of this reunion when, you know, they didn't really feel like opening, you know, opening their arms to us when we were in high school, you know."

Even West Charlotte High School, which was reportedly less hierarchical in terms of cliques because of its history as a black school, the broad range of social class diversity among both whites and blacks, and the fact that the school drew students from so many different junior high schools, had what many graduates referred to as "the Myers Park clique" of white students from one of the most affluent neighborhoods of Southeast Charlotte. Still, as one of the white graduates who lived in Myers Park and was technically part of that "clique" explained, "I had friends that were [of all] backgrounds, but there were definitely cliques, groups, and, you know . . . along racial lines and some of it was along socioeconomic lines, and some of it was just on the cool people . . . the jocks and the cheerleaders and just like every school."

Echoing the views of several of his former classmates, a white male graduate of Muir High School said that there were some racially mixed cliques, particularly what he called "the intellectual cliques" and some of the "burnout" groups. But for the most part, he said, students at Muir gravitated toward the group that most represented what type of person they were, and "You know, you could tell that most of the groups were either, you know, one race or another."

Even the lower-status groups at Muir were fairly segregated by race. A white female graduate described the clique referred to as the "Lodis"—the white "druggie" kids who hung out on the soccer field and smoked; "that was their subculture." While the Lodis were mostly white, she noted, there was another group of black kids who were drug users, but supposedly the two druggie groups—one white and one black—did not mix.

Overall, then, at Muir and the other five schools, graduates and educators reported that cliques were largely divided along lines of race and class, though many cliques had some degree of racial mixing. In fact, one of the more interesting findings to emerge from the Muir data was that most people saw their own cliques as diverse racially but the school as a whole as having mostly racially separate cliques. This finding may relate more to the often somewhat porous boundaries between cliques that looked more rigid to those outside them: graduates often report that they were not really a member of just one clique and that they instead saw themselves as part of many groups.

Four of the high schools we studied—Austin, Dwight Morrow, Muir, and Topeka—had more than a smattering of Latino students back in the 1970s, and in three of these (all but Topeka High) many graduates noted that the Latinos tended to remain more separate from the other non-Latino students—white, black, or Asian. As Geri, the Muir graduate highlighted in the vignette above, noted: "My opinion is that Hispanics at our school, there was a very strong clique; they all hung out together, and they all dated each other." At Dwight Morrow, the graduates also noted, the Hispanic students were more isolated—in part because they were mostly recent immigrants who were not English proficient and often played soccer instead of football or baseball. And at Austin High, several white students commented on how the Hispanic students kept more to themselves. As one West Austin white woman noted: "You know, we didn't have any problems with black people. . . . My opinion was the black people didn't have problems with white people. They called us honky. We called 'em black . . . black people or something like that. It was the Hispanics, as a group, as a whole, who caused more conflict. . . . They ran in groups, whereas the black and white people seemed to intermingle a little bit easier."

Class as Important as Race?

The distinct presence of a small group of white, affluent students with enormous social clout and ability to intimidate other students was by far most pronounced at Austin High and speaks to age-old characteristics of how race and class and gender play out in Texas. Still, there is some evidence that the wealthier white students had a social advantage at most of these schools, leading many graduates we interviewed to conclude that class was more of a dividing factor than race. Of course, so few students of color were from affluent families across these schools that at least at the high end of the socioeconomic spectrum the distinction seems moot. But as we noted above, the social class distinctions were very real among white students from different side of the tracks—or the river, as the case may be.

In Englewood, white students felt such social class distinctions when they were merged with the students from Englewood Cliffs in their first year of high school. While there were wealthy white students in the town of Englewood who lived "up the hill" in the First Ward and near the border with Englewood Cliffs, once the Englewood Cliffs students arrived to attend Dwight Morrow High School and merged with the Englewood students in ninth grade, some of the more middle-class white students from Englewood's Third Ward noted that the social class distinctions across white students became more pronounced.

A white Dwight Morrow graduate who had grown up in the more middle-class Third Ward noted when asked who was popular at his high school that the students from Englewood Cliffs "tended to have their own parties, and they tended to be popular." He said that some of the students from Englewood, especially the ones that lived up the hill in the more affluent First Ward, closer to Englewood Cliffs, would go to these parties. "So geographically the white, rich kids tended to be closer to the Englewood Cliffs kids and quite separate from us in the Third Ward. . . . That divide makes it more complicated. But the popular kids tended to be, to me, tended to be the more affluent white kids, sort of from up the hill."

Students across the sites were quick to point out that social divisions had more to do with money or class than with race per se. As a white Topeka High graduate noted: "I think it broke more along social economic lines than they did on racial lines." In a more illustrative example of how important social class could be to students on a daily basis, a Latino graduate of Austin High who came from a poor family on the east side of town explained:

> I mean, the differences between a high-class family and a struggling poor family are tremendous. I mean, what's he [an upper-class student] going to say, "Hey, I went to play tennis yesterday with Boomer." . . . And what's the [poor] guy going to say, "Well, I went to go do shoeshines down on Sixth Street to get some money for feeding my little brothers and sisters," I mean, what is there to talk about? So I think what happened was, a lot of people in their own cliques talked about their own experiences and they could identify with them.

The powerful contrast this Austin High graduate makes between the experiences of a rich and a poor student reminds us that the focus on class as opposed to race or ethnicity was disingenuous given the many ways in which the two have been intertwined throughout the history of this country. Class distinctions alone may be more important for less affluent whites, but they were too often tightly woven into experiences on opposite sides of racial and ethnic lines for the graduates of color.

Also, it seemed that when white graduates justified racial divisions as merely by-products of social class, the focus often shifted toward other factors that divided students, including different levels of academic achievement or cultural issues. The white graduates saw these other factors as proxies for social class, but given the histories of racial segregation and inequality within these communities, and given what we documented in chapter 3, these other "factors" were strongly related to race and ethnicity and the socioeconomic disadvantage of black and Latino students in particular. A white West Charlotte graduate who enrolled in the highest-level classes explained the social divisions in his high school this way: "I took it to be more social class, and I would say more academic achievement. . . . So you tended to socialize with those that you knew, and you got to know them through your academic classes. Not necessarily so much through gym or homeroom, which were the melting pots, but through peer discussions in AP history or English."

In a related observation, a white Shaker Heights High graduate explained that even as white people were trying to be color-blind, there was still an expectation that other races should assimilate, and whites tended to get along best with the black kids who were "like acting white." He said: "The kids who caused me the most trouble were the ones who were definitely identifying with an urban, poor, lower socioeconomic demographic. And that's still an issue for me. I'm just still . . . you know, we are attracted and get along with people who are similar." Another white Shaker High graduate told us that there was very little talk of the racial or social class divisions in the school—divisions that were far less pronounced in this school than a place like Austin High. He said that it was a question not of white versus black but rather of "professional versus nonprofessional." He explained, "If you're not going to gain acceptance, it's because people who are there came from professional families and expected to interact with professional families. If you do not gain acceptance from that group, it should not be misconstrued because you are black. Do you understand what I'm saying?"

Of course, the relationship between being black in Cleveland, Ohio, in the 1970s and *not* being a professional was quite profound. While blacks who had moved into Shaker Heights at that time tended to be more middle class than those in Cleveland, as we noted in chapter 1, only about 20 percent of all blacks in the 1960s were considered middle class, compared to about 50 percent of blacks in 2005.[5] Thus, even though there were black students with parents who were professionals at Shaker High School, these distinctions based on education, credentials, and access to professional jobs had many racial dimensions.

But what is interesting about this time period when the class of 1980 was in school versus our more recent history as it relates to social class is that distinctions along class lines have become more pronounced in the last thirty years in the United States, as the gap between the rich and nonrich has widened. As we noted in chapter 1, income inequality has grown at an alarming rate since the 1970s, when the average CEO made thirty-seven times what the average worker made. In 2000, the average CEO made 310 times what the average worker earned.[6]

The gap between what Robert Reich refers to as the "fortunate fifth," or the top 20 percent of income earners, and the bottom four-fifths has grown as these graduates have become adults.[7] Thus they note that social class distinctions are far more pronounced today than when they were in school. For instance, several African American Muir graduates commented on the growing gap between the affluent and poor in Pasadena. As a black woman graduate stated: "I really think at the time in the seventies where we were, it was much more evenly keel." One of her classmates, a black male Muir graduate, argued that back in high school it seemed that they were all middle class. "When I was in high school they started to come with designer clothes. Even then there wasn't a big thing, oh, you have to be wearing such and such clothes, or such and such shoes, we did not have that problem, I think that came after my class."

Similarly, a white female graduate of Topeka High who was a teacher in a nearby suburban school district when we interviewed her, explained that today students are much more caught up in having certain kinds of very expensive jeans and sneakers than when she was in school. She noted that when she was growing up her family was relatively wealthy compared to many of their neighbors but that no one would have known that back then because she wore mostly ripped jeans, and one or two styles of sneakers were popular, neither of which cost $120, as many do now. "I see it now with a lot with kids, and you can really tell the differences [in family income] a lot more. . . . I don't know if we noticed that as much." Betsy Hagart, the white West Charlotte High School graduate we discussed in chapter 4, said that her daughter, who was twelve when we interviewed Betsy, would be criticized at her school for wearing shoes from K-Mart, even though Betsy had grown up wearing such shoes and no one had seemed to notice. Betsy said, "I hate the commercialism that we have now, that we really didn't have as much of. . . . I don't think there was so much pressure on us at West Charlotte."

Popular Students of Color

The term *token* came up fairly frequently in interviews with graduates and educators of color when they were talking about the popularity and acceptance experienced by African American, and to a lesser extent Latino, athletes on the major sports teams at these schools. This phenomenon of the popular black or Latino jock had definite gender implications, as far more male than female students of color were popular in the predominantly white schools. Once again, Austin High was the school where these issues appeared to be most pronounced. Articulating the views of many other graduates of color, a Latino graduate of Austin High explained: "I had the luxury of being very popular, and so I never really had any of the real racial problems that you would think about. And I think, my popularity, I guess, stemmed from being a good athlete as well as doing well in school." Similarly, a black female graduate of Austin High noted that it was a rich school and that students of color had a lot of opportunity if they made friends with the rich white people: "[But] if you weren't into sports and cliques . . . then basically you weren't a part of them. . . . If you weren't in sports you were basically a nobody. If you were good in sports and excelled and you were a stand-out, then they [West Austin students] adopted you. . . . If you weren't their token, then you weren't accepted into their little cliques and into their little party stuff."

A former Austin school board member who is African American stated the issue a bit more bluntly. She asserted: "The only [black] people who really were welcome on the campus in terms of not being threatening were the athletes, because they then enabled these [deseg-regated] schools to compete in areas where they really hadn't thought before." Yet this woman further noted the gender dynamic that resulted from this sort of conditional acceptance of black and Latino athletes only: it "left the African American females in bad shape because these other girls flirted with these guys, who were flattered by the attention. And so the ones who suffered the most, probably, were the African American girls."

While these issues were more pronounced in Austin High, where certain sports, such as football, were highly emphasized, they existed at other schools as well. For instance, at Shaker Heights High School as well the most popular students of color were the athletes, although in some ways the bar was set even higher. As one white Shaker graduate informed us, the black students who were most popular not only had to be athletes but had to have a good sense of humor, be good looking, and come from "nice families, their parents were professionals."

At Topeka High School, black students with some kind of special talent—athletic or dramatic—also felt more accepted. As one African American Topeka graduate explained, unless you had something you could do for the school, you were pretty much ignored by the white students. "If you were good in athletics or something like that or you were a good singer, well, they [the white students] don't really mess with you as much. But they will peg you real quick."

Intimidation from Both Sides

Thus far, our focus has been mostly on the ways students in these racially diverse schools were divided by race and on how the white and affluent students (and often adults as well) used their privilege and power to intimidate students of color and less wealthy whites. In this section we talk about the relatively small amount of evidence that the students of color, particularly the black students, found their own ways to intimidate white students—perhaps in retaliation and perhaps in frustration.

The data here suggest that Betsy Hagart's insights were fairly accurate when she reflected back on her bus ride to West Charlotte and what had happened when the black and mostly poor Piedmont Court students got on the bus and intimidated the white students from her middle-class neighborhood. She stated that she recognized that these students too were frightened about getting on a bus with more affluent white students. "They didn't have the money. That's all they had was the attitude."

The point Betsy was making speaks to an important subtheme in this chapter on the social milieu of the schools. Because the students of color, particularly the black students, were often intimidated in these schools by white privilege and money, they would, on occasion try to intimidate white students by playing on whites' racial attitudes and fears of blacks as violent and aggressive. As a black graduate of Austin High explained, the white students at that highly stratified school did not know how to accept the black students. "There is a stereotype that if you're black you are violent and rude, crazy, and you are disrespectful. Even now they think that, and they are intimidated by a lot of our black students."

Black students' physical intimidation of white students was not the norm, and often it had occurred in junior high school, before the graduates' arrival at the high schools. Still, in more than one case, the fear that these incidents instilled remained with these white students. For instance, a white male graduate of Shaker Heights High School had vivid memories of being picked on by black students in junior high school. "These kids were a little rough, and I was a small kid, shy kid, and it, you know, I was an easy target. So, you know, that was not easy." But by the time this graduate got to the high school, the black students from his junior high school had quit harassing him, and there was very little mention of black students intimidating white students at Shaker High in our interviews with graduates or educators there.

Interestingly enough, black students' acts of intimidation against whites most frequently occurred in the predominantly black schools, where white privilege was actually in the shortest supply but also where black students felt more empowered. The two schools where there were more complaints of such intimidation were the two predominantly black schools—Dwight Morrow and Muir—though even in these sites meaningful threats were not common and were seldom followed through. Still, several white graduates, particularly women, from both Muir and Dwight Morrow told us they were sometimes afraid to go to the bathroom or enter certain parts of these schools that were considered to be dominated by the black students. A former Muir teacher recalled that in the late 1970s, when the school was about one-third white, a few white students at that time "might have been getting mugged for their lunch money or taken advantage of." He said he remember those types of complaints and maybe some harassment of some type, maybe a black toward a white: "The very poorest of student, the one that seemed to be really in trouble, could be the type that kind of looked right through you, and you might feel slightly intimidated."

Similarly, at Dwight Morrow, Larry Rubin, the white graduate we introduced in chapter 1, recalled that some of "the white girls sometimes felt physically threatened, 'cause they'd tell me that they felt that way. Who were they threatened by, the black girls. . . . They were tough." One of Larry's African American classmates, Sydney Morgan, whom we quoted in chapter 4, tried to explain what was happening at Dwight Morrow between the white and black girls at the time. She said: "I think what might have happened is you have a situation where everyone's getting along as equals, and then a white person does something that makes the black person feel like they're trying to put them down, and if you weren't in a position to challenge them intellectually, then the next best thing was to challenge them physically."

Indeed, white graduates were more likely to remember threats or unrealized fears of intimidation than actual incidents of being intimidated in high school by students of color. And even when these acts did occur, they tended not to be major events. A white female graduate of Dwight Morrow who lived in Englewood Cliffs and had attended all-white schools until high school explained: "I got bullied a little bit by some of the tough black girls, like I said, [but] it didn't really bother me. I kind of brushed it off." Other white students were less resilient, and even though nothing happened to them at Dwight Morrow they were fearful of some of the tougher and poorer black students and would do all they could to avoid them, including not going into certain bathrooms or hallways.

Meanwhile, the stories of white graduates from some of the other schools remind us that if you are not from the most affluent white group in your school, intimidation can cut more than one way. For instance, a white Austin High graduate from a working- to middle-class family talked about being physically intimidated by Hispanics and blacks in junior high school but feeling more intimidated by rich white girls when she got to high school. She remembered feeling very self-conscious in high school about the clothes she was wearing and whether the elite, affluent white girls were looking at her: "I think it was the whole . . . probably the whole atmosphere. . . . I mean, when you walked into the building and went upstairs, there was a group and they were the popular group, and . . . I mean, so when you walked by they were looking at you, I mean, you knew that they were judging you by, you know, whatever."

EXTRACURRICULAR ACTIVITIES

Despite the many forces working against interracial friendships in multiracial schools, within the more intimate spaces of the extracurricular activities at these high schools some of the most meaningful cross-racial ties were formed. Whether playing on athletic teams or working on student government projects, students in racially diverse schools often came into closer and more meaningful contact with students of other races in these venues than they generally did in their classes or racially separate social spaces.

At the same time, as we discuss in more detail below, a smaller number of "elite" or "ethnic" organizations reinforced the racial divisions within the school by including only white or only black and/or Latino or Asian students. And in some instances athletic teams were also strongly segregated by race, either because the black students were better at that particular sport, as in the case of the basketball team at Dwight Morrow High School, or because the sport was one that mostly affluent (meaning mostly white students) had had access to before high school, as in the case of the hockey team at Shaker High or the tennis teams at Austin High.

Thus two powerful themes emerged from our study regarding extracurricular activities in these six schools. The first was that, on average, athletic teams, clubs, and other organizations such as band, choir, or student government created social spaces that, more than the school classrooms and corridors, students could enter as equals to work toward common goals.[8] The second theme was that, simultaneously, several of these activities were also divided by race. Indeed, the pages of the 1980 yearbooks from these six schools tell the story of a team-by-team and club-by-club mix of racial integration and segregation that is quite striking.

These findings corroborate other studies of desegregated schools and extracurricular activities.[9] For instance, in an article analyzing the content of yearbooks from 193 multiracial high schools, including pictures of 8,849 teams and other organizations, Charles Clotfelter found that the nonwhite students enrolled in those schools tended to be, on average, slightly underrepresented in school activities—they made up 24.9 percent of the students but only 20.7 percent of the members of teams and clubs. Furthermore, because the racial composition of each activity was uneven—a phenomenon that was prevalent in the schools we studied as well—the average white student member was part of an organization that was only 15 percent nonwhite.

Still Clotfelter concludes that the rate of interracial contact for these students, although clearly less than its theoretical maximum given the overall makeup of the schools, "appears to be much higher within these extracurricular activities than what would occur if friendships were the only vehicle for interracial contact outside the classroom."[10] For the graduates we studied, this was certainly the case. These former students recall that participation in many extracurricular activities provided the "integrated moments" that they would have otherwise lacked even in the most multiracial of schools.

Integrated Moments

Across the six high schools in our study, bands—marching and otherwise— seemed to unite more students from diverse racial and ethnic backgrounds and across genders than any other single activity. The types of bands in the different schools varied according to the history, tradition, and demographics of these schools. But whether they were jazzy and rhythmic or stiff and reserved, they served the same integrative purpose.

A white graduate of Dwight Morrow High School who was in the marching band, concert band, and jazz band recalled the young black band director, who was a phenomenal saxophone player and brought in a lot of nontraditional music for the students to play. The graduate, a woman who was living in midtown Manhattan with her husband and young children at the time of our interview, remembered fondly how the Dwight Morrow marching band "used to be the talk of the football games because the other marching bands would go out there and do these real rigid [routines], you know, and our band was doing like this funky music, we were bopping around, nothing rigid; I wish I could see it in video, I wonder if anyone ever had a video of it." She and her classmates described the all-black color guard that would dance with the marching band, and "people would just scratch their heads. . . . It wasn't a normal marching band, there's no way, not at all. . . . Cheerleaders too, same sort of, like, funky cheering, rather than the real rigid, usual type of cheerleading. . . . Yeah, I loved it, I mean, I thought it was great." The marching band at West Charlotte and the drum corps at Muir High School had a similar reputation and style, although Muir's drum corps had very few white students, while Dwight Morrow and West Charlotte's bands were more reflective of the overall student population.

In other performing arts as well, including drama and choir, students came together across racial lines. West Charlotte, in particular, was known for its strong theater program, and the graduates who partici-pated in those productions remember them as very integrated and very rewarding. A white West Charlotte graduate recalled that she "had sev-eral really, really good black friends" who were very active in the theater program with her in both junior high and high school, "and there was a lot of, a lot of talent . . . in West Charlotte. A lot of . . . really, really smart black people . . . and white people. But I mean, you know, to me, that was one of the gifts of West Charlotte, was to see . . . that they're no dif-ferent. Just because the color of their skin happens to be different, it, you know, it doesn't matter."

Graduates spoke in similar ways about student government, which was diverse at all of the schools—in some because of racial quotas for who could be elected and in others by the luck of the vote. Several of the white West Charlotte graduates recalled the discussion on the student council their senior year about the kind of graduation announcements they would order. One of these white graduates from an affluent family on the east side of town explained: "I just remember how some of the black members of the council felt very differently from the white mem-bers of the council about what the graduation announcement should look like. It just seemed a silly, trivial thing, but I think it illustrated that we came from different cultural expectations as to what was traditional or desirable." They ended up ordering the announcements that the black students picked out, which were more colorful—flamboyant, even— than the more traditional (by white upper-class standards) announce-ments chosen by the white students. Another white student who was on the student council at the time said that she and several other students just laughed about the announcements when they imagined what their more traditional and monied relatives and family friends would wonder about the kind of school they were attending.

Beyond the music, drama, and student government, there was the all-powerful arena of sports and cheerleading. The racial makeup of dif-ferent teams, particularly the most high-status high school teams of football and basketball, varied across the schools because of the overall demographics of the schools. Thus far fewer white students were on the football or basketball teams of Dwight Morrow or Muir, and there was much more racial mixing on those teams at the other schools. As Geri, the Latino graduate of Muir High whom we introduced at the beginning of the chapter, recalled the basketball team, "Ninety percent of our team was African Americans and the other 10 percent was Caucasians. So it put me into a whole different circle of friends and people."

Similarly, the cheerleading squads at both of these predominantly black schools were also mostly black—and all-black in the class of 1980's senior year at Muir. Meanwhile, as we noted above, at the end of the 1970s there were few black and Hispanic cheerleaders at Austin High because of the strict racial quota. Similar quotas ensured greater diversity of the squads at Topeka and West Charlotte.

Whether these high-profile sports teams and activities were racially mixed or not, there were always some athletic teams that brought students together across racial lines in each of these schools. According to one white graduate of Austin High who grew up in the affluent part of town, "What I found interesting was the diversity, because I stuck with sports going into Austin High, and that's where I really got to meet a lot of different girls from other parts of town. So that was nice to experience." Larry Rubin, the white graduate of Dwight Morrow described in the vignette in chapter 1, explained that his involvement in several sports was critical to his high school experience:

> I don't know how I would have survived. . . . Sports was so huge for me . . . my ego, my self-esteem, and just fitting in. And I think that's where I never felt physically intimidated, 'cause I was friends enough with enough athletes and football players, and . . . I ran on a lot of relay teams in track, for example, with older guys who were black. . . . So if I didn't play sports I don't think I would have known a lot of these people, I wouldn't have been around them, I don't know what I would have done. . . . It definitely, it broke the color barrier.

Similarly, a white Austin High graduate from the less affluent South Austin noted that despite all the social hierarchies in the school, "Where it was very egalitarian was on the sports teams, [which were] much more egalitarian. . . . So that's why I think football games and baseball games looked so different, because everyone's there for . . . a common good, which in that case was, you know, cheer your team on for victory. And it didn't matter who played where. You know, the kids from East Austin played just as well as the kids from South or West Austin, or vice versa. The kids from West Austin played just as well as the other kids. So there was less division there."

Since popular students tended to be the athletes, especially if they were boys, and the cheerleaders if they were girls, racial diversity of the teams and squads did encourage more integration and more egalitarian access to the high-status activities. In fact, at Topeka High School, even the nominees for homecoming queens and kings had to reflect the diversity of the school, which often put white students at a statistical disadvantage if the blacks or Latinos voted in a bloc while the white student vote was split across several candidates. This was helpful in terms of black and Latino students' gaining access to these coveted positions, but it garnered resentment among some of the white students who wanted a better shot at being king or queen.

Still, overall, the interracial contact that these students experienced through their participation in extracurricular activities—and sometimes in classes or other places in these schools—did over time bring them closer together across the color lines toward their senior years of high school. This gradual coming together, after having experiences that dispelled myths and prejudices, was described by the vast majority of graduates we interviewed. As one white graduate of West Charlotte High School noted, most students coming into this desegregated school, which drew black and white students from all over the socioeconomic spectrum and the county, at least initially hung out with the group they were most familiar with. Then, over the years, students would widen their associations, especially to include students they got to know through activities. Through involvement in a number of activities such as student government, this student and his classmates "got to know people from different areas and were certainly comfortable and had friendships with people who were from some of the other groups that came into West Charlotte." He added that at the time he and his peers developed almost an esprit de corps about school desegregation, in part because they saw themselves as distinct because of it: "Most of us were children of people who grew up during the time when you didn't have that level of desegregation of schools. And probably a little bit of the typical adolescence of wanting to do something just a little bit to make your parents feel uncomfortable and almost embrace it a little bit more than you might have otherwise had."

Something similar occurred over time at the other sites, as the then-teenagers remember things changing the longer they were in desegregated schools. According to a white graduate of Dwight Morrow who grew up in Englewood Cliffs, "It just really changed a lot during the years. The first couple of years, I would say no, it wasn't mixed. The kids from EC, we kind of stayed together and hung out and talked to each other during lunch and all that. As you wound up being more confident, [and being the more] senior people in the school, everybody is a lot more mixed."

As a black graduate of Shaker High School explained, the "rubbing elbows" method of school desegregation was far more efficient and meaningful than a briefing session or a workshop: "Meaning—having experience and seeing that there was some natural divisions at lunch, but being able to bridge that in the classroom, being able to bridge that in intramural sports, be able to bridge that with friendships through those events. Then, that was the best teacher than anybody could have ever provided. You couldn't have taught that in a debriefing sessions from adults, you know, trying to get into the mind of a sixteen-year-old."

Exclusive Clubs and Activities

The other side of the extracurricular issue is that some sports teams and activities further divided the students by race instead of bringing them closer together because not all students had the same ability, access, or desire to be a part of them. In each of the six schools—and in some more than others, depending on the demographics—certain teams and clubs were racially identifiable and segregated. In athletics, across the different schools, teams such as golf, tennis, water polo, swimming, bowling, and hockey—to the extent that a given school had each of these—tended to be all or mostly white. This racial skew clearly reflected who had access to the opportunities to learn these sports as children.

At times issues of access included a lack of information about how to join a certain group or try out for a team. For instance, Christine Almonte from Austin High School noted that it had been very difficult for her to get information on how to join the volleyball team: "I had to do all of that on my own . . . like finding out . . . how to do that. How to go to tryouts, how to do stuff like that. . . . Nothing was ever handed to us, like, 'We're having volleyball tryouts.'" And at times, as Hattie's story about the tennis try out at Austin High reminds us, students felt that the tryouts themselves were not fair.

As we noted above, in the predominantly black high schools of Dwight Morrow and Muir, certain sports, especially basketball and football, had few white players by the late 1970s. This further marginalized the white male students who either were not good enough to make those teams or simply did not try out because there were so few whites. As one black Muir graduate noted, "Sports was again based on race. The water polo team was white, and tennis, and they had a couple of blacks that played tennis. Basketball and football was pretty much black."

We know from Larry Rubin's experience playing football at Dwight Morrow High School that at least some of the white students who played on those teams in the predominantly black high schools found it very rewarding and made close black friends. But sometimes the white boys would not even consider going out for teams that they deemed as being for the black athletes only. Even in predominantly white Topeka High School, the varsity men's basketball team had become almost entirely black, with only one white player in the 1979–80 school year. As a result, a few of the white male graduates we interviewed twenty-plus years later who had played basketball growing up said that they had opted not to try out for the high school basketball team and to play for a municipal league team instead.

In addition to these sometimes segregated athletic teams, certain clubs or organizations were also one-race-only. Some traditionally elite clubs such as Key Clubs were made up of almost exclusively white and often very affluent students; others, especially ethnocentric clubs such as a Black Student Union, were all-black or all-Latino. One of the Latino male graduates of Austin High School remembered being invited to join the

Key Club. He said that he went to one meeting, but "it was all white guys in the Key Club, no Hispanics at all. . . . After that I didn't go because I didn't feel comfortable there, because I just felt so out of place. . . . I didn't fit in, I could tell these were all rich white guys you could tell had a lot of money, and I just didn't feel like I wanted to be a part of that club, so I chose not to be a part of that club." Similarly, a black graduate of Muir explained that his black peers would have considered him a "nerd" if he did anything like Chess Club or State Club: "There was always one or two black kids who did that, and of course they were considered the Oreos of the class."

Several of the schools we studied had female clubs or organizations. For instance, Austin High School had the Red Jackets, which was mostly made up of wealthy white girls from West Austin. At Muir High School there were a couple of service clubs for girls that were the female equivalents of the Key Club. Then there was the group called Interact, a co-ed service club that was very popular with white students as well. Such service clubs are, by definition, more attractive to students who have more family resources and thus the luxury of having their own immediate needs met, which allows them to spend time providing services to others. As a result, at each of these schools the traditional service clubs for the most part attracted white and middle-class or affluent students.

Meanwhile the black and Latino students were gathering together in ethnic clubs such as the Black Student Union or MECHA, which were geared toward supporting these students academically and socially. While the graduates of color were fairly clear about why these organizations were needed, particularly back in the 1970s as the first generation of desegregation moved through the schools, the white graduates were less supportive of them and often noted their segregating effects on the schools. As one white Muir graduate commented, "All the different clubs and organizations seemed to clique—according to racial lines, and there didn't seem to be any . . . anything from the top to try to direct that or within the students." Another white Muir graduate, a woman who was very active in several clubs and organizations in the school asked: "Why couldn't . . . you know, I, as a Caucasian, be able to, you know, be a part of BSU? And probably, if I had pursued it, I probably could've! I don't think they probably would've had any, you know, requirements. . . . Yet, nobody ever, nobody ever challenged it."

Interestingly enough, we rarely heard white graduates critique the predominantly white clubs in this same way, perhaps because their racial affiliation was more subtle. Meanwhile, the students of color who joined these ethnic clubs said they did so to have a place where they could be involved in the school but on their own terms. As one black graduate from Muir explained it, she joined the Black Student Union because "most of the clubs, like the ski clubs and all the other clubs that didn't sound very interesting, most of them were predominately white. . . . So for me it was like, black people don't ski."

Sociologists who study ethnic student organizations on college campuses say that these clubs provide safe spaces where students learn to survive and gain critical navigation skills in a system that devalues their ethno- and sociocultural experiences. Thus ethnic organizations often served an important purpose that white students in many instances did not understand.[11] To the extent that white students in racially mixed schools were less aware of the need for ethnic clubs than were the students of color, they also seemed less aware of the barriers they, their parents, and the larger society had erected to the cross-racial friendships that did develop.

THE LIMITS OF CROSS-RACIAL FRIENDSHIPS

As we discussed briefly in chapter 3, the larger, segregated context of these high schools prevented students from spending much time with students of other racial/ethnic groups outside school. There were logistical challenges to getting students together when they lived across town from each other. The distance between white and black and Latino neighborhoods also meant that individuals were unfamiliar with areas on the other side of the color lines and thus were often afraid to cross them. Also, as we noted in chapter 3, it was often the parents of the white students, in particular, who squelched their children's efforts to bring home friends of other races or to visit classmates who lived in other, racially segregated neighborhoods.

Thus logistics, fear, and prejudice worked against cross-racial friendship development outside the schools. In addition, students often lacked the common experiences or ways of making sense of the world—and its inequality—that allowed them to take their friendships much further. In fact, it became difficult for close cross-racial friendships to develop, given the many forms of "distance" across racial (and class) lines.

Comments by the white graduates illustrate that cross-racial friendships could go only so far. One of the white male Topeka High graduates who had been in the band for several years in high school said he had developed friendships with members of all three racial/ethnic groups, blacks, whites, and Latinos—"and we were all pretty much friends for the most part"—but he qualified this further by adding, "Again, not friends in terms that they would come to my house. . . . I would see them at school and just normal friendships just through those kinds of encounters." Likewise, a white woman who had been involved in theater and chorus at West Charlotte and had made several black friends through those activities noted: "I had a network and groups of friends I feel was pretty diverse there at school, but I didn't necessarily, you know, hang out with them on the weekends."

When students of color did end up at white students' houses, it was often part of a team activity or a party, although many weekend parties at these schools were also segregated by race. According to a white graduate of Austin High, parties or activities on the weekends were rarely mixed: "You know, you're all together at school and you all got along at school, but when you left school you were pretty much [segregated]. I can't think of any instance where I went to a party, say over in East Austin, or in South Austin, for that matter. You know, that I just didn't feel welcomed down in South Austin."

Weekend parties at students' houses tended to be more racially mixed at Dwight Morrow and Muir High Schools, especially by the senior year of high school for this class. As a white graduate of Dwight Morrow who lived in Englewood Cliffs explained: "I mean, my senior year was really when I remember the sort of interracial relationships really sort of flourishing. . . . I do remember, you know, going to all these parties and they were very, you know, integrated."

Another white Austin High graduate who was on the football team recalls bringing as much of the football team as he could, "blacks, Hispanics, and white guys," over to his house to have his family's cook— "a big, extremely large, black lady"—make them fried chicken on the Fridays before games: "The best fried chicken you'd ever taste in your life. . . . Every Friday afternoon my house would have five to ten to fifteen guys in it, of all cultures, eating fried chicken together before games during football season. And it was just great friendships."

These kinds of group activities, tied to a team effort or a larger party, were more prevalent than close personal friendships. Across all the sites and all the racial/ethnic groups, it was very unusual for anyone to tell us that their closest friends were of a different racial/ethnic group from their own. In fact, the following quote from a white Topeka High School graduate was typical: "Well, my three best friends in high school were three other white girls just like me. We were really not in a clique of any kind, and we socialized with and actually we had friends in all three of the main [racial groups]. . . . My personal group of friends was mostly white people, but there were black too, but mostly on the weekends it was just us four."

INTERRACIAL DATING

Like the former students' most intimate friendships, interracial dating was highly circumscribed by race, class, gender, and school: when it occurred, it was almost exclusively between more middle-class male students of color and white girls. Also, as we noted, interracial dating was virtually nonexistent at Austin High School and West Charlotte High, the two most southern schools in the study; it was not at all unusual at Dwight Morrow, Muir, and Shaker High; and at Topeka High it was somewhere in the middle, neither highly unusual nor extremely common. These distinctions had a lot to do with larger issues of race in the contexts of these communities.

In a city like Austin, Texas, in the late 1970s, interracial dating was completely unacceptable. As one Austin High graduate responded when asked if there was any such dating when she was in school: "This is the Bible Belt." We posed the same question to the white Austin High graduate who had invited football players over to his house to eat the fried chicken that his black cook had made. He said: "Not much. It wasn't as accepted. . . . A girl in our group . . . she was white, did better with black guys than she did with white guys, and we all thought she was weird. I remember having a couple crushes on Hispanic girls, but never saying it out loud. . . . I think we were not very accepting of people who went there, which is I guess some hypocrisy on our part."

White graduates of West Charlotte gave similar answers. "Maybe one, two couples," a white West Charlotte graduate told us. "It would've been taboo. . . . I would say interracial relationships were not—if they were there, they were—it was hidden. You know, it was behind a big black cloud or whatever." The behind-the-scenes dimension of interracial dating at West Charlotte High School was confirmed by a black graduate who seemed to think that it was more prevalent than her white counterparts did. She said there was "a lot" of interracial dating, "but then, some of it was behind the scenes and nobody knew about it."

In schools such as Austin High or West Charlotte High, where the taboo against such dating was stronger, the exceptions seemed to have stricter requirements. In other words, the conditions upon which interracial dating could be accepted by the popular white students had to do with the social class, family, and behavior of the student of color involved in the relationship. One white Austin High graduate from an affluent family stated that interracial dating between blacks and whites was "not looked upon well" but recalled an instance of Hispanic-white dating that was okay because of who the Hispanic boy was: "There was a real popular Hispanic guy. . . . He's from South Austin actually, but he went to junior high with us and went through high school. And he dated some white girls. And . . . that was fine. The Hispanics didn't like it, but he was . . . his family was more in the upper socioeconomic class than some of the other Hispanics, and . . . and in fact his brother married a girl in my class. But that wasn't looked upon negatively from the whites' perspective 'cause he was very . . . he was one of us. I mean, he was very well accepted."

In the other four schools where interracial dating was more prevalent, the gender dynamic became more pronounced. Across all of these sites, when such dating did occur, it was almost always white girls dating black boys. Rarely if ever did white boys date black girls, and for the most part, the black boys who dated white girls were often more middle-class and the most athletic and popular of the "jocks." This trend ended up being most problematic for the black girls, who were not being asked out by the white boys and who were insulted by the implication that white girls were more desirable dates. And in schools like Dwight Morrow, where the population of white girls was small, white boys who said they did not feel comfortable dating black girls had fewer white girls to date.

Although the graduates of all racial backgrounds were generally loath to explore the racialized and gendered reasons why the interracial dating followed this consistent trend, a few interviewees suggested that prevailing white norms regarding beauty and culture drove the dating dynamic in favor of white girls, who were seen as prettier and more compliant than black girls. But for the most part, the ways in which white privilege influenced the interracial dating scene, like so many manifestations of white privilege in these schools, went unexplored.

One white female graduate of Topeka said she remembered it was a "big deal" for some of her white friends to be dating some of the jocks, "and a lot of those guys were black." She added, "A lot of the white girls did date them. I know that there were some, and I could hear from some of the black girls that they didn't like that the white girls were dating the black guys." Her black female classmate from Topeka High had a deeper analysis of this situation and why she was opposed to it. "I had a problem with it for the reasons that were being stated that white women were seen as being more . . . or less aggressive and not as demanding, and to me . . . I found that to be personally offensive as making a stereotype and a classification of all black women." She said that looking back on her years at Topeka High she saw the trend of popular white girls dating popular black boys as "demeaning to me."

In the end, several dimensions of the social milieu of racially mixed schools were demeaning to different students at different times across these diverse contexts. This is true, no doubt, in any high school, as adolescence is a difficult time of life, and teenagers are quite often not nice to each other.[12] But adding racial diversity to the process of coming of age, and asking this cohort of teenagers to deal with issues that their parents, for the most part, had not, made the journey that much more challenging.

Since the adults in their lives at that time did next to nothing to help them better understand their place in history or the monumental hurdles they had to overcome if they were to have meaningful and strong relationships across race, the members of the class of 1980 were left to make their way on their own. On their own, they quite often made a friend or two across racial lines and felt quite fulfilled to have had such experiences. But they were not prepared to understand just how fragile these relationships would be or how frequently they would be compromised by the broader racial inequality that framed their lives then and today. As a white male graduate of Shaker Heights explained it, he only began a long struggle of crossing color lines in high school. He said that today he still has some interracial friends but that the segregated nature of our society works against these relationships in many ways. "I like a lot of black people, but at the same time, there are these broader issues," he said, laughing a hopeless sort of laugh. "It will be my struggle till I'm old and gray."

SIX Why It Was Worth It

When she was a student at Shaker Heights High School in the late 1970s, Maya Deller was passionate about changing the world. By the early 2000s, when we met her, this fiery, redheaded white woman was a successful lawyer in a Cleveland law firm. She was divorced with three young children and lived in a community not far from Shaker Heights. And like many adults in their early forties, Maya had modified her life goals. But she still wanted make a difference—a desire she had developed as a young child in Brooklyn, New York, and then as an adolescent in Shaker Heights. In both places she was compelled by the diverse experiences of the people she met.

Taking an early evening break from her work at the law firm one fall day, Maya sat in a wood-paneled restaurant an elevator ride away from her office in one of the city's tallest buildings. She sipped a glass of wine pensively and recalled what she had hoped to accomplish when she was in high school. At the time she had wanted to be an elected official and have "a positive impact on the lives of many, many people." Some of the problems she had wanted to address were poverty, racial and ethnic inequality, lack of education, lack of opportunities, and general issues of injustice. "I actually still don't understand why things have to be that way, and I really, really wanted to change them."

As a grownup with bills to pay and children to raise, Maya said she has become more focused on the local level and the lives she touches each and every day. She said she still tries to make a difference, but more

on an individual basis with the people she comes in contact with personally and professionally: "So it's more of a local-level thing than a
national or international thing, which is not to say that there aren't
people in the world who affect people's lives on a national and international, grossly huge level, but I'm . . . I don't think I'm one of those
people, and it's okay. I found other ways . . . to feel that my place in the
world is meaningful."

Maya described herself as "outgoing," "dramatic," and still a bit high-
strung—"I'm a little less high-strung—believe it or not—than I used to
be!" With this energetic profile, she had taken on one local cause that
might have appeared to be a losing battle to a less tenacious person.
Basically, she was trying to stem the white flight from her school district,
where one of her older children was enrolled and where her third child
would enter kindergarten the following fall. In her inner-ring suburb
next to the Cleveland border and not far from Shaker Heights, more and
more of the white families were either putting their children in private
schools or fleeing to suburbs farther from the city and the African
Americans who live there.

Maya was frustrated by this white flight. She said that the district's
sole high school, which was about 70 percent black and 30 percent white,
was just "great" but that it got a lot of bad press. She said that she thought
the bad press was due to the fact that "there are so many black people
there, which makes me sick to my stomach."

She said that she is determined that her kids will go to that high school
"unless there's a good reason why they can't for some academic reason,
you know, their own personal styles." But she said that the high school
continues to attract fewer and fewer of the white students from the community: "Between the Catholic families sending their kids to Catholic
school and the Jewish families sending their kids to Jewish school and
the rich families sending themselves to really expensive schools, you end
up with a high school that is not reflective of the racial balance of the
community, and it bothers me a lot."

Maya said she realizes that this as an uphill battle because the local
papers fuel the parents' desire to leave by presenting the high school as
a gang school, when she knows from her neighbors' children who

babysit for her that it is not a violent or frightening place. Times have changed, she said, since she was in school, and peoples' priorities are different. She sees white parents and students in particular as less political and more materialistic. "Of course, when we went to school, it was, like, the late seventies, early eighties, and . . . because the seventies, you know, the beginning of the seventies was the war and Watergate and all that kind of stuff, and people were really serious and political . . . but the end of the seventies and into the eighties, people were so done with that."

She notes that her generation was caught in the middle of the more liberal sixties and early seventies and the more conservative eighties and nineties. Having experienced a bit of both eras, she said, "We get all the guilt feelings of being in this really materialistic society when . . . our formation years were really, like, liberal, 'Let's save the world' kind of thing."

Maya spent much of that first half of her life in Brooklyn, New York, from the time she was born until she was eleven, when she moved to Shaker Heights. She recalled that Brooklyn was "really, really racially diverse, and the particular area in Brooklyn that we lived, there were not a lot of white families . . . 'cause it was pregentrification."

Maya is Jewish; she is certain that at the time her family was the only Jewish family in her mostly black Brooklyn neighborhood. Those experiences in New York, she said, profoundly affected her. When she moved to Shaker Heights in the sixth grade, she was struck by how predominantly white her neighborhood elementary school was: "In sixth grade, I remember . . . there were, like, three black people in the whole class, and it was very bizarre for me."

Not until she went to junior high and then high school in Shaker did she have more black classmates. But in junior high, three of the black students—a small group of girls—used to pick on her. She recalled that these girls "were really scary and very tough." She said that she was small for her grade because she was a year younger than everybody else and was not a big person. "Actually, one girl [laughs] threatened to beat the shit out of me! And I was saved by the grace of God or something, 'cause I definitely would have lost a fistfight, no question!"

To this day, Maya is not sure what prevented this black girl from attacking her. But she looked back on that moment in her schooling history as an aberration and something that she would never generalize from to describe her overall experience in racially diverse schools. Yet, she noted, some white people might do that. Maya, on the other hand, will tell you that she also had many more "experiences that were very positive, and so in that way, by knowing not just one person but by knowing a base of people, it was easier not to generalize." She added, "Color is such a visible thing, just like gender is. . . . I mean, race is such a hugely visible thing that I think it makes it so much easier for people to generalize based on [one incident] when that may very well be very unfair."

Maya found Shaker Heights High School to be a calmer place than the junior high, and she did not recall any kind of physical intimidation there. She said that the only sort of intimidation she faced in high school was social rather than physical and that it came from popular and "WASPy" white students rather than from any of the students of color. She remembered, for instance, being very aware of the different "social layering" and the "echelons" and "cliques" at Shaker and seeing that the most popular kids were all "white and blond and WASPy and from money." She explained with a nervous sort of laugh in her voice, "I felt more intimidated from them than I ever felt . . . from anybody who was black at school. . . . I did not feel physically intimidated in high school by black people. I felt socially intimidated by popular, white, bitchy girls."

She went on to explain that these girls were very popular and that everybody knew who they were: "They were very attractive. They probably had lots of dates and boyfriends and went to parties and were in on everything and had the right clothes and looked like they were really fitting in."

Perhaps Maya's most painful memory of high school was when one of these very popular, blonde white girls knocked into her in the hallway and all of her Advanced Placement Modern Civilization books—a large stack of them because she never had time to go to her locker—fell to the floor with a loud thud. "I mean, she knocked all this shit out of . . . my hands—and she just looked at me like I was garbage and that I was in her way and that she owned the halls. . . . I mean, that kind of thing."

In addition to the wealthy WASPy students, many of the Shaker athletes and cheerleaders, whether they were WASPy or not, were very popular, Maya said. She remembered that football was a "big thing": "If you were good in sports, you were popular. And I actually think there were a ton of black people who were really popular, especially the guys who played football."

Maya also remembered not sticking out because of her religion, since there was a fairly large population of Jewish students at Shaker: she guessed that maybe 20 percent of the students, which would have been about a third of the white students, were Jewish. "I would not say that at Shaker . . . that me being Jewish was an issue for anybody."

So, despite the intimidation by some of the popular white girls, Maya has fond memories of Shaker High, in large part because it was big and so diverse that she could just be herself and not try to fit into one particular group or way of being. "You know, this is the beauty of a school like Shaker, which is large, as opposed to schools that are small where there are only a hundred students and ninety of the students totally fit in and then five or ten of the students think they will never fit in anywhere. You can find your friends and find your place . . . and your life doesn't rise and fall on the graces of some blond-haired, blue-eyed person."

Echoing the sentiments of her classmates and fellow graduates at the other high schools, Maya said that issues of race, or the different ways that students across different racial groups made sense of what was happening at their school, were never officially discussed in her classes. Maya saw this lack of a dialogue about race as a missed opportunity because, she said, "Even if there isn't a racial issue in terms of, like, problems . . . you definitely experience the world differently depending on your background and who you are and where you come from. So I can't imagine that people who are women, men, Jews, non-Jews, blacks, whites, Asians, Hispanic, don't experience it differently, and it's just really interesting to hear of their experiences. I mean, it makes you a more sensitive and aware person, so even if it's not a problem, it's so interesting to talk about it."

Like the vast majority of the former students we interviewed across the six schools, Maya, who had been enrolled almost exclusively in the highest-track classes, said that most of her cross-racial connections to students occurred in extracurricular activities. As a member of the Drama Club, she said, "Race wasn't an issue in terms of interactions among the students."

Although Maya was not a big sports fan, she did consider the sports teams and other extracurricular activities to be the "great equalizers and diversifiers" of the school—the places that would bring students together across racial lines even when they were more separated across classrooms. She saw these more integrated spaces of her racially diverse school as being very important: "I mean, it's really good to make connections with people based on interests and not based on how much money your dad makes or what color you are or what religion you are . . . to share interests and values with people who are different than you, and develop friendships along those lines."

A big part of why she is fighting to maintain the racial diversity in her children's school district today, she will tell you, is that she has a strong conviction that learning to cross these racial, social class, and religious dividing lines is a fundamental lesson in preparing children for a diverse society. Maya talked about the ethnic and racial fighting in places such as Bosnia, Africa, and the Middle East and how much of this violence stems from people not really knowing each other. Thus, when asked what could be accomplished by having racially diverse schools in the United States, she began a long and impassioned explanation: "I mean . . . it's a lot easier to be afraid of people you don't really know. When you know that people are just people, they love their families, they care about their kids, they want their kids to learn to read and write and have a future, they want to be happy, they want their kids to be happy . . . how can you be afraid of that?"

At the same time, Maya was aware of the many ways that race mattered in her high school. She said she realized that it had to be "extremely difficult" for a black student who was not an athlete to still be accepted. "I don't know if a black kid could be popular for just being good-looking and nice or whether they had to be in either sports or a cheerleader."

She said she was also aware that black students were sometimes "steered away from AP classes, whereas white kids would be steered towards AP classes." She said that she was sure that the black students at Shaker sometimes felt intimidated too. For instance, she said, in the AP classes, "I can't even imagine what it was like to be one of the two or three or one black students in a class of all white kids. I can't. And I know that there were kids like that."

After graduating from Shaker Heights High, Maya attended a top-ranked college where the few black students who attended were mostly segregated into separate black sororities and fraternities, while the white students were in white sororities and fraternities, some of which were separated into non-Jewish and Jewish. Maya did not join any of these organizations, but she said she suffered as a result of them because so many students were members, and thus the social life on campus was very segregated by race, religion, and social status.

Since Maya graduated from Shaker High, she has lived in several cities, including New York, where she worked as a prosecutor after law school, but she said her exposure to people of color has been much more limited. Even when she has come into contact with blacks as an adult the interaction has been far less intimate and meaningful than it was in high school, where she worked on plays and other activities side by side with black students. She explained that you do come into contact with "tons of people," whether riding the subway or shopping in Toys R Us or whatever, "but you don't have real interaction with those people. When you're in school, you have a group of two thousand, three thousand, one thousand, five hundred, whatever it is, of people you . . . come into more intimate contact with. There are levels of intimacy, and you're not friends with or enemies with everybody, and some people you probably ignored and had very little to do with, but . . . you have more intimate levels of contact with a more diverse group than you normally would just going to work and going home."

Thus, in part because of her memories of more meaningful interactions with African American students when she was at Shaker Heights High School, Maya was determined to educate her children in a racially diverse environment. When her oldest child, her son, was ready to go to school, she said she got some pressure from her in-laws to send him to a Jewish day school. "That was never appealing" to Maya because of the homogeneity of the students in such schools: "I could not imagine taking my kids out and putting them in a school where everybody's white and has money. I think that's a really bad thing to do. I mean, it might be a great thing to do in terms of financially for my kids' future 'cause they all get to hobnob with the future CEOs of real Fortune 500 companies, and so they'll be filthy rich someday, but I don't think it makes them better people or happier people. And I think it's not that interesting a life, to tell you the truth."

Maya is clear that her passion about these issues stems, in part, from her positive encounters with black students on a daily basis in Shaker High. These experiences dispelled any preconceived notions she had had about black people and overrode her one bad experience with the three black girls in junior high. The importance of these daily interactions in school when children are still young enough to move beyond stereotypes is critical, Maya said, and it explains why she is not afraid of people simply because of their race. But, she noted, "If you have no experience with anybody black except for the TV news or . . . some media bullshit thing, then . . . maybe you do get creeped out just because they're black."

Maya still shakes her head when she sees white families moving out of the school district where she lives now and heading to more eastern suburbs: "That's where everybody goes, is east of here, to all-white schools or where there are, you know, two black kids and an Asian kid." She noted that the youth culture in these outer-ring, affluent suburbs is "messed up" in terms of money and kids having a lot of material things, including cars, drugs, and alcohol—"but . . . you never hear about that." She added that in the schools in such suburbs children cannot become friends with people from different racial or social class backgrounds, and everyone is similar in terms of having lots of money, living in huge houses, and "everybody gets a car for their sixteenth birthday." In schools like Shaker High and the schools her children attend, however, "You can be friends with somebody . . . visibly different than you because when your interests are the same, whether it's photography club or drama club or chess club or sports or marching band . . . or choir, you can become friends with people who look different from you because they are there and you have similar interests."

. . . . .

In 2002, Quentin Dennis, an African American graduate of John Muir High School's class of 1980, was living in a large house in a predominantly white and affluent suburb of Los Angeles with his wife and two children. At that time he was enjoying a great sense of accomplishment in terms of where he had come from and how far he had traveled on the path of upward mobility.

Quentin grew up in Altadena, a working-class community that is part of the Pasadena Unified School District. His father was a truck driver with a sixth-grade education, and his mother cleaned wealthy people's houses. In fact, his mother attended Central High School in Little Rock, Arkansas, not long after the National Guard had been brought in to keep the peace when the first nine black students enrolled in that school. Quentin admitted that when he was growing up he sometimes he felt ashamed of his parents because of their lack of education or the way they spoke. But he is also grateful to them for all their hard work and their openness about race and acceptance of all people, which, as we know from chapters 3 and 5, was somewhat unusual for the parents of these graduates. "My parents never had a problem with white people. My brother has gone out with two or three white girls; I used to have white girls and girlfriends—girls I dated and just friends—and they used to come by the house all the time." He said one of his white friends used to refer to his mother as "Mom."

In part because of his parents and in part because of his experiences in public schools in Pasadena, Quentin is in many ways a living testimony to the benefits of school desegregation, and he is not shy about expounding on them to whoever will listen. When we visited, Quentin was doing quite well for himself as a police lieutenant in a nearby town. His wife, who graduated from Pasadena High School a couple years later, also had a well-paying job, and together they were living their version of the American Dream.

He said that a large part of his "making it"—that he "plugged away and did it and did okay"—was due to the diversity of his public schools and the insights he gained there. He said he wants people who read this book to know "that desegregation, despite the fears of the people who didn't want it to happen, can work, can produce good people, can produce good friends, can produce good experiences, and . . . it's a necessity."

But as with most people of color in the United States, Quentin's journey from a working-class neighborhood to this more upper-middle-class area of the L.A. region was consistently fashioned by the dynamics of race and race-specific policies such as school desegregation and affirmative action. Beginning in the fourth grade, Quentin was bused from the west side of Pasadena to Field Elementary School on the far east side of town. More than two decades later, Quentin still had fond memories of that east-side school—the "cool teachers"; the lessons about the stock market in fifth grade; the field day activities, including relay races; and the cross-racial friendships he formed. The adult Quentin smiled and noted: "I just will never forget Field Elementary School."

Quentin became friends with a boy who lived right around the corner from the school. The two boys—one black from the west side and the other white from the east side—would occasionally spend the night at each other's houses: "My parents knew his parents, and it was just, it was—it was a blast."

But when the two boys were assigned to different middle schools and high schools, their cross-racial, cross-town friendship faded—like many such friendships Quentin would form growing up in desegregated schools. Quentin noted that while he had many good friends who were white, for the most part they "didn't last." In contemplating why that was, he said:

> I think it's like I said about, you know, they lived in a different part of town, and so you just didn't get a chance to connect. If you're a young person, you don't have the transportation. Your parents aren't taking you way across town. So you just, you know, you talk on the phone a little bit like—and then after that, it just goes away. And I think that's what happened with [his fourth-grade friend]. . . . We went to, you know, these different middle schools, and then he went to a different

high school, and we just didn't—we just didn't communicate. And so, I—I—that was somebody that I lost.

Despite his lost friends along the way, Quentin managed to make new friends of different racial backgrounds as he matriculated through the school system. He describes himself as shy and not popular in high school and said he had been "petrified" of being called up to the board in class. Still, he managed to make friends in his own spaces, and while the majority of these friends were black students from his neighborhood, he also met white and Latino students through his extracurricular activities, including the fishing and printing clubs.

Quentin recalled that while many of the social cliques at Muir High School broke down along racial lines and students at Muir tended to congregate according to race at lunchtime, there were also groups of students who mixed with others. He remembered that greater cross-racial understanding was occurring as white students, who were in the minority at Muir, were learning, "Wow, this is kind of the way, you know, that black guys and black girls act."

He said, for instance, that some of the activities at Muir, such as the drum corps, were "black" in character and thus distinct in their style from the activities of most other schools in the area. He said that while the drum corps was popular there were no white students involved. Then one of the white students finally made it onto the corps while Quentin and his classmates were at Muir. He said that this white corps member was accepted and popular with black and white students alike—"everybody loved him."

Even though race defined certain dimensions of the school, such as the band and the lunchtime spaces, for the most part the issue was not discussed at Muir. Quentin thought this lack of race talk at the school was particularly odd given that those days were not too long after busing had started in Pasadena and "everybody knew about the race problems." He added: "I think people knew about racism and about some tensions and things, but I think we, at that time, I think the thought was to be quiet, to just not address it unless it came up. And I think that's the way we dealt with it."

Yet there were many moments at Muir High School when race was both painfully obvious and "no big deal." According to Quentin, the pep rallies at Muir provided integrated, all-school experiences that were often quite funny because they included the athletes from different sports, some of whom would get up and start dancing with the band in front of the whole school. This was particularly funny, Quentin recalled, when one of the popular white male athletes would "cross the lines" and get up and try to dance with the black athletes. Quentin explained that it did not matter how well the white guy could dance because everybody would love him for trying. "There were things like that that happened, you know, where people got together and it wasn't a big deal, and—and people laughed. Pep rallies . . . and things like that where people came together," he said.

Similarly, even though Quentin's closest friends were black he continued to make meaningful white friends throughout high school. Yet after graduating he was far less likely to see his white friends from Muir. He noted that he does not see any of his white high school friends on a regular basis. In trying to explain how this happened, Quentin said:

> I think that's partly because my white friends that I met when I was in high school, one, were bused in more than likely, and when we graduated from high school, went back to wherever—their part of town, and then branched out and went other places after that. . . . I could drive into my old neighborhood and see, you know, Preston Travis's house, and his parents still live there. I could drive and see Lee Marcus's house and where his parents live, and I could wave to them. I couldn't do that with the white friends because they lived somewhere else, and I probably never knew where they lived anyway. So I couldn't drive through their neighborhood and see if they were still there.

But the neighborhood where Quentin lived in 2002 is quite different from the one in which he grew up. In theory, he should have had more white friends there than he did in high school because the percentage of white people living in this neighborhood was much higher than the percentage of whites at Muir. His huge house—what might well be classified as a "McMansion"—with a boat in the backyard fit right into the surrounding neighborhood, which was not too far from a university and attracted a lot of professionals. What fit in less readily in his neighborhood was his skin color—he told us that out of the forty-two or so houses in this community, his was one of only two black families.

Quentin and his wife bought this house because, he said, he wanted his two daughters to grow up in a "better community where they would have a better chance of excelling." Quentin is quick to add that he does not mean to imply that his kids cannot excel in a predominantly black community—particularly one that is more middle class and has well-educated professionals. But he thought his daughters would do better in a place that was outside L.A.—"not in a town that has a lot of . . . extraneous activities that are going on—drugs, gangs, and all that kind of stuff." He said he wanted them to grow up in a place where "they could concentrate on their academics and potentially also interact with people who . . . have a higher degree of education."

But perhaps the greatest irony of Quentin's story is that he said he has experienced more racism living in his suburban, upper-middle-class home in the early twenty-first century than he ever did in his racially diverse public schools back in the 1970s. As Quentin put it, "They're not used to having a lot of black people live out here." He has several examples of discrimination and assumptions, including the time he went to enroll his two daughters at the local elementary school and the person at the school district office assumed that his family was from the other side of the school district where there is public housing—a.k.a. "the projects." Quentin describes this encounter in detail:

And so the lady automatically placed us in her mind, . . . and she said, "Well, do you live in the bungalows?" And my wife's like, "Well, the bungalows, where are they?" And she goes, "Well, it's those houses right there on the corner." . . . And I said, "Never heard of it." And she goes, "Well, where do you live?" And I said, "We live in [neighborhood]." . . . And she goes, "Oh, I've never heard of that." And then she goes, "Oh, is that that new community that's up there?" And I go, "Yeah, that's where we live." And she goes, "Oh, my—oh, those are really nice." So now all of a sudden, the whole demeanor changed to "Oh, okay, well, fill this document out."

Such encounters are not isolated or even rare in upper-middle-class suburbia, according to Quentin. In fact, he talks about facing "subtle" forms of racism regularly—for example, getting steered away from buying homes in certain neighborhoods or speaking with a car dealer who assumes you don't know anything about finances. He said that "from real estate to car buying to anything, you've got to stay on top of your game because they will take advantage of you."

Quentin contrasted this more recent subtle racism from what he experienced back in his diverse and predominantly black high school: "Oh, now it's totally different. I mean, back in high school, nobody really said anything that was negative or anything like that. Now you can see all kinds of issues of race. I mean, they're very prevalent."

Even when the same people are transported in place and time from a racially diverse high school of the 1970s to a predominantly white and wealthy suburban neighborhood more than twenty years later, the larger context seems to shape their interactions more tightly than their common history in a particular place at a particular time. For instance, Quentin noted that after his twenty-year high school reunion he discovered that one of his neighbors was a white Muir graduate from his class. At the reunion, the white graduate and his wife, who did not attend Muir, were friendly to Quentin and his wife and appeared pleased to know they live right down the street from each other. But back in the neighborhood, Quentin said, he sees the wife of his classmate at the local public elementary school where they both send their children, and she does not even speak to him. He was still a bit shocked by this white woman's behavior more than two years after the reunion when we last interviewed him. "I'm sitting here saying to myself, you know, we went to the same high school. . . . Now, her husband, he's working all the time, so I see her. So you would think [she would say], 'Oh, wow! You went to school with my husband!' That don't mean nothing."

Still, Quentin is convinced that it does mean something to her husband, who is rarely home because he is working late. Quentin said that if he could change one thing about his experience in desegregated schools it would be to not let the cross-racial friendships formed there fade away after graduation. "We don't know each other anymore. I would not allow that to happen. . . . I would remain friends with them because to me, you can't beat that."

Quentin does have friends and acquaintances of other races that he has made after high school, but mostly, he said, they are people he has met through work and they are not his close friends—for the most part, they do not come to his house or hang out with him. Most of his closest adult friends are black, and some of these friends went to Muir with him.

Despite this odd feeling that most of his cross-racial friendships lasted only so long, Quentin would not trade his experience in a racially diverse high school. He even went so far as to suggest that the mixture of people in his public schools had helped to give him and his classmates a good education. "I think there's life lessons that you learned [when you] sit next to somebody who was different from you." He called it a "great education based on the diversity."

Thus despite some sadness about his inability to hold onto friends who lived across the tracks, so to speak, Quentin unequivocally stated that the "social experiment" of school desegregation had been "worth it." He said that at least, through desegregation, the students had a chance to reach out across the racial divide: "I mean, if we didn't have busing, do you know . . . what we would be right now? We—we'd have more problems than you could ever imagine. . . . It didn't do as much as we thought it would do, but it did a lot. But I think that busing allowed us . . . the ability to see people differently. And I'd say it was an experiment. I feel it was a good experiment. It had some flaws to it, but it was a good experiment."

. . . . .

As Maya's and Quentin's stories illustrate, despite the multiple ways in which racial inequality permeated these six racially mixed high schools, making meaningful integration problematic at best, there is a brighter side to the story of school desegregation. We found that all the graduates— from each of the racial and ethnic groups—expressed gratitude for having had the opportunity to attend a racially diverse school. Reflecting back, these graduates said that their public high school years had given them the rare opportunity to get to know people of other racial or ethnic backgrounds in a meaningful way. Whether they were teammates, working together on student government, or starring in a play together, students in these schools crossed racial boundaries every day and emerged from that experience feeling wiser about racial differences than their parents or their peers from segregated schools. These findings reinforce recent social science research on these issues in schools and other contexts and affirm what Gordon Allport argued several decades ago: positive interactions can undermine stereotypes of people of other racial and ethnic backgrounds.[1] But graduates went further, expressing the conviction that their experiences had made them more capable of connecting not only to people of the other races that they had gone to school with but also more generally to people who differed from them, whether in race, culture, nationality, or other ways. Consequently they felt more prepared than their peers who had not experienced desegregation to live in a highly diverse, global society in which many hold jobs that require them to cross international and thus cultural boundaries all the time.

Further, most of the graduates claimed that their experiences in desegregated schools, which had occurred in some of their most formative years, had stayed with them throughout their lives. As Betsy Hagart (see vignette in chapter 4) told us: "The things that I learned at West Charlotte I have carried with me. . . . Honestly, it taught me not to judge people until I get to know 'em. That has been one of the best lessons I think I ever learned, and I've carried that through, and I definitely learned that at West Charlotte. So that has not changed, thank goodness." In a similar vein, a white Shaker Heights High graduate named Dale Kane (see vignette in chapter 9), who now helps his family run an international business, said that he gets along with people from all over the world because "I don't think that the atmosphere of Shaker has gone away." And a white graduate of West Charlotte High School who told us that her desegregated schooling experience made her "very comfortable with black people" in a way that is still with her as an adult said, "You know, it—it wasn't worthless, it wasn't worthless. I mean, I did not leave West Charlotte and leave everything good about it behind."

Many graduates told us that they realized just how unique their high school experiences had been, and how much they had learned from them, only *after* they graduated. Back when these individuals had been teenagers, they had had difficulty seeing (or hearing) beyond the regular social "noise" of high school—the normal adolescent social angst that is part of that time of life. Further, for many it was only later—in college, in the workplace, in their adult social lives—that they had the opportunity to compare themselves to their peers who had not attended diverse schools. At that point, the graduates said, they realized that their high school experiences had made them more open-minded, less prejudiced, less fearful of other races, and far more adept at reaching across cultures and nationalities. One African American Shaker Heights High School graduate summed up how much of the impact of her high school experiences had been revealed to her in hindsight. She told us that her twenty-year reunion, at which she and her former classmates, both black and white, reconnected, had reminded her that being part of this diverse school had been a lovely and honoring experience. Once you left that environment, she said, "and you went into the world, you realized the gift that you were given. But it wasn't *until* you embarked on the world that you realized the gift that you had, and those are life skills. . . . *The gift of the experience, for me, most of all, was realized once I left.*"[2]

This is a crucial finding because, until now, though a great deal of research has been conducted on the so-called short-term effects of school desegregation on students' achievement or racial attitudes while those students were still in school, few researchers have asked graduates of racially diverse schools how they *as adults* understand the impact of that experience on their lives more broadly.[3] The research on the impact of school desegregation on students' racial attitudes while they are still in school is intertwined with many complications related to the type of interracial contact occurring in schools at the time they were studied. Quantitative studies in particular that try to generalize about outcomes with little or no data on the contexts of students or their schools fall short of depicting the complex settings and understandings that students were experiencing in racially mixed schools.[4] The graduates of such diverse schools—those several years removed from the chaos of adolescence—are the ones who can give us the deepest insight into these issues. Further, qualitative research employing in-depth interviews seems best capable of exploring the wide-ranging and long-lasting effects of school desegregation on the hearts and minds of all students who lived through it— those who historically were meant to feel inferior and those who had historically benefited from their white privilege.

Our research uncovered some important differences across racial and ethnic groups in terms of *what* the students learned about race and how it has helped them as adults. In other words, while both white graduates and graduates of color said that their diverse schooling experiences had taught them to break down stereotypes of what members or other racial/ethnic groups were like and to be more comfortable around people who were racially different from themselves, the specific skills they gained and the meaning they made of the lessons were quite distinct. For instance, the white graduates said they learned to be more comfortable in interracial settings in large part because they had overcome much of the physical fear of people of color that white people tend to carry around in their heads. Meanwhile, many graduates of color stated that one of the most valuable lessons they gained from high school was preparation for the discrimination they would face in a white-dominated society. They believe that their schooling experiences helped them learn how to be less fearful of all-white or racially mixed environments, more confident in their ability to compete in such settings, and better able to cope with prejudice.

Graduates of all races and ethnicities, however, seemed to glean insights about race from their school desegregation experiences that greatly informed their double consciousness. These experiences seem to have lifted the veil of race for students of color so that they could see life on the other side of the color line more clearly (or at least differently) than the blacks of DuBois's day. Meanwhile, the white graduates told us that they could not buy into simplistic notions about ongoing racial inequality in the United States because they had known people of color who did not fit the stereotypes that whites so often attribute to them.

Finally, as we describe in more detail below, the graduates of these schools were quite certain that what they had learned about race had to be learned through daily interactions and experiences within a school setting. Occasional or part-time exposure to students of other racial or ethnic backgrounds would not have had the same effect. They noted that they "had to be there," in the midst of things, to learn what they learned.

Paradoxically, at the same time that these graduates were coming to understand what these day-to-day experiences had meant to them, school desegregation had been curtailed and even eliminated in hundreds of school districts across the country.[5] Our study documents long-term consequences of a policy that the federal government had started to dismantle by the mid-1980s, long before we even understood its impact on those who had experienced it. Our goal here is to explain our findings about what graduates learned from attending racially diverse schools in light of the current trend toward increasing segregation in this country and policy makers' resistance to promoting diversity in public education.

A WORLDVIEW FOR A GLOBAL SOCIETY

With very few exceptions, the graduates we interviewed said that as a result of attending their racially diverse high schools they felt more prepared for a racially diverse society than they would otherwise have been. All of them said that their high school experiences had given them a deeper understanding of people of other backgrounds and an increased sense of comfort in interracial settings. In fact, many claimed that their daily experiences of negotiating race in school were one of the most challenging yet rewarding aspects of their education.

In their work environments, upper-middle-class graduates in particular increasingly find themselves forced to cross many cultural boundaries in order to succeed in international companies. The worldviews that they say they developed in high school are especially important—not to mention lucrative—for the U.S. economy and themselves. Thus perhaps one of the more intriguing paradoxes of our findings is how school desegregation helped prepare white people to succeed in a global economy.

Dale Kane, a white Shaker High graduate whom we quoted earlier in this chapter, is an excellent example of this. He spoke of traveling all over the globe to sell the products that his family's business manufactures in Cleveland. He said he is at a big advantage in doing this work because after attending Shaker public schools, where in addition to the U.S.-born students of different races he recalls many foreign exchange students as well, he is not "freaked out by different groups of people, whether black or more so, other . . . you know, foreigners." Dale explained that he was open to "other places and people and to speaking other languages from Shaker, you know, or being encouraged to [do] it." He said that he has been "on the road," traveling, since 1984 for his work. "I love my job because of the fact that I know eight zillion people all over the world." He spoke about how he befriends many of his clients and builds meaningful relationships: "not buddy relationships, but respectful, professional relationships, and some of them verge on—you know, there's different nuances to each one. . . . It's such a—you know, doing what I do is such a combination of social and science that I do think part of my social skills have come from, you know, the Shaker background."

Similarly, a white graduate of Dwight Morrow from Englewood Cliffs told us that she owes much of her success in her profession as an internationally renowned psychologist to what she learned about people and their differences in high school. She talked about befriending black students in her homeroom class who were musicians and were cutting their first album. One of these artists came into class to tell her about the record, which would become very popular, although they did not know it at the time. Looking back, this white woman graduate said she will never forget that day.

> I have to say that there is something in my heart about having been there . . . not just been there at that time, but like, in the school where this guy, who was really my friend. I mean, he really, you know, sort of chose to tell me this—you know, "Guess what? I made this record." . . . And it just—it's one of those, like, things that—that I hold inside me

that is one of those sort of . . . just seminal experiences, sort of having been a part of something that was just . . . I don't know what—how to describe it, but there was something about being in that school at that time and having these relationships with this incredible diversity of people that just made a huge impression.

This particular graduate had many friends from her Englewood Cliffs neighborhood who went to private high schools instead of Dwight Morrow. But in retrospect she thinks her parents did the right thing to send her to the predominantly black public high school down the hill. "I mean, I feel like . . . I'm a very, very different person." She added that it is hard to say who she would have been had she gone to one of the elite and expensive private schools in the area where many of her friends from elementary and middle school went. She said, "I took such a different course in my life than my friends who went to private school did, and I have to think that part of it, certainly, I think was my personality and me, but part of it, I do think, was that [Dwight Morrow] experience."

Graduates of these six schools stress that even though their high schools may have consisted of only two or three racial groups for the most part, the experience of dealing with diversity on a daily basis taught them lessons in getting along with almost anyone, anywhere. For instance, an African American female graduate from West Charlotte High School said she felt she had gained a useful set of skills that her African American friends who had attended all-black schools had not: "I know a lot of black people have only been around blacks, and they really can't see past being around anyone other than blacks. So, you know, I feel like that has helped me in a way that . . . I was already comfortable enough being around a different racial group, so now, when there are so many different racial groups that I'm around on a daily basis, it doesn't bother me at all." More broadly, a black Dwight Morrow graduate commented that growing up in a diverse, if segregated, community and attending racially diverse schools had taught her how to "actively coexist with people and be respectful of what it is that they do, of how it is that they live their lives. And I think that that probably was the biggest thing for us, so that . . . you don't have a problem, you know, with whatever race people are, whatever their beliefs." Another African American

female graduate from Dwight Morrow similarly explained that attending a desegregated school system and high school had made her able to
adapt to very different social contexts and move in different circles of
people. She said, "I'm not limited in terms of, you know, when I walk
into a place, I can speak the same King's English, I can do that, and I can
speak to my friends on a different level. So I think that it's made me a
diverse person." She said that has translated into her work in the business world, where she has no problem rubbing elbows with people who
are more affluent than she is: "In other words, I don't get nervous when
I'm dealing with someone who is a CEO of a company because his experiences and my experiences are so different. You know, I've been around
certain things that have afforded me a certain confidence."

Similarly, a white graduate of Dwight Morrow High School told us
that the racial diversity in her public schools "was preparation for getting out there into the world." She said that in contrast to her college,
which was much more racially homogeneous, her high school prepared
her for dealing with people from different backgrounds: "So I think it
made it easier . . . having had that kind of upbringing, you know, having
gone to a school that was like that, the whole school system, I think,
helped me prepare better for dealing with lots of different kinds of
people in the world."

While this theme was particularly strong at Dwight Morrow, it was
echoed across the other sites. For instance, a white graduate from Austin
High School said of his experience: "It helped my people skills. It gave
me the ability to relate to just about any person and feel good about it,
and to be sincere—not putting on an act. . . . I can't put enough value on
it." And a white female graduate from Topeka High stated that, as a
result of attending a racially diverse high school, "I can walk into any
room or any situation, and I don't care if they are black, yellow, white,
orange, or whatever. I feel that I can have a conversation with anybody
or not be afraid to talk to somebody just because of their social status or
because of the color of their skin."

Thus the graduates we interviewed expressed, across high school sites
and racial/ethnic groups, a profound belief that attending these diverse
schools helped shape a worldview that would be far more in sync with

the global society they encountered as adults. We do not mean to imply, however, that all these graduates learned exactly the same things in the same ways. As we discuss below, *how* these lessons were learned and *what* these lessons mean to them today differed for the white graduates and graduates of color. They also varied within racial/ethnic groups and across the six high schools, according to their context, in subtle but important ways.

White Graduates

While all of the white graduates we interviewed said they believed attending a racially diverse school had changed them in lasting, positive ways, we found that the more specific lessons that white graduates took away from their school experiences both differed from those of the graduates of color and varied to some degree by school. Though much of what the white graduates told us speaks to the "seeing all people as people" theme discussed in chapter 4, there is some evidence that a few white graduates gleaned a deeper understanding of racial inequality and its relationship to segregation and race relations. But even for those who did not learn these more complex lessons, becoming more comfortable and less fearful of "others" was a valuable lesson indeed, even if it took them only so far in questioning the relative privilege of whites in the United States.

INCREASED COMFORT, DECREASED FEAR

The one consistent finding from our interviews with white graduates across the six high schools was the increased sense of comfort that they say they gained subsequently in racially mixed and predominantly non-white settings as a result of their high school experiences. Many white graduates say that attending a racially diverse high school has made them more at ease as adults in interactions with people of different backgrounds and more willing to engage in conversations with people of color than many other whites they know.

White graduates traced their increased sense of comfort in racially mixed environments as adults to the way in which their experiences with members of other racial groups in high school had challenged their own misconceptions about people of color. Daily, up-close interactions with members of other racial groups in high school, many white graduates observed, allowed them to see through their previously held stereotypes. A white graduate from Topeka High noted that his high school had given him an opportunity to know "some people that were black or Hispanic that are not like stereotypes at all. . . . I think that my ideas about other races at that point in my life had been probably just formed by television stereotypes, and there wasn't any real-life experience before this for me." Similarly, Dale Kane, the white Shaker Heights High graduate who helps run an international family-owned business, said he thinks that people's prejudices get broken down once someone "blows the model" of what a black person or a Hispanic person is "supposed to be like": "The first time you have a black person hold the door for you or be polite or act out of your expectations, . . . the model of prejudice is somewhat taken down a notch or destroyed or minimized."

Most white graduates recalled specific incidents with students of color during their high school years that changed how they viewed those students. As recounted in chapter 4, Betsy Hagart had been afraid of African American students when she started high school because of what other whites had told her about blacks before she knew any, but she overcame this fear early in her first year of high school after several African American students helped her stand up to a white bully. "To this day," she concluded, she is thankful that she attended a desegregated school because "I feel that just with family values, with my friends' ideas, I think I would have been extremely narrow-minded, extremely prejudiced growing up"—a statement reiterated by many of the white graduates we interviewed.

These white graduates said that their feelings of ease around people of color were in large part attributable to their discovery, from their experiences with people of color in high school, that the fears most white people had toward African Americans and Latinos were unfounded—a particularly important finding in light of U.S. culture and media, which often suggest that people of color and predominately nonwhite settings are to be feared and avoided.[6] But the white graduates of racially diverse schools reported that they were less fearful in interracial settings than the whites they knew who had attended all-white schools, including their spouses and relatives. In fact, in each site, white graduates frequently said that they realized how much more comfortable they were in diverse settings only when they encountered racially mixed situations after high school with a friend or spouse who had attended predominantly white schools.

One white graduate of Dwight Morrow High School, for example, recalled an evening when she had attended a retirement party for her mother, who taught in a predominantly black school district. She and her husband, who had gone to mostly white rural schools, had very different reactions to the experience:

> You know, the room is mostly black, the families of the retired teachers, the other teachers that came, and a lot of them were teachers I had growing up, and you know, they'd see me, "Oh, how are you," and I introduced [my husband], and his comment, which was sort of a sad thing later on, he's like, "Wow." He had a great time, everybody was so nice. I don't remember his exact words but "God, they were actually really nice." And I felt bad for him for a minute, I was like, "Yeah, they are." It was funny, but he doesn't know any different than that, and he still has that mind-set, although he's much more open-minded than his family . . . but he doesn't understand, he doesn't know a lot of things, so whenever he doesn't know he reverts back to what he knew growing up.

The point illustrated in this one story is repeated in dozens of transcripts. This distinction between the graduates of the six schools we studied and their spouses was perhaps most pronounced in Austin, Texas, when the affluent West Austin students grew up and married other people from other affluent families—many of whom had attended elite private schools or far more homogeneous public schools.

One such white Austin High graduate married a woman whose parents had actually sent her to an all-white private school to avoid school desegregation. This graduate said he was continually surprised by how nervous his wife was in the few racially diverse settings they found themselves in as adults. For instance, he recalled an experience with his wife not too long after they got married: "We walked into a movie theater and were in, definitely racially in a minority, and it kind of startled my wife. She had not grown up in a desegregated setting, and I felt sorry for her." He said that while his wife's high school education at an elite private school might have been better than his in some respects, the "people skills" he learned at Austin High had been invaluable to him personally and professionally. In reference to his wife, he said, "She did not have a natural ability to relate to people of different cultures. And I remember feeling 'I'm so glad I went to Austin High for that reason right there.'"

A similar story was reported by a white male graduate from Shaker Heights High School who said that he realized how comfortable and unafraid he was around people of color on a recent family trip to Baltimore when he and his wife had gotten on a bus that was filled with African Americans and Latinos. He contrasted his sense of comfort in getting on the bus to his wife's unease: "I think we were the only white people on the bus, there were some Hispanic people, African American. . . . My wife . . . went to pretty much an all-white high school, and to listen to the way her father talks and, you know, he hadn't been around too many minorities . . . but I felt very comfortable, you know, getting on the bus and I really didn't feel out of place. . . . But I could definitely tell that my wife was not, you know, a hundred percent comfortable getting on that bus."

Yet another white male graduate from Austin High who grew up in West Austin and married a white woman who had attended an elite private school in another city said that his wife's lack of experience with students of color had left her extremely fearful in predominately non-white social contexts. He contrasted her fear with his own feelings of comfort, which he feels he gained through daily interactions in high school with members of different racial and ethnic groups:

> If you just hang out with a bunch of white people . . . and you do every-
> thing that you can to say, "I'm going to act like a nice, open-minded
> person when I get around these black folks and Mexican folks," you're
> not going to be as good at it. You're going to be more uptight. You're
> going to be stressed out. It's going to be a problem. There's . . . there are
> all kinds of things. Whereas because I was around black folks and
> Mexican folks and learned that they weren't going to kill me, . . . I can
> go to the . . . to the Texas Relays where my girlfriend, now wife, is

hyperventilating. . . . [I said to her,] "It is correct that we're in a group of twenty thousand people and 75 percent of 'em are black people, but we're going to be all right. They're not going to hurt us. They're not going to knife us. They're not going to kill us. They're not going to rob us. We're going to be okay. Just act nice . . . and treat people the way you like to be treated . . . and you're going to be okay."

An interesting and unexpected finding of this study is that several of the white graduates who reported living through uncomfortable racial situations in high school in which they had felt intimidated or physically threatened by members of another racial group also said that as a result of these experiences they ultimately felt a decreased fear of people of color as adults. In fact, it was the process of overcoming a greater, more immediate fear of the "other" that was long-lasting and sometimes more meaningful. For example, a white graduate of John Muir High School who reported that she had occasionally felt intimidated by the African American students there said that ultimately her high school experience left her with not only a decreased fear of people of color but a longing for more diverse environments than the all-white suburb she currently lives in. She noted that she does not feel afraid when she sees a black person or a Hispanic person walking down the street. In fact, she said, "I feel kind of like . . . nostalgic 'cause it reminds me of growing up. . . . 'Cause around here, all I see are pretty much white people everywhere I look." Thus even white graduates of the two high schools—Muir and Dwight Morrow—in our study in which whites were in the minority say that those experiences ultimately left them more at ease in racially mixed settings, in part because they learned how to handle difficult interracial situations.

INCREASED EMPATHY AND INSIGHT

Another important outcome of attending racially mixed schools, at least for a few white graduates, was the better understanding they say they gained about what it was like to be a person of color in a separate and unequal country. These graduates say that their high school experiences played an important role in opening their eyes to other ways of seeing and knowing the world. Such insights have made it far more difficult for them to accept the simplistic generalizations and stereotypes about people of color that are so often put forth by more racially segregated whites who want to explain away racial inequality in the United States.

The former students expressed their sense of these gains in a variety of ways. One white West Charlotte graduate said that he had learned not only an appreciation for African American culture but also, at least to a small extent, what it was like to be a minority—an experience he realizes that most whites have not had: "And at West Charlotte I . . . I mean, there were times when I felt like I was the minority, and I think that was good for me, you know, in a way, to know a little bit what it feels like to walk down the hall full of these people and feeling like, okay, I'm the odd man out here, and to know what that feels like, you know, to not always be among the majority and on top of your game." Another white graduate, who had attended Topeka High School, stressed his exposure there to different perspectives and points of view. In such a racially diverse setting, he said, "You get a lot of different input from different walks of life. . . . I have never been pulled over [by the police] simply because I met a profile. But I have friends who have. . . . Those are issues that I wouldn't be aware of if I went to a totally Caucasian school."

One Dwight Morrow graduate said that the white people who had the most fun in her high school were those like her, who tried to broaden the way they saw the world and their cultural perspective. She said they would go with the flow and learn how to do the dances the black students were doing and just enjoy different kinds of music and different experiences than most white students had at more affluent and predominantly white schools. She said, "It was really a good time. And going to a racially mixed school was probably the best thing that ever happened to me. It makes you see through the eyes of other people."

Another Dwight Morrow graduate, the woman quoted above who told us how important it had been to hear from one of her black musician friends about cutting a record, expressed similar sentiments. One of the few white students on the Dwight Morrow softball team, she recalled traveling with the team to nearby predominantly white schools where students said negative things to her and other white students about playing on a "black team" and attending a "black school": "I can't even remember exactly what was said, but I do remember sort of there being some . . . you know, sort of ragging on us . . . [and] feeling some, you know, some sense of sort of discrimination, you know, against us for going to . . . Dwight Morrow." This graduate was aware of the racial and social class divisions between the students at Dwight Morrow and worked hard to bridge them, knowing that they were the result of greater inequalities. She recalled wanting to win the trust and friendship of her black teammates and prove to the black students that "I wasn't just this, you know, spoiled, you know, elitist, racist." The acceptance and respect of her black teammates were very important to her, she said, and being part of that community had been the most valuable aspect of her experience at Dwight Morrow. She had developed relationships that she would not have developed otherwise, with the result that she had "more of a sensitivity to different people and different cultures and different life experiences, and . . . I think that that really made a very big impact on . . . the rest of my life."

A white male graduate from Shaker Heights High said his experience in his racially mixed community and in his schools had given him a critique of the larger society and caused him to question why most communities in the United States are so segregated. Growing up, he had developed a sense that Shaker Heights and its racial diversity was the way the world was. But then, he said, "You go out in the world and you realize that that's not the way the world is. . . . Then you can question the way the world is rather than the way Shaker Heights is. . . . So, I think, in a subtle sense, it develops sort of a devil's advocate mentality."

Claims of developing such a "devil's advocate" mentality about ongoing racial inequality and segregation in the United States and across the globe are hopeful coming from white Americans, who, as a group, include many of the most privileged and powerful people on earth. If more white Americans shared this view, meaningful change could occur. And while the finding of reported greater empathy and insight was far from universal across the white graduates, the ability of at least some of these graduates to see—or try to see—the world from the point of view of people of color and even to question the larger social structure was all the more profound because, as we discussed in chapter 3, there was very little discussion about such issues in the schools. The lessons these white graduates learned outside the classroom about racial inequality—often despite their formal schooling experience—attest to desegregation policies' potential to promote a deeper understanding of racial difference and foster greater interracial harmony in our increasingly diverse society.

Graduates of Color

Desegregated schools had a powerful impact on the racial understandings not only of white graduates twenty years later but also of African Americans, Latinos, and other graduates of color. The lessons learned by these graduates, like those of the white graduates, varied somewhat; in particular, the racial makeup of their schools and the behaviors of the teachers and administrators in these schools seemed to matter a great deal.

INCREASED COMFORT, DECREASED FEAR

Like the white graduates, the graduates of color we interviewed said that going to a desegregated high school prepared them for a diverse society in that they had a greater sense of comfort in interracial settings. But in saying things like this many of these graduates of color meant that they were prepared not simply to get along with others but also to function in predominantly white work and social settings—often dominated by powerful whites—that would otherwise have been intimidating to them. As one African American male graduate from Dwight Morrow High School said about his experience with whites in high school, "Today I would say that it makes me feel comfortable, that I can go anywhere and not feel intimidated, I just always feel like I belong and it didn't matter who was in the majority or minority, that I knew how to deal with all of them. . . . It definitely gave me the confidence to know that it didn't matter, people were people, and I could just interact."

Above all, graduates of color say that had it not been for desegregation they would have had little or no exposure to whites as they were growing up. The exposure that they did get in high school gave them a sense of ease and confidence in interracial work and social settings that they find very useful today. For instance, Sydney Morgan, the African American graduate of Dwight Morrow we quoted in prior chapters who went on to law school and, when we last spoke to her, was working in a state agency as a lawyer, said that as an adult she probably feels more comfortable around black people than any other group, but "I don't feel uncomfortable around white people. I'm pretty comfortable with most people." More specifically, she talked about the judges she consistently has cases before—one is from a blue-collar Italian background, and another is from a very affluent WASPy background. Sydney said that she finds a way to get along with and interact with each of these white men but that she sometimes uses different strategies—telling the Italian judge a joke or talking about the plays that both she and the affluent judge have both seen. Without stereotyping these white men, she does try to find ways to connect to each, given the interests they express to her. Comparing herself to "some of my colleagues, my black female colleagues who don't . . . come from the same kind of background . . . as I do," she said they had "a different way of handling situations. They're very reactionary, whereas it's not that I don't react, but I do it in a more calculated way." She sees her ability to gain insights into people different from her, her flexibility in adapting to people, and her ability to "calculate" a strategy rather than simply "react" to difficult situations as skills she began to acquire while growing up in racially diverse public schools.

An African American graduate of Topeka High School similarly noted that his adult experiences in a large city in Texas, where he has lived for nearly twenty years, have highlighted for him the comfort that he gained in interacting with whites in Topeka High School. He says that as a result of attending such a diverse high school he is far less intimidated by whites than the African American people he has met in Texas who have not had the chance to interact with whites in school:

> I remember the first time I came down here, and it was amazing to me . . . the way I thought some of the black people here in the South dealt with white people. I thought they were very submissive, and it seemed like coming from Topeka High and being there and stuff like that, I had already overcome that barrier, you know what I mean? That almost . . . looked to me like they was intimidated. I mean, you know? I don't want to be out here saying they're "Yes sir, master" stuff, but it almost seemed like that mentality. And I was just going like, "Damn, man, you should . . . hell, they probably won't give it to you, but you

should be trying to get it. Why are you afraid?" And so honestly if I had to put kind of something in that whole scenario and say, I think it prepared me to learn how to not to be afraid to talk to a white person because I was so amazed at that concept.

This same African American graduate said that when he taught high school in Texas he was struck by how sheltered some of his Hispanic students were, in that they had attended only all-Hispanic schools and rarely left the Hispanic community. One such student, he said, was afraid even to go to restaurants outside his neighborhood. "Coming out of Topeka High School, I didn't have none of that. And so I really believe that if I had to say how it prepared me for later in life, it would be just that way. I mean, really honestly."

COPING WITH DISCRIMINATION

Graduates of color also reported that their experiences in desegregated schools had taught them lessons about coping with prejudice and discrimination that they could not have learned in all–African American or all-Latino schools. The ways they learned to cope with discrimination differed, however, depending on the high school they attended. For example, several graduates of color from Austin High School said that attending Austin had helped them better deal with prejudice as adults because they had encountered it so often at Austin. A Hispanic male graduate noted that if he had not attended Austin High "I wouldn't know what the word 'prejudice' was. I would have been in like a cocoon. . . . I was prepared. High school prepared me for prejudice. It did. That's what helped me." Other graduates of color said they were better able to cope with the prejudice they encountered as adults because they had had more positive experiences dealing with white students in their high schools and consequently knew firsthand that not all whites were as racist as the ones they met as adults. One African American female graduate of Shaker Heights High School, for example, told us: "It prepared me for the ignorance of college, to understand everyone's not ignorant. I knew that, so it was able to probably help me have more confidence and be able to deal with the racial discrimination I *did* deal with in college [that] I [had] never dealt with in my life. So I think having friends that were not African American probably prepared me for, you know, the ignorance that I had to deal with."

Even those graduates of color who say they had particularly painful racial experiences, such as discrimination by teachers or counselors, resegregation into lower-level classes, or social shunning or intimidation by white students, say they are glad they had the opportunity to attend those schools so they could learn the lessons they did. The reflections of one African American female graduate from Austin High School are representative: "I'm glad I went to Austin High in spite of the pain and difficulty. I'm glad I went to school there. I think it prepared me in some ways for the real world. Not that I necessarily like the real world, the way it is, but you've got to start somewhere."

The comments made by graduates of color in our study show that not all lessons learned in a racially diverse school are positive. In fact, some of the stories we heard from graduates of these schools—of all races and ethnicities—were quite upsetting and no doubt have had a lasting impact. Still, graduates affirmed that these experiences had taught them lessons that they now found valuable as adults navigating a racially divided and unequal world.

YOU HAD TO BE THERE

Perhaps the most important testament to the power of policies designed to promote racial diversity in schools is graduates' strong belief that the lessons they learned in high school about diversity could not be gained through lectures, history books, documentary films, courses on multicultural education, or festivals; they had to be lived firsthand through personal, day-to-day experience in shared spaces and times. The schools had played a role in teaching these lessons, not directly through the official curriculum, but indirectly by providing the spaces in which students of different races spent many years together, getting to know each other and participating in common activities. Indeed, many graduates observed that their friends and spouses who had attended racially homogeneous schools—the type of schools that are rapidly becoming more common in the United States[7]—had had no genuine opportunities for students to learn about race or learn how to negotiate racial differences. As a white female West Charlotte High School graduate said: "You cannot suddenly teach someone how to get along with someone [who's] different from them. You can't learn that from a book!"

Day-to-day high school experiences with members of other racial groups left many of these graduates with a fundamentally altered way of seeing the world that they feel cannot be fully transmitted to those who have not shared those experiences. A white woman who graduated from Dwight Morrow in 1980 and played on several predominantly black athletic teams there concluded, "I think that I learned something there that you can't teach anybody, just learned about people and acceptance of life, things that I don't think you teach, you just have to live that kind of environment, you just know it. . . . I just learned a lot by being around so many different kinds of people. . . . You learn something different from them without them teaching it to you in a book or writing it down, you just absorb so many different things." Similarly, the African American graduate of Shaker Heights High who commented above on "the gift" of having gone to a diverse school explained that while there were some "natural divisions" between the students along racial lines at lunch, the students were able to bridge those divisions and form friendships in classrooms and extracurricular activities. That type of cross-racial interaction, she said, "was the best teacher anybody could have ever provided. You couldn't have taught that in debriefing sessions from adults, you know, trying to get into the mind of a sixteen-year-old." Another black graduate from Shaker Heights High School who now lives in New York City, explained: "There's just stuff you can't take for granted anymore when you have been in a racially diverse environment. . . . You can't just fall into these, like, bland stereotypes of everyone of another race or class if you've just had prolonged personal contact with them." And a graduate of John Muir High School who is of both white and subcontinent Indian descent said that while he faced some interracial conflict in high school and "found [John Muir High School] maybe a little bit harder than somewhere else," he appreciated going there because "I also knew that it was teaching me life lessons that no college can teach you.

And those are invaluable. I know a lot of people who do a lot of college work and they test really well, but you put them out in the real world and . . . they can't make it."

Though some would argue that such lessons about race could be learned at any time in one's life, a number of graduates said that these lessons were all the more powerful to them because they had learned them during their youth. For instance, an African American graduate of Dwight Morrow High School said about her experiences of interracial contact in schools from a young age, "That really put me ahead of the game being exposed to children, innocent children from other groups because there is no pretense about anything. You actually learn what people are about because you are kids, you don't have time to be pretentious."

The importance of "being there" in desegregated schools and letting interracial connections and understandings happen naturally was a popular one that we heard across the sites and across the different racial groups within those sites. While this finding might appear to contradict our claim in chapter 4 that more focus on and dialogue about race would have been helpful in these schools, it actually does not. These graduates are saying that in day-to-day interactions, especially in activities in which they had shared goals, such as those on an athletic team, they did not require lectures on how to get along. Spending time together and working on projects or sports together constituted enough of a lesson in how "people are people" that it could change these students' feelings about others of different racial and ethnic backgrounds. Such experiences, however, when not backed up by larger understandings of the structural inequalities that made their lives outside school so different, were not enough to help them change the broader society that surrounded them. This is why, we believe, all but a handful of the graduates of these six schools told us that attending such a diverse school was one of the best things that ever happened to them, yet in the next breath struggled to explain why their adult lives were far more segregated. They had learned the necessary first step toward greater racial understanding, and it had definitely changed them; but a more race-conscious curriculum would have helped Maya and others like her change the world.

CHANGED HEARTS AND MINDS

The comment made by graduates of all races that they often appreciated how valuable their diverse schooling experiences were only once they left high school and interacted more with peers who had not attended diverse schools highlights the need for policy makers and the public to pay attention to the voices of these 1980 graduates now—in their adult years—in evaluating whether desegregation was a success or failure and whether to reconsider our national retreat from policies designed to foster diversity in public schools. As graduates of all racial backgrounds repeatedly pointed out, the deep-seated lessons about race and racial differences they gained in high school could be learned only by "living through it" and would not have occurred without the policies that made their schools diverse. Yet these are the policies that have been under attack for the past several decades both politically and legally. In fact, we know that public schools are currently in the process of becoming more and not less segregated racially. Meanwhile, very little has been done to improve segregation in housing, leading to patterns of white flight from the inner-ring suburbs that are similar to those we saw in urban neighborhoods forty to fifty years ago.

The broader policy context has clearly affected the graduates' adult lives, making it more difficult for them, no matter what they experienced in high school, to live adult lives surrounded by the kind of diversity they had in their high schools. Yet clearly one of the most prominent findings to emerge from our data is the ways in which graduates' hearts and minds—their understanding of themselves and one another—have been altered by attending racially diverse public schools.

Thus, although our study shows that these graduates have not changed the world—in fact many white graduates in particular have (often unwittingly) done their part as adults to perpetuate our segregated society—their experience of attending racially diverse schools may at least help to break down the cycle of segregation by giving them increased comfort in racially mixed settings and decreased fear of racially mixed environments. The fact that these skills were learned in schools that were often segregated academically and socially and situated in extremely segregated communities illustrates the power of racially diverse schools—however flawed—to promote a more racially understanding society.

An African American graduate of West Charlotte High School provided the most optimistic take on such findings, suggesting that as his generation of people in their forties become the leaders in this country—a process that is already occurring and is symbolized by people such as Barack Obama—the experiences of school desegregation will have an even more profound effect: "So, I guess, us as future . . . one-day leaders of society . . . we would have an opportunity to make a change or make a difference, you know, and be accepting of everyone. Once all those old bigots and stuff like that die off and get out of the picture."

Yet as the next two chapters illustrate, the solution to societal segregation and inequality may be far more complicated than the passing of the baton from the older baby boom generation to the younger one. It may require those on the tail end of the baby boom—the classes of 1980, 1981, 1982, et cetera—to take a hard look at their own adult lives and their role in perpetuating the structures that keep them on one side of an enduring color line.

SEVEN More Diverse Than My Current Life

Henry Delane was born and raised in Topeka, Kansas, where his family had been part of the black community for generations. Like his father and uncle and cousin before him, Henry went to Topeka High School. But unlike prior generations of Delanes, Henry experienced a Topeka public school system that was considerably more desegregated, both across and within school buildings, even though it still had a long way to go to achieve meaningful integration. In the fall of 1977 Henry entered Topeka High School, which was grades 10–12 at the time, with a sense of pride. He said, "I was excited about just being there."

He had grown up attending Topeka High football and basketball games and band concerts with his father and felt familiar with the school. He had been to both all-black and predominantly white elementary and junior high schools, so the racial makeup of Topeka High at that time— 69 percent white, 20 percent black, 8 percent Latino, and the rest a mixture of American Indian and Asian—did not faze him.

Still, Henry, like many of his classmates, noted that he had been in "awe" of the school building itself. As we noted in chapter 2, Topeka High is a beautiful Gothic structure built in 1931 and thought to be the first million-dollar high school in the United States. It resembles a New England college or prep school campus and thus seems a bit out of place at the center of Topeka, the Kansas state capital, where drab government buildings predominate.

The class of 1980 arrived on the doorstep of this high school during a relatively quiet era in its history. The civil rights movement and the ensuing protests for equal rights had led to unrest in the school district from the late 1960s through the mid-1970s, but as we noted in chapter 3, by the time Henry and his classmates got to Topeka High the turbulence had subsided. Educators were worn down. Some, though not most, of the changes that students of color had fought for had occurred, and Henry noted that in the late seventies students were already becoming more apathetic. Still, Henry resented that the teachers and administrators did not discuss race or incorporate different racial perspectives into the curriculum.

Henry recalled sitting through upper-level history classes, where he was one of only two or three blacks, and hearing little about African American history—not even the landmark *Brown* decision that some would argue should have been central to the study of the history of Topeka and Kansas. He recalled, "We never talked about, you know, accomplishments of . . . blacks in history. . . . But you sure as hell would talk about George Washington."

His parents inspired him to explore his own history more. He remembered that whenever he had a research paper for which he could choose his topic, he would write about an African American such as Frederick Douglass. Ironically, he said, since he was one of the few blacks in his upper-track classes, his perspective was not seen as threatening: "I don't think that . . . it really bothered [the teachers], just because I was a minority amongst a majority."

He and other black students were sometimes intimidated in the predominantly white high-level classes. "You get some of the top white students, and they [would] just yak, yak, yak," he said, while the black students would not say very much. He added that he thinks the black students were afraid that it would seem like "we didn't know and that we were stupid" if they tried to speak up more.

He also recalled that the African American students were less involved in activities and in student government leadership, in part because the white students had a greater voice and were more connected to the process. But Henry was popular. He had friends of all races, he said, and was a "very upfront person" who did not fake anything. He was elected a member of the Homecoming Court and participated in two bands, the Spanish Club, football, basketball, wrestling, and the Black Student Union. Through extracurricular activities he got to know more white students and find more "common ground."

While his closest and longest-lasting friendships were with other black students, Henry, like many of his classmates—black, white, and Latino—remembered having been proud of the racial diversity of the high school, especially compared to the more white and affluent Topeka West High across town. Henry noted, "Topeka West was seen as the elite school, and Topeka High School was seen more as a melting pot."

The two schools had an intense rivalry. It was not unusual for Topeka West students, in typical high school fashion, to go to the Topeka High campus the night before a football game and paint the trash cans the Topeka West colors. But this rivalry had another dimension: Topeka West students often referred to Topeka High as "Congo High"—a not-so-subtle racial slur. Henry remembered seeing these words painted on Topeka High walls and seeing bananas strewn across the ground. The bananas, he explained, were "their indication of monkeys, Africa and that kind of thing."

That angered him and his fellow students—the African Americans in particular. Topeka High administrators, he said, never did anything about these pranks, which occurred on a regular basis, although he remembered their having the words washed off the walls. He thought the situation somewhat ironic, given that Topeka High was predominantly white. But Topeka West had so few black students in comparison "you could count them on two hands."

The ups and downs of attending a racially diverse high school, Henry said, prepared him well for adult life; he graduated from a predominantly white university and now works and lives in predominantly white settings. The subtle racism he encountered at Topeka High readied him for the attitudes of many of the white students he met in college, most of whom had not had much exposure to people of different racial backgrounds.

Today, Henry is the vice president of a bank in a midwestern town not far from Topeka. He handles commercial and real estate lending and thus must interact with a mostly white clientele. He is one of only a handful of African Americans working at this bank, and all of his black co-workers are in lower-level positions. Henry, who has determinedly overcome racial barriers while climbing the ladder, recalled the beginning of his career as a loan officer. "I was . . . the only black . . . loan person in [my town] in any bank. And these older white customers would walk in, and I'd step out of my office and I'd say, 'Can I help you?' 'Oh, no. We're going to wait for Bert over here.' All right. One did that, another did that. Finally . . . I realized what was going on, and I walked out one day, and I had in my mind that I'm not going to let 'em say no to me."

Henry explained the different tactics he used to find "common ground" with his white customers. In much the way he had established connections with white students in high school through shared interests, Henry would show the elderly white grandparents pictures of his children—"and boom, there was common ground. They got grandchildren. I got a kid. . . . Next thing I said, 'Well what is it that . . . I'm going to do for you today?'" One white customer at a time, Henry said, he broke through with his message: "I'm a black guy over here, but I can help you. I can do it."

Finding that common ground with some of his mostly white neighbors has been more challenging. When he, his wife, and their three children moved in, not many people welcomed them. They have since met a few friendly neighbors, and his children have made some friends nearby and in the predominantly white public school. But one family will not even wave to him when they drive by, so when he is outside and sees them coming, he said, he will stand out by his mailbox and wave at them. "I make them wave. I mean, they have to be . . . very blatant *not* to wave at me."

Then there are the white neighbors who say hi and tell Henry and his family that they are going to have them over for a barbecue sometime. "We've been here since 1997," he said. "Haven't been to a barbecue yet."

Behind Henry's somewhat comical description of these interactions is a sense of disappointment that race still matters so much in this society. When he is not at work, most of his social life revolves around his family and his African American church, where he is very involved with the youth group. Church is vital to him, he said, "so I think that has a lot to do with, you know, just who I spend most of . . . the social time with."

He noted ironically that this is the same as when he was in high school—that most of his free time was spent with his African American friends. And this, he said, speaks to the color line that school desegregation itself could not dissolve:

> Going to a desegregated high school . . . [from] the black perspective gave us an opportunity to intermingle and see some of white culture. . . . Now, you did give [blacks] access to the same books and things like that, which I think is good. . . . But there was nothing that was done there that would create a different social pattern. . . . And so, you know, if you don't do something to create a different social setting, then you're always going to get that—even . . . in the professional [world]. I don't care if you work in a predominantly white workplace, if you don't change something social there, then when you leave work you're going to go your separate ways still.

· · · · ·

Henry's story demonstrates the many degrees of racial separation that graduates of racially mixed high schools experience as adults. Indeed, Henry, who was popular in high school and took predominantly white high-track classes, leads a more racially integrated adult life than the vast majority of graduates we interviewed—black, white, or Latino. He works in a predominantly white bank, where much of his clientele is white; he lives in a predominantly white neighborhood and sends his children to predominantly white schools. At first blush, Henry would appear to be a poster child for the long-term effects of school desegregation—a man who left a desegregated school for a more racially diverse and integrated "real world."

But when we scratch a bit below the surface of Henry's predominantly white world, we see that he spends most of his free time with other African Americans, because even once Henry found the mostly white job and neighborhood, his social networks and key social institutions such as his church remained segregated by race. Furthermore, his white neighbors are not exactly twisting his arm to spend more time with them.

Meanwhile, his former classmates from Topeka High, in general, have even less exposure than he does to people of other races. This is true in particular of the white graduates from all six high schools. As one of Henry's white classmates from Topeka High School explained, "I don't have as many black friends today, but that's not by choice. Again, it's where I live. . . . It had nothing to do with where I chose where I live."

Thus, despite the high value that the graduates placed on their desegregated high school experiences, one of the most important findings from our study was the contrast between the schools that these students attended and the very segregated society that they encountered when they left high school. Indeed, we learned that as adults in their forties, class of 1980 graduates, especially the white graduates, for the most part have found themselves leading racially segregated lives. Of the white graduates, 75 percent reside in racially segregated neighborhoods with few if any neighbors of color. The numbers are more optimistic for the graduates of color: 56 percent of African Americans and about 65 percent of Latinos live in neighborhoods that they describe as racially diverse or predominantly white. But about 20 percent of the African Americans living in diverse communities said that their white neighbors are moving out and their neighborhoods are becoming more segregated. As we discuss below, these figures reflect broader trends, which show that as more blacks and Latinos move out to the suburbs temporary desegregation is followed by the movement of whites either back into gentrified areas of the cities or to suburbs and exurbs farther out from the suburbs that are becoming more racially diverse.[1] In fact, the data from these graduates of color (but not the white graduates) suggest that they live in more racially integrated neighborhoods than the general public in the United States. According to one study of 2000 Census data from sixty-nine metro areas in which African Americans are a dominant minority, more than two-thirds of whites live in areas that have less than a 5 percent black population. In these same urban areas, more than half of the blacks live in neighborhoods that are 50 percent or more black.[2]

Virtually all the adult graduates of the schools we studied attend one-race churches or temples and share most or all of their friends' ethnic or racial backgrounds. And like the general population in the United States, they are most likely to interact and associate with people of other racial and ethnic backgrounds at work. But although their workplaces tend to be more integrated than their churches or neighborhoods, many of these graduates, especially the white graduates, still work in environments in which they have little contact with people of other races.[3] Even when graduates work in settings that are more diverse, they are often segregated internally, with more white employees in the managerial or professional positions and more employees of color in the lower ranks. While this stratification along racial lines somewhat reflects the tracking system in the high schools these adults attended, it is often worse because too often their work environments have nothing analogous to electives, athletics teams, or other extracurricular programs to bring together employees who are on different rungs of the corporate ladder. A white Shaker Heights High School alumnus who went to desegregated schools from kindergarten through twelfth grade echoed a common sentiment among the adult graduates. About his years in public school, he said: "I've never had as diverse a daily experience."

Fairly frequently, a 1980 graduate would point out the irony that desegregated schools back in the 1970s were supposed to prepare students for the "real world" but that their adult worlds now are in general far more segregated than their high schools were. As one white graduate of Dwight Morrow High School commented, "Yes, you think it's [your high school is] this wonderful place, and it *is* this wonderful place, but when you get out you realize the rest of the world is not like that." Another white class of 1980 graduate from Shaker Heights echoed this sentiment: "I've thought about it a lot over the years. It's still a bummer that we couldn't make more of a difference than we thought we could and that the world hasn't changed as much as I thought it should, in terms of both women and other races being more widely accepted and integration being more of a commonplace occurrence. It's a bummer."

This contrast between their high schools and the segregated "real world," which many of the graduates regret and could only fully recognize long after they had left high school, helped to explain why most of them began to lead more segregated lives as adults. Thus, even though they said that their school experience helped them understand and interact with people of other racial and ethnic backgrounds, this has not always translated into leading more integrated adult lives in terms of where they live, work, and attend church or temple or what their adult social networks look like. Perhaps the themes embodied in this chapter are best represented by a white graduate of Shaker Heights High School who recalled that at her twenty-year high school reunion a group of class of 1980 graduates—"all different religious faiths and different races"—were sitting around until the "wee hours" of the morning talking. "And we were reflecting on our lives now—that we feel as though the settings that we're in are less integrated than they were back in high school, which was real sad for all of us to say that."

In many ways, these findings speak to the important issue of how much schools could be expected to accomplish in the context of a highly segregated and unequal society. This chapter presents some of our analysis regarding the segregated adult lives of the graduates of these six high schools.

Our interview data suggest that, for the most part, graduates of all racial backgrounds entered more segregated worlds after high school. This path toward a more segregated adulthood, although not consistent across every interview and slightly more pervasive for whites than for graduates of color, usually began immediately after high school graduation and was especially pronounced for those who went on to college.

SEGREGATION ON COLLEGE CAMPUSES

One of the most unexpected findings from this study was that the graduates' path toward a more segregated adulthood—while not consistent across every interview and more pervasive for whites than graduates of color—usually began immediately after high school graduation and was especially pronounced for those who went on to college. Indeed, the graduates who transitioned directly into college talked about the social milieu being far more segregated than that of their high schools. Students of different racial and ethnic groups occupied different areas of the campus, with few opportunities to interact as they had in high school through extracurricular activities and common spaces.

Although most predominantly white college campuses had at least a small percentage of black, if not Latino, students enrolled by the early

1980s, what struck the graduates we interviewed who had attended college was the highly pronounced segregation within those campuses: virtually all their college classmates gravitated toward same-race friendships, activities, organizations, and even housing. As a white Muir High School graduate who had studied accounting at one of the California State University campuses said of the startling contrast between her high school and her college: "All I really focused on [in college] was accounting, but that was mostly white. Yeah, so then I graduated [from Muir] and I was like, 'God, I'm surrounded by white people!'" An African American graduate similarly reported that when she left Muir High School for Cal State Northridge she "got culture shock" because basically "the black people hung out with the black people. The white people hung out with the white people—there were smaller groups that were only black or only white." While this form of self-segregation was not unheard of in the high schools they had just left, as we noted in prior chapters, the separation on the college campuses was more pronounced, according to the graduates, and the physical space across which the students were spread was greater.

Further, as we mentioned briefly above, many of the college-educated graduates that we interviewed were shocked to encounter so many college peers, of all races, who seemed to have had very little experience interacting with or engaging people of other racial backgrounds. Most of their college classmates, they discovered, had not experienced desegregated high schools and had arrived on these campuses without ever having had their racial stereotypes or prejudices challenged. The white graduates in particular noted that the vast majority of their white college classmates were from very segregated and sheltered—and often privileged—backgrounds. One white male graduate of Shaker Heights High School said his experience at a large urban and selective university was very disappointing in this regard: "I remember going to college . . . and expecting it to be a very cosmopolitan and sophisticated, you know, place of higher education . . . and meeting, you know, my white classmates who had never gone to school with any black people, you know. And likewise my black classmates who, by and large, had not gone to school with any white people, or else had been, you know, like the one black guy at, you know, Andover, or something." Another white Shaker High graduate was equally surprised in college to realize that "the rest of the world didn't live like Shaker did at that time." This graduate, who went to a large state university in a small rural town in the Midwest, remembered pulling out her Shaker Heights yearbook to show her white dorm mates: "They couldn't believe how many black kids we went to school with, and there were pictures of, you know, kids kind of arm in arm and hugging, and . . . they just asked a thousand questions, like 'How did you do that?' and 'Didn't that bother you?' And I sat there and I thought, 'Oh, my God! Where are these people coming from?'"

But many African American college graduates as well expressed this kind of culture shock. For instance, an African American graduate of Dwight Morrow High School noted that she had attended a predominantly white private college and that "because of the type of high school I went to, it was a real awakening, because I just assumed that everybody was as comfortable with different types of people as I had been growing up." She recalled having a comfort level in her racially diverse high school as she and her classmates learned about different cultures. "I really didn't understand anti-Semitism until I went to college because I always had a lot of Jewish friends growing up, and so when I go to [college] and I hear people make comments, you know, and black and white, I'm like, oh, this really is an issue, because where I came from it wasn't an issue."

Such interactions with college classmates from more racially segregated settings taught the graduates of desegregated schools just how unique their experiences had been and how much they had learned. Still, such segregation in higher education was more than these graduates could change. Graduates of different racial or ethnic backgrounds from the same high school who went to the same college campus often found their cross-racial friendships hard to maintain. For instance, an African American graduate of West Charlotte High School recalled that her relationship with a white male classmate from high school who attended the same university was severed in college because of racial tensions and the degree of racial segregation on campus. She explained that although she and this white high school classmate, John, had been "very, very close" in high school this closeness was hard to maintain in college, where they

lived in separate, racially distinct dorms. This black West Charlotte graduate noted that blacks were such a minority on campus—only about
three hundred students out of more than four thousand—that they
tended to stick together and to be angry because they felt marginalized
and discriminated against. As a result of this somewhat hostile and segregated context, when she and John tried to maintain their close relationship, "some of the African American guys on campus did not like
that. And so when John visited me one night, they were very rude to
him, and every time we tried to get together, it was a problem."

Every graduate we interviewed who went on to a residential college—
about 50 percent of the total and a larger percentage of whites than students of color—talked about physical segregation on campus. For
example, housing was almost always racially segregated by dorm building or floor or by fraternity or sorority house. Often the vast majority of
students of color lived in one or two dorms or certain floors in those
dorms that were physically separated from the predominantly white
dorms or floors.

This physical and social segregation on college campuses was mentioned time and time again and was corroborated by different graduates
who had attended the same universities. For instance, the many West
Charlotte graduates who went on to University of North Carolina at
Chapel Hill all recalled the north campus as being almost entirely white
and the south campus as the place where the majority of black students
and many of the athletes lived.

To be sure, most of the college classes, particularly introductory
courses taught in large lecture halls, were often more diverse than these
graduates' high-tracked high school classes had been. Yet in terms of the
social realm, especially the extracurricular activities that had brought
students together across racial lines in high school, the colleges were
generally more segregated. The Greek fraternities and sororities in particular added yet another degree of separation across racial lines. For
example, one white Austin High School graduate noted, "[I] hung out
more with my fraternity, which was 99 percent white, and we had a
couple of Hispanics." "I always felt kind of sad about it," said one white
West Charlotte graduate about the racial segregation, in terms of both

housing and extracurricular activities, that she had experienced at Chapel Hill. "I mean, it felt like I'd gone backwards a little bit. I mean, like . . . but part of it, you know, I did myself, I chose to live on north campus, I mean, I didn't know that much about it at the time. . . . I joined a sorority my sophomore year, and it was all white." A typical statement on the social life in college of white graduates who had attended diverse high schools was that of a Dwight Morrow graduate who told us, "I would say that in college that it was mostly white friends. I really didn't see very many black people at all in college."

Graduates of color from the diverse high schools who had attended college told us a similar story. As one African American graduate from Shaker Heights High School recalled: "It was different, in college. . . . No socializing or anything, and I had classes with [white students]. I didn't have any kind of study groups or anything with them. At [high] school the comparison is, it was easier for me to develop a personal relationship with someone at high school who was a different race versus college, because I wasn't living on campus and I saw them in classes I was assigned to, and that was it." In fact, in part because of these more rigid racial boundaries on the college campuses, a segment of the black students who attended these six high schools and were able to go to college afterward began to immerse themselves in the black college community and seek to develop a stronger racial identity.

Still, time and time again, whether in interviews with African American, Latino, or white graduates from these six high schools, we heard how racially segregated and separated students had been on their college campuses and what a sharp contrast this had been to their high school experiences. Given what we know about the extent of resegregation in the six high schools, this suggests that the college campuses were organized around a fairly extreme form of racial segregation.

The specifics of what racial separation at college looked like or how it related to the social experiences students had there did vary across the different contexts. For instance, a white Dwight Morrow graduate who left her predominantly black high school and headed to a mostly white college campus in New England spoke of encountering a lot more "cattiness" in college, as white girls were busy putting down and talking about

other white girls. She did not remember that kind of backbiting or petti-
ness at Dwight Morrow:

> When I went to college, I had this shock of being around, like, all of these
> white people. And to be honest, like, especially the social scene . . . there
> was, I mean, I don't know the right word, but it was like, this cattiness
> or this . . . nonsense, in a sense . . . that I wasn't used to. 'Cause we
> didn't have that. And that was the beauty of our high school, so that
> when I went to college and I found this . . . these social difficulties . . .
> and to me, it was shocking because . . . it was like these whites with
> whites having these social difficulties, you know, talking about
> people, you know. Probably all the high school nonsense that people
> talk about, you know, like "Oh, that's so high school," and you know,
> girls talking about girls and you know, you don't fit into this group
> and that group. . . . And it was shocking to me because it was, like,
> white on white! You know, and . . . and I felt like it was stronger and
> meaner.

While their college experiences taught them just how unique their
high schools had been, they also seemed to set the graduates off along a
much more segregated trajectory—into an adult world that would look
less like their high schools and more like their college campuses. As one
particularly insightful white graduate of Dwight Morrow High School
explained, during his high school years he and his white classmates were
temporarily "taken off our paths as mainstream white kids for a short
period of time," but "once we were ejected back in college, we continued
on that same path. So we just merged with kids that had gone to the private schools or the parochial schools or came from public schools that
were all white and privileged."

HOUSING SEGREGATION
IN THE "REAL WORLD"

As the class of 1980 entered adulthood, they found jobs in a rapidly changing labor market and, in most instances, decided to settle down, get married, buy a home, and have children. Clearly, not all the graduates we
interviewed had done all of the above: less than 20 percent of them had

not married or had children, and an even smaller percentage had not purchased homes. But whether they were married or not, only a handful still lived with their parents, meaning that 99 percent had made choices about where they would live. For the vast majority of white graduates—three-fourths of those we interviewed—such choices led them to communities that they themselves described as virtually all white. Meanwhile, as noted above, less than half—44 percent—of African American graduates and only about 35 percent of Latinos lived in neighborhoods they described as "racially segregated" or mostly composed of people of the same race/ethnicity as themselves.

These findings suggest that at least the graduates of color who attended these racially diverse schools were more likely than the "average" black or Latino to move into a racially desegregated neighborhood. Indeed, research on housing segregation finds that, on average, about 56 percent of people in this country would have to move to create a racially integrated society. In other words, 56 percent of the time, the average American is living in a highly segregated neighborhood. This is an improvement from the late 1960s and early 1970s, when nearly 75 percent of Americans would have had to move to create a society in which we were all evenly spread across neighborhoods.[4] Thus, in the years that the class of 1980 entered adulthood and the housing market, the rate of residential segregation had decreased by nearly 20 percent from its peak in the late sixties and early seventies.

Still, these cross-racial, universal averages hide the differences across racial groups. Indeed, as mentioned in chapter 1, the average white person in the United States now lives in a neighborhood that is 80 percent white and only 7 percent black, while the "average" African American lives in a neighborhood that is only 33 percent white and more than half black.[5] Though we did not ask the graduates of these six high schools to estimate the more precise percentages of their neighbors by race, the statistics above, along with prior research on the long-term effects of school desegregation on African Americans, suggest that graduates of color that we interviewed were somewhat more integrated in terms of their neighborhoods than the average black or Latino resident of the United States but that the white graduates of these schools made neighborhood choices that were more in line with those of the average white person in the United States. This speaks to broader trends toward more movement of people of color out of segregated urban neighborhoods and subsequent white flight to outer suburban and exurban communities or back into expensive housing in gentrified urban communities. In the middle of these shifts, there are moments of greater integration in inner-ring suburbs.

In other words, the housing market that the class of 1980 entered was marked by further expansion of suburbs to more remote, outer-ring locations. It was also characterized by housing patterns in which inner-ring suburbs were shifting from predominantly white to predominantly black and Latino as more people of color were moving to the suburbs, followed by old patterns of white flight. Indeed, according to the 2000 Census, 40 percent of African Americans now live in suburbs. In major metropolitan areas—those with populations of more than five hundred thousand—blacks and Latinos combined constitute 27 percent of suburban residents. Yet the rapid suburbanization of African American and Latino graduates has not, for the most part, led to an equal increase in housing integration. Instead, the suburbs are offering a repeat performance of the urban white flight that occurred in the fifties, sixties, and seventies, so that these blacks (and to a lesser extent, Latinos) have remained highly segregated in their new suburban homes. Affluent whites and Asians are more likely to live in predominantly white suburbs. As noted in chapter 1, we have become more segregated by social class in this country, thanks in large part to the fallout of the global economy.[6]

Thus predominantly white and Asian exurbs and gated communities far from city centers were becoming more common as the 1980 graduates of desegregated schools began shopping for their first homes.[7] It should not be too surprising, therefore, that many of the more economically successful white graduates in particular have moved into these exclusive communities.

These trends also explain why 20 percent of the African American graduates who said they lived in diverse neighborhoods also said their white neighbors were moving out and their neighborhoods were becoming more segregated. For example, a black graduate of Dwight Morrow who lived in a suburb just outside Chicago described her middle-class neighborhood this way: "When I moved into this neighborhood it was actually very mixed. It was white and black, then we had the white flight, so the neighborhood is changed."

Still, the data suggest that graduates of desegregated schools do not reside in more segregated neighborhoods than the rest of the society; indeed, overall, African American and Latino graduates in particular are more likely to reside in diverse neighborhoods than the average American. But they find themselves in a housing market with limited choices of diverse and stable communities. Meanwhile, white graduates of deseg-regated schools have strong economic incentives to be drawn to less racially diverse neighborhoods, even as they voice frustration about how racially segregated their lives are as adults.

The theme that comes through in the data, particularly with the white graduates, is that their housing choices were driven by factors of economics, perceived safety, and convenience. While these factors clearly overlap with race and class to move them in the direction of predominantly white and not racially diverse neighborhoods, for the most part, aversion to racially "diverse" neighborhoods—at least in the abstract—does not appear to be the primary factor in their decision. Indeed, these forty-some-thing white adults, most of whom live in segregated neighborhoods, talk as if race were not an issue in their housing decisions at all. Yet when they talk about housing segregation in their neighborhoods and towns, they seem very aware of how racially diverse or homogeneous these communities are. For example, a white graduate of Muir High School told us: "Pasadena is a segregated city. . . . [My neighborhood] is, you know, like, 90 percent white, [and] I'm not entirely comfortable with that. But the reason we live here is that . . . while I was working on my PhD, we were renting the house that my wife grew up in from my father-in-law, so we get subsidized rent. [laughs] And . . . so, you know, I mean, Pasadena as a whole . . . the residential segregation is persistent. . . . And so when you stop the active effort to overcome that, . . . it gets screwed again."

The way in which this white graduate separates his personal housing choice from the larger trend in Pasadena is not uncommon in our data. Many of our graduates seem genuinely unaware of how the housing market and the factors that contributed to their housing choices operate in a racialized way to keep neighborhoods highly segregated. This is probably true of most white Americans, not just the ones we studied. Whites' "benign" way of seeing their housing choices and thus *not* seeing the connections between those choices and racial segregation is a typical manifestation of white privilege.

We do not think that claims of "color-blind" neighborhood choice are entirely believable, given how tightly intertwined race is with all of the factors that do more explicitly matter to these graduates and other whites in terms of where they live. But it is quite plausible that these white graduates have more tolerance for racial diversity in their neighborhoods than the average white person has, according to the research on such preferences. For instance, as we noted in chapter 1, the social science literature suggests that whites, for the most part, are unwilling to live in neighborhoods that are more than 20 percent black.[8] Our evidence suggests that all but a handful of white graduates from desegregated schools are more open-minded than that, although they note that neighborhoods with more diversity are very hard to come by.

In fact, the white graduates who did live in racially diverse communities when we interviewed them said that they had actively sought out those communities and that they were not always easy to find. For instance, a white graduate of Dwight Morrow High School who married a Latina said he and his wife had looked in several suburbs before finding a racially diverse community with diverse public schools for their children. He said that part of the reason why they ended up where they did was the value of homes. "But we were looking for a diverse area, . . . and there were very few places we really found. . . . I think [it is] one of the very few towns in all of the U.S. that really has a real good mixing and not just . . . a co-existence."

Still, it was the combination of the home values and the racial mixing that drew this graduate to his suburban community, not the diversity alone. For those graduates of any race who have the income to make real estate investments, the value of the property—clearly related to the race and class of their neighbors, though they do not like to admit that— often drives them away from more diverse communities. Thus they too perpetuate a segregated housing market that goes against some of the most important lessons they learned in desegregated schools.

Because of the efforts in the Shaker Heights community to create more housing as well as school integration, the graduates of this high school often talk about how they used to live in neighborhoods that were racially diverse, even if not as diverse as their school, and how as a result they are taken aback by others' matter-of-fact acceptance of housing segregation. For example, one African American graduate of Shaker Heights High School who now lives in a predominantly black neighborhood in New York City commented on the blacks he knows who have an attitude that "Well, the white people live over there, the black people live over here, there's this line, you know, we mix a little bit at work, but we're just totally—you know, we—our community, their community." He said this way of thinking about the world puzzles him because he did not grow up "with that consciousness." Further, like many other Shaker High graduates, he indicated that the combination of a more diverse community and a distinctly diverse school had not prepared him for the "real world." He had to get used to people who were not comfortable hanging around people of other races, and he had definitely had his moments of feeling, "'Oh, my God, I just didn't know that the rest of the country was like this.' . . . But—and at the same time, there was that feeling of, like, you know, we were wrong. The rest of the country is not like we thought it was. It's not like the way we grew up, and you know, maybe . . . we should have been a little bit more informed."

Others, like Geri Delgato, the Latino graduate of Muir High School who married an Asian woman and now lives in a fairly homogeneous white neighborhood (see chapter 5), felt that where they now lived should not be interpreted as a success or failure of their racially diverse schooling. Geri, who has been very successful in the business world and earns a salary that allows him a great deal of choice in where he lives, said, "The community that I chose was not based on race. It was based on the schools, the safety of the neighborhood, and economically, what we could afford. That's what it was based on, and so I don't think it's a fair assessment to say, because I don't live in a diverse community, that John Muir didn't prepare me."

Despite the value that these graduates place on diversity, then, the segregated housing market in this country has led to a situation in which the majority of them—60 percent overall—live in areas where they seldom come into contact with people of different racial groups. As adults, many class of 1980 graduates, especially the white graduates, find themselves leading racially segregated lives. Even those who have actively sought more racially diverse environments—more typically the men and women of color than the whites—have found few options. Racial segregation has proved more powerful than the good intentions of this cohort of graduates, many of whom carried high hopes that their adult lives would be more like their lives in high school.

The neighborhoods of these graduates are, on average, far more segregated than their high schools were two decades ago. This is especially true of Englewood, New Jersey, where many of the Dwight Morrow High School graduates we interviewed commented on the contrast between their high schools and their current neighborhoods. As one white graduate of Dwight Morrow High School noted, his current neighborhood in a very exclusive suburban section of the state has absolutely no racial diversity, just "different shades of white."

Furthermore, it seems that any nonwhite residents in the predominantly white communities where most of the white graduates now live are not African American or Latino but Asian. For instance, a white graduate of Austin High School who now lives in a very large, newly constructed suburban home outside the Austin city limits said her neighbors are "diverse" in an international sort of way. The people who live in her immediate neighborhood, which attracts those employed in Austin's high-tech industry, are "very multicultured, not black. We have a lot of Chinese. We have a lot of Korean, a lot of, you know, there's Russian down at the end of the street. There's a family from Russia . . . and even in the school . . . same thing." But there aren't really any blacks or Latinos, just one family of Africans "like from South Africa, or something like that." Similarly, Larry Rubin, the white alumnus of Dwight Morrow we discussed in chapter 1 who now lives in a very affluent New Jersey suburb, said that although there are many Asians in this predominantly white area, there are virtually no blacks:

I wish the population in town was more mixed, you know. When my kid plays soccer, there's not a black face on the soccer field. That bothers me. So I wish it was an environment where he was exposed to different kinds of people, but there are a lot of different types of people in town, . . . black people in town, you know, I want them to be exposed to black people. . . . There's an Asian population, and there are people from India, . . . and a white population of many different religions, so they are exposed to a lot of different people, but they're really not exposed to black people. There's no community that looks like my fifth-grade class.

Many of the white graduates we interviewed, like Larry, expressed a sense of loss or dismay when discussing their current, more segregated lives, not just in terms of where they live but also in terms of the people with whom they socialize and work. One white Austin High graduate who had moved to a white and affluent suburb outside the city of Austin said she was "shocked" at "how white it is. . . . I mean, you go into the grocery store and there . . . if you see a Hispanic person he's a worker. . . . You don't see any black people." And a graduate of West Charlotte told us, after some reflection on her answers to questions about her adult life that revealed how little contact she had with people of other races, "I need more color in my life."

MORE DIVERSE BUT OFTEN STRATIFIED WORKPLACES

The one place that graduates of diverse schools are most likely to interact with people of different racial and ethnic backgrounds is at work. Research on racial diversity in the workplace shows that whites in particular are far more likely to have co-workers of other races than to have neighbors of other races. Indeed, by the 1990s, according to measures of black-white occupational and residential segregation, the average white worker in the United States was almost twice as likely to have black co-workers as she was to have black neighbors.[9] This is also true for the graduates we interviewed. They are more likely to interact with members of other racial and ethnic groups at work than in other dimensions of their adult lives, but for nearly 50 percent their workplace also remains fairly segregated.

In making sense of this segregation, many of the white graduates described it as the result of their industry, the labor market, the supply of qualified job applicants among people of color, or discrimination and prejudice on the part of those in charge. For instance, a white graduate of Shaker Heights High School who is now employed by a construction company said about his workplace: "We have a unique situation here. We don't seem to want to hire anyone of a different racial group here; I can't impact that. Ultimately it's not my decision. But it was told to me quite clearly that that was not gonna happen because the individual who owns the company felt that the exposure wasn't worth the risk." When asked, he explained that *exposure* meant "legal exposure," implying that the owner of the company could get sued if a black or Latino worker was hired and it did not work out.

Many graduates we interviewed said that while the companies they work for in sales, education, or other service industries are not racially diverse, their work involves interacting with customers of different race or ethnic backgrounds on a regular if not daily basis. As we noted in chapter 6, when graduates work in such global and diversified industries, their relatively high comfort level with people of very different backgrounds is a huge asset. For instance, a white Dwight Morrow graduate who grew up in Englewood Cliffs and went on to start his own computer company on the West Coast talked about having clients and distributors all over the world—in Asia, Europe, and South America in particular. Thus, he said, he and his business partners have "all of these different people that you're dealing with all the time, and . . . things are never totally divorced from racial and cultural things; you just can't avoid it." He added,

> So being sensitive to it, understanding what's important, learning about other people's . . . quirks or, say, differences from your culture, it's very important to selling them on you, selling them on what you do, and kind of getting past these . . . stereotypes and fears and apprehensions. . . . So I've always been very sensitive to kind of knowing who the audience is, who you're dealing with. . . . And again, it very much came from my exposure at Dwight Morrow, that

was my first . . . exposure in a living way to this heterogeneous population outside of Englewood Cliffs, New Jersey.

For white graduates like this one, the past experience of attending a
racially diverse high school does seem to play an important role in their
professional lives, even when their co-workers and employees are not
diverse in terms of race.

Even in the more diverse workplace settings, graduates describe a
workplace hierarchy in which they tend not to be on an equal footing with
co-workers of different racial backgrounds, since people of color are more
likely to be in subordinate roles and whites are more likely to be in leadership or management positions. That dynamic mirrors the tracking in
desegregated high schools and challenges meaningful cross-racial interactions on equal terms. As a white Austin High graduate noted, in the prestigious law firm where he works, "We've got two Hispanic lawyers and
one who just started about five months ago, and so that's a problem. . . .
We've got a couple Hispanic secretaries and one black secretary, one black
receptionist. . . . But you know, sadly, it's a . . . we're, to a large extent,
we're a lot of white guys at this firm and a lot of white women, and . . .
that's just kind of the way it's worked out." This same graduate went on to
recall that many of the "runners" or college students who run errands for
the lawyers and make photocopies and do filing—the workers who get
paid seven dollars an hour—are more diverse racially but that this has not
thus far translated into more diversity at the top of the firm.

> I mean, it sounds really, and I guess it is, snobbish, but we're . . . we're
> a very high-powered, select law firm around here. . . . Myself and
> the other lawyers around here, I mean, we all finished in the top,
> like, 5 percent of our law school class . . . and most of us clerked for
> judges, and . . . I mean, it's just . . . quite frankly, we're one of the top
> five firms in town that you go to when you've got big-ass litigation
> matters. And . . . there's just not . . . we haven't . . . we should do a
> better job of getting more minorities into the firm, but we . . . it's never
> been something that we've really made a priority, and we're quite
> frankly real selective about the people that we bring into the firm.

Many of the white graduates who were business owners had African
American or Latino employees, and it was not unusual for these

employer-employee interactions to be the white graduates' most common exposure to people of color on a regular basis. One white Dwight Morrow graduate who lives in a predominantly white and afflu-ent suburb and owns his own company noted that the one person of color he interacts with on a daily basis is an employee, an African American man named Dwayne. He reflected on how his relationship with Dwayne is different from his relationships with black students at Dwight Morrow, where he recalled having black friends: "I mean, we have an employee-employer relationship, and I've fired him and rehired him on several occasions . . . [for] being late, not showing up, you know, this, that and the other thing, but . . . you know, being an employer, it's kind of like being an officer in the army, you know, you . . . it's not oblig-atory, but it's best to keep a certain distance because it's still a business, and it's just the way that it goes. . . . Here I'm in control, you know, I'm the man. I don't take advantage of that, you know, but I could."

Some graduates, particularly graduates of color, were more critical about the racial hierarchy in their workplace. One of the most articulate interviewees on this topic is Sydney Morgan, the African American grad-uate of Dwight Morrow High School whom we have quoted several times throughout this book because of her insights and the connection between her experiences and the central themes that have emerged from our data. Sydney, who is also a lawyer but who works for the govern-ment and not a private law firm, noted that there are very few minority attorneys in her office, even though it is not a high-level private law firm. The support staff is primarily minority, and there are a lot of women, but "It's not as diverse as it could be or should be." She added that she works in the area of family law dealing with child abuse and neglect cases, where "primarily the defendants that I'm dealing with are minorities." But, she noted, "Our office is very comfortable with not hiring minorities to do this type of work. I find it very disturbing."

It was not at all uncommon for the graduates of color from these diverse public schools to find themselves in situations where they felt that they or other blacks or Latinos were being treated unfairly or singled out because of their race. One African American graduate of Shaker Heights High School who had moved to California to work in the film industry cited this kind of treatment by his co-workers and said he became especially frustrated because "You know, I'm like, I don't want to—I'm not talking about being friends with these people. I'm talking about trying to get my job done, you know, . . . and people are . . . assuming that I probably don't know what I'm talking about, you know?" Similarly, an African American graduate of West Charlotte High School who had joined the air force said that when he returned to Charlotte to get a civilian job,

> I found out that sometimes society has still got a long way to go. . . . The professional world still looks at race. . . . It's not stated, or they don't come out with saying it, but sometimes you're limited on the resources that you can have because of the color of your skin, . . . especially down here in the South no matter what. . . . I've gone to college now and did well, you know, and traveled the world and . . . and you know, did well in the air force. . . . I was at the top of my profession in the air force, but coming back here and applying for a job, you know, they don't care about . . . they don't look at that. They just look at the color of your skin.

Furthermore, we found that often even when white graduates are working in what they call racially or ethnically "diverse" settings, this diversity refers, not to African American or Latino co-workers, but instead to various Asian, Middle Eastern, or other "minority" ethnicities. Thus one white graduate of Topeka High stated that at her job in an office she is not exposed to the same racial mix she was exposed to every day in high school but added, "I work in an office and I see perhaps more Lebanese people than I do blacks or Hispanics. We have a pretty good-size Lebanese community here." Another white Topeka High graduate who now works in the sciences explained that his field is not very racially mixed but added, "Well, I should qualify that. There just aren't very many African Americans in the sciences. And so I had a lot more interaction and exposure with African Americans when I was in high school. I mean, now, in my company, I think a third of the company is Chinese and a third of it is from India, and I got people from all over the world, but— and that was, you know, the people that I was most associated with in college and graduate school and postgraduate school." In the workplace, as in neighborhoods and schools, the term *diversity* has taken on new meanings that can exclude African Americans or Latinos entirely. Basically, while workplaces tend to offer these graduates of desegregated high schools their most diverse settings, these settings differ in fundamental ways from their schools.

SEGREGATED SOCIAL LIVES

Across racial groups, the 1980 graduates of desegregated high schools are struck by how segregated their friendship groups and social networks are. As one white Shaker High graduate remarked, "I've never had the [same] sort of [diverse] social experience as I did when I was in high school"; most of his friends today, he said, are white. Though graduates say they are much more comfortable in racially diverse social settings than friends and spouses who attended more racially homogeneous schools, it turns out that many of them, particularly the white graduates, say they have had few opportunities to actually spend time in such settings. Given the larger context of segregation around them, they are also more comfortable in same-race social networks, which are easier to access. And in many instances, these networks assist them in maintaining their own racial privilege, which translates into economic power in an increasingly economically divided world. Meanwhile, the graduates of color are more likely to seek refuge from the prejudice and closed doors they encounter in the larger world by joining predominantly black churches or same-race/ethnicity organizations. And they trust their souls only to their very closest friends, who are, far more often than not, of the same race.

Churches, temples, and social circles seem to be largely segregated for these graduates, even when they would wish the situation to be otherwise. The white Austin High School graduate quoted above who is now a lawyer in a prestigious and mostly white law firm expressed regret when talking about how he has stayed in touch with many of his white friends from high school but not his African American or Mexican friends: "I mean, the fact of the matter is I don't have as many black friends. . . . I had a whole bunch of very . . . good buddies that were black folks and Mexican folks when I went to Austin High, and a large part of that was playing on the football team. And . . . now that I'm a lawyer, . . . as far as close friends that I . . . stay in contact with and see on a regular basis, I don't have that many black friends. And it . . . and it sucks . . . and I don't like that." He went on to explain that there is a real tendency to stay with your own racial group and that his Presbyterian church has basically all white parishioners. "It's all white folks, and we do things with black churches. We like black churches, but it just kind of seems to be the way things work out."

Even those white graduates who have managed to find housing in integrated neighborhoods and jobs in racially diverse businesses told us that their social circles, including their churches and most of their close friends, tend to be white. And as Henry Delane's story at the beginning of this chapter illustrates, even when graduates of color live in predominantly white neighborhoods and work in predominantly white offices, they spend most of their free time with family and people from their churches or other mostly black institutions or networks. An African American graduate of West Charlotte High School commented that although she works in a racially diverse setting where she interacts with plenty of whites in different capacities, "it's basically professional and there's not any personal things going on." Her current social network of friends is mostly black. "I had more white friends in high school," she told us, "and when I see them, it's like we are back at West Charlotte, but we don't call each other." Quentin Dennis, the African American graduate of Muir High School whom we described in chapter 6, similarly said that even though he now lives in a predominantly white neighborhood and works in a diverse setting, most of his close friends are black because "We can relate to each other. I mean, you know, you don't always have— I mean, you don't always have to play a game. I mean, there are some games you got to play, but it's just easier." Finally, a Latina graduate of Austin High School stated that while she interacts with people of different races and ethnicities at work, she does not feel the need today to make the kind of cross-racial connections that she did when she was in high school. She said: "We had to do what we had to do when we were in school. Those were the people we knew then. Once you get out into the real world, you know, you develop other relationships, or you just simply go back to what you're comfortable with, you know. Unless you're living, you know, in an area, in a community where, you know, you develop friendships with neighbors or stuff like that, I . . . I just think you go back to your comfort zone."

This trend of same-race friendships is so strong in our qualitative data that the few exceptions to the rule stand out. Hattie Allen, the black Austin High graduate described in chapter 5, is one of them. She told us that of her four closest friends, two are white and two are black. The tendency for people to have only same-race friends, she said, is "reflective of this country. . . . It's the way that we are. I think that people like me are the exception to the rule. I think white people separate and segregate themselves, and black people do that, and Hispanic people. Part of it, again . . . it's just where they're comfortable. And people don't push themselves past their comfort zone."

These findings speak to the pervasiveness of racial segregation and inequality in the society that these graduates entered when they left their high schools. They also suggest that although school desegregation could affect the hearts and minds of the students who lived through it, these graduates of desegregation entered a society in which the racial status quo was entrenched and in which white graduates would, on average, benefit far more than their fellow graduates of color.

Yet some of the white graduates of racially diverse schools know that larger social issues are at stake here, even as they benefit from racial segregation and its impact on the housing market in predominantly white neighborhoods. One white Dwight Morrow graduate commented:

> I think that—I—I really, really do believe that in this country, if people ever want there to be more tolerance, less . . . racism and prejudice, the only way to do it is to have communities and schools that are more integrated because then you're just always fighting an uphill battle, helping— you can't really, truly understand another person, you know, just through books or through reports on, you know, different ways of living or being. . . . Anyhow, I'm sorry, I'm going on and on, but I—I—I really, I feel actually very strongly about that, and we're not gonna make much progress as long as communities are—are segregated as they are now.

THE LIMITS OF SCHOOLING

Larry Rubin, the white alumnus of Dwight Morrow described in chapter 1 who now lives in an affluent and mostly white suburb not far from Englewood, is, for the most part, no longer in contact with his black friends from high school. We quoted him as saying: "We went to school with each other. . . . We got along nice, we all threw our hats up together, and then we don't talk [to] or see each other anymore, so I think we failed. . . . We didn't make the world an integrated place. It's just not. They forced people to go to school together, but they don't force you to live together, so other than that—the races, where do they commingle? Tell me."

We repeat this quote here to underscore the racial separation that occurred across the sites after high school. But unlike Larry, a frustrated but financially successful white graduate who lives in a beautiful suburban home, we are more hesitant to point fingers at individual graduates and blame their choices about friends, housing, and jobs. While there are points in their lives where many, particularly the well-educated white graduates, could have made different choices, the social forces that push all of these graduates toward more segregated adult lives must be examined as carefully as individual choices.

The findings presented in this chapter speak to the major themes from this study, namely that school desegregation did change the individuals who lived through it but that eventually those individuals left their racially diverse schools and were filtered back into a highly segregated and unequal society. To the extent that the white and more middle-class and affluent graduates have benefited economically and professionally from this unequal playing field in the "real world," they have—advertently and inadvertently—helped to perpetuate these conditions. But having lived through desegregation at a young age, they feel a sense of loss about the long-gone days of desegregation. Their double consciousness about race, inequality, privilege, and segregation remains a part of them, whereas their black and Latino classmates have a clearer understanding of how these factors play out in their daily lives and thus why they often need refuge from the storm.

EIGHT **But That Was a Different Time**

The history of school desegregation in the United States includes many instances of white students never showing up to their newly assigned racially mixed public schools. This was not at all uncommon in the South, where "segregation academies"—private schools for white children— opened just in time to enroll students who were fleeing desegregated schools.

Yet in Charlotte, North Carolina, the focus of a famous 1971 Supreme Court case that allowed districts to transport students, or "bus" them, to achieve racial balance, relatively few whites fled the public schools. Many attribute this to the role that several affluent and prominent white families played in supporting the desegregation in Charlotte—in some cases, putting their own children on buses to attend a historically black high school.

In Charlotte and other cities across the country, as we noted in chapter 3, the black students were most likely to bear the burden of busing, since they were more likely to be reassigned to white schools and at a younger age. But when it came to the historically black West Charlotte High School, a source of pride in the city's African American community and the only black high school the district had not closed down, the district leaders knew desegregation would be possible only if white students were reassigned there—and if they showed up.

The Charlotte-Mecklenburg School Board and several community leaders agreed to a plan that sent white high school students from some of the wealthiest and most influential families on the east side of town to the black community that was West Charlotte's home. Reassignment to West Charlotte of some of the district's best teachers—along with the establishment there of a special program called the Open Program—helped entice white students.

Hannah Monroe was one of hundreds of white students who, in the mid-1970s, along with Betsy Hagart, was assigned to West Charlotte High. Hannah's parents, unlike Betsy's, supported desegregation in Charlotte and never questioned whether she would go to her newly assigned school. In fall 1977, she and several of her friends from her afflu-ent white neighborhood set out for West Charlotte and did not look back.

Hannah, who is cheerful, warm, and outgoing ("My husband and my children laugh at me because I talk to anybody, anywhere"), said she had not missed her neighborhood high school, Myers Park, which people in her community had attended for generations. It was seen as the most desirable school in the district, and some white students from Hannah's neighborhood who had been reassigned to West Charlotte tried to appeal the transfer. Some families moved to keep their children in Myers Park. As Hannah explained it, "When you pull a group of people, and a pretty small group of people, [who] . . . had focused most of their life on attending a school that perhaps their parents attended, it is a big change."

The change had cultural and other dimensions, many of which Hannah and her white classmates ended up embracing. For instance, as we noted, West Charlotte's band and cheerleading squad had a different, more fluid style than those of the white schools. Although, as discussed in chapter 3, much of the tradition and pride of the old West Charlotte High School was hidden or at the very least downplayed, the new West Charlotte of the late 1970s, with a student body that was about 50 percent black and 50 percent white and a long tradition of serving the black com-munity, was not going to become just another white school. According to Hannah, West Charlotte was an important part of the black community, so certain traditions were not going to die easily. "So assemblies and things, [we] just did the way they'd always been done, and that didn't bother anybody."

Hannah laughed, noting that West Charlotte was in many ways different from the predominantly white Myers Park: it was a more forward-looking, more "hip" high school. For instance, Hannah noted that the school play at West Charlotte one year was *Godspell*, whereas the Myers Park production was *The Sound of Music*. "In a lot of ways it was a more sophisticated environment we were in, and it was more fun."

Hannah became a member of the West Charlotte Student Council, but not without the help of affirmative action for white students. After the school was desegregated, a student government election process was established to ensure that the three students of each race—white and black—who received the most votes would be elected. After that, the three students—black *or* white—who received the next highest vote totals won the last of the nine seats. In the year that Hannah ran, the student body voted in six black council members and three white ones. The school administration decided that more white students were needed to provide more balance, so the fourth- and fifth-ranked white students were assigned two "extra" seats. Hannah was one of those.

At her first student council meeting, she recalled, she had spoken up with an idea, and one of the black students had snapped: "Honey, as somebody who wasn't even supposed to be on this council, you don't get an opinion." The remark stunned Hannah, but it also forced her to step back and realize that before she tried to exert any influence she had to build friendships and trust in the black community.

Hannah excelled academically at West Charlotte, enrolling in the top-tier classes, which contained a far smaller percentage of black students than the 50 percent schoolwide. She graduated near the top of her class and won a prestigious scholarship to a state university. She had few complaints about her education, even though she felt herself a victim of affirmative action when a black classmate, lower in the class ranking than she, was accepted to a prestigious private university that rejected Hannah.

Looking back on her three years at West Charlotte High School, she has no regrets about going there and thinks she is a better person for it. What's more, she thinks that Charlotte as a community is better for having desegregated its schools and students. She said that if the goal is to "have cross-cultural, cross-racial relationships, you've got to work at it. And . . . the Charlotte-Mecklenburg school system did that."

At graduation, Hannah was approached by the black student who had said she didn't have the right to an opinion on the student council. By then they had become friends. Hannah recalled, more than twenty years later, "She told me that I was the damn nicest white girl she ever met. And . . . that probably meant more to me than any other . . . I mean, I get teary eyed when I tell you about it 'cause it was just like, okay, we've really, you know, built a bridge there."

Hannah and her classmates graduated from West Charlotte in spring 1980 feeling that they had been an important part of the city's efforts to build more long-needed bridges across the racial divide. To an extent, these connections remain. For instance, Hannah knows more African Americans her age in Charlotte than she would have attending an all-white school. She sometimes runs into black fellow alumni through her work in the community. She also talked, as did virtually all the white graduates we interviewed for this study, about being more comfortable in racially mixed settings and black neighborhoods than many white people she knows.

But for the most part Hannah's classmates returned to a segregated society, with most of the whites living in predominantly white communities and most of the blacks living in predominantly black communities. Meanwhile, since the late 1970s, the city of Charlotte has doubled in population and grown physically and economically at an alarming rate. This made the commute across separate black and white communities more problematic in the decades that followed, but logistics was not the greatest force working against school desegregation.

Many of the newcomers, especially whites from the North, had little patience for the desegregation plan. They demanded "better" but not necessarily racially diverse public schools for their children. That reduced political support for the policies that had transported Hannah from the white to the black side of town. Meanwhile, in the years since her graduation, the country had changed politically, leaving the goal of racial integration and equality behind.

In 2002, most of what was left of Charlotte's desegregation policies was dismantled after federal judges declared that the district had done all it could do to desegregate its schools. Today Charlotte's public schools are more separate along racial lines than they were when Hannah was in high school. West Charlotte High School is only 2 percent white.

Hannah, her husband, and their four sons live in the same house in which she grew up. The neighborhood is still predominantly white and affluent. Hannah's husband attended an elite private school in Charlotte, and her three school-age children were enrolled there when we interviewed her.

Coming from a family that strongly supported public schools and integration, Hannah struggled with the decision to put her children in private school. She and her family tried to make the public school option work but felt that the neighborhood elementary school where her children were assigned—the same school she had attended as a child—did not have what her oldest sons, who are twins, needed. She wanted them in separate classrooms with equally good teachers, and one of the kindergarten teachers at that school was considered superior to the other. Even Hannah's mother, who was a public education advocate, told her to do what she thought was best for her children, saying, "It's a different day and time in the city."

In fact, it appears to be a different day and time in most metropolitan areas, for segregation prevails in much of the housing market and in public school systems, with little or no emphasis on correcting it.[1] While Hannah has fond memories of her experience at West Charlotte High School and says she might move her children to public schools as they get older, she sees many differences between today and when she went to school. For instance, she says that our society today is much more materialistic and there is much less emphasis on equality: "The things that are important to the students these days are different. I mean, even the idealism we sort of grew up with and carried over is gone."

She adds that she is "very sad" that the Charlotte-Mecklenburg school system is moving away from race-based school assignments. "I just think it's not . . . good for our community. It's . . . an easy fix, for something people perceive as a problem that will have long-term detrimental effects on our community."

· · · · ·

Our findings related to where the graduates send their own children to school speak directly to the contrast between the social, political, and economic context of the early twenty-first century and that of the 1960s and 1970s. By the time these graduates became adults, few political leaders focused on equity, equal educational opportunities, and racial harmony. Since the late 1980s, our leaders have stressed mostly account-ability, high-stakes testing, and market forces as the solution to any prob-lems in public education.

The graduates we interviewed are caught, as several have pointed out, between then and now. Many reflected on these political and social differences with a sense of remorse, noting that the focus today is much more on individual gains and less on changing society for the better. As a white alumna of West Charlotte explained, "Things seem a lot more materialistic to me now. . . . We were all coming off the sixties and seven-ties. . . . There was still a lot about women's rights, and . . . people were still looking for equality and their place in the world, and that seemed to be more what was important."

With this shift in focus has come a very real shift in wealth and privi-lege since the class of 1980 left their diverse schools. As we have docu-mented several times in earlier chapters, income inequality has grown tremendously in the last two and a half decades, leaving the haves—primarily upper-middle-class and upper-class professionals and busi-ness owners—more focused than ever on maintaining their status by giving their children educational opportunities that other children lack.[2] Caught in this "fear of falling" syndrome, the vast majority of the most affluent graduates of these six high schools have felt a great deal of pres-sure to enroll their own children in the "best" schools, as defined almost exclusively by state tests and rankings. These wealthier graduates, who are usually but not exclusively white, recounted how much less pressure their parents had felt about getting them into the "right" school.

Looking back, however, virtually all these graduates said that what they had valued most when they were in school was a broader under-standing of "good" schools that included everything from creative teach-ers to strong theater and music programs to winning sports teams to the racial diversity of their classmates. But as parents in this "different time" of greater emphasis on narrow accountability measures and significantly more testing of students, many interviewees said they felt compelled to put test scores or other measures of academic "excellence" before diversity when choosing a school for their daughters and sons.[3] Despite their heartfelt testimonies, captured in chapter 6, on the value of racially diverse schools in preparing them for the "real world," only half of the white graduates we interviewed contemplated the possibility that a school could be both "excellent" and diverse.

The growing gap between the rich and nonrich in this country has driven more affluent families like Hannah's toward elite and exclusive, separate and unequal private schools. A white graduate of Muir High School noted how back in the 1970s even the most affluent families in Pasadena sent their children to public schools, including Muir, which was 50 percent black at the time; one "very wealthy" family from Altadina sent all their kids to Muir. He said, reflecting on how things have changed over the years, "I don't think that would happen today."

At the same time, these graduates said that diversity in public schools was still a very important goal. In this respect they agree with the majority of parents of all races polled in large surveys. In one national survey from 1998, a majority of white parents, 66 percent, said it was "very" or "somewhat" important for their children to attend a diverse school, and only 16 percent said that racial integration was "not important at all." The poll showed that 80 percent of African American parents believed it was either "very" or "somewhat" important for their child's school to be racially diverse and only 10 percent said it was "not important at all."[4] Similarly, a 2003 telephone survey of more than 3,421 adults found that a strong majority—57 percent—believed that going to an integrated school was better for their children and only 33 percent believed that it made "no difference."[5]

Thus the double consciousness of graduates of desegregated schools becomes clearer in their struggles to do the right thing by their own children. White graduates who could not stop talking about the benefits they had obtained by going to a racially diverse high school struggled to explain why they had enrolled their own children in "disgustingly" white and affluent schools. Similarly, graduates of color talked about the difficulties they faced in finding schools for their children that were both academically rigorous and diverse in the sense that their children would not be the only minorities in their classrooms. They knew that schools enrolling larger numbers of white students were more likely to have more resources, the most qualified teachers, and a challenging curriculum—the white powerful parents would ensure this. At the same time, they did not want their children to be "tokens" in schools that catered to the demands of white families. These hard choices and the values, political shifts, and demographic trends they reflect are not unique to graduates of racially mixed schools—they are only somewhat more frustrating and conflicted.

"A DIFFERENT TIME" IN AMERICAN EDUCATION

These graduates of racially diverse high schools have not been making educational choices for their own children in a vacuum. In fact, since the class of 1980 graduated from high school, two overlapping and very powerful trends have profoundly shaped the U.S. educational system: an increase in racially isolated schools for black and Latino students and an unprecedented rise in the use of standardized tests to hold both educators and students accountable for higher levels of achievement. While the relationship between these two trends is unclear and may be more coincidental than causal, we argue that the accountability movement, which has mandated significantly more student testing and an increased emphasis on school rankings according to test scores, has significantly narrowed the definition of school quality in a way that works against racial diversity in education, at least diversity that includes blacks and Latinos in the same schools as white and Asian students.[6] In other words, the broader measures of school quality that the graduates recalled when they reminisced about their own schools have been overshadowed as parents have come to pay more attention to school rankings on state-mandated test scores. According to these rankings, a school cannot be "good" if it is not at the top in standardized test scores, no matter what other programs or accomplishments it boasts. And since schools with more racially and socioeconomically diverse student bodies have, on average, lower overall standardized test scores than do more affluent and predominantly white and Asian schools, statewide accountability systems grounded in such tests feed perceptions that more racially diverse schools are not as good.

While we cannot generalize from the specific experiences of people affiliated with the six school communities we studied to every school across the country, we think that the threat posed by the proliferation of standardized tests and rankings to school-level diversity should be more carefully considered. Our evidence sustains a powerful theme about how parents today tend to define good and bad schools for their children and how too much emphasis on narrow indicators of school quality works against efforts to sustain racially diverse schools.[7] Yet as we explained in chapter 6, adults who attended such diverse schools said they had learned valuable lessons about how to function and thrive in a global society.

Of course, there are claims that the testing mandates put in place via the federal No Child Left Behind Act of 2001 (NCLB) may indeed promote more equity because they force schools to be accountable to all families and not just the high-achieving students who are in the running for National Merit scholarships and Ivy League college admissions.[8] Indeed, under NCLB, states are required to disaggregate test score data to better understand how students of different racial and social class backgrounds and other characteristics (e.g., limited English proficiency, special education status) are performing on tests. In theory, such accountability measures could be used to force schools to focus more closely on how they serve *all* of their students.[9]

Yet these accountability systems purport to distill the quality of a school down to such a narrow criterion that, given the correlation between test scores and race and socioeconomic status, the wealthiest schools and those serving very high percentages of white and Asian students are most likely to consistently rank near the top on average scores. And those scores, we argue, are an important criterion that parents who have other educational options will examine when choosing to flee from or stay in diverse public schools.

It is not a coincidence, we believe, that of the six schools in our study, those that were in contexts in which standardized test scores were most strongly emphasized were also most likely to experience white and middle-class flight between the late 1970s and 2000 (see table 2). Indeed, three of the six schools we studied have lost virtually all of their white and more affluent student population. Two additional schools were losing these students when we were collecting our data from 1999 to 2005. In all five of these sites, state-mandated tests appear to have played a role in this white and middle- and upper-middle-class flight, which occurred in these schools at the same time that state mandates and media focus began to reduce the meaning of a "good school" to a single test score. When this happened, broader definitions of "good" schools were obscured or discounted, definitions that included such factors as performing arts programs, athletic teams, number of National Merit scholars or Ivy League college acceptances, and the school's diversity itself. The one high school we studied that has maintained its racial diversity without a significant decline in white students over the last twenty-five years—Topeka High School—was the only site where state accountability measures were less highly publicized and less salient to the way in which interviewees and other community members made sense of school quality issues.

We do not want to claim that the accountability systems single-handedly created white and middle-class flight from the schools in our study. At each school other social and political factors contributed to the loss of white and more affluent students. Still, test scores, which were lower than those of neighboring districts, had become the main rationale for white flight by the eighties in the three high schools we studied that had lost virtually all of their white and affluent students. In fact, these scores were regularly cited as the definitive evidence that these schools were "bad," despite much counterevidence that the schools remained strong on several dimensions. Too often, however, as we noted in chapter 3, once the families with resources and political clout left a school, the self-fulfilling prophecy of its being "bad" or inferior became a reality. We know from reams of social science research that predominantly black and Latino schools are more likely to have high concentrations of poor students, less qualified teachers, more teacher turnover, a less rigorous college prep curriculum, fewer social networks with employers and

Table 2   Racial demographics then and now in six high schools

	Late 1970s		2000s	
Austin High School	African American	15%	African American	8%
Austin, TX	Hispanic	19%	Hispanic	37%
	White	66%	White	54%
			Asian/Pacific Isl.	2%
Dwight Morrow	African American	57%	African American	60%
High School[a]	Hispanic	7%	Hispanic	36%
Englewood, NJ	White	36%	White	2%
			Asian/Pacific Isl.	2%
John Muir	African American	50%	African American	49%
High School	Hispanic	12%	Hispanic	40%
Pasadena, CA	White	34%	White	9%
	Asian/Pacific Isl.	4%	Asian/Pacific Isl.	1%
Shaker Heights	"Minority"	39%	African American	52%
High School	(mostly AA)		Hispanic	1%
Shaker Heights, OH	White	61%	White	43%
			Asian/Pacific Isl.	3%
Topeka High School	African American	20%	African American	20%
Topeka, KS	Hispanic	8%	Hispanic	15%
	White	69%	White	61%
			American Indian	3%
			Asian/Pacific Isl.	1%
West Charlotte	African American	48%	African American	89%
High School	White	52%	Hispanic	6%
Charlotte, NC			White	2%
			Asian	3%

SOURCE: Amy Stuart Wells and Jennifer Jellison Holme, "No Accountability for Diversity: Standardized Tests and the Demise of Racially Mixed Schools," in *School Resegregation: Must the South Turn Back?* ed. John Charles Boger and Gary Orfield (Chapel Hill: University of North Carolina Press, 2005), pp. 187–211.

a. Not including the Academies@Englewood (see chapter 2). Data from the Institute on Education Law and Policy, "New Jersey's Interdistrict Public School Choice Program" (report to the New Jersey State Department of Education, November 2006), http://ielp.rutgers.edu (accessed September 27, 2007).

colleges, less political support, and less status in the communities and with college admissions offices.[10]

These are the issues that the graduates we interviewed struggled with on a regular basis. For graduates we interviewed who still lived in or near the school districts in which they had grown up, it was interesting to hear their many reasons why their own children were enrolled in different schools—often in different school districts—than they had attended, schools and districts that typically were less racially diverse than the graduates' own schools. Meanwhile, even the graduates who had moved to other cities and metropolitan areas faced similar dilemmas about where to enroll their children, dilemmas that were intertwined with issues of race, class, test scores, and privilege.

GRADUATES' SCHOOL CHOICES
FOR THEIR CHILDREN

Though graduates of these six high schools strongly valued their experiences in desegregated schools, we found that about 50 percent of white graduates described their children's schools as virtually all white. This was not the case, however, for the graduates of color, a majority of whom had sought out more diverse schools in both the public and private sectors.

The other half of the white interviewees who had school-aged children had enrolled them in schools that they described as at least somewhat racially diverse. Although more of the black and Latino graduates had children who were enrolled in racially diverse schools—about two-thirds—many noted that these schools were becoming less diverse as desegregation plans ended and their communities experienced white flight.

In light of recent trends toward greater racial segregation in public schools, the graduates' children are not nearly as segregated as they could be. According to research on the resegregation of students in U.S. public schools, white students tend to be the most racially isolated group. In fact, the "typical" white public school student in this country attends a school that is nearly 80 percent white. Meanwhile, growing numbers of black and Latino students attend public schools that are between 90 and

100 percent "minority." In the highly segregated northeastern and mid-western parts of the country, approximately 50 percent of black and Latino students attend such schools. Thus the graduates of desegregated schools that we studied are on average more likely than their same-race counterparts across the country to place their children in racially diverse schools. Still, given that 100 percent of these adult graduates attended such schools, the cross-generational trend is toward more racial isolation.

On the other hand, the graduates' self-reporting on the racial diversity of their children's schools suggests more integration in these schools than in the neighborhoods in which they and their children reside. It appears that now, as when these graduates were in school, the public schools are more diverse than their neighborhoods.

The explanations that the graduates gave for their choice of schools varied across racial and ethnic lines, with white graduates placing a great deal of emphasis on academics and school quality, often over and above "diversity," as the key variable in their choice of schools for their children. What's more, white graduates were far more likely to talk about academic excellence and racial diversity as mutually exclusive characteristics of a school. Meanwhile, the graduates of color regularly cited "diversity" as a key factor in their school choice decision and made the link between school quality and the racial makeup of the school in their assessment. In other words, the graduates of color often offered a more sophisticated assessment of the old adage that "green follows white," whereas white graduates, particularly those with children in racially isolated schools, tended to downplay the role of race in their school choices. What is clear, especially in the way that the white graduates make sense of the contrast between their school experiences and their children's, is that this is indeed a different time from the late 1970s.

White Graduates: Academics Trumps Diversity

An underlying theme that clearly influenced the way in which the white graduates talked about their own school choices for their children was their acute awareness, in most instances, of just how much times had changed. The stakes are higher, they say, for students today versus when they were in school to achieve academically in order to get into a good college and succeed, so they seek schools with the necessary academic rigor to help their children "make it."

Many of the responses of the white graduates to our questions about their school choices for their own children mirror conclusions from the 1998 national study of parents' attitudes toward school diversity that we cited above.[11] As we noted, two-thirds of the white parents surveyed in the 1998 national study—66 percent—said it was "very" or "somewhat" important for their children to attend racially diverse schools. Yet this study, which included focus groups and a survey, also asked black and white parents whether they would rather have their child attend a school with high academic standards or a school that was racially and ethnically diverse—as if high academic standards and racial diversity had to be mutually exclusive. Forced to choose between these two options, the vast majority of parents, both black and white, said that the quality of the academic program was more important.[12]

In our own study, the proportion of white parents who thought that racial diversity was a very or somewhat important aspect of their children's education was even greater than in the national study, nearly 95 percent, demonstrating once again the long-term impact of their own school experiences. But the dilemma posed by the national study of having to choose between two characteristics of a school for your child that you think are important without being allowed the option of having both, was the way that about half of the white graduates from our study who had school-age children made sense of their school choices for their children. Feeling the pressure of the times to help their children attain the highest academic credentials, these white graduates made choices guided by their sense of urgency about academic excellence.

On the other hand, the vast majority of the white graduates who enrolled their children (or planned to enroll them in the future) in racially diverse schools told us that they had done it because they considered racial diversity to be critical in preparing their children for a diverse society. In other words, their explanation was the same as the one they had given for valuing their own experiences in diverse schools.

Comments by two of the graduates we studied illustrate these contrasting choices and their motivations. One white Austin High graduate with young children said that he has thought a lot more about the type of school he wants them to go to in terms of the racial and ethnic diversity than his parents did when he was young: "I think that maybe enters into my mind more than it did, say, for example, my father's mind. . . . I don't want my kid to be in a private school where he is surrounded by everybody that's like him because the time will come, either, you know, during school years or when he's out in the workplace, that's he's not going to have that. And I want him to be comfortable with people, you know, and . . . other ways."

In contrast, a white graduate of Topeka High School who lives in a middle-class, predominantly white, and sparsely populated school district outside the city of Topeka said he wants most for his children to be ready for the changing labor market, since the educational requirements for various jobs keep going up and more and more employment opportunities require some higher education. This graduate, who attended a couple semesters of college but did not graduate and now works as a firefighter, lives in a modest ranch house on a semirural stretch of road. He said he values having gone to a school as diverse as Topeka High because it prepared him to work in almost any environment. But when asked how important it was for him to have his three children attend racially diverse schools, he said, after a long pause, "Going to a racially diverse school, from my perspective and being a parent now, it would be good. But being racially diverse isn't going to get you a job."

White graduates in particular tended to talk about academic quality of a school as a decontextualized and easily measured characteristic. Clearly, the current educational policy framework, with its strong emphasis on testing and accountability, has led more and more parents to believe that "objective" and quantifiable measures of student achievement provide the best indications of "good" versus "bad" schools. Others make more subtle assumptions about the relationships between the race and socioeconomic status of the student body at a particular school. In other words, many are quick to distinguish diversity from school quality, despite what they say about how valuable their own school desegregation experiences have been.[13]

At the same time, these graduates are being bombarded with news reports and information on how critical it is for high school and college graduates to be competitive in the current high-skilled job market. As the Topeka High graduate above reminded us, the stakes are higher for future workers to have more and better educational credentials. Believing that it is fairly easy to figure out which schools are the best in terms of academics and that strong academic credentials are important for their children's future, the white graduates—even those with children in diverse schools—are quick to assert that they will not sacrifice their children's education to make sure they are exposed to racial diversity, much as they value that diversity.

The white graduates who have children in more homogeneous schools say that their choice of school for their children had nothing to do with race and everything to do with "quality." For example, when we asked a white 1980 graduate of Dwight Morrow if the racial makeup of his children's schools had been a factor when he and his wife were deciding where they would live, he said clearly, "No." The only thing he was interested in, he said, was securing for his children the best opportunity to succeed, which he explained as providing them with the "best" education as defined simply by state test scores. He noted that the more recent state practice of ranking all the school districts according to test scores had assisted him and his wife in deciding what the best district would be. "That was what brought us. . . . That was the tail that wagged the dog, really."

This particular graduate of Dwight Morrow, a reflective man who grew up in Englewood Cliffs and now lives in a very affluent community in New Jersey, contemplated why his own parents, who could have afforded to send him to a private high school, allowed him to attend the predominantly black high school in Englewood instead. He noted that today raising and educating children is "supercompetitive, compared to like our generation . . . at least that's what the perception is. . . . I'm like gearing up with my kids already to like teach them everything because everybody is like so competitive, you know, like they have to know how to read by the time they're three, you know, otherwise they're behind the curve already, you know, at least in [inaudible] where I live. . . . A bunch of uptight overachievers, but overachieving not for the pure sense of overachieving, but just the competitive sense."

This graduate did admit that living in such a community puts a lot of pressure on his family. He and his wife at one point considered moving somewhere else for that reason—to "maybe not have to subject our children to like this . . . 'cause I really hated . . . like I told you, that individual peer pressure and stuff." But they decided not to leave because their school district is rated number two in New Jersey, and "You've got to believe that like it's rated that because . . . you know, it's got the highest percentage of children that go to Ivy Leagues. . . . Any statistic that you take that meters educational success solely, in that particular school system, is, you know, outstanding."

Thus this graduate, like so many we talked to, seemed to buy into the current focus on test scores and outcome measures as the best judge of "a good school," even if he wondered whether the pressure was worth it and whether his children might be missing out on other dimensions of a quality education. But when asked about the life experiences he had in high school—experiences that he had told us he valued but that his children would miss out on in their virtually all-white suburban schools—he was quick to say: "They can gain life experience through life. Education is more important than it was twenty years ago."

Similarly, a white Austin High School graduate who was a strong supporter of diverse public schools and who said that he greatly valued his experience in a racially mixed high school put his own children into an elite, virtually all-white and affluent private school because he was concerned about academic rigor; the decision, he said, had "nothing" to do with race and "everything" to do with education. He said he is not impressed with the level of teaching and learning in the public schools, although he admitted he has little specific information on what is going on in those schools. "So this is ironic. I'm not giving my children the opportunity I had. I mean, they have a different opportunity. They're getting a much better education. I do math with my daughter every night and think, 'I wish I'd had this. I could have been good in math if I had this kind of education.' . . . So educationally they're getting a much better education, but they're not as exposed racially, and I feel . . . that's the part that's the downside for me. . . . It's a very white school. It's a very white, disgustingly affluent school."

A white Shaker Heights graduate offered a similar explanation for why he and his wife had decided to stay in a predominantly white school district after moving out of Shaker. He said that the district where he lives now has what is considered to be one of the top three high schools in northwestern Ohio and that in general its public schools have an excellent reputation based on various measures he has read in the newspaper, including "test scores, graduation rates, you know, the proficiency exams at the different grade levels, they also do . . . [teacher]-to-student ratios and per capita student spending, that type of thing." In contrast, Shaker Heights public schools, on the basis of those indicators, appear to have slipped over the last several years.

The majority of the white graduates whose children are in practically all-white schools are doing well economically, living in very affluent communities and holding high-paying jobs. As graduates of racially diverse public schools themselves, they do not appear to have suffered in the long run from their school experiences. But they are convinced that this is indeed a very different time. For instance, a white Dwight Morrow graduate commented on what her parents would have done if they were choosing her high school in the current context: "Going to DM—now, it would not have been discussed."

Even the white graduates who currently have their children enrolled in diverse public schools told us that while they greatly value the racial and socioeconomic mix of these schools, they would have no qualms about pulling their children out of their schools and putting them in more racially homogeneous schools if they thought for a minute that the quality of the education was not good enough or that the diverse schools were unsafe. One white Dwight Morrow graduate with children in diverse public schools explained that he would not send his kids to Dwight Morrow High School because it is "too tough a school." He added, "I will deal with that as the kids get older. I mean, they're going to diverse schools now, but I'll definitely deal with it in high school. If . . . they keep the academics and there isn't any, you know, safety concerns, that's where they'll go. I think it'll be good for them. But whenever they say, 'I'm not gonna have my kids be an experiment,' well, as a parent, that's when you realize what that means."

Still, the vast majority of white graduates we interviewed said that they valued their own experiences in racially mixed schools and wanted their sons and daughters to attend schools that reflected the diversity of our society. And, as we noted, about half of the white graduates with school-aged children managed to find such schools for their children. Some of these class of 1980 graduates were even passionate about the issue. One white graduate, for instance, told us that her decision to send her children to a Spanish-language immersion school had sprung from her commitment to having her children in a diverse environment, which was "definitely a legacy of my . . . high school." Another white mother who graduated from Shaker Heights High School and who currently sends her children to racially mixed public schools in Shaker explained to us why she had chosen to move back to this still-diverse community and enroll her children in these schools, even as a growing number of her white neighbors were opting for more homogeneous private schools: "I wanted to support the community and keep the community strong, and . . . it was very important for me to have my children have that type of worldly experience. I think what a lot of the neighbors forget is when their kids get out there in twenty years or fifteen years, whites will probably be in the minority, and they don't realize it because they weren't raised in a community that promoted cultural diversity."

But the actions of this graduate's neighbors indicate the pressures that the white graduates across the six sites tend to feel and the fears that they express as a result of that pressure. Even those who embrace diversity are clear that in the current context this commitment goes only so far and that if they have concerns about the perceived quality of a diverse school they will opt out and choose a "better" school. Though graduates with children in virtually all-white schools may lament that their kids will not learn about people of different racial and ethnic backgrounds in school the way they did, their sense of loss about this lack of diversity does not outweigh their anxiety about helping their children "get ahead."

ATTITUDES ABOUT DESEGREGATION POLICIES

Even those white graduates who are strong supporters of racially diverse public schools do not agree with many of the past government policies used to achieve such balance in schools. They told us that although many of them participated in school desegregation plans that reassigned them to more racially diverse public schools, such policies are no longer legitimate, and they want more control over where their children attend school. They do not want their children bused across town unless it is by choice to attend superior schools.

This finding provides further evidence that for the white graduates we studied, today is indeed a "different time." Their indignation at the idea of the government reassigning their children to schools outside their neighborhood to accomplish desegregation is a sharp contrast to how they describe their parents' reactions to busing—as a policy that most did not like but most did not feel they could successfully fight.

Many of the white graduates who harbor the strongest feelings about this issue are those who grew up in school systems with such mandatory reassignment policies or court orders. For instance, a white graduate of Muir High School in Pasadena talked about wanting his biracial son to attend a racially diverse public school but added, "I don't know that I necessarily agree anymore with the forced desegregation where they're busing people to a certain place, and you know? I think all that does is create more of the 'us' and 'them.'" Similarly, many of the white graduates of West Charlotte High School, which was desegregated via a comprehensive student assignment plan, are adamantly opposed to having their own children bused involuntarily to achieve racial balance across the schools. One such graduate argued that while he thinks it is important for his children to be around diverse cultures,

> I don't want to have to force my child to go . . . to be somewhere where they don't need to be. I mean, if, you know, if everything works out to where everybody wants to be around each other, that's great; if they don't, don't force it. I want my kid to go to a neighborhood school. Now, if my neighborhood is racially mixed, that's great, go to school where it's racially mixed. If my neighborhood is 90 percent white, go to that school; if it's 90 percent black, . . . go to that school. I think that's pretty healthy.

When asked about the recent changes in Charlotte that were going to return the system to more neighborhood school assignments and thus more racial segregation, he said, "Suits me. Suits me, sure does."

What is most interesting about the white West Charlotte High School graduates and the time frame in which they were interviewed for this study—as the last remnants of the mandatory student reassignment plan, or busing, were being dismantled—is that even the staunchest supporters of desegregation in that district did not want their own children bused out of their neighborhoods the way these graduates had been. Most of them were all right with having African American students bused into their neighborhoods to maintain diversity in their children's schools, and most were supportive of "voluntary desegregation," in which families were offered a choice of different racially diverse public schools. But even their support for such desegregation policies went only so far in the face of a broader political and legal effort to dismantle most of the race-based student assignments in that district. As a white mother explained to us, she was angry about the court case that was bringing an end to most of the desegregation policy in Charlotte at the time we interviewed her, but she had limited time and resources to fight the decision:

> And I—when I first—when I first started talking about [the recent court case], I sent an e-mail to the whole school board and told them, you know, my experiences as a public school graduate in this city and how important they are to me. And I kind of thought, "Okay, that's all I can do," and that's all I did [laugh in voice]. And then I kind of stuck my head in the sand and said, "Let me know when it's over!". . . I didn't have the time or the energy to, you know, do a whole lot more than that. So . . . here we are, you know.

It is fairly clear from our data that while white graduates of racially mixed high schools valued their own school experiences, there are limits to how far most of them will go to recreate those diverse school conditions for their own children in this era of more testing and accountability.

DEFINING "GOOD DIVERSITY"

Another theme to emerge from our data on the white graduates is that while virtually all of them attest to the fact that diverse schools are good, they are somewhat cautious in how they define "good diversity" today. We learned that many of these graduates have a lower tolerance of predominantly black schools than they or their own parents did in the 1970s. Because both Muir High School and Dwight Morrow High School were 50 percent or more African American when the class of 1980 attended, it is interesting to listen to the white graduates of these schools as they talk about what they see as acceptable levels of racial diversity for their own children. For example, we interviewed a white Muir graduate who is in the process of deciding where his son will go to school after he leaves his diverse but majority-white elementary school in a majority–black and Latino public school district. This graduate has already ruled out sending his son to a school that is 50 percent or more black, as Muir was when he was in school. He explained that he will continue to seek diversity in the schools where he will send his son but that schools that have become "predominantly Afrocentric" are "not inclusive."

Indeed, for some, "too many" black students in a particular school is something to avoid. Predominantly black schools seem to symbolize "bad" schools, even though several of these white graduates graduated from such mostly black schools themselves.

Furthermore, we found a shift toward defining "good" diversity not as much in terms of a mix of white, African American, and Latino students as in terms of "international" diversity. Several white graduates noted that this country is far more diverse racially and ethnically now than when they were in school and that although they want their children to be exposed to students of different backgrounds, they do not mean just black or Hispanic students. Related to this are the many different—and often preferable—forms of "diversity" and "multiculturalism" that white graduates now find for their children. As one Dwight Morrow graduate noted, her children are exposed to a great deal of multiculturalism in their suburban schools because of the large number of affluent immigrant families that live near her. Yet they have very little exposure to African Americans or Latinos except for their volunteer work in an urban soup kitchen. Indeed, we are struck by the shifting meanings of "diversity" that these white graduates are defining and developing in our increasingly diverse society and how these meanings can, in some instances, help legitimize the increasing rate of school segregation for black and Latino students, the two largest minority groups, in the United States.

Even Larry Rubin, whom we introduced in chapter 1 as one of the graduates who misses the black friends he had in high school, noted that certain kinds of exposure to certain kinds of diversity are, for him as a father, more appealing than others. He said that if you are a doctor or a researcher and you're going take your family into Zimbabwe, and you bring your kid and send him to a school where he is "the only white face in the school, that's a whole cultural experience." But, he said, if you can afford to live around here at the beginning of the twenty-first century, you're not going to choose to send your white child to Dwight Morrow, where he would be one of the only white faces, and make him "a guinea pig." That, said Larry, "is not a cultural experience."

Graduates of Color: A Different Understanding of Diversity

Some of the graduates of color from the six high schools in our study echo their white counterparts in emphasizing academics more than diversity when it comes to choosing schools for their own children. Still, most of them see a more complicated relationship between race and school quality than their white counterparts. For instance, a Latino graduate of Muir High School explained to us, in much the same way that the white graduates cited above did, that he would sacrifice some degree of diversity to ensure that his daughter was in a school with a strong academic program. He explained, "I have got to be honest with you, I would sacrifice—if the choice were mine—some diversity for quality of education. The bottom line for me is that my daughter is going to be going away to college in eight years."

GREEN FOLLOWS WHITE

Yet when graduates of color describe the choice of sacrificing some degree of "diversity," they are talking about enrolling their children in schools where there are often very few other students of color, so that their children will have little opportunity to be with students like themselves. White graduates who talk about enrolling their children in nondiverse schools are talking about settings where their children will be with many students "like them" in terms of race.

Further, although graduates on both sides of the color line noted a relationship between the racial makeup of their children's schools and the academic opportunities available in those schools, the graduates of color tended to have deeper, more insightful ways of making sense of this relationship. For instance, these graduates of color were more likely to imply that they understood an old desegregation adage that in a predominantly white society "green follows white"—meaning that predominantly white schools are more likely to have the resources and curriculum (not to mention the social status and prestige) to help students achieve to high levels and matriculate to better colleges and universities.

Graduates of color had a much clearer sense of the complicated way in which race overlaps and intersects with school quality (or perceived school quality) issues. As one African American graduate of Dwight Morrow and mother of two children who attend a predominantly white Catholic school explained while reflecting on whether she would send her children to Englewood schools today:

> Would I send my kids to Englewood schools now? Probably not, because there is no integration, and I just think . . . I am not going to say that I don't want them to be around black kids, but whenever a community or school system turns to be 98 percent black, people don't care anymore, and the money stops going into the schools and the legislation is not really going into it. People don't care what really happens. I would say that wherever you have a large amount of white people your kids are going to learn, and that is just my opinion. That is why they didn't go to Englewood, because the people have given up on it and they don't really care.

This understanding on the part of graduates of color helps to explain why a larger percentage of them (compared with the white graduates) have put their children into private schools. Given the still very segregated housing situation described above, these graduates are often forced to seek out private schools to keep their children out of predominantly black or Latino schools.

The arguments that graduates of color make when discussing what they want for their own children are much like the ones they made in chapter 6 for the benefits they themselves experienced from being exposed to people of different races and ethnicities from an early age. One African American Dwight Morrow graduate explained: "Because of my experience, it is important to me that they know children of all different cultures. See, my husband came from a different experience where he came from a black high school, and he wants the kids to be exposed to all different kinds of people." Similarly, a black graduate of Topeka High School, who echoed many other graduates of color when he proclaimed, "I think everybody should go to a racially integrated school. Everybody," said that in searching for a school for his daughters, "I'd like them to be somewhere that was integrated, you know, so they really get a, you know, chance to interact and see what it's like, you know, what people are like." Then, in the next breath, he added, "But my daughters, I just want them to be somewhere where they can learn, that's somewhere that has a good academic program, hey, I don't care what color the kids are."

This Topeka High graduate's comments reflect a theme that emerged from our interviews with many graduates of color, particularly African American graduates: the struggle to find the right balance between diversity and racial isolation. Many of these graduates, particularly those who attended college as the man quoted above did, want the most challenging curriculum for their children, but they also want a form of "diversity" that does not translate into their children being the only students of color in their classes.

As one African American Muir graduate pointed out, diversity in schools is necessary, but too few African American students is not good. She said that she chose a private school for her daughter because it was more diverse than any of the other schools she looked at. One school she looked at had a student body that was only 1 percent black in her daughter's grade, "and that was just not enough for me."

CHASING SCHOOL DIVERSITY IN A SOCIETY THAT NO LONGER SUPPORTS IT

The other important theme to emerge as the graduates of color talked about their efforts to find "good" schools for their children was that racially diverse schools are not always easy to find or maintain. More than a third of the graduates of color talked about the challenges they faced in choosing the best schools for their children. They also talked about shifting demographics in some school districts, with racially diverse schools losing white students and becoming more heavily black and/or Latino.

One example of this phenomenon was articulated by a black graduate from Shaker High who had moved to a midsized midwestern city and had been living in a racially diverse neighborhood—which he likened to Shaker Heights—for thirteen years. He said that the local public school his children attended was very mixed, with black and white students, and that he had chosen to live in that area for that reason—because of the diversity. Yet he noted that some of his white neighbors had been talking about moving out and going to a different school in another district that was more predominantly white. He noted, "My wife and I, we just, you know, it's crazy! People are running, and you know, to me, it seems like they've had a different experience than I have. I think that's great to be in a diverse school." As a result of these shifts, the school that his children were attending at the time was losing many of its white students and was becoming predominantly black. He said, "And as we would talk to parents, you know, they really had no reason to leave except for that, to me, it just seemed like there were more blacks in the school, and for some reason that caused fear."

In these interviews, white flight from racially diverse school districts and an increase in Hispanic populations moving into some communities were common themes related to the demographic shifts evidenced in the U.S. Census data and discussed in chapters 1 and 7: as more blacks and Latinos move out of segregated urban neighborhoods into inner-ring suburbs, whites tend to move farther out to exurbs or else back into high-end gentrified neighborhoods in the cities. A Latina graduate of Muir High School noted about her children's school district in a Michigan suburb: "The racial makeup, it's, I mean, most of it is just white. I don't— I'll say between 70 and 80 percent are white. And blacks, it's maybe . . . 10 or 15. But as the time goes on, I mean, there's a lot more Hispanics moving into—into this part of Michigan." And a black Shaker Heights graduate who has moved to Southern California commented on how many of the parents in the racially and ethnically diverse school district where she is living choose which schools they will enroll their children in by the demographics and not by features like the quality of the teachers. She described the school her children attended, right up the street from her house, as diverse, but she said that many of her white neighbors are taking their children out of that school because of the growth of the Mexican population:

> A lot of people in this area where we are now have taken their children over here to this school and to that school. I'm like, I am not running all over . . . just to get it right. I have trust in the teachers, and if there are "too many Mexican kids" over there, that's not my problem. I can't get off into that, and that is what happens down here. "Too many Mexican kids!" "Too many Asian kids!" So I'm just going to the school that's right here, right down the road . . . because I just don't buy into that kind of stuff and maybe because I came from a racially mixed school. I'm not that uptight with it!

THE COLOR LINE IN A DIFFERENT TIME

In the end it is clear that white graduates *and* graduates of color think that "racial diversity" is an important component of their children's schools, but they examine these issues from very different standpoints—on opposite sides of the color line. While both white graduates and graduates of color sense that predominantly white schools are generally "better" schools, they have different ways of making sense of that and what it means for their children.

Further, these understandings lead them to think differently about the relationship between racial diversity and "academic quality" of particular schools: about half of the white graduates want academic quality first and foremost, even if it comes with very little or no diversity, and most of the graduates of color want diverse schools that are predominantly white but have at least a critical mass of students of the same race or ethnicity as their children.

It does seem odd that the white graduates of racially mixed high schools, who talk at length about how much they value their experiences at these schools and how much they learned there about living in a racially diverse society, have not felt more impelled to find racially diverse schools for their own children. And, given that so many of them have been professionally and economically successful, one might think that more of them would be critical of the narrow ways in which "good" schools are defined these days.

As we mentioned in chapter 1, as of 2005, the school-age population in the United States was less than 60 percent white. How can these graduates, of all people, not believe that sending their own children to a predominantly white and nondiverse school would be doing them a disservice? Clearly, the pull to chase after the highest test scores is incredibly strong—taking them far from what they said was most important to them when they were growing up. We must all pay close attention to a policy agenda and an unequal society that take so many parents so far from their gut instincts and core beliefs.

Meanwhile, the white graduates who have sought out racially diverse schools for their own children, and their African American and Latino counterparts who have done the same, are swimming against a strong tide toward segregated public schools in this country. Interestingly enough, these parents stated that their children's schools are "good" as well.

NINE

The Souls of Desegregated Folk

Sydney Morgan, an African American graduate of Dwight Morrow High School whom we have quoted several times in prior chapters, has seen racism from many sides now. When we spoke to her, more than twenty years after her graduation from Dwight Morrow, she was a lawyer living in a predominantly white suburb of New Jersey, not too far from Englewood or the affluent community where Larry Rubin, her former classmate, lived. On a warm summer evening, Sydney sat on her screened-in porch and considered the many and ongoing forms of discrimination she has experienced both in the Englewood Public Schools and beyond.

Sydney's complexion is a light, caramel color, and her eyes are a brilliant hazel-green that flashed when she told us her more painful memories. As we noted in chapter 3, Sydney was a high-achieving student from a two-parent, middle-class family, and her mother was very active and vocal in the local public schools. All of these factors combined made Sydney stand out among her black peers in Englewood, many of whom, she said, were poorer, from single-parent families, or in low- or mid-level classes. To make matters even more complicated, Sydney was fairly shy, and she had been accelerated two grades in junior high school, which meant she was much younger than her class of 1980 peers.

The combination of several of these factors made Sydney an easy target, especially in high school. Some of her classmates thought she was stuck up and snotty. Her black classmates, in particular, she said, were sometimes hostile toward her because she was smart and quiet and minded her own business. "That was interpreted as being snotty, and . . . so it was almost as if people would, you know . . . pick at you to cause confrontations."

Sydney said she felt that a few of the white teachers, particularly those who taught higher-level classes, had treated her differently from the white students and that some of the black teachers had also treated her unfairly. Sydney said that while she hated to admit it, she believes that the black teachers who hated her did so because of the issue of skin color among African Americans.

But it was a few white teachers who most blatantly made her feel like a second-class student. She recalls that when she took chemistry as a senior the class was racially mixed to begin with but that as the semester went on the other black students dropped out. "I ended up being the only minority student left in the class, and because of where I was sitting I was on one side of the room by myself, and the rest of the class was on the other side of the room because the teacher wouldn't allow me to change my seat, so as people dropped out around me, I was just [by myself]. . . . He was a piece of work. . . . I really got the impression that he took pleasure in seeing the minority students drop out."

The white students, particularly the more affluent, high-achieving, and competitive white students, were for the most part nice to her but sometimes made her feel as if whatever she accomplished would just be due to her being black and getting preferential treatment via affirmative action programs. She felt this in particular when it came time to apply to college and the top students felt a lot of pressure to get into the best schools. At that time Dwight Morrow still had a reputation for sending large numbers of students to Ivy League universities and other top schools. Sydney recalled that by their senior year "there was some tension in the sense that some of my white classmates would make comments like 'Well, you don't have anything to worry about, Sydney, in terms of getting into college because they have quotas.'"

Even some white parents were petty. Sydney recalled one very high-achieving white boy who had a nervous breakdown in their senior year and was out of school for a while. She said he got into an Ivy League school in the end, and Sydney ended up getting a full scholarship to a top-ranked college but not an Ivy League school, as her older brother had the year before. After her graduation, she remembered, the mother of the boy who had the nervous breakdown came up to her and said, "Well, you didn't do as well as your brother, but you did okay."

Sydney recalled that at that moment she felt sorry for the woman's son because he must have had so much pressure on him to achieve according to her standards. And despite the discrimination she faced, Sydney made it through Dwight Morrow with flying colors. She was ranked in the top quarter of her class, and she attributes much of her academic success to her mother's persistence in making sure her children got what they deserved. This, Sydney said, made her mother stand out among the African American parents in Englewood at that time, for many of them were too intimidated or overwhelmed to play such an activist role in the public schools. Furthermore, by the late 1970s, well after the struggle in the 1960s to desegregate the Englewood Public Schools, the forms of discrimination black students faced, such as tracking and low expectations, were far more subtle and difficult to fight. Sydney recalled her mother participating in school board meetings, school activities, and parent groups alongside the white parents. In fact, Sydney's mother worked in the school system as a teaching assistant at one of the elementary schools. Thus her mother knew what was going on, and many of the administrators and teachers knew who she was, so they would treat her children "with a certain type of respect."

Thus, Sydney reflected, things could have been a lot worse for her if she had not had the extra respect her mother garnered. Furthermore, Sydney learned the importance of parent involvement in education first-hand, and while she did not have any children of her own when we interviewed her, she did encounter a lot of troubled families in her work as a lawyer in a state government agency. She bemoaned the fact that by the early 2000s she saw fewer intact families in the African American communities she worked with than she had when she was growing up in Englewood. She noted that once a community has a lot of children who are growing up in single-parent households, many social issues arise: "They've got young parents, they've got drug-involved parents, substance-using parents, they're being raised by grandparents who probably are well intentioned but are too old to deal with the issues that are coming up. And I think that we have a generation of kids that are kind of out of control. When they get to school, they don't come to school prepared to learn. And schools aren't prepared to deal with the social problems that the kids have. . . . So school becomes a question of maintenance and baby-sitting as opposed to true education going on."

While Sydney is quick to see the problems in poor black communities, she also has a clear understanding of broader issues of inequality and discrimination in the United States that makes her very thoughtful about the difficulties of dealing with these "out of control" children and their parents. When contemplating the role that race plays in this society, she was quick to say that race does *not* matter in terms of what people are capable of accomplishing, but she added, "I think that race matters in terms of white people—and I'm just going to say white people as a group—have benefited from the oppression of people of color, and have this advantage, you know? . . . As long as you have nepotism, an old-boy network that controls access to the jobs, to housing, to education, then it's going to remain that way."

The persistence of oppression of people of color and of the advantages that white people often have, Sydney explained in her double-conscious way, is why programs such as affirmative action are still necessary. She said that "racism is still a problem," so even though "affirmative action is not perfect and is not a cure-all, for a lot of people it's the only way they're going to get their foot in the door. Once you have your foot in the door, it's up to you to demonstrate what you can do. But without that, you would—you might not even get that opportunity."

But Sydney added that race-conscious programs such as school deseg-regation and affirmative action can be a double-edged sword because blacks lose credibility when whites imply that they got where they are only because of such programs. Her concern about this is reflected in her discussion of how she got into her university with a generous scholar-ship. Sydney noted emphatically that she does not believe she was accepted for affirmative action reasons. But she does believe, she said, that affirmative action helped her: "I might not have otherwise gotten in simply because of who I am? Yeah, sure. That I definitely believe. But I don't believe that I got something that I . . . hadn't earned or wasn't entitled to.

I think it just helped to make sure that I got what I deserved." This is complicated reasoning in a world that insidiously discriminates against people of color and then chides and belittles them for using what few tools are available to help them gain greater access, as Sydney recognizes:

> It's a double-edged sword, though, because I think, for example, like the supervisor that I have at work, I think she's the type that feels, you know, "Oh, well, they get in because of affirmative action, they're not really qualified." See, it feeds into that. When you're looking for an excuse to think less of people, then it unfortunately helps. Now, quite frankly, I don't really care what other people think because I've seen—I've been in situations where I have seen white people cheat and lie in order to get ahead academically and professionally. So I have no qualms about benefiting from affirmative action because I don't cheat and I don't lie.

Sydney's perceptiveness about the complexities and the double consciousness involved in being an African American in the United States in the twenty-first century springs partly from her dual-identity background as the daughter of a man from rural Texas, a descendant of sharecroppers, and the daughter of a woman from an affluent Caribbean family. She got her sense of entitlement and pride from her mother and her keen awareness of racial oppression from her father, and the two have been blended throughout her life in educational and other institutions. This is the double vision of a black woman who is a product of the civil rights movement, is poised to benefit from what it accomplished, and can articulate specific instances in which she has been discriminated against or put down by whites because of the color of her skin.

At least, she said, being the product of racially diverse schools helps her navigate this complexity and interact with whites in a more sophisticated way. She said that the cross-racial understanding she developed through having classmates of other racial backgrounds was extremely important in preparing her for higher education and adulthood in a diverse but still predominantly white society. Sydney noted that although her white supervisor at work, who is a woman, refuses to acknowledge her hard work and accomplishments, the "flip side" is that most of the white male judges she comes before in her cases have great respect for her. So nothing is straightforward, she said.

She learned to be more discerning about white people and their various agendas and biases at Dwight Morrow, where, she recalled, white students would sometimes ask her questions about herself or blacks in general.

> I learned to distinguish between someone who was curious and someone who had some sort of malice. I mean, I had—I remember in Spanish class one time, a white student asked me how come I'm so light-skinned with light eyes. And I'm like, ". . . We come all different kinds of ways. We're mixed with all different kinds of things," you know? I mean, I was just really amazed that—but she wasn't asking out of meanness, she really was just curious. And the simple fact that she didn't know something like that, I found, you know, in a seventeen-year-old, pretty amazing, you know? Just things like that.

Sydney noted that in some ways attending racially diverse schools was like "suspended animation" before entering the more cut-throat world of work in a capitalist society in which a very small percentage of people control the wealth. Attending a high school that was segregated by race across classrooms gave her and her classmates their first opportunity to see the stratification and division of the larger society, but at the same time, because they were students and still "kids," they could interact in a safer, less competitive way than their parents, "who were out there earning an income." This less stressful environment, Sydney noted, gave students an opportunity to reach across the color line and thus allowed them to see certain things they would not have otherwise come to know. These were helpful lessons, even though they did not single-handedly alter the overall power structure of the larger society.

"I think," Sydney said, ". . . what it really boils down to is that we were the first generation to grow up with all of the advantages of the civil rights movement. And so for minorities, that made a huge difference. For my white classmates, I think that you know, they already started off at an advantage, and they were simply able to maintain that."

·   ·   ·   ·   ·

While Sydney was feeling unfairly treated by some of her teachers and classmates, both black and white, Dale Kane was at Shaker Heights High

School raising Cain. Dale, a white graduate whom we have quoted in prior chapters as well, was, in his words, "a discipline problem." As an adult, Dale still has a rebellious streak that sometimes plays out in a double-conscious and reactive way against policies and practices designed to help African Americans, while at the same time he is a staunch supporter of the Shaker Heights Public School, in large part because of its racial diversity.

Dale's double consciousness in terms of race and inequality apparently began at an early age, when his teachers, instead of consistently demoting him to remedial classes because of his insubordinate behavior, often interpreted his problem as boredom from not being challenged. So he ended up with what he called a "weird mix" of high-level classes and lower-level classes that he said everyone referred to as "ghetto classes" because they were almost entirely black. He said that in such classes, as long as you were quiet and turned in what you were supposed to turn in, you'd get a good grade.

In another "weird mix" of events for Dale, during his school years in Shaker Heights his family went from being simply middle class to being much more affluent because his father's business, which he would later join, took off. As a result they moved to the other, more expensive side of town and joined a local country club, where Dale would run into the "snooty little rich kids" from one of the nearby elite private schools. He remembered, "My dad had gone from having nothing to suddenly having money and joining the country club. . . . I got to that country club, and, you know, in seventh grade, having already competed against some of these kids in Little League . . . I hated them. I had such disdain for the country club."

In fact, Dale's parents had considered transferring him to the elite private schools for high school because of his discipline problems, but he refused to go. He wanted to stay in the public schools and attend Shaker Heights High School. Twenty-plus years later, he was still a staunch supporter of the Shaker public schools. He convinced his wife, who had attended an established private school in Connecticut, to move to Shaker Heights and enroll the eldest of their two children in the local public elementary school. He said that his wife, who was soon to be his ex-wife at that point, "thinks the only way you can get a good education is to go to a private school." But Dale had put his foot down and said he was not putting his children into a private school—not just because of the cost but because the private schools are "really rich," and "really white" and, "you know, if they need a ball player, they'll throw a scholarship at some black kid, you know, and I don't want that. And frankly, I don't even think they give them as well-rounded an intellectual education, not just the social end of it. . . . I've met a real lot of dummies from [the local private school]."

As a young person growing up in Shaker Heights, Dale's best friend was (and still is) a black guy named Ned. He said that Ned would come to his family's house "all the time" and his father would always say, "Ned's the kind of black person that, you know, I want you to be around. You know, he's a normal black person." According to Dale, his father "loves" Ned and holds him up as "what black America should strive to be . . . even to the point of revealing his racism in front of Ned by saying things like that, you know?"

At some points in our two long interviews with Dale, he critiqued his father and the way he talked about blacks or race in general. At other times, Dale appeared to be quite a chip off the old block, so to speak, seemingly buying into his father's way of seeing the world. Dale's double vision of race and racism seems especially poignant in his discussions about his still-very-good-friend Ned, whom he referred to in an affectionate way as "the whitest blackest man I've ever met."

Still, there were many moments when Dale sounded like a much more reasonable person than his father—a tough man of German descent who would think nothing of whacking his son on the head with the handle of his butter knife if he received an angry phone call from one of Dale's teachers during dinner. Remembering this routine, Dale noted that "at dinnertime, even when I was married . . . my wife noticed every time the phone rang, I'd jump." Some of Dale's other significant memories of growing up with his father include the time he "yanked" the family out of the church they had been attending because the focus there was "too much" on helping black families in the ghettos who "wouldn't help themselves. So we stopped going to church." Dale also remembers that his father would not let him or his brother go to school the day Jesse Jackson came to Shaker Heights High School to talk about his Project Push to help black students. He said he remembered "my mother fighting him on that because she had seen Martin Luther King speak at Miami University in like the mid-fifties, and she saw a, you know, [the Jackson speech as] paralleling that." Then there was senior prom night, when Dale was allowed to take ten couples to the country club for dinner before the dance. One of the couples was a white girl and her black date. Dale remembered this being a big deal—both for the people who ran the country club and for his father, who "threw a fit" because he had not known that there would be a black student there, much less a black male with a white date. According to Dale, his father "just threw a conniption about that, and, you know, I'm like, oh, you didn't tell me I had to have a guest list for this thing."

These were just a few of Dale's many stories of his father, who is now also Dale's employer in the family business. Thus Dale is a good case study for considering the out-of-school influences on white graduates of racially mixed schools and how someone's experiences in such a school can make them less racist, at least in a way, or at least less racist than their parents.

Since high school Dale has tried to figure out where he stands on issues such as race and how distinct he is from his father. Clearly, he does not hit his children on the forehead with the handle of a butter knife, nor is he at all likely to keep them from hearing Jesse Jackson speak. But in some ways, Dale admitted, he is becoming more and more like his father. For instance, he said that the book that has been his "bible" is Ayn Rand's *Atlas Shrugged*. His father gave it to him in seventh grade and told him, "It's the most important book you'll ever read." Dale said that he has probably read the book fifty times since then, and what he finds compelling about the book is Rand's idea that "you get what you earn, you get what you deserve, you—you should do what's right. And you do it for self—you do everything for selfish reasons, and as long as you're a good person, your selfishness reasons should fit in with society."

He said that the characters in the book who work for the government are "leeches" and drains on society—a segue for him to talk about various government policies or programs that make him angry. One such program encourages corporations to purchase from minority share-held distributors instead of his father's white-owned business. He said that every time his father's business loses a customer because of such a policy, which he sees as a sham and not a meaningful way to help the black man, he empathizes with his father. He said: "So, you know, in a lot of ways I know where he's coming from. He's felt fucked over by being a white male all the time, and here we've finally got a business where we're contributing to [a major corporation] . . . and they beat us up, cut your prices 5 percent every year, but the minute they want to buy in a more politically correct fashion, they don't mind spending 22 percent more for our product [from a minority-owned firm]."

Furthermore, though Dale talked about what a "fuckup" he had been back in high school, he was careful to distinguish between his own position as a bad white boy and the position of some of his black classmates who were also deemed to be "discipline problems." The black students, Dale said, were displaying "ghetto culture," while he was just a "fuckup." When asked for a more comprehensive distinction between the two, he said that being a "fuckup" was something you could control: "It's not caused from where you are; it's behaving how you're choosing to behave and going from area to area or . . . you know, I knew when I was misbehaving for the most part. There were times when it was, you know, uncontrolled or acting without thinking, but you consciously knew it was wrong, whereas the ghetto culture, for the most part, the actions were coming out of 'No, this is normal. This is how it's okay to do this.'"

Thus Dale's analysis suggests that white boys acted out by choice and black boys acted out because of who they were and their culture—that they not only had no choice in the matter but were compelled to be "bad boys" because of their family values and where they came from. The same "ghetto" culture, Dale argues, is what keeps blacks who attend schools like Shaker Heights High from succeeding professionally and economically. It begins quite young, he said, if black students have parents who do not read to them (although Dale admits that it was not his parents but an old lady who was a friend of the family who taught him to read). "It depends," he said, "on what they were handed, what their parents' prepping or motivation [and] tenacity was."

The solution, he said, to ongoing racial inequality in the United States is not policies such as corporate incentives to do business with minority share-held companies or affirmative action or busing or reparations for all blacks who are descendents of slaves. These tools, he said, are "very arbitrary and nonsophisticated ways of attacking the problem." He said that the reparations movement in particular was problematic, based on an argument that "'Hey, my grandfather was a slave; I deserve money' kind of thing that takes it—the perversion and the help factor to only a level that I think creates resentment. And you know, how much, how . . . many times do we have to pay for the sins of my grandfather or forefathers?"

In the end Dale admitted, at different times in the interview, that he can see these issues from both sides now. He is not his father, in large part, he said, because he went to Shaker public schools, yet he is also a product of his family. He convinced his wife to put their son in a racially diverse Shaker elementary school, but he does not know how long that will last in a climate of high anxiety about school inequality on the part of upper-middle-class white parents. He is not very optimistic about the future of the country in terms of racial or social class divisions. When asked about the relationship between race and class in this country, Dale began singing a song he said was called "National Brotherhood Week" by Tom Lehrer (as he somewhat imperfectly remembered it), moving his medium-frame, wiry body to the beat and pushing up his wire-framed glasses on his nose:

> Well, the rich folks hate the poor folks,
> And the white folks hate the black folks.
> All my folks hate all your folks
> It's American as apple pie.

> But during National Brotherhood Week
> National Brotherhood Week,
> Do-do-do-do-do-do 'cause it's very chic
> Take the hand of someone you can't stand
> And kiss them on the cheek, if you can try.

. . . . .

By the late 1970s, much of the hard work to get black, white, and Latino students together under one school roof had been done. The struggle for desegregation and greater racial equality needed to go to the next level, which would have included not just the public schools but also policies such as housing integration. Unfortunately, the schools were left, in essence, holding the bag as the country abandoned broader social change.

Once these graduates left their racially diverse high schools, desegregation and greater racial equality were not national priorities. In fact, dismantling school desegregation became a much higher priority.[1] And there was the class of 1980 in the school desegregation version of "all dressed up and nowhere to go"—more prepared for racial integration than any cohort before them but in the midst of a society that was in many ways moving in the other direction.

It is important to contrast the experiences of these graduates in racially diverse public schools with the political agenda of the last almost three decades, which has encouraged and rewarded a tighter focus on material gain and individual advancement than on racial equality and social justice. Public schools that have managed to continue to bring people of different racial backgrounds together for even short periods of time have been working against the prevailing trends.

Thus, amid their fond memories and valued experiences, many of these graduates have gone on to lead far more segregated lives—coming of age in a time of greed, individualism, and growing gaps between the haves and have-nots. They have embarked on careers, married, had children, and settled down in an era that tells them to focus more on themselves and their own accumulation of wealth than on the problems of others or the greater good. Their politically schizophrenic life span—in which they left high school at the end of the seventies and became adults during the eighties and nineties—has contributed to the confusion and contradiction in the voices of the African American, Latino, and white graduates we interviewed.

The voices of the class of 1980 are thus in many ways symbolic of the political and social soul of this country and the shifts and changes it has endured since the early sixties. While they do not seem to have any more answers to racial problems in the United States than most adults, they do express more regret about the seemingly never-ending racial divide in our society. Virtually all the graduates we interviewed—black, white,

Latino, and Asian—expressed a sense of loss when contrasting the racial diversity of their high schools with their current, mostly segregated lives. They all said they interacted with more people of different racial backgrounds in their high schools than they have in any other period of their lives since. They laugh at the notion that desegregated schools were supposed to prepare them for the "real world" when the world outside their high schools is so much more racially divided.

Through the stories of these middle-aged graduates more than twenty years later, we come to understand what they learned—or did not learn—about race in America from their high schools and their current struggles to do right by their own children. These stories may help us better understand the missed opportunities of the 1970s, especially in light of the move back toward more racially segregated schools. In these graduates' sense of loss about what they once had in high school, we can see a glimmer of the possibilities for a renewed agenda for social justice and future race-conscious public policies.

These graduates of racially mixed high schools from more than two decades ago can help researchers, policy makers, and educators understand the many ways in which school desegregation was compromised by a broader society that placed so much of the burden of creating greater equal opportunity on the public schools while leaving too many other domains separate and unequal. They also tell us why school desegregation policy, limited though it was in changing the society as a whole, was worth the effort.

In this way, the graduates teach us a great deal about race and double consciousness in America and the American dilemma at the beginning of the twenty-first century. For one thing, they help us understand why, after so many setbacks and disappointments on the road to desegregation, the vast majority of African Americans will continue to choose racially diverse schools for their children whenever they can. As we noted in chapter 8, despite prejudice and rejections, 85 percent of black parents today still state that placing their children in racially diverse schools is either "very important" or "somewhat important."[2] Clearly, these parents know what many civil rights lawyers have argued for years: in a society that has historically been racially divided and in which one race possesses so many of the resources and opportunities, there is no such thing as "separate but equal."

Furthermore, African Americans and Latinos who have led desegregated lives can attest to the importance of crossing color lines and reaching across the racial divide. They argue that such connections across race make for a more democratic society in which DuBois's vision of American Negroes' effort to merge their double selves into a better and truer self—less conflicted but still watchful and insightful—emerges more clearly than in any other scenario of race relations in the United States. Only through some degree of integration between blacks, white, Latinos, and Asians and greater understanding and, hopefully, greater equality across racial lines will an African American or Latino be allowed to "be both a Negro [or person of color] and an American, without having the doors of opportunity closed roughly in his face."[3]

This double consciousness—of being both a person of color and an American, despite the constant struggle that such coexistence entails—was articulated quite clearly by Quentin Dennis (profiled in chapter 6), the African American graduate of Muir High School who, by the early 2000s, was working as a police lieutenant and living in a predominantly white neighborhood in a large house. Contemplating the issue of race in American society today, Quentin explained that in many ways it is important to see race, although, he said, it is important for blacks to realize that not all white people, on an individual, person-to-person level, dislike you. "Not all people dislike you. Not all people want to see you fail; there are a good number of people who want to see you do well. So I've learned that. So don't judge a book, as they say, by the cover. Give everybody a fair shot."

Yet Quentin is not naive about the broader systemic and more insidious forms of racism that still pervade the everyday lives of African Americans in this country. He said that racism is still alive and well in America and that it has merely changed its form:

> It's not always the cross on the front lawn. . . . It's not always gonna be, you know, yelling and name-calling. It's gonna be the subtle things that sometimes happen, and some of them are intentional, some people do it because they know it, it's cognizant. Other people do it because they

have some ignorances, and they do it because they don't know any better. So it's intentional and then unintentional, but it's very injurious. It's very hurtful. . . . We don't realize [that racism] is not always, you know, go and beat somebody up. It's, you know, following you around at JC Penney's, thinking you're gonna steal something simply because you're black, when the majority of shoplifters are not African American.

This more subtle racism, Quentin says, plays out in a context of a still-unequal playing field in which whites like to talk about equality but those in positions of power—those who "have the ability to make us equal"—are not willing to share the wealth of this country, particularly with African Americans and Hispanics. Thus, Quentin notes, while an individual white may treat an individual black or Latino decently, the larger inequality that perpetuates racial segregation and the concentration of wealth and power in the hands of relatively few people, most of them white, continues.

At the same time, Quentin, like many of his fellow graduates of color from the class of 1980, complains about his fellow African Americans who continually get in trouble. As a police official, Quentin said, he gets tired of taking young African American males and Hispanic males to jail. He said he just wants to tell them how to stay out of trouble, "how to get yourself together and get an education, how to get off the street corner, how to stop slinging drugs, how to have somebody that is in a position that can help you."

Quentin said that while he understands subtle racism and he is aware of the unequal distribution of power and money in this white-dominated society, he still thinks that many blacks and Latinos could make other choices about what to do with their lives. In fact, he even thinks that if he does not try to change some of the young people he arrests and books for various crimes, he is failing to give back to his community: "That is my job. If I don't do that, I'm failing. . . . I'm failing John Muir, I'm failing black folks, I'm failing in a number of areas. You can't get to a certain position and then not be able to go back and help somebody. And I get tired of [people] just not doing that. You got to do that."

At the same time, the double consciousness of whites described in chapter 1, which allows whites to simultaneously espouse color-blindness and racial equality while maintaining their own racial privilege, can be challenged only through greater racial integration. The white graduates we studied are highly conflicted about the current paradigm and racial discourse used politically to justify the dismantling of any race-specific policies in the United States. The vast majority of white graduates we interviewed—with three exceptions across the six sites—do not completely buy into the simple explanations of ongoing racial inequality in this country—for example, the explanation that the problem lies entirely in the immorality and lack of family values and work ethic in black and Latino communities. While many of them will lapse into such explanations when they lack other ways of making sense of what they know, when they think back to their friends and teammates from high school who were black or Hispanic they begin to contradict themselves and search for different, more complex explanations. In their contradictions and confusion, there is hope.

A white Muir High School graduate explained his interpretation of racial issues in America this way: "I think my experience growing up and attending a racially mixed school had an impact . . . gave me, perhaps . . . some insight into, you know, America's dilemma. And I find that . . . as someone who teaches history, the civil rights struggle, I think, is one of the most inspiring moments in American history. And it's one that's not complete."

At the same time, a white graduate of Topeka High School named Kelly Lynch continues to struggle through her sometimes contradictory ways of making sense of race in the United States. On the one hand, she has touted the benefits of racially diverse schools to her friends who have a child starting kindergarten. She said that her friend's son was signed up for kindergarten in a racially diverse school in Topeka but that this friend was thinking about moving to a more predominantly white school district as his son got older. Kelly, who grew up in a middle-class family and attended only a couple semesters of college but who has kept her own children in the Topeka Public Schools, including Topeka High School, explained that her friend really wants to "yank" his son out of diverse schools for junior high and high school: "I go, why? You're not preparing him for life and you know there's blacks, Mexicans, mixed, Orientals, Asians, or whatever no matter where you go now. No matter where you go, why not prepare him now?" Going even further, she stated: "What America is made of, I think that different races can make beautiful partners in everything. Otherwise I think it will end up a civil war again if you try to keep people from knowing one another and understanding each other's cultures."

Yet Kelly is highly opposed to policies that would help facilitate racial diversity in public schools. Like many of her fellow white graduates across the six schools we studied, she is adamantly opposed to busing even when it is voluntary on the part of the students. She said: "There should not be busing because this is a free country and you choose where you want to live. If you want your child to go to a certain school, then you need to pay for the transportation to get them there."

What is missing from Kelly's and many other graduates' critiques of busing and the argument that you can live wherever you want is an understanding of the more structural issues of housing segregation and the intertwined relationship between segregated schools and housing and of how this prevents many people of color from meaningful choice, whether in the public or private educational systems. The one white graduate with the best grasp of these critical housing segregation issues was Maya Deller from Shaker Heights High School. Maybe it was her undergraduate major in history or her law degree, but Maya seemed to grasp the structural inequality issues far better than her peers. Clearly part of it was her background as a Jew who has thought long and hard about the legacy of the Holocaust on Jews who were not yet born when it happened. She said that feelings of oppression get passed down from one generation to the next: "I mean, you know, I don't know any Jewish people—any!—who aren't profoundly affected by the Holocaust. Now, I was not alive during the Holocaust. I am profoundly affected by it. My children . . . will be . . . even though it wasn't in our lifetime." She said that on the basis of understanding this intergenerational effect she can imagine how the kind of racism and oppression blacks have faced in the United States historically and even in the more recent past would affect black students and their families today.

Maya knows she is an exception because most white people cannot seem to see beyond individual experience. "And it's hard to imagine that

there are structural issues, like, housing discrimination or . . . like, institutional racism. It's hard for people to see that and understand that
because it's abstract to some level in terms of your personal experience.
It's not something you touch and feel every day." Yet even Maya, when
asked to explain the current conditions of income inequality and black
poverty rates, goes back to a focus on the individual, especially as she
struggles to articulate a "solution." She said that maybe the inequality is
residual from slavery and Jim Crow. "Who the hell knows? I mean . . .
look. People have to take responsibility for themselves, whether they're
white, black, or purple. They have to—you pull yourself up; I know, you
know, you get yourself together. There's opportunity, there are black
people who started with nothing in much worse racial climates than we
have today who have achieved amazing things. So is it an excuse? No. Is
it a reality?"

Meanwhile, a white classmate of Maya's from Shaker Heights tried to
explain away ongoing racial inequality in the United States by
adamantly refusing to believe that history plays a critical or central role
today. This graduate explained that she has always loathed that "what
your people did to my people type of thing" that she has heard blacks
bring up. She said that growing up in Cleveland where there wasn't any
slavery, at least not by the time of the Civil War, she wanted to know
from the blacks she grew up with, when they complained about the past,
whether they had any relatives who had been in slavery. If they could
not think of anyone offhand, her response was: "Okay, well, then what's
your problem? . . . It [slavery] was not necessarily a proud moment in
history, but it happened, there's nothing we can do to change it type of
thing. . . . I grew up down the street from you my entire life, so did my
family, and the family before them, so don't tell me that, look what my
family did to your family, 'cause I don't have any relatives that ever lived
in the South, and neither do you."

It is problematic that this woman and other white graduates of desegregated schools apparently never learned enough American history to
know that most of the blacks who live in Cleveland and most northern
cities today did not arrive there until the twentieth century as part of the
great migration of slaves and sharecroppers from the South to the North

and from the farms to the cities. The fact that they arrived for the most part poor and uneducated and then faced tremendous housing and job discrimination when they got there, most of them shortly before the class of 1980 was born, should not be unknown to a middle-aged white person with a high school education. In fact, some have argued that this great migration of blacks to the northern cities in the middle of the last century is one of the most important demographic changes ever to occur in the United States.[4] Its relationship to current conditions in northern cities is something any educated adult should have considered.

In part because of what they do not know or understand, the graduates of these schools have not changed the world—in fact, many have (sometimes unwittingly) done their part as adults to perpetuate our segregated society. In their sense of loss about the racial diversity they once enjoyed, there is indeed hope that the United States need not always be so separate and unequal. But someone or something—like a social movement—will need to take their sense of loss forward to press a new reform agenda around issues of diversity in public schools and neighborhoods. As one white graduate of Dwight Morrow noted, after school integration occurred and proved to not be sustainable in the manner it had been carried out in the 1970s, "Nobody . . . had like second gear for the civil rights movement . . . for the society as a whole, you know." A white Shaker Heights High School graduate similarly commented, "I believe that we thought we were on the cusp of being the new way of how it was gonna be, and it didn't pan out that way, it was a great disappointment." Another glum assessment came from a white graduate of West Charlotte High School who noted, in a discussion of the recent retreat from school desegregation in that city, "It's amazing to me that . . . my parents went through segregation, I went through integration, and potentially my daughter might go back to segregation."

But a white classmate from West Charlotte argued that there is a huge difference today in racial attitudes and acceptance and understanding, a change that he attributes largely to the kind of school desegregation policies he experienced. He said, "I think it's got a long, long, long way to go, but I think just changing the attitude and people's willingness to look at it differently is what integrated schools helped accomplish. And I think the benefit of that is just now being . . . starting to be realized, and will be realized by the time we're older, and our kids are my age." If this last graduate is even partially right, the next section, on policy implications and recommendations, may help direct us toward a different future for our increasingly diverse society.

POLICY IMPLICATIONS
AND RECOMMENDATIONS

This small ray of hope is reflected in the U.S. Supreme Court's 2003 ruling in *Grutter v. Bollinger.* The Opinion of the Court stated that "student-body diversity is a compelling state interest." Although the ruling applied to a law school admissions policy, it was believed, until June 2007, to have major implications for K–12 education, where, it can be argued, the state interest is even more compelling. But as we noted in chapter 1, in June 2007 the Supreme Court issued a complicated ruling on this issue as it applies to K–12 public schools in its *Parents Involved* decision regarding two voluntary integration cases from Louisville, Kentucky, and Seattle, Washington. Because of Justice Anthony Kennedy's swing vote in this decision, it appears that the "compelling state interest" argument—or the rationale for the "ends" to be achieved by school districts in term of racial balancing—is hanging on by a very thin thread. The means by which school district officials can attempt to achieve these ends are narrowed significantly, making the ends that much more elusive.[5]

As we move forward in a post–*Parents Involved* era, we need to keep in mind the many forces that should compel policy makers to work around the recent Supreme Court ruling and address issues of racial segregation. For instance, as we noted above, polls show that the vast majority of parents—black or white—support the concept of racially mixed public schools, but they strongly prefer voluntary or choice-based desegregation policies to mandatory reassignments. In this era of school choice policy proliferation, it should be fairly easy to give parents what they want. Indeed, when we combine the legal argument of a state interest in diverse educational settings with the opinion poll data and the voices of people who have lived through school desegregation, we can clearly see the demand for public policies to support rather than dismantle desegregated schools.

How would we get there? The answer seems to be voluntary school desegregation and greater housing integration, which policy makers could facilitate in several ways.[6]

1. *Broaden measures of school quality and accountability to include indicators other than standardized test scores. For instance, racial and other forms of diversity could be considered one measure of a "good" public school in an increasingly diverse society.*

Growing public frustration with President Bush's education policy, the No Child Left Behind Act, shows that Americans are tiring of testing and retesting students as the single instrument of enforcing school, teacher, and student accountability.[7] The collective wisdom of the American public and the voices of the class of 1980 show a yearning for a fuller understanding of what makes a school good. While tests can be one very important indicator of student learning, our interviewees never mentioned "high test scores" when reflecting on what they valued most about their school experiences.

We have seen in our study that these narrow testing measures—used as the sole criteria for judging "good" and "bad" schools—work against the kinds of schools that these graduates attended. As parents, they have come to pay increasing attention to school rankings on state-mandated test scores in newspapers. And standardized tests, on which white and wealthy students generally score higher, often feed perceptions that racially diverse schools are inferior and not worth sustaining.[8]

Some people argue that new testing systems may promote equity because they force schools to be accountable to all families, not just those of high-achieving students destined for Ivy League colleges.[9] Indeed, under the No Child Left Behind Act, states are required to disaggregate test score data to better understand the performance of students of different racial and social backgrounds (and students who, for example, have limited English proficiency or receive special education). In theory, these accountability measures could compel schools to focus on serving all of their students.[10]

At the same time, these accountability systems still judge the quality of a school by the narrow criterion of testing. Only the wealthiest schools, and those serving high percentages of white and Asian students, consistently rank near the top in terms of average score.[11] Our data suggest that affluent parents and/or white parents are less likely to keep their children in a diverse public school that has lower average test scores even if it is succeeding according to other important measures.

Such narrow measures of accountability also undermine efforts to "untrack" racially diverse public schools. Students constantly feel they are in competition for the few spaces in the best classes. Such competitive models seem to run counter to efforts in corporations to create more cooperative working environments, and they certainly work against efforts to create more democratic and equal schools.

We know from our research that the reputations of racially diverse public schools are fragile and need to be bolstered—not shot down— by state policies. Legislators could, in collaboration with local school and community leaders, enforce accountability *and* foster racial diversity. One possible means would be to devise accountability measures that more accurately reflect the range of experiences of students within racially diverse schools and give racially and otherwise diverse schools credit for reflecting the "real world" and swimming against the tide of segregation. Such measures are supported by recent research showing that students who attend racially diverse schools learn more and gain deeper insights into issues and social problems by participating in class discussions that encompass many different perspectives.[12]

This shift in thinking about accountability would open many democratic possibilities and give schools and communities more input into efforts to define public school accountability. In other words, we need an accountability system that more clearly reflects what parents and students say are important characteristics and goals of public schools. One of these would be racial and other forms of diversity.

2. *Amend current public school choice policies, including charter school laws, to make them more supportive of parents and educators who want to start and maintain racially diverse schools.*

We acknowledge the political popularity of the many newer forms of school choice polices in states across the country. Most won passage in the 1990s and were touted as measures to infuse greater competition and choice into the public school system. But many of these deregulated school choice options—including interdistrict choice plans, charter schools, and vouchers—raise far more problems than they solve, especially in terms of equity and greater access to the best schools for poor students of color. They are, by definition, "color-blind" school choice policies that do not require any racial balancing and in fact make such balancing difficult because of their laissez-faire style of recruitment and their lack of transportation to bring students from segregated neighborhoods together. Furthermore, we find that when government oversight diminishes and choice is left to vagaries of the market, inequality and fraud arise.

The most well known of the 1990s-era school choice policies is charter school reform. With charter school laws on the books in forty-one states and nearly four thousand charter schools that serve more than one million students up and running, the idea of giving schools public per-pupil funding but allowing them considerable autonomy from the public system has obviously caught on.

Yet despite broad-based and bipartisan support for charter schools, the public policies under which the schools operate tend to serve a narrow set of interests—those of free-market advocates who want public education deregulated and privatized. Nomenclature in the charter school world defines "strong" laws as those that allow more deregulation and spawn the largest number of charter schools. Conservative backers of charter school laws argue that "strong" charter school laws should include the following provisions: no cap on the number of charter schools allowed, multiple charter-granting agencies, no requirement for formal evidence of local support before start-up, greater legal and fiscal autonomy, automatic waiver from state and district laws, exemption from collective bargaining and work rules, and a guarantee of per-pupil funding (but no more and no special support for schools serving poor students).[13]

Missing from this definition of a "strong" charter school law is any thoughtful discussion of the question "'Strong' for what?" If strong charter school laws are simply those that spawn the most schools regardless of the quality of those schools or whether some of them can help to further the goal of racial integration, then we as a society should question how appropriate such definitions are. But the goal of racial diversity, despite strong political support in the general public, appears not to be part of the agenda for those who have the most influence in the statehouses across the country. Thus most charter schools lack any method to broadly disseminate information about their programs. Nor do most of them have the public transportation they would need to bring in students from different communities, the way magnet schools do. Furthermore, unlike magnet schools, many charter schools have admission criteria that do not take into account the goal of racial diversity. These and other characteristics of so-called strong charter school laws have contributed to the growing consensus in the research literature that charter schools are more racially and socioeconomically segregated than regular public schools.[14]

But charter school laws could be amended to help encourage racial, ethnic, and other forms of diversity. For instance, good or "strong" laws could provide financial and other incentives for educators and parents who want to start racially, ethnically, or socioeconomically diverse charter schools. Following the Supreme Court ruling in the Louisville and Seattle voluntary integration cases, it is most likely not possible for charter schools to use the racial identities of individual students as a mechanism to create racially or ethnically diverse schools. But they can, according to Justice Kennedy's key opinion in that case, make a concerted effort to draw students from racially identifiable neighborhoods, which would be helpful in reducing some degree of racial segregation.

Under such laws, state governments would also need to (a) pay for student transportation to and from diverse charter schools, especially for students who live far from the school and whose parents lack the means to ferry them each day; (b) prohibit charter schools from having narrow admissions criteria or requiring parents to sign contracts with the schools (such prerequisites are too reminiscent of private school practices, and there is no good justification for tax dollars going to schools that exclude students because their parents work two jobs, etc.); (c) ensure that information on charter schools is widely distributed and that word-of-mouth recruitment is no longer the primary means by which families learn about charter school opportunities. Indeed, such outreach efforts should include the targeted recruitment of students from racially isolated communities that are underrepresented in the charter school, which Justice Kennedy condoned and even recommended for schools struggling to achieve the goal of a racially diverse school.

In addition to charter school laws, since the late 1980s, forty-four states have passed interdistrict "open enrollment" school choice laws that allow nearly five hundred thousand students to choose to enroll in a public school in a different school district. These plans, like most of the deregulatory choice policies of late, make parents shoulder the entire burden of finding a new school, applying for admission, and providing daily transportation to and from the distant school. In about half the states, schools and districts choose whether they want to participate in the program and accept choice students. In the other half, the districts are "mandated" to participate, but they can argue against accepting choice students on the basis of lack of space.[15]

Little research exists on these politically popular state policies. However, in a recent review of the evidence on these open enrollment plans as they compare to interdistrict desegregation plans, Holme and Wells found that the open enrollment choice plans consistently led to more racial and social class segregation while the interdistrict desegregation plans fostered more integration.[16] For instance, one important study on Massachusetts's open enrollment choice plan found that these programs tend either to maintain the status quo in terms of segregation and inequality or to worsen the situation by allowing families to use the programs to move to more segregated schools.[17]

But interdistrict school choice policies, like charter school laws, could be amended to provide incentives and transportation for families that want to use them to foster greater racial and other forms of school-level diversity. We know from our experience with magnet schools and voluntary transfers under school desegregation plans that parents can make choices that fulfill academic expectations *and* support the goal of desegregation. Parents, students, and our society deserve public policies that provide for the choices of individuals as well as serving the greater good.[18]

3. *Increase the often pitiful federal and state support for school districts that are trying to maintain desegregated schools.*

One of the most obvious implications of our research is that communities and school districts that are currently operating under school desegregation court orders or desegregation plans that they adopted voluntarily deserve support from federal and state governments.

While the era of mandatory reassignment of students for desegregation purposes is ending, hundreds of school districts across the country still struggle to maintain diversity in at least some of their public schools. For instance, most urban school districts continue to operate magnet schools, which are public schools of choice designed to attract students of different racial and ethnic backgrounds. Most of them have curricular themes such as math and science or the performing arts, and they are generally popular. Magnet schools, which preceded charter schools, continue to receive nominal federal support through a grant program that has been funded at the same low level—between $100 and $120 million—for more than a decade. Federal funding for charter schools and other choice programs, including interdistrict open enrollment choice programs, that are not aimed at desegregating students, and in fact often exacerbate segregation,[19] now totals almost three times what the federal government is spending on magnet schools. The federal government must be held accountable for such imbalances.

Other important, but fragile, voluntary options include interdistrict transfer plans that allow students to cross urban-suburban boundaries in order to desegregate schools. Operating in a handful of metropolitan areas, including St. Louis, Milwaukee, and Boston, these school choice plans are at critical stages and depend on the goodwill of their state legislatures or the suburban school districts that accept the urban transfer students. Policy makers at the federal, state, and local level should listen to the voices of the people we have interviewed and renew their commitment to such important and successful programs.[20]

4. *Pursue noneducation goals, such as housing integration and suburb diversification, that will facilitate the creation of more diverse public schools.*

Our study demonstrates that school desegregation accomplished a great deal but that it could have accomplished much more if the "real world" outside the schools had made similar gains—for example, in housing and income equality. The Clinton administration's "Moving to Opportunity" program, which helped low-income families relocate from poor urban neighborhoods to more affluent suburban ones, was a step in the right direction.[21] But such programs must be expanded beyond a handful of metropolitan areas and a small number of families.

Also essential are policies to help maintain racially diverse suburbs and their suburban school districts. The vast majority of urban school districts are now less than 20 percent white. So the effort to create and sustain racially diverse public schools in the cities is all but over for the foreseeable future, save for a few stellar specialized schools or elementary schools located in predominantly white neighborhoods. Today the responsibility to fulfill the promise of Brown belongs more to suburban than urban school districts, as increasing numbers of blacks, Latinos, and Asians cross urban-suburban lines. As we noted in chapter 1, according to the 2000 Census, 40 percent of African Americans now live in suburbs. In major metropolitan areas—those with populations of more than five hundred thousand—blacks and Latinos combined constitute 27 percent of suburban residents.[22]

Recent evidence suggests that the suburbs are offering a repeat performance of the urban white flight that occurred in the sixties, seventies, and eighties. Thus, as blacks (and to a lesser extent, Latinos) are moving out of the cities, they are remaining highly segregated in their new suburban homes because, as we noted, more and more whites are fleeing these communities for more remote suburbs or gentrified urban areas. Asians, meanwhile, particularly those of Chinese, Japanese, and Korean descent, are more likely to live in predominantly white suburbs.[23]

Policy makers could stem this tide before it is too late. Large urban school districts cover many square miles and include hundreds of schools and populations that are often disparate in terms of income. Suburban districts are smaller and more homogeneous in terms of social class, so they could racially balance schools with relatively modest—and thus politically palatable—student movement. Some ask, If racial integration cannot happen in suburbia, where in American society can it happen? Are the suburbs the last hope for the integrationist's dream?

From among the graduates of the class of 1980—and those who graduated from high school shortly after or just before—a new generation of leaders is emerging. This book has tapped into the spirit of that generation, too long ignored and underresearched, but one with a crucial and powerful message.

Far into the future, the political choices made and the priorities set in the coming years will dictate the course for this nation, increasingly diverse yet still separate in many ways. We can continue in our current direction. Or we can choose to listen to the voices of those who experienced the benefits of school desegregation firsthand—men and women who know in their hearts and minds that our increasingly diverse society need not be evermore separate and unequal. This generation of forty-somethings has seen our racially divided society from both sides. They know that it is not easy to bring people together across the color line, but they also know that we can do so much more than we are doing now, and that it is worth doing.

In closing, we provide a quote from a 1980 graduate of Muir High School, Geri Delgato, a Latino whom we profiled in chapter 5. When asked to reflect on his experience with school desegregation in Pasadena, Geri summed up many of the major themes in this study: "Could the programs have been improved? Of course they could have been improved. Were they better than what we had? Without a doubt! But I also think quite honestly, we just didn't stick with it long enough."

Notes

CHAPTER 1

    1. The names of all the graduates cited in this book have been changed to protect their confidentiality.

    2. Robert Reich, Secretary of Labor in the Clinton administration, referred to the top 20 percent of American income earners—those making more than $93,000 in 2000—as the "fortunate fifth" because between 1973 and 2000 this group enjoyed a 61.6 percent increase in real income, well above the percentage increase for lower-income workers. Peter Drier, John Mollenkopf, and Todd Swanstrom, *Place Matters: Metropolitics for the Twenty-First Century*, 2nd, rev. ed. (Lawrence: University of Kansas Press, 2004), p. 25.

    3. Amy Stuart Wells et al., "How Desegregation Changed Us: The Effects of Racially Mixed Schools on Students and Society" (final report from the Understanding Race and Education Study, Teachers College, Columbia University, New York, March 30, 2004), www.tc.columbia.edu/desegregation (accessed January 4, 2008).

    4. The Court's belief in the growing significance of education and educational opportunity in providing mobility in our mid-twentieth-century society was underscored in its opinion, written by Chief Justice Earl Warren: "Today, education is perhaps the most important function of state and local governments. Compulsory school attendance laws and the great expenditures for education both demonstrate our recognition of the importance of education to our democratic society. It is required in the performance of our most basic public responsibilities, even service in the armed forces. It is the very foundation of good citizenship. Today it is a principal instrument in awakening the child to cultural values, in preparing him for later professional training, and in helping him to adjust normally to his environment. In these days, it is doubtful that any child

may reasonably be expected to succeed in life if he is denied the opportunity of an education. Such an opportunity, where the state has undertaken to provide it, is a right which must be made available to all on equal terms." *Brown v. Board of Education*, 347 U.S. 483.

5. See Amy Stuart Wells et al., "How Society Failed School Desegregation Policy: Looking Past the Schools to Understand Them," *Review of Research in Education* 28 (2005): 47–100.

6. Wells et al., "How Desegregation Changed Us."

7. See "Brief of 553 Social Scientists as *Amici Curiae* in Support of Respondents," *Parents Involved in Community Schools v. Seattle School District No. 1 and Meredith v. Jefferson County Board of Education* (Nos. 05–908 and 05–915), 2006, www.civilrightsproject.ucla.edu/research/deseg/amicus_parents_v_seatle. pdf (accessed January 20, 2008); Amy Stuart Wells and Robert L. Crain, "Perpetuation Theory and the Long-Term Effects of School Desegregation," *Review of Educational Research* 64 (1994): 531–55.

8. See Melvin L. Oliver and Thomas M. Shapiro, *Black Wealth/White Wealth: A New Perspective on Racial Inequality* (New York: Routledge, 1995); Thomas M. Shapiro, *The Hidden Cost of Being African American* (New York: Oxford University Press, 2005); Heather Beth Johnson, *The American Dream and the Power of Wealth: Choosing Schools and Inheriting Inequality in the Land of Opportunity* (New York: Routledge, 2006).

9. U.S. Census Bureau, "State and County QuickFacts," 2007 (for the year 2006), http://quickfacts.census.gov/qfd/states/00000.html, and National Center for Education Statistics, "Digest of Education Statistics," 2006 (for the year 2004), http://nces.ed.gov/programs/digest/d06/tables/dt06_040.asp (both accessed January 4, 2008).

10. See Amy Stuart Wells and Erica Frankenberg, "The Public Schools and the Challenge of the Supreme Court's Integration Decision," *Phi Delta Kappan*, November 2007, pp. 178–88.

11. Rajiv Sethi and Rohini Somanathan, "Inequality and Segregation," *Journal of Political Economy* 112 (2004): 1296–1322.

12. Ibid.

13. Mary Patillo, "Black Middle-Class Neighborhoods," *Annual Review of Sociology* 31 (2005): 305–29; Drum Major Institute for Public Policy, "Injustice Index: The Black Middle Class," 2004, www.drummajorinstitute.org (accessed August 8, 2005).

14. Douglas S. Massey et al., *The Source of the River: The Social Origins of Freshmen at America's Selective Colleges and Universities* (Princeton: Princeton University Press, 2003), p. 42.

15. Kimberly Atkins, "Mapping the Quiet Divide: Suburban Housing Segregation," *Boston Globe*, March 9, 2003, www.boston.com (accessed August 10,

2005); Patillo, "Black Middle-Class Neighborhoods." Also see Christopher Leinberger, "The Next Slum?" *Atlantic Monthly,* March 2008, www.theatlantic.com/doc/200803/subprime (accessed March 6, 2008).

16.   Richard Rothstein, "Must Schools Fail?" *New York Review of Books,* December 2, 2004, www.nybooks.com (accessed December 5, 2004).

17.   Roger Barnes, "Income and Poverty: Demographic Statistics for African Americans," *Black Enterprise,* October 2001, p. 34.

18.   National Urban League, *The State of Black America 2005* (New York: National Urban League, 2005).

19.   John Schmitt, "Recent Job Loss Hits the African-American Middle Class Hard" (briefing paper, Center for Economic and Policy Research, Washington, DC, October 7, 2004), www.cepr.net/publications (accessed August 5, 2005).

20.   National Urban League, *State of Black America 2005;* Oliver and Shapiro, *Black Wealth/White Wealth.*

21.   Rothstein, "Must Schools Fail?"

22.   Sethi and Somanathan, "Inequality and Segregation."

23.   David M. Cutler, Edward L. Glaeser, and Jacob L. Vigdor, "The Rise and Decline of the American Ghetto," *Journal of Political Economy* 107 (June 1999): 455–507.

24.   John E. Farley and Gregory D. Squires, "Fences and Neighbors: Segregation in 21st-Century America," *Contexts* 4 (Winter 2005): 34.

25.   Sethi and Somanathan, "Inequality and Segregation"; Farley and Squires, "Fences and Neighbors," p. 5.

26.   Drier, Mollenkopf, and Swanstrom, *Place Matters;* John Logan, "Ethnic Diversity Grows, Neighborhood Integration Lags Behind" (report, Lewis Mumford Center, Albany, NY, April 3, 2001), www.albany.edu/mumford/census (accessed February 21, 2002).

27.   Cutler, Glaeser, and Vigdor, "Rise and Decline."

28.   Logan, "Ethnic Diversity Grows," p. 1.

29.   Patillo, "Black Middle-Class Neighborhoods."

30.   John Logan, "Separate and Unequal: The Neighborhood Gap for Blacks and Hispanics in Metropolitan America" (report, Lewis Mumford Center, Albany, NY, October 15, 2002).

31.   Keith R. Ihlanfeldt and Benjamin Scafidi, "Whites' Neighbourhood Racial Preferences and Neighbourhood Racial Composition in the United States: Evidence from the Multi-City Study of Urban Inequality," *Housing Studies* 19 (May 2004): 325–59.

32.   Ibid., p. 356.

33.   Thomas Piketty and Emmanuel Saez, "The Evolution of Top Incomes: A Historical and International Perspective" (Working Paper No. 11955, National Bureau of Economic Research, Cambridge, MA, January 2006), www.nber.org/papers/w11955 (accessed September 21, 2007).

34. Paul Krugman, "Losing Our Country," *New York Times,* June 10, 2005, p. A2.

35. Bob Herbert, "The Mobility Myth," *New York Times,* June 6, 2005, www.nytimes.com (accessed June 7, 2005).

36. Drier, Mollenkopf, and Swanstrom, *Place Matters;* Logan, "Ethnic Diversity Grows."

37. Drier, Mollenkopf, and Swanstrom, *Place Matters;* Logan, "Ethnic Diversity Grows."

38. Logan, "Separate and Unequal."

39. Janice Petrovich, introduction to *Bringing Equity Back,* ed. Janice Petrovich and Amy Stuart Wells (New York: Teachers College Press, 2005).

40. Thomas Byrne Edsall, *Chain Reaction: The Impact of Race, Rights, and Taxes on American Politics* (New York: Norton, 1993).

41. Thomas Frank, *What's the Matter with Kansas? How Conservatives Won the Heart of America* (New York: Metropolitan Books, 2004).

42. David Grissmer, Ann Flanagan, and Stephanie Williamson, "Why Did the Black-White Score Gap Narrow in the 1970s and 1980s?" in *The Black-White Test Score Gap,* ed. Christopher Jencks and Meredith Phillips (Washington, DC: Brookings Institution, 1998), pp. 182–226.

43. See ibid. and Gary Orfield, *The Growth of Segregation in America Schools: Changing Patterns of Separations and Poverty since 1968* (Washington, DC: National School Boards Association, 1993).

44. Chungmei Lee, "Is Resegregation Real?" (working paper, Civil Rights Project, Harvard University, Cambridge, MA, October 2004), www.civilrightsproject.ucla.edu/research/resego3/mumfordresponse.pdf (accessed January 5, 2008).

45. Gary Orfield and Chungmei Lee, "Why Segregation Matters: Poverty and Educational Inequality" (working paper, Civil Rights Project, Harvard University, Cambridge, MA, January 2005), p. 12, www.civilrightsproject.ucla.edu/research/deseg/Why_Segreg_Matters.pdf (accessed January 5, 2008).

46. Ibid., p. 16.

47. Ibid., p. 4.

48. U.S. Department of Education, National Center for Education Statistics, "Enrollment in Elementary and Secondary Schools, by Level and Control of Institution: Selected Years, Fall 1970 to Projections for Fall 2014," *Digest of Education Statistics, 2005* (Washington, DC: U.S. Department of Education, 2006), nces.ed.gov/fastfacts (accessed July 10, 2006).

49. John R. Logan, "Resegregation in American Public Schools? Not in the 1990s" (report, Lewis Mumford Center, Albany, NY, April 26, 2004), www.albany.edu/mumford (accessed May 11, 2005).

50. Lee, "Is Resegregation Real?"

51. Christopher Cross, *Political Education: National Policy Comes of Age* (New York: Teachers College Press, 2004).

52. Linda Darling-Hammond, "From 'Separate but Equal' to 'No Child Left Behind': The Collision of New Standards and Old Inequalities," in *Many Children Left Behind*, ed. Deborah Meier and George Wood (Boston: Beacon Press, 2004), pp. 3–32; Theodore R. Sizer, "Preamble: A Reminder for Americans," in Meier and Wood, *Many Children Left Behind*, pp. xvii–xxii.

53. Eric Robelen, "'No Child' Remains at Top of Bush Record," *Education Week*, September 29, 2004, pp. 1, 23–24; David E. Sanger, "Bush Defends Financing for Schools," *New York Times*, September 9, 2003, www.nytimes.com (accessed September 6, 2004).

54. "Bush Warns against the 'Soft Bigotry of Low Expectations,'" *Education Week*, September 22, 1999, www.edweek.org (accessed June 14, 2005).

55. Stan Karp, "NCLB's Selective Vision of Equality: Some Gaps Count More Than Others," in Meier and Wood, *Many Children Left Behind*, pp. 53–65; Richard Rothstein, *Class and Schools* (Washington, DC: Economic Policy Institute, 2004).

56. Julian E. Barnes, "Unequal Education: Now the Focus Shifts from Integration to Achievement for All," *U.S. News and World Report*, March 22, 2004, pp. 67–75; see also Greg Winter, "50 Years after *Brown*, the Issue Is Often Money," *New York Times*, May 17, 2004, pp. A1, A19.

57. Orfield and Lee, "Why Segregation Matters."

58. See Barnes, "Now the Focus Shifts"; Wells et al., "How Society Failed."

59. See Wells et al., "How Society Failed."

60. See Jennifer L. Hochschild, *Facing Up to the American Dream* (Princeton: Princeton University Press, 1995).

61. See Kelly Bagnishi and Marc R. Sheer, "*Brown v. Board of Education:* Fifty Years Later," *Trends and Tudes*, Newsletter of Harris Interactive, June 2004.

62. Gunner Myrdal, *An American Dilemma*, 2nd ed. (New York: Harper and Row, 1962).

63. Michael J. Klarman, *From Jim Crow to Civil Rights* (New York: Oxford University Press, 2004).

64. Gary Orfield, "Public Opinion and School Desegregation," *Teachers College Record* 96 (1995): 654–70.

65. Amy Stuart Wells and Robert L. Crain, *Stepping over the Color Line* (New Haven: Yale University Press, 1997).

66. See Edsall, *Chain Reaction;* Bruce J. Schulman, *The Seventies* (New York: Free Press, 2001).

67. See Edsall, *Chain Reaction,* and Schulman, *Seventies.*

68. Charles Murray, *Losing Ground: American Social Policy, 1950–1980* (New York: Basic Books, 1984).

69. Hochschild, *Facing Up to the American Dream.*

70. Ibid., p. 74; Bagnishi and Sheer, "*Brown v. Board of Education.*"

71. W.E.B. DuBois, *The Souls of Black Folk,* 100th Anniversary ed. (Boulder, CO: Paradigm, 2003).

72. Ibid., p. 2.

73. Charles Lemert, foreword to DuBois, *Souls of Black Folk,* p. xv.

74. Lawrie Balfour, "'A Most Disagreeable Mirror': Race Consciousness as Double Consciousness," *Political Thought* 26 (June 1998): 349.

75. DuBois, *Souls of Black Folk,* p. 2.

76. Henry Louis Gates, "Both Sides Now," *New York Times Book Review,* May 4, 2003, p. 31. We credit Gates with giving us the idea for our title.

77. While much has been written about black double consciousness and, more recently, whiteness and whites' racial dualism, far less has been published (at least in English) about the consciousness of Latinos. Still Gloria Anzaldúa's concept of "mestiza consciousness" speaks to the issues of oppositional culture and consciousness not only in terms of race and ethnicity but also in terms of social class, gender, and sexual orientation. See Gloria Anzaldúa, *Borderlands: La Frontera,* 3rd ed. (San Francisco: Aunt Lute Books, 2007), and Theresa A. Martinez, "The Double-Consciousness of Du Bois and the 'Mestiza Consciousness' of Anzaldua," *Race, Gender and Class* 4 (October 2002): 158.

78. Martinez, "Double-Consciousness of Du Bois," p. 158.

79. Howard Winant, "Behind Blue Eyes: Whiteness and Contemporary U.S. Racial Politics," in *Off White: Readings on Power, Privilege and Resistance,* 2nd ed., ed. Michelle Fine et al. (New York: Routledge, 2004), pp. 3–16; Shelly Fisher Fishkin, "Interrogating 'Whiteness,' Complicating 'Blackness': Remapping American Culture," *American Quarterly* 47 (1995): 428–66.

80. See Hochschild, *Facing Up to the American Dream;* Wells and Crain, *Stepping over the Color Line;* Joe L. Kincheloe and Shirley R. Steinberg, "Addressing the Crisis of Whiteness: Reconfiguring White Identity in a Pedagogy of Whiteness," in *White Reign: Deploying Whiteness in America,* ed. Joe L. Kincheloe et al. (New York: St. Martin's Griffin, 1998).

81. Derald W. Sue, "Racism and the Conspiracy of Silence," *Counseling Psychologist* 33, no. 1 (2005): 100–114.

82. Winant, "Behind Blue Eyes," pp. 3, 4.

83. Ibid., p. 4.

84. Ibid., p. 5.

85. Paul M. Kellstedt, "Media Framing and Dynamics of Racial Policy Preferences," *American Journal of Political Science* 44 (April 2002): 239–55.

86. Walter R. Allen and Angie Y. Chung, "Your Blues Ain't Like My Blues: Race, Ethnicity, and Social Inequality in America," *Contemporary Sociology* 29 (2000): 796–805. Also see Ian F. Haney Lopez, "A Nation of Minorities: Race,

Ethnicity, and Reactionary Colorblindness," *Stanford Law Review* 59 (2007): 985–1063.

87. See Balfour, "A Most Disagreeable Mirror," p. 355.

88. Linda Greenhouse, "Court Reviews Race as a Factor in School Plans," *New York Times*, December 5, 2006.

89. *Parents Involved in Community Schools v. Seattle Public Schools* and *Crystal D. Meredith v. Jefferson County Board of Education*, 551 U.S. (2007), Opinion of Chief Justice Roberts, p. 28.

90. Ibid., p. 35.

91. *Parents Involved in Community Schools v. Seattle Public Schools*, 551 U.S. 2007, Opinion of Chief Justice Roberts, p. 40.

92. Eduardo Bonilla-Silva, *Racism without Racists* (Lanham, MD: Rowman and Littlefield, 2003), p. 3; also see Eduardo Bonilla-Silva, *White Supremacy and Racism in the Post–Civil Rights Era* (Boulder, CO: Lynne Rienner, 2001).

93. See Michael K. Brown et al., *Whitewashing Race: The Myth of a Color-Blind Society* (Berkeley: University of California Press, 2003).

94. Bonilla-Silva, *White Supremacy and Racism*, p. 162.

95. Bonilla-Silva discusses Bobo and Essed's work in ibid., pp. 138–39.

96. For a meta-analysis of this literature, see Thomas F. Pettigrew and Linda R. Tropp, "Does Intergroup Contact Reduce Prejudice: Recent Meta-analytic Findings," in *Reducing Prejudice and Discrimination*, ed. Stuart Oskamp (Mahwah, NJ: Lawrence Erlbaum, 2000), pp. 93–114. Also see Peter B. Wood and Nancy Sonleitner, "The Effect of Childhood Interracial Contact on Adult Antiblack Prejudice," *International Journal of Intercultural Relations* 20, no. 1 (1996): 1–17; T. Towles-Schwen and Russell H. Fazio, "On the Origins of Racial Attitudes: Correlates of Childhood Experiences," *Personality and Social Psychology Bulletin* 27 (February 2001): 162–75.

97. See Gary Orfield and Chungmei Lee, "*Brown* at 50: King's Dream or *Plessy*'s Nightmare?" (working paper, Civil Rights Project, Harvard University, Cambridge, MA, January 2004), www.civilrightsproject.ucla.edu/research/reseg04/brown50.pdf (accessed January 5, 2008); Gary Orfield, "Schools More Separate: Consequences of a Decade of Resegregation" (working paper, Civil Rights Project, Harvard University, Cambridge, MA, 2001), www.civilrightsproject. ucla.edu/research/deseg/separate_schools01.php (accessed January 5, 2008); Civil Rights Project, Harvard University, "Resegregation in American Schools," *Civil Rights Alert*, 2002 (accessed October 12, 2003), www.law.harvard.edu/civilrights/alerts/reseg.pdf.

98. Orfield, "Schools More Separate"; Erica Frankenberg and Chungmei Lee, "Race in American Public Schools: Rapidly Resegregating School Districts" (working paper, Civil Rights Project, Harvard University, Cambridge, MA, 2002), www.civilrightsproject.ucla.edu/research/deseg/Race_in_American_Public_

Schools1.pdf (accessed January 5, 2008); Civil Rights Project, Harvard University, "Resegregation in American Schools"; David Rusk, "Trends in School Segregation," in *Divided We Fall: Coming Together through School Choice*, ed. Century Foundation Task Force on the Common School (New York: Century Foundation Press, 2002), pp. 61–85.

99. We realize that after 1974, when the U.S. Supreme Court ruled in *Milliken v. Bradley* that court-ordered urban-suburban school desegregation was possible only when plaintiffs could prove that suburban districts helped to create the racial segregation in the cities, the possible impact of school desegregation on poor urban school districts was highly limited. But for the students who were living school desegregation during this later era at the end of the 1970s, things were better, more hopeful, and certainly calmer in their communities than they had been before.

100. Orfield, "Public Opinion," p. 663.

101. See Edsall, *Chain Reaction*.

102. Eduardo Porter and Greg Winter, "04 Graduates Learned Lesson in Practicality," *New York Times*, May 30, 2004, pp. 1, 24.

103. Schulman, *Seventies*.

104. Eric Foner, *The Story of American Freedom* (New York: Norton, 1998).

CHAPTER 2

1. The epigraph is from Raymond W. Mack, "School Desegregation: Case Studies of Conflict and Change," in *Our Children's Burden: Studies of Desegregation in Nine American Communities*, ed. Raymond W. Mack (New York: Vintage Books, 1968), p. 459.

2. See Amy Stuart Wells et al., "How Society Failed School Desegregation Policy: Looking Past the Schools to Understand Them," *Review of Research in Education* 28 (2005): 47–100.

3. See Sharon B. Merriam, *Qualitative Research and Case Study Applications in Education* (San Francisco: Jossey-Bass, 1998).

4. Ibid.

5. Sarah Lawrence-Lightfoot and Jessica Hoffman Davis, *The Art and Science of Portraiture* (San Francisco: Jossey-Bass, 2002).

6. "Commissioner Librera Praises Local and County Officials for Launch of Academies @ Englewood," press release, New Jersey State Department of Education, September 5, 2002, www.state.nj.us/education/news/2002/0905eng.htm (accessed September 20, 2007).

7. Institute on Education Law and Policy, "New Jersey's Interdistrict Public School Choice Program" (report to the New Jersey State Department of Education, November 2006), http://ielp.rutgers.edu (accessed September 27, 2007).

8.   James Smith, "Report Card Narratives: Dwight Morrow High," 2006, New Jersey Department of Education, http://education.state.nj.us/rc/rc06/narrative/03/1370/03-1370-040.html (accessed 9/20/07).

9.   Anthony J. Lucas, *Common Ground: A Turbulent Decade in the Lives of Three American Families* (New York: Vintage Books, 1986).

10.   See "Brief of the Swann Fellowship, Former School Board Members, Parents and Children from the Charlotte-Mecklenburg Schools as *Amicus Curiae* in Support of Respondents," *Parents Involved in Community Schools* v. *Seattle School District No. 1, et al.,* and *Crystal D. Meredith* v. *Jefferson County Board of Education, et al.* (Nos. 05–908 and 05–915) (Sp. Ct. 2006), www.law.unc.edu/documents/civilrights/briefs/swannbrief.pdf (accessed January 22, 2008).

CHAPTER 3

1. . When quoting people from Austin about Latinos in Texas and at Austin High School, we generally use the term *Hispanic* instead of *Latino* because that is how our interviewees from this city describe people from Central America and their descendants. But in general throughout the book we prefer the term *Latino* and use it most of the time. Similarly, many of our respondents from Texas refer to whites as *Anglos.* We try to vary these terms depending on whom we are quoting or paraphrasing.

2.   Amy Stuart Wells and Erica Frankenberg, "The Public Schools and the Challenge of the Supreme Court's Integration Decision," *Phi Delta Kappan,* November 2007, pp. 178–88.

3.   See Amy Stuart Wells et al., "The Space between School Desegregation Court Orders and Outcomes: The Struggle to Challenge White Privilege," *Virginia Law Review* 90, no. 6 (2004): 1723.

4.   Ibid., p. 1723.

5.   Ibid., p. 1724.

6.   See ibid., p. 1729; Amy Stuart Wells et al., "How Society Failed School Desegregation Policy: Looking Past the Schools to Understand Them," *Review of Research in Education* 28 (2005): 85.

7.   Wells et al., "Space," p. 1729; Wells et al., "How Society Failed," p. 85.

8.   Wells et al., "Space," p. 1729; Wells et al., "How Society Failed," pp. 85–86.

9.   See Charles Vert Willie and Sarah S. Willie, "Black, White, and Brown: The Transformation of Public Education in America," *Teachers College Record* 107, no. 3 (2005): 475–95.

10.   See Alvis V. Adair, *Desegregation: The Illusion of Black Progress* (Lantham, MD: University Press of America, 1984); Derrick Bell, *And We Are Not Saved* (New York: Harper Collins, 1987) and *Silent Covenants: Brown v. Board of Education and*

the Unfulfilled Hopes for Racial Reform (New York: Oxford University Press, 2004); Mwalimu J. Shujaa, ed., *Beyond Desegregation: The Politics of Quality in African American Schooling* (Thousand Oaks, CA: Sage Publications, 1996).

11. Wells et al., "Space," p. 1730.

12. See ibid.

13. Vanessa Siddle Walker, personal communication, March 27, 2008.

14. See Adair, *Desegregation;* Bell, *And We Are Not Saved.*

15. See Adair, *Desegregation;* Bell, *And We Are Not Saved* and *Silent Covenants.*

16. *Swann v. Charlotte-Mecklenburg,* 402 U.S. 1 (1971).

17. *Swann v. Charlotte-Mecklenburg,* 402 U.S. 1 (1971), pp. 29–31.

18. R. Halpren, "Urban Renewal and Public Housing: A Decade of Mistakes," in *Rebuilding the Inner City: A History of Neighborhood Initiatives to Address Poverty in the United States* (New York: Columbia University Press, 1995), pp. 57–82.

19. See chapter 5 for a more detailed discussion of extracurricular activities at the six schools and how they related to race and class.

20. Pierre Bourdieu, *Distinction: A Social Critique of the Judgement of Taste* (Cambridge, MA: Harvard University Press, 1984) and "Cultural Reproduction and Social Reproduction," in *Knowledge, Education, and Cultural Change,* ed. Richard Brown (New York: Harper and Row, 1973), pp. 487–501.

21. Amy Stuart Wells and Robert L. Crain, *Stepping over the Color Line: African American Students in White Suburban Schools* (New Haven: Yale University Press, 1997).

22. Gordon Allport, *The Nature of Prejudice* (Reading, MA: Addison-Wesley, 1954).

23. Julie Kailin, "How White Teachers Perceive the Problem of Racism in Their Schools: A Case Study in 'Liberal' Lakeview," *Teachers College Record* 100, no. 4 (1999): 745.

24. See chapter 5 for more detail on this as well.

25. See Susan Yonezawa, Amy Stuart Wells, and Irene Serna, "Choosing Tracks: 'Freedom of Choice' in Detracking Schools," *American Educational Research Journal* 39 (Spring 2002): 37.

26. See Floyd M. Hammack, ed., *The Comprehensive High School Today* (New York: Teachers College Press, 2004). Ch. 1, "What Should Be Common and What Should Not?" by Hammack, notes that Advanced Placement began in 1954 and was ubiquitous by 2002 (p. 19). Ch. 5, "The Comprehensive High School, Detracking and the Persistence of Social Stratification," by Jeannie Oakes and Amy Stuart Wells (pp. 87–113), notes that AP had become widespread by the 1980s. This chapter also talks about unequal access to AP in poor versus rich schools.

27. See Jeannie Oakes, *Keeping Track: How Schools Structure Inequality,* 2nd ed. (New Haven: Yale University Press, 2005).

28. Beverly Tatum, *Why Are All the Black Kids Sitting Together in the Cafeteria?* (New York: Basic Books, 1997).

29. Peter Drier, John Mollenkopf, and Todd Swanstrom, *Place Matters: Metropolitics for the Twenty-First Century*, 2nd, rev. ed. (Lawrence: University of Kansas Press, 2004).

30. See Amy Stuart Wells and Erica Frankenberg, "The Public Schools and the Challenge of the Supreme Court's Integration Decision," *Phi Delta Kappan*, November 2007, pp. 178–88.

31. Amy Stuart Wells and Jennifer Jellison Holme, "No Accountability for Diversity: Standardized Tests and the Demise of Racially Mixed Schools," in *School Resegregation: Must the South Turn Back?* ed. John Charles Boger and Gary Orfield (Chapel Hill: University of North Carolina Press, 2005), pp. 187–211.

32. Wells and Frankenberg, "Public Schools."

33. See Wells and Crain, *Stepping over the Color Line.*

CHAPTER 4

1. Thomas Byrne Edsall, *Chain Reaction: The Impact of Race, Rights, and Taxes on American Politics* (New York: Norton, 1991).

2. See Eduardo Bonilla-Silva, *White Supremacy and Racism in the Post–Civil Rights Era* (Boulder, CO: Lynne Rienner, 2001).

3. Sam Dillion, "Schools' Efforts on Race Await Justices' Ruling," *New York Times*, June 24, 2006, www.nytimes.com (accessed June 24, 2006).

4. On more recent forms of color-blindness, see Howard Winant, "Behind Blue Eyes: Whiteness and Contemporary U.S. Racial Politics," in *Off White: Readings on Power, Privilege and Resistance*, 2nd ed., ed. Michelle Fine et al. (New York: Routledge, 2004), pp. 3–16.

5. See Ray Rist, "Race, Policy and Schooling," *Society* 12, no. 1 (1974): 59–63; Janet Ward Schofield, *Black and White in School: Trust, Tension, or Tolerance?* (New York: Teachers College Press, 1989).

6. Signithia Fordham, "Racelessness in Private Schools: Should We Deconstruct the Racial and Cultural Identity of African-American Adolescents?" *Teachers College Record* 92 (Spring 1991): 470–84.

7. Eduardo Bonilla-Silva, *Racism without Racists* (Lanham, MD: Rowman and Littlefield, 2003), p. 3.

8. Janet Ward Schofield, "Promoting Positive Peer Relations in Desegregated Schools," in *Beyond Desegregation: The Politics of Quality in African American Schooling*, ed. Mwalimu J. Shujaa (Thousand Oaks, CA: Sage Publications, 1996), 105.

9. Schofield, *Black and White in School* and "Promoting Positive Peer Relations."

10. Schofield, "Promoting Positive Peer Relations," p. 105.

11. See Van Dempsey and George Noblit, "Cultural Ignorance and School Desegregation: A Community Narrative," in Shujaa, *Beyond Desegregation*, pp. 115–37.

12. Bonilla-Silva, *White Supremacy*, pp. 12, 89–120; Fordham, "Racelessness in Private Schools"; Schofield, *Black and White in School* and "Promoting Positive Peer Relations."

13. Amanda E. Lewis, *Race in the Schoolyard: Negotiating the Color Line in Classrooms and Communities* (New Brunswick: Rutgers University Press, 2003); Mica Pollock, *Colormute: Race Talk Dilemmas in an American School* (Princeton: Princeton University Press, 2005); Schofield, *Black and White in School*.

14. Bonilla-Silva, *White Supremacy*.

15. Gary Orfield, "Schools More Separate: Consequences of a Decade of Resegregation" (working paper, Civil Rights Project, Harvard University, Cambridge, MA, July 2001), www.civilrightsproject.ucla.edu/research/deseg/separate_schools01.php (accessed January 5, 2008).

16. Dempsey and Noblit, "Cultural Ignorance."

CHAPTER 5

1. Murray Milner, *Freaks, Geeks, and Cool Kids: American Teenagers, Schools, and the Culture of Consumption* (New York: Routledge, 2004), p. 124.

2. See Penelope Eckert, *Jocks and Burnouts: Social Categories and Identity in the High School* (New York: Teachers College Press, 1989).

3. See Maureen Hallinan and Richard A. Williams, "Interracial Friendship Choices in Secondary Schools," *American Sociological Review* 54 (February 1989): 72–76; see also Charles Clotfelter, "Interracial Contact in High School Extracurricular Activities," *Urban Review* 34 (March 2002): 41–43.

4. Beverly Daniel Tatum, *Why Are All the Black Kids Sitting Together in the Cafeteria?* (New York: Basic Books, 1997).

5. National Urban League, *The State of Black America 2005* (New York: National Urban League, 2005).

6. Peter Drier, John Mollenkopf, and Todd Swanstrom, *Place Matters: Metropolitics for the Twenty-first Century,* 2nd, rev. ed. (Lawrence: University of Kansas Press, 2004).

7. Ibid., p. 20.

8. Gordon Allport, *The Nature of Prejudice* (Reading, MA: Addison-Wesley, 1954).

9. See Clotfelter, "Interracial Contact," pp. 25–46.

10. Ibid., p. 25.

11. Daniel G. Solórzano and Octavio Villalpando, "Critical Race Theory, Marginality and the Experience of Students of Color in Higher Education," in

Emerging Issues in the Sociology of Education: Comparative Perspectives, ed. Carlos Torres and Theodore Mitchell (Albany, NY: SUNY Press, 1998), pp. 211–24.

12. See Eckert, *Jocks and Burnouts,* and Milner, *Freaks, Geeks.*

CHAPTER 6

1. "Statement of American Social Scientists of Research on School Desegregation Submitted to U.S. Supreme Court," Civil Rights Project, October 10, 2006, www.civilrightsproject.ucla.edu/news/pressreleases/amicus_brief-10-10-06.php (accessed January 21, 2008); "Brief of Profs. Amy Stuart Wells, Jomills Henry Braddock II, Linda Darling-Hammond, Jay P. Heubert, Jeannie Oakes, and Michael A. Rebell and the Campaign for Educational Equity as *Amici Curiae* in Support of Respondents," *Parents Involved in Community Schools v. Seattle School District No. 1* and *Meredith v. Jefferson County Board of Education* (Nos. 05–908 and 05–915), October 10, 2006, www.naacpldf.org/content/pdf/voluntary/both_parties/Amy_Stuart_Wells_et_al._Brief.pdf (accessed January 21, 2008).

2. Emphasis added.

3. Janet Ward Schofield, "Review of Research on School Desegregation's Impact on Elementary and Secondary School Students," in *Handbook of Research on Multicultural Education,* ed. James A. Banks and Cherry A. McGee Banks (New York: Macmillan, 1995), pp. 597–617, and "School Desegregation and Intergroup Relations: A Review of the Literature," *Review of Research in Education* 17 (1995): 335–409.

4. Schofield, "School Desegregation"; Amy Stuart Wells and Robert L. Crain, "Perpetuation Theory and the Long-Term Effects of School Desegregation," *Review of Educational Research* 64 (Winter 1994): 531–55.

5. Gary Orfield, Susan E. Eaton, and Harvard Project on School Desegregation, *Dismantling Desegregation: The Quiet Reversal of Brown v. Board of Education* (New York: New Press, 1996); Gary Orfield and Chungmei Lee, "*Brown* at 50: King's Dream or *Plessy's* Nightmare?" (working paper, Civil Rights Project, Harvard University, Cambridge, MA, January 2004), www.civilrightsproject.ucla.edu/research/reseg04/brown50.pdf (accessed January 5, 2008).

6. Lena Williams, *It's the Little Things: The Everyday Interactions That Get under the Skin of Blacks and Whites* (New York: Harcourt, 2000).

7. Orfield and Lee, "*Brown* at 50."

CHAPTER 7

1. John Logan, "Ethnic Diversity Grows, Neighborhood Integration Lags Behind" (report, Lewis Mumford Center, Albany, NY, April 2001), www.albany.edu/mumford/census (accessed February 21, 2002); Seth Ovadia, "The

Dimensions of Racial Inequality: Occupational and Residential Segregation across Metropolitan Areas in the United States," *City and Community* 2 (December 2003): 313–33. Also Lance Freeman, *There Goes the Hood: Views of Gentrification from the Ground Up* (Philadelphia: Temple University Press, 2006); Loretta Lees, Tom Slater, and Elvin Wyly, *Gentrification* (New York: Routledge, 2007).

2. "Report Finds Crisis of Housing Segregation," *Journal of Housing and Community Development* 62 (May/June 2005): 23.

3. See Correspondents of the New York Times, *How Race Is Lived in America* (New York: Times Books, 2001); Ovadia, "Dimensions of Racial Inequality"; Bruce J. Schulman, *The Seventies* (New York: Free Press, 2001); Leonard Steinhorn and Barbara Diggs-Brown, *By the Color of Our Skin: The Illusion of Integration and the Reality of Race* (New York: Penguin Putnam, 2000); Lena Williams, *It's the Little Things: The Everyday Interactions That Get under the Skin of Blacks and Whites* (New York: Harcourt, 2000).

4. Ovadia, "Dimensions of Racial Inequality."

5. David M. Cutler, Edward L. Glaeser, and Jacob L. Vigdor, "The Rise and Decline of the American Ghetto," *Journal of Political Economy* 107 (June 1999): 455–507.

6. Peter Drier, John Mollenkopf, and Todd Swanstrom, *Place Matters: Metropolitics for the Twenty-first Century,* 2nd, rev. ed. (Lawrence: University of Kansas Press, 2004), p. 25; Logan, "Ethnic Diversity Grows."

7. Joel Garreau, *Edge City: Life on the New Frontier* (New York: Anchor Books, 1992).

8. Keith R. Ihlanfeldt and Benjamin Scafidi, "Whites' Neighbourhood Racial Preferences and Neighbourhood Racial Composition in the United States: Evidence from the Multi-City Study of Urban Inequality," *Housing Studies* 19 (May 2004): 325–59.

9. Ovadia, "Dimensions of Racial Inequality."

CHAPTER 8

1. Gary Orfield, "Schools More Separate: Consequences of Decade of Resegregation" (working paper, Civil Rights Project, Harvard University, Cambridge, MA, 2001), www.civilrightsproject.ucla.edu/research/deseg/separate_schools01.php (accessed January 5, 2008); "Brief of *Amici Curiae* Housing Scholars and Research and Advocacy Organizations in Support of Respondents," *Parents Involved in Community Schools v. Seattle School District No. 1, et al.* and *Crystal D. Meredith v. Jefferson County Board of Education, et al.* (Nos. 05–908 & 05–915) (Sp. Ct. 2006), http://prrac.org/pdf/HousingScholarsBrief.pdf (accessed January 20, 2008).

2. See Peter Drier, John Mollenkopf, and Todd Swanstrom, *Place Matters: Metropolitics for the Twenty-first Century,* 2nd, rev. ed. (Lawrence: University of Kansas Press, 2004); Jeannie Oakes and Amy Stuart Wells, "The Comprehensive High School, Detracking, and the Persistence of Social Stratification," in *The Comprehensive High School Today,* ed. Floyd Hammack (New York: Teachers College Press, 2004), pp. 87–113.

3. Amy Stuart Wells and Jennifer Jellison Holme, "No Accountability for Diversity: Standardized Tests and the Demise of Racially Mixed Schools," in *School Resegregation: Must the South Turn Back?* ed. John Charles Boger and Gary Orfield (Chapel Hill: University of North Carolina Press, 2005), pp. 187–211.

4. Steve Farkas and Jean Johnson, *Time to Move On: African-American and White Parents Set an Agenda for Public Schools* (New York: Public Agenda, 1998).

5. See Metropolitan Center for Urban Education, "'With All Deliberate Speed': Achievement, Citizenship and Diversity in American Education" (report, Metropolitan Center for Urban Education, Steinhart School of Education, New York University, NY, 2005), p. 23, http://steinhardt.nyu.edu/metrocenter/brownplus/reports.pdf (accessed January 20, 2008).

6. Wells and Holme, "No Accountability for Diversity."

7. Ibid.

8. See Richard Riley, "Reflections on Goals 2000," *Teachers College Record* 96, no. 3 (1995): 380–88.

9. See Lynn Olsen, "Final Rules Give States Direction, Little Flexibility," *Education Week,* December 4, 2002, www.edweek.org (accessed February 29, 2003).

10. See Amy Stuart Wells and Erica Frankenberg, "The Public Schools and the Challenge of the Supreme Court's Integration Decision," *Phi Delta Kappan,* November 2007, pp. 178–88.

11. Farkas and Johnson, *Time to Move On.*

12. Ibid.

13. Jennifer Jellison Holme, "Buying Homes, Buying Schools: School Choice and the Social Construction of School Quality," *Harvard Educational Review* 72 (2002): 177–205.

CHAPTER 9

1. See Gary Orfield, Susan Eaton, and Harvard Project on School Desegregation, *Dismantling School Desegregation* (New York: New Press, 1997).

2. Steve Farkas and Jean Johnson, *Time to Move On: African-American and White Parents Set an Agenda for Public Schools* (New York: Public Agenda, 1998).

3. W. E. B. DuBois, *The Souls of Black Folk,* 100th Anniversary ed. (Boulder, CO: Paradigm, 2003), p. 2.

4. Nicholas Lemann, *The Promised Land: The Great Black Migration and How It Changed America* (New York: Vintage Books, 1992).

5. Amy Stuart Wells, *Racial Diversity in K–12 Education and the Supreme Court: When the Ends Do Not Justify the Means* (Boulder, CO: Paradigm Press, forthcoming).

6. An earlier version of these recommendations appeared in Amy Stuart Wells et al., "How Desegregation Changed Us: The Effects of Racially Mixed Schools on Students and Society" (Final Report from the Understanding Race and Education Study, Teachers College, Columbia University, New York), www.tc.columbia.edu/desegregation.

7. See David J. Hoff, "The View from Rockland," *Education Week*, February 7, 2007, pp. 22–25; Alyson Klein, "School Board Members Hit D.C. to Weigh In on NCLB," *Education Week*, February 7, 2007, pp. 19–20.

8. Amy Stuart Wells and Jennifer Jellison Holme, "No Accountability for Diversity: Standardized Tests and the Demise of Racially Mixed Schools," in *School Resegregation: Must the South Turn Back?* ed. John Charles Boger and Gary Orfield (Chapel Hill: University of North Carolina Press, 2005), pp. 187–211.

9. See Richard W. Riley, "Reflections on Goals 2000," *Teachers College Record* 96, no. 3 (1995): 380–88.

10. See Lynn Olson, "Final Rules Give States Direction, Little Flexibility," *Education Week*, December 4, 2002, pp. 1, 26, 27.

11. See John R. Novak and Bruce Fuller, "Penalizing Diverse Schools?" (Policy Brief 03–4, Policy Analysis for California Education, Berkeley, CA, December 2003), http://epsl.asu.edu/epru/documents/EPRU-0312-48-RW.pdf (accessed January 18, 2008).

12. Michal Kurlaender and John T. Yun, "The Impact of Racial and Ethnic Diversity on Educational Outcomes: Cambridge, MA School District" (working paper, Civil Rights Project, Harvard University, Cambridge, MA, 2002), www.civilrightsproject.ucla.edu/research/diversity/cambridge_diversity.pdf (accessed January 18, 2008); "Statement of American Social Scientists of Research on School Desegregation Submitted to U.S. Supreme Court," October 10, 2006, www.civilrightsproject.ucla.edu/news/pressreleases/amicus_brief-10-10-06.php (accessed January 18, 2008).

13. Amy Stuart Wells, ed., *Where Charter School Policy Fails: The Problems of Accountability and Equity* (New York: Teachers College Press, 2002).

14. Amy Stuart Wells et al., "Charter Schools and Racial and Social Class Segregation: Yet Another Sorting Machine?" in *A Notion at Risk: Preserving Education as an Engine for Social Mobility,* ed. Richard Kahlenberg (New York: Century Foundation Press, 2000), pp. 169–222; Wells, *Where Charter School Policy Fails;* Erica Frankenberg and Chungmei Lee, "Charter Schools and Race: A Lost Opportunity for Integration," *Education Policy Analysis Archives* 11 (September 5,

2003), http://epaa.asu.edu/epaa/v11n32/ (accessed January 18, 2008). Also Amy Stuart Wells and Allison Roda, "Colorblindness and School Choice: The Central Paradox of the Supreme Court's Ruling in the Louisville and Seattle School Integration Cases," paper presented at the annual meeting of the American Educational Research Association, New York, 2008.

15.   Jennifer Hochschild and Nathan Scovronick, *The American Dream and the Public Schools* (New York: Oxford University Press, 2003).

16.   Jennifer Jellison Holme and Amy Stuart Wells, "School Choice beyond District Borders: Lessons for the Reauthorization of NCLB from Interdistrict Desegregation and Open Enrollment Plans," in *Improving on No Child Left Behind*, ed. Richard Kahlenberg (New York: Century Foundation, forthcoming).

17.   See Kathryn McDermott, Susan Bowles, and Andrew Churchill, "Mapping School Choice in Massachusetts, Data and Findings, 2003" (report, Center for Education Research and Policy, MassInc., Boston, 2003), ERIC 476565, p. 300. Also see Jennifer Jellison Holme and Amy Stuart Wells, "School Choice beyond District Borders."

18.   Holme and Wells, "School Choice," and Wells and Roda, "Colorblindness and School Choice."

19.   See Frankenberg and Lee, "Charter Schools and Race"; Casey Cobb and Gene Glass, "Ethnic Segregation in Arizona Charter Schools," *Education Policy Analysis Archives* 7, no. 1 (1999), http://epaa.asu.edu (accessed June 9, 2004); Wells et al., "Charter Schools."

20.   See Holme and Wells, "School Choice," and Amy Stuart Wells and Robert L. Crain, *Stepping over the Color Line* (New Haven: Yale University Press, 1997).

21.   Susan J. Popkin, James E. Rosenbaum, and Patricia M. Meaden, "Labor Market Experiences of Low-Income Black Women in Middle-Class Suburbs: Evidence from a Survey of Gautreaux Program Participants," *Journal of Policy Analysis and Management* 12, no. 3 (1993): 556–73.

22.   John Logan, "Ethnic Diversity Grows, Neighborhood Integration Lags Behind" (report, Lewis Mumford Center, Albany, NY, April 2001), www.albany.edu/mumford/census (accessed February 21, 2002); Seth Ovadia, "The Dimensions of Racial Inequality: Occupational and Residential Segregation across Metropolitan Areas in the United States," *City and Community* 2 (December 2003): 313–33.

23.   Logan, "Ethnic Diversity Grows"; Ovadia, "Dimensions of Racial Inequality."

Index

accountability systems, test-based, 271–73, 278, 312–13

Advanced Placement (AP) classes, 99, 100, 178, 202, 205

affirmative action, 18, 25, 30, 32, 127, 208, 266, 293, 295–96, 302

African Americans, 2–3, 6, 7, 24–25, 37, 38, 98, 112, 200, 223–27, 241, 263, 285–86, 298, 303–4; in Austin, 46, 78, 80, 88–90, 155–57; at Austin High School, 42, 47–51, 81, 82, 90, 140, 145–46, 149–50, 155, 157–62, 173, 181, 182, 188, 195, 196, 231, 262; busing of, 87–99, 126, 173, 208; in Charlotte, 72, 91–98; choice of schools for children of, 270–71, 275–77, 286–91; in cliques, 166–76, 178–84; in college, 205, 238, 243–47; color-blind perspective and, 32–35, 126, 131, 137, 138–43, 145, 150, 154; cross-racial friendships of, 105–6, 157–58, 160–62; "desegregation fatigue" of, 86; double consciousness of, 24, 26–29, 156, 161, 270, 295–96, 304–6, 326n77; at Dwight Morrow High School, 2, 3, 42, 43, 56–59, 100, 101, 107–8, 110, 139–41, 168–69, 171, 183–86, 191, 197, 219–20, 226–29, 232, 233, 245, 250–51, 258, 285, 287, 288, 292–94, 297; economic disparities between whites and, 11–13, 17; in Englewood, 52–55; extracurricular activities of, 185–93, 203, 204; Fourteenth Amendment rights of, 85; in housing industry, 122; interracial dating by, 166, 196, 197, 207; interviews with, 44; intimidation of white students by, 182–84, 201–2; at John Muir High School, 42, 43, 61–63, 107–10, 142–43, 162, 163, 168–69,

171–72, 175, 179–80, 183, 188, 191–93, 207, 209–10, 212, 213, 244, 285, 288, 305; long-term benefits of desegregation experience for, 216, 219–20, 228–35; middle-class, 11–12, 15, 18, 31, 53, 94, 176, 179, 181, 207–8, 238–39, 292; migration to North of, 52, 309–10; in Pasadena, 60, 61, 91, 164, 208; in racially and socioeconomically isolated schools, 19–22; residential segregation of, 13–16, 26, 34, 39, 249–55, 318; scapegoating by whites of, 24, 26, 124–25, 127, 129, 307; segregated social lives of, 260–62; in Shaker Heights, 65–66; at Shaker Heights High School, 42, 66–68, 146–47, 171, 178–79, 181, 190, 202–6, 215, 230–32, 253, 258, 288–89, 301; skin color issues among, 292–93; and test-based accountability systems, 271–73; in Topeka, 236; at Topeka High School, 43, 69, 70, 105, 170, 181, 189, 191, 194, 195, 197, 229–30, 236–40, 288; tracking of, 63, 66, 67, 99–104, 151, 205, 237, 240; at West Charlotte High School, 43, 73–75, 89, 93–99, 103–4, 115, 117–19, 121, 141, 167, 168, 175, 182–83, 187, 189, 194, 196, 235, 245–46, 259, 261, 264–67; in workplace, 255–60

Allen, Harriet (Hattie) (pseudonym), 49, 86, 155–62, 164, 174, 191, 262

Allen, Walter, 32

Allport, Gordon, 98, 214

Almonte, Christine (pseudonym), 77–84, 88, 101–2, 173, 174, 191

Altadena, California, 162, 207, 270

American Creed, 24, 27

American Indians. *See* Native Americans

Anderson High School (Austin, Texas), 47, 88–90
Anzaldúa, Gloria, 29, 326n77
Asians, 2, 7, 21, 121, 138, 172, 176, 203, 290, 307, 318; in Austin, 46; at Austin High School, 51; at Dwight Morrow High School, 59; extracurricular activities of, 185; interviews with, 44, 151, 304; at John Muir High School, 42, 63, 163, 171; residential segregation and, 15, 250, 253–55; and test-based accountability systems, 271–72, 313; at Topeka High School, 43, 70; in workplace, 259
athletes, 16, 104, 214, 242, 273; cross-racial friendships of, 158–60, 162–63, 165, 184, 185, 187–89, 191–92, 204, 210, 226–27, 238; interracial dating by, 196, 197; social status of, 165, 168, 180–81, 203
attendance zones, alteration of, 47, 55
Austin, Texas, 41, 45–46, 77–83, 155–57, 254; busing in, 48, 88–91, 94; social class distinctions in, 174, 177–78, 223. See also Austin High School
Austin High School, 42, 45, 47–51, 86, 107, 155, 278; changing racial demographics in, 274; choice of schools for children of graduates of, 278, 280; cliques at, 50, 157–58, 168, 173–74, 176, 178, 180–82, 184; college experiences of graduates of, 246; color-blind perspective at, 130, 132–35, 137, 140, 142, 143, 145–46, 149, 150; cross-racial friendships at, 105–6, 157–58, 194, 195; extracurricular activities at, 158–60, 188–89, 191, 102; interracial dating at, 161, 195, 196; long-term benefits of deseg-regation experience at, 220, 223–24, 230–31; segregation in adult lives of grad-uates of, 254, 255, 257, 260–62; tracking at, 101–2
Autobiography of Malcolm X, The, 140

Baldwin, James, 32
Balfour, Lawrie, 27
band. See performing arts
Bergen County Vocational School District (New Jersey), 58–59
Black History Month, 142
blacks. See African Americans
Black Student Union (BSU), 70, 191–93, 238
Bob, Larry, 34
Bonilla-Silva, Eduardo, 33–34, 153
Boston: conflicts over desegregation in, 135; interdistrict transfer plan in, 317
Bourdieu, Pierre, 97–98
Brooklyn, New York, 201

Brown v. Board of Education (1954), 8, 11, 22, 23, 25, 36, 69, 71, 85, 107, 138, 237, 318, 321n4
Bush, George H. W., 32
Bush, George W., 22, 23, 47, 312
busing, 25, 42, 48, 56, 61, 72–74, 87–99, 115–26, 209, 213, 284, 302; cliques and, 169, 173; cross-racial friendships and, 106, 208; opposed by graduates of inte-grated schools, 283, 308; white flight and, 87, 91, 264

cafeterias, racial separation in, 57, 169, 170, 172
California, University of, Los Angeles (UCLA), 37
California Institute of Technology (Cal Tech), 60
California State University system, 244
Catholic schools, 200, 287
Caucasians. See whites
Central High School (Little Rock, Arkansas), 207
Charlotte, North Carolina, 41, 72, 73, 266–68, 284; busing in, 73, 74, 91–98, 106, 115–25, 264–65; color-blind perspective in, 126; workplace segregation in, 259. See also West Charlotte High School
charter schools, 313–16; federal funding for, 317
cheerleaders, 166, 175, 186–89, 203, 204, 265; racial quotas for, 134, 158, 159, 188
Chicago, residential segregation in, 14
chorus. See performing arts
Chung, Angie, 32
churches, one-race, 240, 241, 261
Cinco de Mayo, 142, 143
Civil Rights Act (1964), 11
civil rights movement, 24, 25, 29, 30, 35, 56, 237, 296, 297; backlash against, 26, 31–32, 37, 127
Civil Rights Project, 19
Civil War, 139
class. See social class
Cleveland, Ohio, 64–66, 199, 200, 309–10; res-idential segregation in, 14, 64; social class distinctions in, 179
Clinton, Bill, 318, 321n2
cliques, 50, 104, 157–59, 163–84, 202–3, 209; class determinants of, 176–80; racially distinct spaces and, 169–73; token stu-dents of color in, 180–84; white privilege in, 173–76, 202, 203
Clotfelter, Charles, 185–86
Cold War, 25

colleges and universities, 205, 238; academic standards and admission to, 277, 278, 287; affirmative action in, 266; information for students about, 101; segregation in, 67, 243–48. *See also* Ivy League universities

color-blindness, 32–35, 120, 121, 125–54, 306; of curricula, 137–44; to defuse racial tensions, 132–36; in housing choices, 252; personal investment of educators in, 136–37; questioning, 144–50; in school choice programs, 75, 314; social class distinctions and, 178

comfort, increased sense of, 221–25, 228–30, 267

Committee to Save Our Neighborhood Schools, 54

competitive racism, 34

Congress of Racial Equality (CORE), 54

Constitution, U.S., 32; Fourteenth Amendment, 85

Cortinez, Roy, 62

curriculum, 55, 66, 231, 233, 237, 271, 288; college prep, 49, 101, 273, 287; color-blind perspective and, 63, 121, 131, 137–44, 149, 150; of high-poverty schools, 111; of magnet schools, 59, 317; multicultural, 112, 139–42

dating, interracial, 161, 166, 195–97, 207, 300

de jure segregation, 69

Delane, Henry (pseudonym), 236–41, 260

Delgato, Geri (pseudonym), 162–64, 253, 319

Deller, Maya (pseudonym), 127, 128, 148–49, 151, 153, 199–207, 213, 233, 308–9

Dennis, Quentin (pseudonym), 61, 207–13, 305–6

Depression, 68

"desegregation fatigue," 86

Detroit, residential segregation in, 14

discrimination, coping with, 230–31

double consciousness, 24–26, 80, 271; black, 26–29, 156, 161, 295–96, 304–6, 326n77; white, 29–35, 126, 129, 152, 263, 298, 299, 306–11

Douglass, Frederick, 237

drama clubs. *See* performing arts

drug use, 171, 175

DuBois, W. E. B., 24, 26–30, 33, 216, 305

Dwight Englewood School, 52

Dwight Morrow High School, 2–4, 42, 43, 53, 55–60, 146, 242, 292–94, 297, 310; changing racial demographics in, 274; choice of schools for children of graduates of,

279–80, 286–88; cliques in, 168–71, 173, 176, 177, 183–84; college experiences of graduates of, 245, 247–48; cross-racial friendships in, 194–95; declining reputation of, 107, 108; extracurricular activities in, 186, 188, 190, 191; interracial dating in, 195, 197; long-term benefits of desegregation experience in, 216, 218–20, 223, 225–28, 232, 233; magnet school on campus of, 53, 59, 111; multicultural curriculum in, 112, 139–42; negative media coverage of, 109–11; segregation in adult lives of graduates of, 250–52, 254, 256, 258, 262, 263; tracking in, 55, 100, 101, 139, 141, 293

East Cleveland, Ohio, 64

East Mecklenburg High School, 99, 115

Economic Opportunity Act (1964), 11

educational achievement, gap in, 19–20

educational attainment, racial disparities in, 11–12

educational policies, 22–24, 283–84; implications and recommendations for, 311–19; shift away from desegregation in, 303; test-based, 271–73, 278

Eisenhower, Dwight D., 237

elementary schools, 62, 65, 69, 105, 115, 119, 155–56, 165, 201, 211–12, 236, 285, 294, 298, 302; busing to, 42, 61, 94, 208; color-blindness in, 144; cross-racial friendships in, 156–57, 208; private, 91, 219, 268; student reassignment to, 42, 54–55; tracking in, 99, 103, 104; urban, 318

Elliott Junior High School (Pasadena), 61

empathy, increased, 225–28

Englewood, New Jersey, 1–3, 41, 51–54, 59, 294; busing in, 56, 94; residential segregation in, 53, 54, 254, 287; social class distinctions in, 177. *See also* Dwight Morrow High School

Englewood Cliffs, New Jersey, 2, 42, 56–59, 177, 190, 219, 256, 257

Essed, Philomena, 34

Eurocentric curriculum, 138–41, 150

extracurricular activities, 104, 242; cross-racial friendships in, 158–60, 162–63, 165, 184–93, 204–7, 209; high-status, 165; racial quotas for, 134–35, 159, 187

fear, decreased, 221–25, 228–30

federal funding, 317

Field Elementary School (Pasadena), 208

Florida, racial tensions in, 135

"fortunate fifth," 179

friendships, cross-racial, 104–6, 129, 151, 153, 155–98, 208–10, 212–13, 266, 267, 299; cliques and, 157–59, 167–84; dating and, 195–97; in elementary school, 156–57, 208; in extracurricular activities, 148–60, 162–63, 165, 184–93, 204–7, 209, 226–27, 237–38; in junior high and middle school, 187, 208; limits of, 193–95

gangs, 200
gated communities, 14, 163, 250
Gates, Henry Louis, Jr., 28
gender issues, 29, 148, 166, 176; in cliques, 180, 181; in interracial dating, 195, 197
gifted programs, elementary and middle school, 103
global society, 214, 217–21
Great Society policies, 25, 26
Green v. School Board of New Kent County, Virginia (1968), 11
Grutter v. Bollinger (2003), 311

Hagart, Betsy (pseudonym), 97, 99, 105, 115–25, 151, 180, 182, 214, 222, 265
Highland Park High School (Topeka), 69, 70
high-poverty schools, 19, 21, 111; No Child Left Behind and, 22–23
Hispanics. See Latinos(as)
Holocaust, 308
honors classes, 99, 103–4
household income, racial disparities in, 11–13
housing integration, 16, 303, 312, 317–18; in Shaker Heights, 64–65, 253. See also residential segregation

identity formation, racial, 105, 172
income inequality, 11–13, 17–18, 179, 269, 270
insight, increased, 225–28
interdistrict choice plans, 314, 316; federal funding for, 317
Iranian hostage crisis, 26, 37
Italian Americans, 52
Ivy League universities, 3, 56, 65, 272, 273, 280, 293–94, 312

Jackson, Jesse, 299–300
Jacobs, Calvin, 118–20
Jet Propulsion Laboratory, 60
Jews, 2, 127, 200, 201, 205, 206, 245, 308; Orthodox, 52
Jim Crow segregation, 5, 25, 30, 32–35, 54, 61, 309
John Muir High School, 42, 43, 60–64, 207, 209–10, 212, 270, 305, 306, 319; changing

racial demographics in, 274; choice of schools for children of graduates of, 283, 286, 288, 289; cliques in, 168, 171, 172, 175, 176, 179, 183, 209; college experiences of graduates of, 244; color-blind perspective in, 132–35, 138–39, 146–48; cross-racial friendships in, 162–64, 194, 209–10, 212, 213; declining reputation of, 107–9; extracurricular activities in, 188, 191–93, 209; interracial dating in, 195; long-term benefits of desegregation experience in, 225, 232–33; multicultural curriculum in, 112, 142; negative media coverage of, 110–11; segregation in adult lives of graduates of, 251, 253, 261; tracking in, 63
Johnson, Lyndon B., 35
Johnston High School (Austin), 77–81
junior high and middle schools, 57–58, 62, 65, 69, 78, 105, 115, 138, 158, 165, 168, 175, 196, 236; busing to, 61; color-blindness in, 144; cross-racial friendships in, 187, 208, 308; intimidation of white students in, 50, 182–84, 201–2, 206; private, 83, 219, 298; racial unrest and tension in, 71; school choice programs for, 123; student reassignment to, 42, 55; tracking in, 103, 292

Kailin, Julie, 98
Kane, Dale (pseudonym), 146–47, 214, 222, 297–302
Kennedy, Anthony, 10, 311, 315, 316
Key Clubs, 165, 191–92
King, Martin Luther, Jr., 35, 300

La Canada, California, 60, 62, 108
laissez-faire racism, 34
Latinos(as), 6, 7, 28, 37, 38, 98, 112, 121, 160, 172, 184, 206, 224, 240, 263, 285–86, 303–4, 306; in Austin, 46, 77, 88; at Austin High School, 42, 47–51, 77–82, 101–2, 158, 173–75, 177–78, 180–81, 188, 191–92, 230, 261–62; busing of, 87–89, 91, 173; in Charlotte, 72; choice of schools for children of, 275–76, 286–91; cliques and, 166, 173–78, 180–81; in college, 243, 247; color-blind perspective and, 32–33, 126, 138, 141–43, 145, 150; cross-racial friendships of, 105–6, 162–64; "desegregation fatigue" of, 86; double consciousness of, 24, 29, 305; at Dwight Morrow High School, 2, 42, 57, 59, 107; economic disparities between whites and, 17; in Englewood, 52, 53; extracurricular activities of, 185, 188, 189, 191–92; Fourteenth

Amendment rights of, 85; interracial dating by, 166, 196; interviews with, 44; at John Muir High School, 42, 61, 63, 107–10, 162–64, 171, 253, 286, 289, 319; long-term benefits of desegregation experience for, 228–35; in Pasadena, 60, 91; in racially and socioeconomically isolated schools, 19–22; residential segregation of, 14, 15, 26, 34, 249–55, 318; scapegoating by whites of, 24, 26, 124–25, 127, 129, 307; segregated social lives of, 260–62; and test-based accountability systems, 271–73; in Topeka, 70; at Topeka High School, 43, 70, 170, 189, 194; tracking of, 63, 99, 101–3, 151; in workplace, 256–60
Lee, Chungmei, 21
Lehrer, Tom, 302
Lemert, Charles, 27
Little Rock school integration crisis, 207
Louisville, Kentucky, 9, 32, 127
lunchtime spaces, 171, 209. *See also* cafeterias
Lynch, Kelly (pseudonym), 307–8

Mack, Raymond W., 39
magnet schools, 53, 59, 74, 172, 265, 316, 317
majority-to-minority (M-to-M) transfer program, 47, 50, 90–91
Martinez, Theresa, 29
mass transportation, lack of, 106
Massachusetts, open enrollment plan in, 316
McMillan, James B., 73
MECHA, 192
Mecklenburg County School District (North Carolina), 72, 92
media, negative reporting by, 109–11, 200
median net worth, racial disparities in, 13
Meredith v. Jefferson County Board of Education (2007), 9, 32, 127, 311, 315
mestiza consciousness, 29, 326n77
Metropolitan High School (Charlotte), 92
Mexicans and Mexican Americans, 46, 70–71, 77, 79, 80, 83, 106, 162–64, 224, 260–61, 290, 307
Miami University, 300
Milliken v. Bradley (1974), 328n99
Milner, Murray, 168
Milwaukee, interdistrict transfer plan in, 317
minority share-held companies, preferences for, 301–2
mixed-race interview subjects, 44, 232
Monroe, Hannah, 265–68
Morgan, Sydney (pseudonym), 56–57, 139–41, 183, 228–29, 258, 292–97
Morrison, Toni, 141
"Moving to Opportunity" program, 318

multicultural curriculum, 112, 138–42
Myers Park High School (Charlotte), 265, 266
Myrdal, Gunnar, 24–27

National Association for the Advancement of Colored People (NAACP), 54
National Center for Education Statistics (NCES), 20, 21
National Merit scholarships, 65, 272, 273
Native Americans, 21, 43, 70, 138
neighborhoods, segregated. *See* residential segregation
New Jersey State Department of Education, 58–59
Newsweek magazine, 37–38
New York City, 51, 52
New York Times, 28
No Child Left Behind Act (2001), 22, 272, 312
North Carolina, University of, at Chapel Hill, 246–47

Obama, Barack, 235
open enrollment plans, 316; federal funding for, 317
Orfield, Gary, 21
Orthodox Jews, 52
"other," racialized, 126; overcoming fear of, 225

Pacific Islanders, 42, 63
Parents Involved in Community Schools v. Seattle School District No. 1 (2007), 9, 32, 127, 311, 315
Parker, Sarah Jessica, 56
parochial schools. *See* religious schools
Pasadena, California, 41, 60–62, 270, 319; busing in, 61, 91, 94, 208–10; residential segregation in, 251; social class distinctions in, 179. *See also* John Muir High School
Pasadena High School, 61–63, 110, 207
Peace Corps, 92
performing arts, 16, 104, 204, 205, 209, 214, 238, 265, 266, 273; cross-racial friendships in, 185–87
Phoenix, Arizona, 163–64
Plessy v. Ferguson (1896), 23
"popular crowd." *See* cliques
poverty, 13, 21–23, 35, 52–53, 111, 273, 295; educational achievement gap and, 19; residential segregation and, 15; scapegoating blacks and Latinos for, 125; war on, 25–26
Presbyterian church, 261

private schools, 52, 67, 68, 115, 200, 219, 248, 278, 279, 282, 298–99; avoidance of desegregation through enrollment in, 91, 223–24, 264; charter school practices and, 315; children of integrated school graduates in, 83, 268, 270, 287. *See also* religious schools

privilege, white, 60, 80, 84–87, 95, 151, 160, 162, 164, 216, 221, 227; and choice of schools for children of graduates, 275; in cliques, 168–76; color-blindness and, 126, 128, 141–43, 147, 150, 306–7; on college campuses, 244, 248; double consciousness and, 29, 31, 33–35, 126, 263, 306; and increasing income inequality, 269; and intimidation by blacks, 182, 183; interracial dating and, 197; institutions and policies maintaining, 26; residential segregation and, 252; self-fulfilling prophecies in absence of, 111–12; social class and, 50–51; tracking and, 99, 100, 104

Project Push, 300

Protestants, 51

public perceptions, negative, 109–11

quotas, racial, 134–35, 159, 187, 266. *See also* affirmative action

race-conscious policies, Supreme Court ruling against, 9–10

racial identity politics, 153

racial profiling, 129

Rand, Ayn, 300

Reagan, Ronald, 26, 32, 35–37, 127

Reich, Robert, 179, 321n2

religious schools, 52, 200, 206, 248, 287

reparations movement, 302

residential segregation, 13–16, 46, 53, 54, 60, 69, 122, 276, 287; in adult lives of graduates, 151, 241, 248–55, 267; cross-racial friendships and, 105–6; school choice programs and, 314. *See also* housing integration

restrictive covenants, 60

reverse discrimination, 30, 32

Robert E. Lee Elementary School (Austin), 155–57

Roberts, John, 32

Rothstein, Richard, 13

Rubin, Larry (pseudonym), 1–5, 10, 56, 77, 139, 183, 188, 191, 254–55, 263, 286, 292

scapegoating, 24, 26, 124–25, 127, 129, 307

Schofield, Janet, 130–31

Scholastic Aptitude Tests (SATs), 74, 101

school choice policies, 284, 313–16; color-blind, 75, 123–24, 314; federal funding for, 317; race-conscious, 9–10

Seattle, Washington, 9, 32

Second Ward High School (Charlotte), 92–94

self-fulfilling prophecies, 107–12, 273

"separate but equal" doctrine, 22–24

Shaker Heights, Ohio, 41, 64–67; busing in, 94; elementary and junior high schools in, 201; housing in, 65, 253. *See also* Shaker Heights High School

Shaker Heights High School, 28–29, 42, 43, 65–68, 199, 201–7, 242, 243, 297–302, 308–10; changing racial demographics in, 274; choice of schools for children of graduates of, 281, 282, 289; cliques in, 168, 171, 172, 178, 179, 181–83, 202; college experiences of graduates of, 244–45, 247; color-blind perspective in, 127, 135, 148–49, 153; cross-racial friendships in, 167, 198; declining reputation of, 107; extracurricular activities in, 190; interracial dating in, 195; long-term benefits of desegregation experience in, 216, 222, 224, 227, 230–32; segregation in adult lives of graduates of, 253, 256, 258–60; test scores in, 67–68; tracking in, 66–67, 100, 102, 204; twenty-year reunion of students from, 214

single-parent households, 294–95

Sister Souljah, 56

slavery, 30, 46, 309; reparations for, 302

smoking, 171, 175

social class, 122–23, 206, 263, 298, 302, 318; in Austin, 46, 49–51; cliques and, 157, 164–65, 167–68, 173–80, 182, 184; and crisis of "whiteness," 31; educational opportunity and, 19, 21; in Englewood, 52–53, 59–60; and growing income inequality, 17–18; interracial dating and, 196; and reputation of school, 107; residential segregation and, 15, 250; tracking and, 100, 101; and test-based accountability systems, 272–73, 278, 313. *See also* income inequality

social interaction: in adulthood, 260–62. *See also* cliques; dating; friendships, cross-racial

Spangler v. Pasadena Board of Education (1976), 62

special education, 57, 312

sports. *See* athletes

standardized testing, 67–68, 74, 271–73, 278–81, 291, 312–13

Stephen F. Austin High School. *See* Austin High School
stereotypes: breaking down of, 214, 222, 225–26; negative, 126, 172
St. Louis, interdistrict transfer plan in, 317
student government, 16, 104, 165, 214, 237; cross-racial friendships in, 184, 185, 187, 189; racial quotas for, 134–35, 187, 266
suburbs, 12, 51, 68, 180; affluent, 19, 56, 207, 258, 263, 279–80; African Americans and Latinos in, 12, 211–12, 241, 250, 289; in consolidated school districts, 72, 92; diversity in, 252, 285, 317–18; domination of state legislatures by, 23; inner-ring, 64, 234, 289; institutional advantages of schools in, 49; residential segregation in, 13, 14, 225, 241, 250–51, 254. *See also* white flight
Sue, Derald, 30
Supreme Court, U.S., 8, 9, 23, 25, 32–33, 127, 264, 311, 315, 321n4, 328n99
suspension rates, 131
Swann v. Charlotte-Mecklenburg Board of Education (1971), 11, 91–94, 264

Tatum, Beverly Daniel, 172
Tenafly High School, 57–56
test scores. *See* standardized testing
Texas, University of, at Austin, 46
theater programs. *See* performing arts
Topeka, Kansas, 41, 68–70; busing in, 94. *See also* Topeka High School
Topeka High School, 42–43, 68–71, 107, 236–38, 240–41; accountability measures at, 273; Black Student Union in, 70; changing racial demographics in, 274; choice of schools for children of graduates of, 278, 279, 288; cliques in, 168, 170, 171, 173, 176, 180, 181; color-blind perspective in, 130, 132–34, 138; cross-racial friendships in, 105, 106, 194, 195, 237–38; extracurricular activities in, 189, 191, 238; interracial dating in, 195, 197; long-term benefits of desegregation experience in, 220, 222, 226, 229–30; segregation in adult lives of graduates of, 259; tracking in, 237, 240
Topeka West High School, 69, 70, 238
tracking, 16, 55, 63, 66–67, 204, 237, 266, 293, 294, 313; color-blind perspective and, 130, 139, 141, 151; social class distinctions and, 178; unequal access in, 99–104; workplace racial stratification and, 242
Travolta, John, 56
"turf," racial, 168–73

unemployment, 13; scapegoating blacks and Latinos for, 125
universities. *See* colleges and universities
urban renewal, 93

Vietnam War, 25, 36
Voting Rights Act (1965), 11
vouchers, 314

Warren, Earl, 321n4
Washington Junior High School (Pasadena), 61
Watergate scandal, 25, 201
West Charlotte High School, 43, 72–75, 89, 111, 113, 114, 214, 264–70, 310; busing to, 92–99, 115–25, 264–65; changing racial demographics in, 274; choice of schools for children of graduates of, 283–84; cliques in, 168, 172, 175, 180, 182; college experiences of graduates of, 245–47; color-blind perspective in, 120–21, 130, 132–34, 139, 141, 144, 153; cross-racial friendships in, 105, 167, 194; declining reputation of, 107; extracurricular activities in, 187–89; interracial dating at, 195, 196; long-term benefits of desegregation experience in, 219, 226, 232, 235; magnet program in, 74, 172, 265; segregation in adult lives of graduates of, 255, 259, 261; tracking in, 103–4, 112, 266
Westlake, Texas, 51
white flight, 53–55, 57, 58, 63, 200, 206, 241, 250–51, 289; busing and, 86, 91, 264; self-fulfilling prophecy of, 107–9, 111–12, 273; suburban, 318
whites, 38, 68, 98, 165, 200–201, 240–43, 303–5; in Austin, 46, 82, 83, 88–91; at Austin High School, 42, 43, 47–51, 77, 78, 80, 81, 86, 131, 143, 158–61, 165, 168, 173, 174, 181, 182, 184, 188–89, 192, 194–96, 220, 246, 254, 257, 260, 278, 280; backlash among, 18, 24, 25, 126, 127, 129; business and neighborhood interactions with, 238–40; and busing, 87–99, 182, 264–65; in Charlotte, 72–74, 91–98; choice of schools for children of, 268, 270, 275–86, 291; in cliques, 166–84; in college, 205, 243–48; color-blind perspective and, 126–29, 131, 137–39, 145; cross-racial friendships of, 105–6, 129, 157–58, 160–62; double consciousness of, 24, 29–35, 129, 152, 263, 298, 299, 306–11; at Dwight Morrow High School, 2, 3, 42, 56–59, 100, 101, 108–10, 139, 145, 169–71, 177, 183, 184, 186, 188, 190, 191, 197, 218–19, 223, 225–28, 232,

whites (continued)
242, 247–48, 252, 254, 256, 258, 262, 263, 279–81, 285, 292–94, 297, 310; economic disparities between nonwhites and, 11–13, 17; economic success of, 6–7; in Englewood, 51–55, 59, 177; extracurricular activities of, 185–93; interracial dating by, 166, 196–97, 207; interviews with, 44; intimidation by black students of, 182–84, 201–2; at John Muir High School, 42, 62, 63, 108, 109, 142, 143, 147–48, 163, 169, 171–72, 183, 188, 191, 193, 209–10, 212, 225, 244, 270, 283, 285, 307; long-term benefits of desegregation experience for, 216–28; in Pasadena, 60–62, 91, 208; race-conscious school choice policies challenged by, 9; racial dualism of, 326n77; in racially and socioeconomically isolated schools, 19–22; residential segregation of, 14–16, 26, 34, 39, 249–55, 318; scapegoating of blacks and Latinos by, 24, 26, 124–25, 127, 129, 307; segregated social lives of, 260–62; in Shaker Heights, 64–67;

at Shaker Heights High School, 42, 66–68, 146–49, 167, 168, 178, 182–83, 199–207, 214, 215, 218, 222, 224, 227, 242, 243–45, 256, 260, 281, 282, 297–302, 308–10; and test-based accountability systems, 271–73, 312–13; in Topeka, 69; at Topeka High School, 43, 69–71, 105, 168, 170, 171, 177, 180, 189, 194, 197, 220, 237–38, 240–41, 278, 279, 307; tracking of, 63, 66, 67, 99–104, 151, 205; at West Charlotte High School, 43, 73–75, 93–99, 103–4, 115–25, 134–35, 144, 145, 153, 172, 175, 178, 180, 182, 187, 189, 196, 214, 232, 246–47, 264–69, 283–84, 310; in workplace, 255–60. See also privilege, white
Winant, Howard, 30–31
workplace, interracial contact in, 16, 241–42, 255–60
Works Progress Administration (WPA), 68
worldview, influence of desegregation experience on, 217–21

zoning, restrictive, 60

Text: 10/14 Palatino
Display: Univers Condensed Light 47 and Bauer Bodoni
Compositor: International Typesetting & Composition
Indexer: Ruth Elwell
Printer and Binder: Sheridan Books, Inc.